DESPERATELY SEEKING SHAH RUKH

'How many books do you know that effortlessly navigate Shah Rukh Khan's movies, recent economic theories, data on jobs, juicy gossip about the peculiarities of Delhi playboys, sociological narratives and a deep dive into the love lives of young Indian women? This intelligent, charming and quirky book, an illuminating portrait of the dire state of gender relations in contemporary India, does all that and more. Read it.'

—**Abhijit Banerjee**, Nobel Laureate for Economics and author of
Poor Economics—FT Business Book of the Year

'Welcome to a brilliant new writer; I felt overwhelmed by her genius, the writing reminded me of Ruth Jhabvala who dissected as well as gave beautiful glimpses of Indian society in her books.'

—**Devaki Jain**, Padma Bhushan awardee for contributions to social justice, feminist economics and women's empowerment, and author of *The Brass Notebook*

'The personal and professional lives of Indian women across social classes come alive in these gripping stories, anchored to our common love for Shah Rukh Khan. A must-read for anyone who wants to make sense of contemporary India.'

—**Snigdha Poonam**, PEN America Literary Award longlist for
non-fiction writing, and author of *Dreamers*

'Brilliant on the fantasies and heartbreak of women ... a decade-defining book.'

—**Nilanjana S. Roy**, novelist and columnist

'*Desperately Seeking Shah Rukh* is a pioneering work, combining a world of human emotions with data and analysis on women and their place in the modern economy. With piercing candour and brilliant insights, Shrayana Bhattacharya takes us through the lives of working women in India, across class and caste boundaries, presenting a picture at once unsettling but also marked by tales of determination and will.'

—**Manu S. Pillai**, author and historian

'A remarkable book. Fascinating idea and beautiful prose. Loved the way Shrayana has dealt with a cross-section of voices. Genuine and personal.'

—**Akshaya Mukul**, author of *Writer, Rebel, Soldier, Lover: The Many Lives of Agyeya*

'Bhattacharya's is a bold new contribution, an intricately told tale of why the status of women has changed so little, even when so much else has changed so much. Her focus on gender struggles through the lens of Shah Rukh fandom leads to dazzling insights. This is social science at its very best—enjoyable and deeply empathetic.'

—**Lant Pritchett**, development economist, Blavatnik School of Government, Oxford University

'Shrayana offers a fascinating glimpse into the lives of contemporary Indian women with refreshing lightness of touch, backed by data presented in an immensely readable way. She is brave to weave her own story! SRK is the golden and magical peg.'

—**Prof. Ashwini Deshpande**, leading scholar on women's employment in India, Ashoka University, and founding director of Centre for Economic Data and Analysis

'This genre-bending book looking at women in post-1991 India draws you in from the word go ... it does much more than just giving a peek into the iconic status of one of India's favourite film stars, Shah Rukh Khan. It presents a powerful commentary on the lives of Indian women and the ways they deal with inequities. Most importantly, it provides women a toolkit to navigate the changing landscape of economy and society in their search for freedom and happiness. What makes this work special is Shrayana's ability to use heartwarming, everyday stories to provide a relatable view of complex economic phenomena.'

—*The Hindu*

'Very rarely does a book appear as if it was written just for you, as if every word and line had been carefully crafted to help you make sense of your life. *Desperately Seeking Shah Rukh* is one of them. Bhattacharya's approach to gender is unique. Economic theories and data blend beautifully with her anthropological approach. Her writing stirs up emotions in a way that is hard for an academic book to do.'

—*The Indian Express*

'Effortlessly creates a unique space for itself as a distinguished anthropological work of its time.'

—*Business Standard*

'Quirky, witty and written with striking clarity, the book is a must-read for anyone seeking to gain insights into the curious world of the female gaze.'

—*The Telegraph*

'A fresh and unique perspective of Indian women and the extent to which they fight to keep their inner flame on.'

—*Deccan Herald*

'Defies easy classification ... a book that endears and enlightens ... a book to be celebrated ...'

—*Open* magazine

'[*Desperately Seeking Shah Rukh*] is no hurried survey. It spans nearly two decades of encounters, conversations and friendships with single, married or somewhere-in-between women in northern India. They are Hindu, Muslim and Christian; happy and unhappy homemakers; content and frustrated working women; and resigned and restless working-class women. They are united only by their fandom ... Until I read this book, I never fully appreciated the quiet rebellion in my mother and aunt's sheer enjoyment of a trip to the cinema nearly every Friday for the late-night show.'

—BBC.com

'This remarkable book is about the challenges faced by Indian women ... But Bhattacharya takes that idea and adds so many layers to show it's not just a story of struggle: it's a story of aspiration and competing interpretations of freedom which is sometimes won through incremental negotiation and compromise and sometimes through rebellion. Some can be complicit in their own discrimination. What she shows subtly is a point many economists ignore: love and desire are not variables to be ignored. They are central to our understanding of the economy.'

—Mint Lounge

'Our economic lives and romantic lives are closely intertwined, Bhattacharya notes in this book, and Khan's films provide women with a different life to aspire to: one where they are free to do what they want and where men will treat them with respect, share the load of caring for a large, multi-generational household, and acknowledge that they, too, need to go out and have fun. To buy their own movie ticket and go to the cinema in a country where a significant percentage of women aren't allowed to leave the house and visit the local market alone.'

—Bloomberg

'Deeply engaging, and as a reader, or at least a male one, will take your minds down many paths which you did not know existed. As an analysis of the world of 30-something metropolitan professionals, regardless of gender, it's a therapeutic read.'

—The Wire

'The writing style and the narrative do not make you lose interest even in the drier topics. There is always a heartwarming incident or a joke mentioned. We know, of course, of the impact of cinema on society. What this book does is that it humanizes these stories. Told from the perspective of fans, we really understand cinema's power to comfort, help, and unite. Especially, the power of Shah Rukh Khan.'

—Firstpost

'Whoever would have thought that Shah Rukh Khan would make an excellent—and effective—research vehicle to track the freedoms of women in middle-class India? Shrayana Bhattacharya has pulled that experiment off wonderfully.'

—The News Minute

'This is narrative non-fiction at its empathetic best.'

—**Sreevatsa Nevatia**, *India Today*

'Bhattacharya's book is compelling because she writes about a fandom that she is part of. This makes her gaze and voice less judgmental than someone reporting from the outside. She is funny, self-deprecating, fond of clever sentences.'

—**Chintan Girish Modi**, News 9

'An important piece of work ... thoughtfully layered, intersectional, just as a contemporary book on India should be. Humour, the use of Hindi words sometimes not translated into English (thankfully) ... chiding herself now and then, fattening all arguments with statistical research and sizing up every character in the luck, longing and language of post-liberalized India, make this a winner.'

—**Shefalee Vasudev**, Voice of Fashion

'[Shrayana] is able to brilliantly link love, sex and romance with economics in an eminently readable way. The insights are rich in details, unselfconscious and make for a granular treatment of the question of gender.'

—**Sucharita Sengupta**, The Book Review

'... an up-close glimpse into how Indian women perceive work, wages, social mobility, economic aspirations, employment, and other seemingly personal issues, like intimacy, loneliness, bargaining power within families, dignity, etc.'

—The Unassuming Economist

'What stands out most is Bhattacharya's ability to weave statistics smoothly into her storytelling, making it both accessible and compelling reading ... a definitive, refreshing account that is at once a sociology text, a historical artifact, a fandom treatise, an economic development study, and a laborious love letter to this self-made Badshah of Bollywood, Shah Rukh Khan.'

—desibooks.co

'[Shrayana's] detailed ethnographic analysis is systematically peppered up with valuable econometric insights—her specialty—to put observations from the ground in perspective with the bigger picture. The unembarrassed multidisciplinary approach of the book, borrowing with equal ease from sociology, anthropology and popular culture, results in a very refreshing comment on Indian society.'

—*Books and Ideas,* Insititut Français

DESPERATELY SEEKING SHAH RUKH

INDIA'S LONELY YOUNG WOMEN AND THE SEARCH FOR INTIMACY AND INDEPENDENCE

SHRAYANA BHATTACHARYA

HarperCollins *Publishers* India

First published in hardback in India by HarperCollins *Publishers* 2021
4th Floor, Tower A, Building No. 10, Phase II, DLF Cyber City,
Gurugram, Haryana – 122002
www.harpercollins.co.in

This edition published in India by HarperCollins *Publishers* 2022

2 4 6 8 10 9 7 5 3 1

P-ISBN: 978-93-5629-214-7
E-ISBN: 978-93-5489-201-1

Typeset in 11/15.2 Adobe Caslon Pro at
Manipal Technologies Limited, Manipal

Printed and bound at
Thomson Press (India) Ltd.

For Ma, Baba, Mashi, Dia

And I am quite free, well-free from three crooked things—mortar, pestle and husband with his own crooked thing.

—Mutta, Therigatha, 600 BC

The economic gender gap runs particularly deep in India ... only one-quarter of women engage actively in the labour market (i.e. working or looking for work)—one of the lowest participation rates in the world.

—World Economic Forum 2020

Their fantasies are—can I get married and be happy? Can I own a small car and not worry about petrol prices? Life can be very hard in India, so for two hours, I'll give them real *fantasy*.

—Shah Rukh Khan, 2013

Contents

III: Work from Home

IV: Mannat

Per Cent Share of Population (Fifteen Years and Above) in the Indian Labour Force: 1993–2017

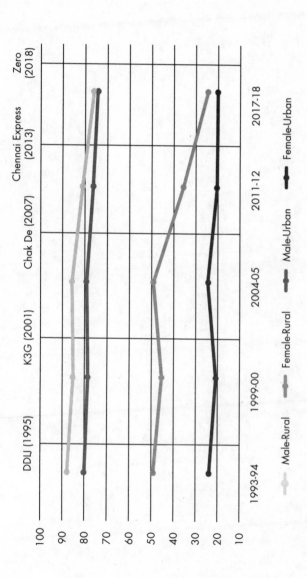

Acknowledgements

Before I tell you about my travels with Shah Rukh, my fellow fangirls and their fantasies, I must tackle your expectations with a few acknowledgements and caveats. In writing about the labours and loves of others, I present facts where available (chronology, dates, wages). Locations are accurately identified, other than the name of a few villages in Jharkhand in the eleventh chapter. This was done to adhere to ethical clearances received by the research project through which I encountered the women I write about. The character in the first chapter is a fictional composite of stories from five women. The short discussion with the Historian in the fourth chapter is also a composite representation. I have changed identifying details such as names to respect the privacy of those who shared their tales of fandom. Due to the personal nature of accounts presented in this book, I returned to respondents who did not read English to narrate and share how I understood and wrote their lives. I have incorporated changes they requested to protect anonymity. This book is a product of their generosity. The events chronicled are based on facts, but I have relied on my own abilities to translate and relay another person's inner experiences and emotional states. Any errors of describing and ascribing remain solely mine.

In collecting stories of how a period of rapid socio-economic transformation manifests in the love lives of women, I am attempting an ambitious project: sketching an intimate history of women in post-liberalization India. And I am no historian; I am barely a scholar. So, I owe a great debt to all those who helped me get my bearings. First to the remarkable Shruti Debi, my agent and guide, for her provocations and encouragement, for helping me publish this book on my own terms. Much gratitude to my brilliant editor Shougat Dasgupta, who is now a Shah Rukh aficionado. I thank all those who made time for repeated readings and my interview questions—Yamini Aiyar, Abhijit Banerjee, Urvashi Butalia, Anupama Chopra, Sapna Desai, Jean Dreze, Emmanuel Farhi, Bijoy Jain, Renana Jhabwala, Naila Kabeer, Anushree Majumdar, Nasreen Munni Kabir, Siddharth Roy Kapur, Supriya Nair, Yamini Lohia, Rohini Pande, Manu Pillai, Lant Pritchett, Varun Rana, Nitya Rao, G. Raveendran, Raja Sen, Mayank Shekhar and Alex Travelli. Special thanks to Udayan Mitra, Ananth Padmanabhan and Amrita Mukerji at HarperCollins India. I want to acknowledge the painstaking work done by statisticians and surveyors engaged in the several data sources I was able to use. I am grateful to Rosa Abraham, Rajib Acharya, Ishan Anand, Amit Basole, Tarun Jain, Anjana Thampi, Jayan Jose Thomas and Sutirtha Sinha Roy for sharing their analysis. To avoid distracting footnotes, I have tried to cite sources in a separate section at the end of the book. Beware that these data have their own limitations. Since I do not aim to write a technical book, I have simplified for easier presentation and provided suggestions for further reading. I am eternally grateful to Ratna Sudarshan and all her colleagues at the Institute of Social Studies Trust—without their efforts, this book would not exist.

These writings have enjoyed friendship and feedback from Jai Arjun Singh, Sam Ashworth, Taneia Bhardwaj, Raaghav Chanana,

Gopikaa Davar, Rehaan Engineer, Nathaniel Gaskell, Amulya Gopalakrishnan, Shalini John, Neha Kaul Mehra, Sumayya Kassamali, Zhen Liu, Swati Lohia, Varun Madhok, Rinku Murgai, Snigdha Poonam, Meenakshi Reddy Madhavan, Salim Riaz Khan, Manasi Subramaniam and Kelly Stone. I am immensely indebted to the senior management and colleagues at my workplace.

This is no ethnography. I don't claim to exhaustively document the everyday lives of the women I met. My stories rely on all that I have gleaned from fifteen years of eavesdropping, phone calls, film screenings, weddings, watching women love and labour—a tapestry of encounters that allowed me to explore how leisure, fandom and fantasy help ordinary women navigate discrimination and loneliness in modern India. Finally: I fully recognize that a film icon is no individual star. Rather, an icon is a constellation formed by multiple stars (co-actors, journalists, musicians, singers, film production crews, make-up artists, writers, producers and directors). When I write about Mr Khan, I salute all those who have helped create his magical filmography.

Author's Note for the Paperback Edition

This book was written as a love letter to women who walk away from conventional scripts of 'good' Indian womanhood and all its inherent self-denial. This book was also a love letter to Shah Rukh Khan and the power of social-science research. Following the book's release, in every interview or talk, I was asked if it had reached Mr Khan. In April 2022, it finally happened. Unbelieving, I walked into Mannat and hand-delivered the book to its research anchor and framework. In a short note he inscribed in the moment, he expressed gratitude to all the women who had participated in the research. He said it was 'heartening to learn about "the economics of things" in such an entertaining and informative way'.

This book was never about the person, career or persona of Shah Rukh Khan. I am too ordinary a fan to 'analyse' his work and celebrity. Instead, my writing was a deep dive into the lives of India's female workforce; the actor understood that. He thanked me for putting him to 'some good use' and I am forever in his debt for catalysing the unusual mode of inquiry I was able to implement in my research.

I owe the largest debt to all the women who played some part in this book. My hope is to use the resources I earn from its success to build spaces for fun and rest for the communities I've surveyed. Finally, in a world where the exploration of women's voices, pleasures and enthusiasms continues to be dismissed as shrill and unserious, I wish to thank all those who have read, reviewed, platformed and recommended this work. As I write this note, the 2022 World Economic Forum Gender Gap Index has placed India in the global bottom five in women's economic opportunities and participation. I hope this book can help you understand how we ended up becoming one of the most gender-unequal economies in the world, by making some sense of these numbers and their nuances. By capturing stories behind the depressing statistics, I hope this book offers you a way to understand the role families, films and each one of us can play in shifting norms. We are all part of the problem; we can be the solution.

Preface
Sheltering with Shah Rukh

Koi na koi chahiye, pyar karne wala
(I need someone to love me)

—*Deewana (1992)*

We really don't need more people around us than the ones we feel like
talking to while we are locked up.

—*Shah Rukh Khan, 2020*

My life has always been heteronormative hell. I've spent many of my adolescent and adult years pining for the attention of some Great Man or another. I am one of those women your friends talk about. You know, the woman from the infamous refrain, 'So many great single women but so very few great single men.' At work, I am competent and composed. At love, I am a fumbling failure.

Sadly, the market for mates has left me scrambling for cover. Bruised and burned, I oscillate along the spectrum of a banal romantic mania. Some days, the pursuit of sexual romance feels tired and odious. On occasion, monogamy has felt like a fetishized scarce commodity, making a committed relationship the most coveted contract. I lack the poise and insouciance required for romance in Delhi. I'm not cosmopolitan or cool enough to grasp the codes of international mating rituals. A spiritual and bodily shame disrupts my love affairs. I experience a consistent discomfort with who I am. My quest for love is doomed. For who can find an iota of love in the world outside if they can't broker some ease within themselves?

In 2019, I entered my mid-thirties with a literary agent, financial independence and no prospect of a partner. Still, I reckoned I would be fine. My life would be a series of monogamous adventures. Yes, I thought, there would be days lost to self-pity and unrequited desire. Perhaps, I would meet someone. But meaningful work and close friends would help forge a truce with the romantic monkeys on my back. In any case, I had become cynical about love. A stable and equal romantic partnership seemed like a fantasy. My love life had become a subordinate part of my identity. I was a working professional, I was a fan, I was a committed friend, I was the primary caregiver for frail parents, I was an upper-caste English-speaking Indian living a life of guilty luxury in a poor country. These experiences defined who I believed I was. Not being someone's partner or wife did not sting as much as it did in my late twenties. Smug in my productive solitude, I felt prepared to live in equanimity with my singledom. Then, in the middle of March 2020, India stopped.

In its early days, the development crisis triggered by SARS-CoV-2 kept even half-economists like me frenetically busy. The hours were dizzying, filled with video calls and virtual meetings with government functionaries. I tried to serve the system as best as I could. Blitzed by a barrage of frantic emails and WhatsApp exchanges with transatlantic colleagues, I was hardly ever alone, though I was in lockdown. Deadlines kept me company. As the weeks passed, like many Indians,

I struggled to comprehend the apparent global collapse—the once-efficient systems of advanced Western countries were breaking down. In India, militant Residents' Welfare Association aunties were using social distancing as an excuse to give free rein to their casteism. On TV, technocrats discussed 'fiscal space'. On the internet, people vented their anger against each other and their governments. Calm doctors preached hygiene and patience, while COVID-deniers and lockdown sceptics screamed conspiracy; hungry workers, tired of pleading for transport back to their villages, took to their feet. As career civil servants offered sincere efforts or cynical excuses, communities came together to cook meals for the elderly. Less hearteningly, millions were losing jobs, employers were withholding wages and those of us with resources were drinking away our pain and fear with liquor delivered to our homes. Little did we know then that the full horror of the pandemic in India had yet to manifest itself. In a year, all our fears, structural injustices and dysfunctions would magnify and meld into an all-encompassing spectre of death and dismay.

I was desperate to have unscheduled spontaneous conversations about it all. To hold someone through this catastrophe. Instead, I was resigned to plan virtual dates with friends, where our intimacy was consistently compromised by patchy internet connections. My best friend, also single, felt as I did. But our mutual love and solidarity, expressed through words and facial cues on a screen, could scarcely calm the panic within. Each night, as I reflected on the day that had passed, I experienced a mix of solitude blended with a lingering sense of loneliness.

Seated on an ergonomically challenged chair, I received the world through screens and windows. I watched women wage war against the virus—wives caring for their in-laws, mothers reprimanding children for not washing their hands, an underpaid female army of community health workers, nurses and contact tracers performing essential services. In my own neighbourhood, so reliant on the labour of domestic workers, wives now cooked and cleaned for large families with no help from their husbands. The men would spend hours on loud phone calls with office colleagues and clients, anxious to signal great productivity. They were eager to return to their workplaces, the core of their personhood. Married women retreated into endless hours of domesticity. For some, this was business as usual. 'We are used to being at home,' a colony housewife told me, 'but the work without my maid is much more. This lockdown is toughest on men and children— they go out a lot more than we do.' As we exchanged pleasantries across our rooftops, she hung clothes up to dry. Data shows that the majority of Indian women have sacrificed careers and the world beyond their homes, all for their family and children. If anything, the virus made this sacrifice feel more thankless and laborious. Domestic violence inflicted by male partners was rising through the lockdown; women were exhausted with no time to themselves.

Witnessing these online and offline scenes, I felt self-satisfied and blessed. From the vantage point of my veranda, I stared at the toiling mothers, restless husbands and irate children, thanking myself and my exes for sparing me a life of domestic suffocation. I felt grateful that I was doing fewer dishes and had the freedom to participate in the world as a paid professional. On social media and on virtual friend-dates, I would spot the rare equal partnership—husbands washing dishes, wives conducting webinars. These exceptional relationships felt as unreal to me as the romantic fantasies sold in Hindi films, at least compared to the domestic imbalance on display in my immediate environment. But on occasion, even on my traditional street, within the unfair homes, I could see exhausted wives chatting companionably with their husbands. I envied these couples, although I would never wish to be them. They had conversations without appointments. The rules of traditional Indian marriage mandated them to take each other to the doctor. These couples embodied a kind of easily accessible support I could only fantasize about.

The crisis has coloured my singledom. I am on my own. No siblings, no husband, no inheritance, no friend commune, no familial safety net other than my ageing parents. These facts no longer feel as comfortable as they did before the world locked down. The surge in registrations for online matrimonial sites through the health crisis in India suggests that my discomfort is shared by many. The pandemic won't propel me into becoming a marriage-obsessed fiend. I'm not moving in with my friends either. Weaving a human infrastructure from the fabric of friendship is costly and uncertain. A group of my closest single friends joke that we'll rent an apartment building, with each one of us on different floors. But this is far in the blurry future. Over the next decade, as we reassemble and build our post-pandemic selves anew, my friends will no doubt continue to lead their independent lives. And while my faith in self-reliance has been shaken, I have no reason to think I won't continue to prefer living alone.

On good days, my singledom feels like a hard-won ally. She allows me the space to design my life as I please, to be selfish and embrace a more public role than most women in my country can enjoy. On bad days, my singledom becomes my nemesis, reminding me that I never chose her, that I am alone because love never arrayed itself into my life. She chastises me for failing to settle for a sensible man. At her very worst, she resurrects buried fantasies of finding a partner and love. As the fantasies resurface, so do old doubts. My singledom conjures images from failed romances, asking uncomfortable questions, tearing into past choices. As you'll soon discover, not very long ago, I spent too much of my time obsessing over some idealized-gentry-type or another. Encouraged by my singledom to wallow in past misery, I excavate the ugly remains of my romantic past. Why didn't he pick me? Why couldn't I have been the One? Why is no one madly in love with me? Am I not good enough? Am I too picky? A map replete with signposts of romantic rejection haunts me. I must endeavour to exorcize my ghost.

In my darkest teary-eyed moments—and there have been countless—there He is. This hazy image, there is Shah Rukh. Arms wide open, promising the ultimate refuge in love and conjugality, yet mocking the sham of my filmy fantasies and expectations. His image serves as a constant reminder of how far I've travelled—chronically dissatisfied with the men I keep trying to be worthy of. I am tired, I am disappointed and I am desperate, but as I have learned over the past decade, I am also not alone.

From the drawing rooms of Jor Bagh to the forests of Jharkhand, across diverse classes and communities, Shah Rukh Khan appears as recourse in many teary-eyed moments triggered by the drudgery and ignominy of being a woman in modern India. While visions of Shah Rukh might serve as mere escapism in the plush homes of Lodhi Road, indulging in fandom becomes a form of assertion, even protest, amongst poor and working-class women. The ability to watch films and buy iconography independent of the family is a freedom bestowed by employment. Espousing the virtues of Shah Rukh marks a woman's enthusiasm for expressing desire rather than *becoming* desirable. Daydreams, posters and cinema tickets signal hidden peeves and protestations. Saddled between expectations, exhaustion, desperation and dissatisfaction, constantly yearning to be free…I am joined by the lonely working women of India.

Through fifteen years of my professional life, talking to women across the country, I pieced together a fan club that turns to Shah Rukh in times of turbulence and heartache. None of the club's members know one another; they'll never meet. The club only exists in my head. However, each member curled up with Khan's tweets and films during the COVID-19 crisis. In seeking out Shah Rukh, they're not seeking entertainment alone. Sure, they're looking to have fun. But they're also looking for new scripts and metaphors, new ways of relating to men, money and marriage.

This book isn't about Shah Rukh Khan. Rather, I hope to reveal how female fans use his icon to talk about themselves. Their stories will illustrate how his films, songs and interviews are invoked to frame a feminine conversation on inequality within families, workplaces and contemporary romances.

Life can often be described as the distance we travel between the people we are and the people we want to be. In one of Shah Rukh's greatest films *Swades* (2004), his character returns from the United States to India to reconnect with his roots. As he drives to a remote village to find his childhood nanny, he offers a sage a lift. Together, they sing a song, composed by A.R Rahman and written by Javed Akhtar. The song says, 'Just keep travelling. Life is a vehicle and time is the wheel.' *Yuhin chala chal raahi. Jeevan gaadi hai, samay paiya.*

My primary interest is to shed light on the trajectories of a few Indian women as they travelled from the 1990s into the 2020s with a film star for companionship. These journeys are as far from feminist principles as Shah Rukh's films are. Their politics may not live up to progressive ideals. But the messy beliefs on display serve as important guides to understand the lived experiences of Indian women without active Twitter handles, those considered too ordinary to find mention in the news.

I present each woman's journey based on her location in the Indian wealth distribution. Part I of this book introduces the actor and the fantasies he inspires in elite women. The stories touch upon the lives of fans like myself, Vidya (a Brahmin engineer), a 'Rajput Philosopher' and composites of various upper-class women I interviewed. Part II presents the 'Accountant', an ambitious government clerk, and Gold, a lonely sleepless flight attendant—both of whom are the first women in their conservative business-caste families to hold paid jobs outside the home. Part III follows women from India's low-income precariat: Zahira, a community organizer and informal worker in the slums of Ahmedabad; Manju, a garment worker bored stiff by her life in semi-rural western Uttar Pradesh; Sandhya, a Bengali part-time cook and housecleaner; and Lily, a tribal Christian domestic worker who migrates between rural Jharkhand and the posh Delhi neighbourhood of Jor Bagh. Part IV starts with a debrief with various scholars and activists. I conclude by talking with fans—a syncretic mix from different faiths, classes and countries—who have lined up outside Shah Rukh's mansion in Mumbai, hoping to catch a glimpse of their favourite star.

The chapters that follow chronicle a paradoxical fan club: full of hopeless romantics born in the 1980s, fantasizing about an impossibly idealized kind of love they'd seen an actor perform on-screen. Yet, all their real-world efforts were extremely pragmatic, often sacrificing the love they fantasized about as a price for earning status, security and financial freedom. These women relied on Shah Rukh when they found the real world and all its pandemics and practicalities inhospitable. Because only the deepest dissatisfaction with reality drives us to dwell in fantasy.

So, what does this club look like? What realities are these women running away from? Where do their fantasies take them? From economic liberalization to an economic lockdown, what did their days and daydreams amount to?

I
Fantasies

1

A Loveless Landscape

Uljhan bhi hoon teri, uljhan ka hal bhi hoon main
(I am your problem. But I am also your problem's solution.)

—*Zero (2018)*

Imagine an expedition. We are a team of explorers, journeying deep into the inner monologue of a heartbroken woman, the subterranean conversation she conducts with herself. The landscape of romantic bereavement is hardly alien to any of us, full of familiar sights and sounds. On the surface, our subject is cool, perhaps even flippant. But we hear her private thoughts, we see her grapple with the aftermath of loss. She is nursing a broken heart and an injured spirit. We decide against dismissing her heartache as banal. Our expedition starts surveying the pictures she draws; we become students of the stories she tells herself.

As we step into her mindscape, we begin to understand how she sees the world. She likes her job. Her professional life elicits a fierce loyalty. She feels a warm attachment towards clients and colleagues who've helped her survive and succeed. We sense deep gratitude for champions and mentors who have guided her through office life, its

3

hierarchies and casual politics. She is proud of her achievements as a working professional of some import and value to her workplace. That pride—of being visible and valued in a system designed to sideline her, to render her voiceless—offers a reservoir of worth and meaning.

She has just had an important week at work—a project she had helmed was released successfully into the world. We might expect her to be thrilled by this triumph. Instead, as we rummage about in her thoughts, we find that she is queasy, berating herself for her inadequacy. She is preoccupied with the sudden and surprising death of a long-distance romance. The joy of making a productive contribution to the world seems completely obliterated by the sting of romantic rejection. She had gradually revealed herself to this man, and felt he did the same. They were building an intimacy, paying attention to the humdrum matters in each other's lives. There was such a charge between them, it electrified dinner tables. Sadly, pragmatism plundered all prospects of emotional exploration and discovery. Distance, respective life goals, many sensible motifs were invoked. Six hours before she boarded a flight from New York to London, en route to New Delhi, he had subjected her to the tired platitude of 'it's not you, it's me'.

Sprawled on a hotel bed, she reminds herself that this connection was never expected to evolve into marriage or a lasting commitment. The logistics of the affair were impossible to begin with—an Indian woman with a rewarding career in New Delhi dating a white Western man in the midst of an equally rewarding career in New York. Despite the odds stacked against them, she had never expected that the end would be so brutal, that his attitude would be so utterly cavalier. Weeping would help, but her body won't oblige. She clings to the hotel linen, unable to physically manifest her pain through tears. We listen closely: she isn't grieving the demise of her quasi-relationship as much as how it ended without exacting any visible emotional toll on her ex.

We hear her ego whine and wail. *He was so nonchalant and inarticulate. The sex and continuous conversation must have meant very little to him, I must have misread the depth of our relationship. Was the sex bad? I don't remember it ever being bad for him. He never took me very seriously. If he really cared an iota about me or what I think of him, he wouldn't do this a few hours before I boarded a flight. He would have ended it properly. Instead, he looked like he had been sleepwalking through our entire affair. When I said we were wasting our connection, he suggested we have dinner the next time I visit New York. Dinner!*

The hotel reception interrupts her angry ballad, informing her that an airport pick-up will arrive shortly. She stares at the room, memorizing all its details, like a detective investigating a crime scene. She has been the victim of a brutal emotional crime, she tells herself. The forensics suggest otherwise.

Wordless, her mind meditates on images. She recalls how they had entered the hotel room. She'd expected pre-departure sex. Instead, he said he didn't want this, didn't want her anymore. Initially, he complained about the distance. After a few half-formed sentences, he changed his plan of attack. He muttered something incoherent about the need to 'figure out his life'. He claimed to be a 'complicated person'. Recollecting the scene, she laughs out loud. He isn't all *that* complicated, we hear her say.

She knows his kind. He is a prototype of the Western cognitive universe, where calibrated composure is strictly preferred to any display of vulnerability. A man of tremendous promise and perfection, collapsing under the weight of his own potential. A simple and decent man, his love life is steeped in the robotic rituals of serial monogamy. A man who has forged and forsaken intimacy so many times that he is inured to romantic aches and niggles. A man stuffed full of accolades, yet starving for meaning. A strategic man, his cold calculus of self-actualization has classified her as inconvenient and incompatible.

We fear she is an untrustworthy witness to her own victimhood. Her recollections bounce without a coherent sequence. All through the conversation, she had been distracted by a gaping hole in her stocking. *No wonder he left me; what kind of man desires a woman with faulty hosiery?* While concealing her stocking malfunction, she heard him say, 'Don't you ever feel like you just want to be alone?'

She had answered in the affirmative. But now, a few hours later, her heart dwells on the harsh unspoken truth: *He doesn't desire freedom from all humans, he desires independence from me, from our intimacy.* His quest for solitude feels like a scam. *Perhaps he's just not that into me,* she thinks. *Perhaps I'm just not that into myself.*

The quasi-ex had tried to pepper the conversation with praise, joking that he felt no need to 'butter her up'. Our team hears her struggle: *I am supposed to believe that I am terrific, although this man no longer desires to touch me. That I am so great, so damned terrific, that after weighing his options, he decided that he could easily do without talking to me ever again.* We notice that her raw feelings of rejection have no interest in considering the other's conflict or interiority.

She relentlessly replays their parting scene in her head. After an hour of listening to him make increasingly incoherent excuses, she had suggested he leave the hotel room. She remembers his response being a khichdi of boredom, guilt and relief. 'Are you sure? Is that what you want? What would you like? Some people want to talk, some people don't want to talk at all,' he had offered, as if he were a restaurant waiter reciting from a menu. *Madam, what kind of break-up would you prefer? Sunny side up or scrambled?* Scrambled.

When they started to exchange their final farewells, she drew on all her maturity and wished him the best. 'I'll miss you,' she said. He said nothing. All goodwill between them evaporated in that room, dried up by his lack of language and her expectation of an empathetic ending. We realize that no real crime has occurred here. Her break-up was so cliché, it would make clichés blush. One person unexpectedly decided to jettison another without using too many words or without much affect. While the asymmetry of romantic power is unbearable, it is yet to be declared a criminal offence.

After clearing airport security, she dials her best friend and seeks counsel. 'If you expect a man to offer sensible words for a break-up, to show you how he actually feels, you're expecting too much. Anyhow, nothing he says will ever make you feel better. Life is not like one of those ridiculous Hindi film romances you love, where Shah Rukh cries and always knows what a girl needs to hear and how to say it. In real life, men are sex-crazed robots who can barely express themselves. I'm sorry for what happened but it's probably for the best. Don't torture yourself with what he did or did not do,' her best friend says on the phone. But she is in no mood to absorb sensible advice. As she boards her flight, the sadness of separation gives way to humiliated rage. She sips her champagne, unable to cry, unable to sleep.

Our subject is not foolish enough to believe that she alone can see things as they are. She doesn't harbour hardened, cynical views on many things other than the chronic lovelessness that is the fate of successful women in her city. Her firm belief in the romantic inequality between men and women of privilege is unshakeable, frozen through years of experience. She thinks: *Have I manufactured my own romantic misery? Am I expecting Shah Rukh in real life? Am I implicated in this mess? All my relationships seem to follow a pattern—I choose to exclusively care for a man while he chooses to exclusively care for himself.*

She is so very afraid. Afraid that she is designed to prefer selfish men. Afraid that all her feminism, friendships, hard work, will, strength and success cannot shield her from the unequal markets of love. Guilty that she's not enlightened enough to reject the need for a pair-bond. Nervous that her quest for love is nothing but a quest to love the structures that oppress her. She feels a desperate need to howl and cry but her tear ducts are blocked by pride and rage. *How did I become this person?*

We hear her catalogue the unequal prospects for personal happiness between her and the men in her milieu. Her quasi-ex's life, an international one of acclaim, allows the confidence of knowing he'll always meet interesting and suitable people. He can casually let go of any romantic connection because the probability of finding a substitute is not scarce for him. She too, can play the field. Sadly, her field is not as open and unconstrained. Patriarchy, geography and her preference for handsome men who take an interest in their partner's career ensure that she will occupy the romantic doldrums of Delhi, where sex is plentiful, but chances of an authentic connection are rare and depleting.

But she refuses to bargain with her romantic expectations. *Maybe it is all those silly Shah Rukh films and interviews. I have mad standards, I am expecting a movie star in real life*, we hear her say to herself. The price she pays for these 'standards' are loneliness and some social discomfort. Her exes don't face such terrible odds in love, they'll do all right. No man in Delhi with the same attributes as her will face the same shallow pool of romantic options, and the resulting fears and predicaments. *If I were a man with the same job and degree, I would be swimming in a sea of dates and attention. But I am not a man.*

We watch her trying to fidget her way to freedom. As she speeds past immigration, she wonders: *Is struggling to find a boyfriend a suitable feminist grievance?*

A sense of shame accompanies her along the taxi ride from Heathrow to her London hotel. Somewhere between Hounslow and Central London, the chatty Moroccan driver asks if she is Indian. He asks if she knows Shah Rukh Khan.

Of course she knows Shah Rukh. She loves him. In fact, at this point, she's convinced that loving him is part of her problem. Her problem and her solution. A formative influence, Shah Rukh was the man who had fooled the child in her into giving primacy to romantic love. The taxi driver waxes lyrical about Shah Rukh's fanbase in North Africa and the Middle East. 'Even Nadia Murad is a fan, amazing lady, and Malala. Both Nobel Peace Prize winners. I saw that. You know them? You know that?'

He continues, 'Don't mind but I feel like I can talk to you about these things. Looks like Shah Rukh will have to move to Dubai soon. You've seen what's happening in your country, right? I don't understand it, but seems like they cut internet in the capital and want to kick Muslims out?'

'It doesn't sound good,' she responds.

It's January 2020, a month since several parts of India had erupted in protests over legislation that outlined a path towards citizenship for 'illegal' immigrants, as long as they were not Muslim. Students, artists and thousands of ordinary citizens took to the streets to defend India's secular credentials and ethos. Her own friends, she knew, had joined the protests. Many were upset at icons like Shah Rukh for failing, for example, to publicly condemn the violence unleashed by police on students in Jamia Millia Islamia University, his own alma mater. Yet, all this talk of Shah Rukh and Indian current affairs don't divert her. Instead, we see her withdrawing further into her own private heartache. She has no emotional energy to reckon with politics. *These are important fights. And here I am, with my self-indulgent first-world worries.*

The driver continues, oblivious to her reticence: 'Let's hope it all becomes all right soon. But if he wants, Shah Rukh can come to Morocco as well. We love him back home. I have some of his songs on my phone, shall I play them?'

She is quick to refuse. 'I just had a bad break-up, I'm not really in the mood for Shah Rukh,' she says. A silence falls in the cab. When they reach the hotel, the driver helps with her bags. He smiles and says, 'It'll be okay—you, Shah Rukh and the country. You'll see. *Kabhi khushi, kabhi gham*; did I say that correctly?'

'Yes, you did. Thank you.'

He was referring to Shah Rukh's grand 2001 movie, the title of which translates roughly to 'Sometimes Happiness, Sometimes Sorrow'. The mention of that film provokes some self-acceptance within her: *It is my time to be sad—no current affairs, no books, no feministic rhetoric or moving images of resistance can prevent the pain.* No matter how trivial, she starts to realize how the standard hetero game was failing her, how she was failing herself. At a time when several of her friends had sent her messages about how 'Shah Rukh was failing the country with his silence', she wonders: *Has Shah Rukh failed me? Did he deliver me to this loveless place?*

After a quick shower, with immense spiritual purpose, she walks to the Madame Tussauds wax museum to commune with the waxwork of Shah Rukh. Now, he stands in front of her. A wax composition of all her self-pity and personal failure. She takes a breath and talks to him.

It's your fault. You're probably like all the idiot men of Delhi yourself. But I've grown up watching you, listening to you. You with so many words, always emoting, always talking, so much said with your face. You with your teary eyes. I know it's 'acting', that I am a fool to expect men in real life to be so emotionally literate. But I can't give up the fantasy.

She prays to Shah Rukh for release from the torment of romantic failure. She is a fan, a new-age devotee. While people in her country may want the flesh-and-blood version of Shah Rukh to speak on their behalf, to echo their personal outrage with the political weight his voice carries, she simply wants this wax figure before her to ferry a metaphysical message up above. For the time being, this wax statue has acquired mystical properties. She believes it is her intermediary, her means of communication with the higher power responsible for arbitrating romantic justice in the world.

The complainant argues her case. She tells him that this break-up feels unfair, that she is struggling to remember that a man's love is secondary to her life's work. *Why aren't family and friendship enough?*

Why doesn't my professional life make me as happy as my ex did? Why does a man's love matter so much? It's one thing to read, retweet and recite great feminists. It's quite another to live their lessons every day as a scared single woman in Delhi. I am sorry for being this self-obsessed when women in our country are protesting and struggling, but I can't deny my hurt. Where can I deposit it? Can you help me?

We watch her complaining morph into a fan prayer. She seeks his blessings and bursts into a fit of ugly crying in public. Now, the tears won't stop. She runs to her London hotel and cries the day away. We sense a transformation; her sadness has been cleansed of shame. On the second and final day of her London layover, the *Gully Boy* album is her companion for long walks in the city. She feels like a traitor, relying on Ranveer Singh as a soundtrack for her sadness. But it's impossible to listen to a Shah Rukh song and avoid another tearful scene outdoors.

On her flight to Delhi, she musters up the courage to invoke Shah Rukh through the miracle of aeroplane Wi-Fi. In a flash, he is on her mobile phone, offering quotes and wisdom, smiling and offering assurance, a picture of masculine vulnerability.

This time she cries herself to sleep.

Bleary-eyed, she lands at Delhi's Terminal 3 airport and gazes around at the humans collecting their luggage from the baggage carousel. She wonders if those near her need an icon to help them nurse failure or rejection. She wonders how they survive, where do they find diversion and comfort to tackle the emotional wounds modern life inflicts on all of us.

Our expedition continues. We study her thoughts till the middle of 2021. Through this time, a predictable recovery routine ensues, amidst the most unpredictable time in the world. She works through the multiple lockdowns. She argues about politics on her family WhatsApp groups. She tries to be productive, with intermittent periods of wallowing and weeping. At the peak of the second wave of the pandemic, she helps strangers find hospital beds and vaccination slots. She loses loved ones and co-workers. Surrounded by news of death, she feels nostalgic for her time in that hotel room where our survey of her interior life began, for a time when romance was the sole cause of pain. Eventually, she realizes that the universe and her quasi-ex have done her a massive favour. They've conspired to ensure she avoids participating in an unhappy relationship with a man who withholds himself. She returns to Shah Rukh's films and interviews; her demand for care and connection are invigorated. And she continues her irrational quest through virtual dates. She is desperately seeking Shah Rukh, desperately seeking an escape from this landscape of endless romantic disappointment.

We walk away from our expedition, puzzled. The typical tropes of Bridget Jones, *Fleabag*, the women from *Sex and the City* and other modern cultural totems representing the angst of privileged thirty-something working women don't feature the female protagonist crying at a Bollywood actor's shrine. What's going on here?

Who is Shah Rukh? Why does she turn to him in her most desperate moments? What does the love of his icon say about the modernity of modern Indian women?

I'll start with the easiest question.

2

Who Is Shah Rukh?

First, the Bombay film is a spectacle, not an artistic endeavour.
To accuse it of not being artsy is to chastise Muhammad Ali for not
being Charlie Chaplin.

—*Ashis Nandy, 1981*

I sell dreams and peddle love to millions of people back home in India, who all
assume that I am the best lover in the world.

—*Shah Rukh Khan, 2017*

If you haven't heard of Shah Rukh Khan, you stand to be judged as provincial and clueless in the places I come from. So global, so pervasive is his fame that it has become tradition for foreign politicians and pop stars to pay homage to him during their encounters with India. '*Senorita ... bade bade deshon mein*,' Barack Obama said in a speech during his presidential visit to Delhi, instantly winning the crowd's goodwill by quoting a famous Shah Rukh line from *Dilwale Dulhaniya Le Jayenge* (*DDLJ*; 1995). Popstar Zayn Malik and footballer Mesut Ozil are Shah Rukh fans. Actor Riz Ahmed tweeted about 'geeking out' when he received praise from Khan. Korean soap

13

stars and boybands love him, recreating his songs and moves. He has active fan clubs from Nigeria to Peru. Singapore has named an orchid after him. At Davos in 2018, he won the World Economic Forum's Crystal Award with Elton John and Cate Blanchett. The actor was awarded for his 'leadership in championing children's and women's rights in India'. The tallest building in the world, the Burj Khalifa in Dubai, is lit up in honour of Shah Rukh on his birthday. As Fatima Bhutto wrote in *New Kings of the World*, her study of the growing reach of Asian popular culture: 'Today, Khan though little known in the West, is one of the icons of a vast cultural movement emerging from the Global South ... Truly global in its range and allure, it is the biggest challenge yet to America's monopoly on soft-power since the end of World War II.'

It feels impossible to write anything original about an icon as self-aware and intelligent as Mr Khan. During an interview in 2019 with the American late-night legend David Letterman, the actor described himself as an 'employee of the myth of Shah Rukh Khan'. In 2016, the actor entered into an uncanny dialogue with his own celebrity in a film titled *Fan*, in which he played both a fanboy and the fanboy's favourite film star. Popular Indian film critic Baradwaj Rangan described the film as a 'risky deconstruction of his inherent Shah Rukh-ness'. Many commend the film as being one of the actor's greatest performances. In 2009, he starred in *Billu*, a film which shows the electrifying effect a star very similar to Shah Rukh has on village life and young rural women. One of my favourite Shah Rukh fan-service films is a small-budget movie called *Shahrukh Bola 'Khoobsurat Hai Tu'*. The film, released in 2010, features a remarkable performance by Preetika Chawla as a young woman who sells flowers on the street. A mad Shah Rukh fan, she yearns to meet her hero. One magical day, she happens to sell flowers to Shah Rukh himself. The actor appears in the film for a minute-long cameo. As he pays for the flowers, Shah Rukh tells the young girl that she is beautiful. When she narrates these events to her friends, they scoff, especially when she tells them Shah Rukh complimented her appearance. The plot is focused on how the fan daydreams and fights to prove that her story is true—she met Shah Rukh, and she is beautiful.

In 2017, Shah Rukh delivered a TED talk in Vancouver. He drew an amusing parallel between the journey of humanity and his own journey as an ageing film star, emphasizing the need for compassionate love as an overarching principle for how humans should approach global policy, automation and each other. In our world of emotional cowardice, censored thoughts and cynical actions, his call to compassion didn't feel clichéd. Lofty romantic notions are radical these days.

Mr Khan introduced himself to the Canadian crowd, many of whom were unaware of the extent of his fame, as a fifty-one-year-old movie star, 'the Muslim son of a broke freedom fighter'. In a light-hearted display of vulnerability, characteristic of his public persona, he says, 'Before this talk, I decided to take a good, hard look in the mirror. And I realized that I'm beginning to look more and more like the wax statue of me at Madame Tussauds. In that moment of realization, I asked … do I need to fix my face?'

I tear up a bit as I write this, because it must take unimaginable bravery for an icon celebrated for his youthful romances to acknowledge age on his face. That too, amidst a roomful of strangers. Then I laugh. Because I've heard many Shah Rukh detractors repeat the *exact* same criticism about him, of how he's become a caricature of himself, how he is too old and too haggard to play the lovelorn hero. Do they learn their insults from the self-deprecating things Shah Rukh says about himself? Or is he acutely aware of how people see him? I suspect it's the latter. The man displays a remarkable understanding of his own cult and celebrity.

So, it's tough to say anything new here. Because no one seems to interrogate their own icon with as much scrutiny as Shah Rukh himself. But let me introduce you to some private and public facts.

Through the years, I've come to know many people who've met the man or interviewed him. I've even had friends who've delivered TED talks on an Indian television show hosted by Shah Rukh. At the risk of sounding unhinged, I've begged for details from anyone I've known to have encountered the actor. What did I learn? I learned that he smokes Classic Milds. Each person I spoke to walked away from their time with him feeling like a superstar themselves, having been subjected to a relentless charm offensive. Not every interaction was necessarily pleasant—some of my interlocutors had been bruised by his humour and fierce dedication to his work—but everyone felt that Shah Rukh was kind, quick-witted and deeply conscious of his media image. Journalists in Mumbai said that the actor changed the energy of any room he walked into. Anushree Majumdar was a film journalist at the *Indian Express* in 2018 when she interviewed Shah Rukh. I interviewed her about her interview. 'My thirty-five minutes,' she said, 'was like being in a movie with him. He makes you feel that you're the most important person in the room and is so sharp and present that you never have to repeat a question or a word, he gets it all the first time. He has the ability to see something in you in that first moment and he tailors himself to your personality, without changing what is expected of him. He's truly special.'

Another journalist-fangirl recalled an embarrassing episode. She was asked to interview Shah Rukh in 2016 for a magazine. At the close of her interview, she asked him about his perspective on romantic love. 'I don't know why I asked him,' she told me. 'I wanted to stop myself, but I couldn't. It's not like he is a scholar on the subject, nor is he my therapist. But you know, I had to know what he thought of love. He defined love for our generation. I could not help myself. It was my one and only chance.' Shah Rukh politely replied, telling her that love contained multiple shades of all the characters he'd played over the decades. That love was silly, obsessive, playful, sweet, jealous and heartbreaking. He then obligingly filmed a short video greeting for the journalist's mother, a fellow fan, making both women ecstatic.

An American friend, unfamiliar with Shah Rukh's films or star status, spotted the actor at a party in London. She described him as 'a brown Cary Grant', and has been a loyal fan ever since. Of all the stories about selfies and fan moments I've been privy to, my envy was most provoked by an economist-policy wonk fangirl who bumped into Shah Rukh at Heathrow. She trailed him through the fast-track immigration queue and they chatted about her job as an economist at a leading commercial bank. He promised her a selfie after they cleared passport controls. Once past immigration, she found Khan waiting patiently to pose for their photo, which she promptly shared with her husband and friends.

Now, let me try and paint a portrait of Shah Rukh strictly based on information that is available to us in the public domain. Who is Shah Rukh Khan? The internet tells you that he is the 'biggest movie star in the world', 'bigger than Brad Pitt', 'the Tom Cruise of India'. A true-blue legend of modern India, he has been in the movie business since 1992. His films arc through Hindi cinematic history, grossing vast amounts of money and acclaim. Film critics and historians credit him with being one of the most media-savvy icons of independent India, revolutionizing Indian celebrity culture. Khan is an entrepreneur as much as an actor, at the head of an empire of endorsements and film-production plans fuelled largely by his persona.

He forms, alongside Aamir and Salman Khan, a third of the famous Bollywood Khan triad that looms so prominently over Indian cultural life. Of the three, Shah Rukh has featured in the most romance films. His filmography contains love stories that have become foundational to Hindi romantic lore, the standard to which all Bollywood love stories aspire. For those born before the 1990s, he embodies all the symbols and gestures of desi romance. It is an accomplishment that Shah Rukh appears to equally enjoy and mock. For instance, in a 2007 film, the actor parodied his on-screen romantic superpowers as 'Mohabbat Man' (literally Love Man). A forty-year-old marketing head for India's largest online matrimonial service said to me: 'The man, for good and bad, has defined romance for most Indians born in the 1980s. When we think of love, we don't even realize how much we think of him.'

Salman plays self-confident men, offering few words in his public appearances, directing attention instead to his biceps. He is wry and witty, and features in Indian news for court cases and relentless legal proceedings. Aamir's career conforms to a traditional understanding of the craft. He has evolved from early successes playing youthful lovers to becoming an actor synonymous with engaging stories, method and skill. He has steadily built a public profile of being a dedicated 'perfectionist'.

But understanding the nature of Hindi film celebrity requires us to take a broader view than an actor's filmography or his acting prowess. These men are heroes, not mere actors doing a job. Film stars in India enjoy, as one scholar put it, 'godlike fame in a land given to deification.' Actors and their films shape how ordinary Indians speak, dress and interact. They have an important cultural footprint. While a new generation of educated moviegoers is more interested in content than charismatic stars, a large swathe of the viewing public continues to expect cinematic spectacles from the Khans, not only in their films but also in their public appearances. These fans mimic the actors' mannerisms. They avidly follow every aspect of the Khans' careers—the TV shows they host, the advertisements in which they appear, their social-media posts and every news headline they make and interview they give. Salman and Shah Rukh, in particular, rely on their public charisma, infusing the roles they play on-screen with who they appear to be off-screen. The process is cannibalistic, where the actors repeatedly draw on popular gestures and mannerisms performed in previous films for future work and are often seen as simply playing themselves in every part. It's what their fans want.

If Aamir's celebrity is composed of competence and excellent film choices and Salman's of brash masculine confidence, Shah Rukh exudes anxiety and vulnerability. He usually plays fragile figures—the fragile lover, the fragile hero, the fragile husband, the fragile Muslim, even the fragile villain. In his films, Shah Rukh is rarely at ease with himself and those around him. The insecurities that bother Shah Rukh's characters have evolved through the progress of a career spanning three decades. In the early 1990s, his characters were worried about finding love and success. We see Shah Rukh portray the anxiety of being a bumpkin in the big city in *Chamatkar* (1992), the anxiety of sexual competition in *Deewana* (1992) and *Kabhi Haan Kabhi Naa* (1994), middle-class moral anxieties in *Raju Ban Gaya Gentleman* (1992), the toxic anxieties of unrequited love in *Darr* (1993) or the violent anxiety unleashed by an attack on one's family honour in *Baazigar* (1993). In a beautiful essay about Khan's career, published in the *Indian Express*, journalist and film-maker Paromita Vohra described his '90s on-screen persona as a 'social outsider, wounded by rejection from the club of adarsh men'.

From the second half of the '90s, as Shah Rukh steadily retired a wardrobe of oversized shirts and baggy jeans, his fashion choices were in service of slicker characters whose outer sleekness couldn't mask their nerves about love and overseas migration. There is the anxiety of navigating tradition and romantic freedom as a non-resident Indian (NRI) in *DDLJ*, the anxiety of an adopted child unsure of his elite father's love in *Kabhi Khushi Kabhie Gham* (2001) and *Pardes* (1997), of being a single parent in *Kuch Kuch Hota Hai* (1998) and the anxiety triggered by imminent death in *Kal Ho Naa Ho* (2003). Shah Rukh's anxious oeuvre extends well into the new millennium. Refined as his clothes and body become, bearing all symbols of globalized wealth, he still suffers the anxiety of marital infidelity in *Kabhi Alvida Naa Kehna* (2006), of nation-building in *Swades* (2004), *Phir Bhi Dil Hai Hindustani* (2000) and *Main Hoon Na* (2004), of being Muslim in *My Name Is Khan* (2010), *Raees* (2017) and *Chak De! India* (2007). The past few years have seen unusual films, where the actor no longer plays the undeniably desirable male. Instead, his characters are brimming with the anxiety of falling for spirited women who outrank them in terms of social status or accomplishment in *Jab Harry Met Sejal* (2017) and *Zero* (2018).

In his films, the resolution of the hero's anxieties about himself or his place in the world can range from faux-cool and ridiculous slapstick to sexist commentary. Anxiety also manifests as murder. His characters are often emotionally destitute, unable to feel fully loved and unwilling to let go of their need to find love. The love Shah Rukh's characters seek is not only the traditional love of a woman; they desperately seek the love and approval of fathers, friends and fellow countrymen. The men he plays feel deeply, are constantly vulnerable to the gaze of the Other and shed many, many (many) tears. His personal story of losing his parents at a young age has amplified the narrative of Shah Rukh being a fragile and sympathetic figure. The sight of him winning his first important movie award in the early '90s, raising the award to the sky with tears in his eyes, expressing gratitude to his deceased mother watching him from the heavens, felt very much like the culminating scene from a Bollywood family saga. But we never feel sorry for Khan; he seems to enjoy his fame far too much for that. Shah Rukh has crafted a deliciously arrogant and poised public persona, forever seducing us with moments of self-disclosure followed by self-deprecating intellect and bitter sarcasm. For his fans, he is an unknowable package of sex appeal, wisdom and witty quips. And in all his quotes and jokes about himself and the world, there is always the hint of a man hiding his vulnerabilities.

Shah Rukh's image deviates from standard masculine tropes. Both Aamir and Salman have captured many male hearts because they have made their bodies archetypes of phenomenal physical strength. A casual online search will yield many videos on how they gained muscle, providing instruction and aspirational goals to even the most sedentary male. Shah Rukh did join the body-building game. His late acquisition of six-pack abs made it to the front pages of newspapers and magazines. And the actor continues to bulk up for his upcoming 2022 release *Pathan*. However, for most of his career, he has been lighter of frame, less visibly muscular. He is built differently from the other two Khans, with a gentler physical presence on screen. Even his take on the murderous criminal from the *Don* series is more psychological menace than physical muscle. Khan decides to have fun with a role meant to be a strong and stoic man (originally portrayed by Amitabh Bachchan) by playing him flirtatious and rather camp in various moments. Nasreen Munni Kabir, an acclaimed film writer and documentary film-maker, said that he had 'sad eyes' that made women want to protect him.

Rumours about his sexuality run rife. The actor feeds the trolls. On a TV show, he quoted Samantha from *Sex and the City* and described himself as 'try-sexual, as in I'll try anything'. Shah Rukh, patron saint of the South Asian Metrosexual, became the first male icon in India to endorse women's beauty products. Aamir has been married twice. Salman remains a bachelor, his relationships with women fodder for tabloid gossip. Shah Rukh has been married to his high school sweetheart for thirty years.

Shah Rukh also appears more 'middle class' than the other two Khans. Sociologists have written countless books and papers on how he personifies the neoliberal ethic, an example of how to 'make it' in India's mythical meritocracy, rising to the top in a nepotistic industry. While Aamir and Salman belong to illustrious and old film-industry households, Shah Rukh has no venerable lineage to prop up his success.

Google Trend data gives you a flavour of Shah Rukh's international fanbase beyond south Asia. His fans live in some of the most conflict-ridden zones in the world—Bolivia, Tanzania, Syria, Iraq, Yemen, Sudan, Egypt and Morocco feature in the list of the top twenty-five countries where his name is most searched. Within India, his following is ubiquitous. The isolated islands of Andaman and Nicobar report the second highest share of Shah Rukh searches in the country, after West Bengal. While Salman wins the search contest in the Hindi heartland, Shah Rukh remains more searched in the southern tip of India, in Puducherry, Kerala and Tamil Nadu, where women's well-being and social mobility outcomes are better than in the rest of the country. In 2019, I visited the city of Kochi to understand why it was one of the cities reporting an overwhelmingly higher number of searches for Shah Rukh than Salman. On my first day, outside a café in the touristy Fort Kochi area, I saw a group of young headscarf-clad women debating where to have lunch. I walked up to them and asked who their favourite actor was. They started to giggle and could not understand why I was interested. Demonstrating some sympathy for my lunacy, they responded in unison: Shah Rukh. 'He is a good man,' one of the girls said.

Far removed from the patriarchal cow belt of the north, these women in the south adored Shah Rukh because he fit their notion of what it meant to be a good man. I asked this young woman why she thought Shah Rukh was 'good'. More giggling. Then a response: 'I saw his Davos speech and TED Talk online and I see his interviews. His films are okay, but he is intelligent and speaks well about life and women. I like that.' Her friend added, 'He seems like a God-loving man also, that is nice.' We talked some more, and I discovered that the girls were a group of college friends. They had recently finished their first-year exams and were spending a Sunday in Fort Kochi, visiting the ongoing Biennale. They were all college-going Muslim women from families with Gulf migrants. None of the women in their families had attended college before them.

Journalist Rana Ayyub—author of an award-winning book about the 2002 Gujarat riots —once wrote a piece suggesting that India thank Shah Rukh for his 'big brave message', demonstrated through repeated interventions on secularism and the Muslim identity. Reading his interviews and scanning his films, you sense that Shah Rukh has become more Muslim than the other two Khans in his public persona. On multiple occasions, the release of his films have been sullied by attacks from Hindu right-wing groups angered by his condemnation of religious intolerance. Perhaps Shah Rukh's most powerful performance came in *Chak De! India*, in which he played a Muslim hockey player who faces accusations of throwing a game against Pakistan. His character decides to redeem himself by coaching the Indian women's hockey team to an important victory. India breaks his heart, and he collaborates with a motley group of underappreciated athletes to use sporting success as a tool for recovery and reconciliation. In 2010's *My Name Is Khan*, a film about a Hindu-Muslim couple in post 9/11 America, he essays the role of a Muslim man with Asperger's. His character, Rizwan Khan, loses his beloved stepson to a hate crime in the US. In response to his son's death, Rizwan decides to find the American president, so he can tell him and the world that Rizwan's family does not harbour terrorists, that he himself is not a terrorist. *My name is Khan, and I am not a terrorist.* In a revealing article in *Outlook* magazine, Shah Rukh wrote, 'I became so sick of being mistaken for a terrorist that I made a movie to prove a point, but was still, with no small irony, held at a US airport when I travelled for its premiere.'

In an infamous episode in Khan's career, the actor was banned from entering the Wankhede cricket stadium in Mumbai in 2012. The Mumbai Cricket Association claimed he had started a fight with a few officials after a cricket match. The story hit the headlines; a photo of him looking unusually aggravated has probably been seen by every Indian. Eventually, the Mumbai police found no merit in the complaints made against the actor, and the ban no longer holds. In a later interview with Rajat Sharma on the TV show *Aap ki Adalat*, Shah Rukh explained that he was angry at security guards who were manhandling his children. When he arrived to collect them from the field, the actor was subjected to an unsavoury comment about his religious identity. Sharma's show was filmed with a live audience that offered sympathetic applause when Shah Rukh described the episode and his annoyance. For most of his career, the actor had always been called upon to play the Adarsh Moderate Muslim by the media. Historically, he has seamlessly played the part—reminding us of our secular traditions, his inter-faith marriage, his stage debut at a Ram Leela in Delhi, his reading of all major religious texts and how he continues to celebrate Hindu festivals. But in 2013, he grew irate and wrote, 'I am one of the voices chosen to represent my community in order to prevent other communities from reacting to all of us as if we were somehow colluding with or responsible for the crimes committed in the name of a religion that we experience entirely differently from the perpetrators of these crimes.'

If *My Name Is Khan* offered viewers a glimpse into Shah Rukh's feelings about the 'war on terror', in 2015 he spoke for himself, without recourse to the medium of cinema. In the first Twitter town hall held in India, Shah Rukh told Rajdeep Sardesai that he was concerned about the 'extreme intolerance' in the country and was saddened that as an Indian Muslim you had to often 'explain your Indianness'. In a follow-up interview with Barkha Dutt, he expressed solidarity with students protesting the appointment of Rashtriya Swayamsevak Sangh (RSS) members to positions of power at India's premiere film institute. The 'students were right', Shah Rukh said, before offering remarks on self-censorship and religious intolerance in India. Sounding frustrated, the actor commented, 'The fact that we need to keep on talking about the three Khans to prove how secular India is means that India is not [all that secular].'

The interviews with these well-known television journalists were intended to mark Shah Rukh's fiftieth birthday. Immediately after the telecast, the national general secretary of the Bharatiya Janata Party (BJP) denounced Shah Rukh for being a 'deshdrohi', a traitor to the country. The current chief minister of Uttar Pradesh was a serving member of Parliament in 2015; he compared Shah Rukh's comments and language to that of the terrorist who planned the Mumbai 26/11 attacks, proclaiming that if the 'majority community' boycotted Shah Rukh's films, the star would be forced to wander the streets like a 'common Muslim'. At the time, opposition parties and even official spokespersons for the BJP criticized these comments against the actor, while the national government distanced itself from what was said. A month later, reflecting on the threats to disrupt the release of his films and the controversy that followed his remarks, Shah Rukh told Mumbai's *Mid-Day* newspaper that he had not meant that India was intolerant, rather he was giving advice to Indian youth to help create a more secular and progressive future. 'I talk about something,' he said, 'and it is misconstrued, and I get into trouble. That's a nuisance.' Since then, Shah Rukh has been guarded about making any interventions on religion and national politics.

In Kochi, at random, I walked into a canteen managed by the state government of Kerala as part of a public digital literacy initiative. It was full of men using the free Wi-Fi to browse YouTube videos and job advertisements on their smartphones. Under the guise of research, I asked some of them about their favourite actors. No one mentioned Salman. This was the first time I had ever visited a place where there were no Salman Khan fans. I asked them why this was, and one of the young men grinned: 'In Kerala, we Malayalis watch good movies with good stories. People in the north like Salman for his muscles and being manly. But here we have actors like Mohanlal and Mammootty. Even for muscles we have Rana Daggubati and Prabhas from Telugu films. No need for Salman.' The men started

to laugh—southern muscles for southern men. I asked them about
Shah Rukh and they said they 'respected him' but enjoyed watching
his interviews more than his films. They felt the way he presented
himself was instructive and watched his media interactions for tips
on how to impress themselves upon job recruiters. And 'women like
him', they all agreed.

Minority at the Movies

To check my own bias, as a fan, I interviewed some of India's leading
film writers and critics, all of whom work for major publications.
When we talked about Shah Rukh's celebrity, each one had a common
thing to say: he is a female icon. 'He is a women's hero,' said Mayank
Shekhar, whose reviews have been published across the mainstream
press. Another critic said, 'No one has the effect on women, of all
ages, that he does.'

I spoke to Anupama Chopra, one of India's most prominent film
writers and critics and the director of the MAMI Mumbai Film
Festival. She has written several award-winning books on Indian
cinema. In 2007, she wrote about the rise of Shah Rukh in *King of
Bollywood: Shah Rukh Khan and the Seductive World of Indian Cinema*.
I asked her why Khan's imagery felt distinctly more female-friendly
(despite portraying men who harm women and generally toe the
traditional patriarchal line) than that of any Indian actor of the past.
'It's not about feminism,' she said, 'as much as how he treated women
in a dignified and respectful way. He played guys who were super
rich and super charming, but who would also be helping women
with housework and in the kitchen.' It was a trope, she pointed
out, through his work: 'In his breakthrough romantic role as Raj,
in *Dilwale Dulhania Le Jayenge*, his character played rugby with the
boys and raced aeroplanes but also helped an aunt select which saree
to buy. He fasted on Karva Chauth with Simran, so that it wasn't the

usual one-sided ritual, and served guests like women are expected to do. We'd never seen a combination like that before. He redefined masculinity on screen. It was such distinctive imagery. We loved it so much that we ignored the times that his characters did shitty things to women. So, I'm not really sure if it (his imagery) was explicitly about feminism or women's issues—there were films in which where he was killing and hurting women. But in his romantic films, particularly starting with *Dilwale Dulhania Le Jayenge*, his characters offered private moments of emotional support to women. He broke the mould with a more progressive and modern take on what makes a real man.'

In 2017, six out of ten audience members at an Indian cinema hall were men. A national survey in 2015 found that only eight per cent of adult women reported visiting a cinema hall at least once a month. On the other hand, the same survey found that twenty-two per cent of men reported making a monthly visit to a cinema hall. By catering to a massive female fanbase with his portrayal of a loving man, Shah Rukh has always served the fantasies of a minority group at the movies. While economic precarity and the decline of low-cost single-screen theatres have constrained the ability of most Indians to watch films, women do struggle more than men, particularly to experience cinema on the big screen. Limited access to media devices or lack of independent incomes, no free time for fun, unfriendly public spaces and rising ticket prices conspire to restrict the number of women who can enjoy a film. Men have more money to pay for the content they want to see.

As Shah Rukh aged out of youthful romances, though, he did succumb to the temptation to play the strong man. Between 2013 and 2015, his filmography is littered with mindless action films in which he exchanged few words with interesting women. He seemed to be busy playing catch-up with the hyper-masculine demigods who ruled India. At the time, the most commercially successful Hindi films were character studies of self-obsessed man-children—musicians, cops, photographers and mafia dons with hearts of gold. Vulnerability vanished from men in the mainstream movies. Shirtless Salman and unsmiling activist Aamir (also often shirtless) reigned supreme. When the six-pack substituted sentiment and flat abs won accolades, Shah Rukh was our only hope. Sadly, young men preferred Salman's antics, buying into a world in which love for a woman was demonstrated through brute strength and muscular gyrations. Romance involved barely speaking to the heroine, all the while protecting her by beating other men black and blue. Shah Rukh's *Chennai Express*, released in 2013, played a similar tune and amounted to his biggest box-office hit. Female fans were disappointed. Commentators felt that the actor was letting his traditional urbane 'multiplex' fans down in favour of 'mass' hits.

You'll hear this often about Shah Rukh. Film critics highlight that he has always been a multiplex-friendly hero, popular with sophisticated, urban audiences as opposed to the mass appeal of icons like Salman. Having met Shah Rukh fans in small towns and rural communities, those who could not dream of buying a ticket at an expensive multiplex cinema in Delhi or Mumbai, I've always been sceptical of this mass–multiplex divide.

I took my questions about mass versus multiplex audiences to Siddharth Roy Kapur, producer of some of Hindi cinema's most successful and stylistically innovative movies. At the time of our meeting in 2019, he was the president of the Film & Television Producers Guild of India. Among Roy Kapur's triumphs is *Dangal*, a 2016 film about the successes and strains faced by a pair of female wrestlers. Featuring remarkable performances by young women, the film includes a charming hat-tip to Shah Rukh. When the lead character, Geeta, leaves her home to train at a national sports academy, her fellow female wrestlers insist on watching *DDLJ* on TV after dinner. Geeta declines; she would rather sleep. In response, her friend, a co-trainee says, '*Shah Rukh ko na nahin bolte, paap lagta hai.*' You never say no to Shah Rukh. It is a sin. This exchange is followed by a short sequence of these future sportswomen swooning and whistling while watching a famous scene from *DDLJ*. *Dangal*, much like *DDLJ*, is one of the top ten most commercially successful films in Hindi cinema history.

I asked Roy Kapur to walk me through the difference between multiplex and mass films. He replied by cautioning against easy labels. 'In the industry,' he said, 'we're quick to label things before understanding their nuances. These niche films, which are targeted to more educated audiences, existed in the past. It's just that the audience for these films has expanded as the audience is more educated now.' We agreed that there was no neat mass–multiplex binary and settled instead on a simple definition: that a mass film simply meant a film that has a large budget and distribution network, a film that you, your mother, your mother's presswallah and your mother's presswallah's extended family have a chance to see before its television premiere. A multiplex film is more targeted to an urbane, Westernized and wealthier audience like me and my friends, often released on restricted numbers of screens. The latter audience prefers realistic cinema with characters and plots they can 'relate' to. The female Shah Rukh fans I knew did not care if they could relate to the films they watched. Given the aggressively masculine spaces these women inhabited, they yearned for an escape from reality. Sadly, Bollywood fantasies were primarily designed for men.

Discussing the share of women watching Hindi films in Indian theatres in 2019, I asked Roy Kapur for a guesstimate. He said, 'I think there was a time when the audience was eighty per cent male. It's improved in some pockets. But I think it is still largely male, say sixty to seventy per cent depending on where you are.' We talked about how difficult it was for women to watch films at the cinema and whether this inequality surprised him. 'Honestly,' Roy Kapur admitted, 'it doesn't surprise me. It saddens me. But we all know the kind of country we live in. How can we expect the way we watch cinema to be an exception?'

For the Shah Rukh fangirl, Hindi movie romance between 2013 and 2015 had become stale. The manic energy of on-screen millennial love tired her. Hrithik was too perfect for sex. Ranveer was all swag and sex. Ranbir was all swish and sex. Ayushmann was too sweet for sex. She cheered the few remarkable films in which women learned to love themselves instead of men. Shah Rukh's cosmopolitan fans relied on foreign media to see grown-up men loving grown-up women. Seated in a cinema hall, watching our hero in action films with fast cars and few women, the anatomy of many Shah Rukh fangirls became frail. Our icon had abandoned us. We found ourselves marooned on an island within Indian popular culture, unable to find any connection to the images transmitted. Anupama Chopra, recalling how Shah Rukh characters were once invariably a lovesick Raj or Rahul, closed her review of his 2013 *Chennai Express* with the plea, 'Now come back, Rahul. All is forgiven.'

After his detour into high machismo, our hero would return to us in 2016 with a female director at the helm. He would play a sexy shrink to a young woman. From then on, he would persist in talking to women on-screen and acting in films where women had more than half the share of dialogue. It was a radical departure from most commercial Hindi cinema in which the loud, overbearing presence of a male superstar inevitably drowned out the voices of women.

In the late 2010s, audiences had their pick of niche multiplex films and web series in which women were given room to speak. However, 'mass' films with equal female dialogue would no longer rule box-office records. A *DDLJ*, with tons of women's voices, was the biggest hit of 1995 and one of the biggest all-time box-office successes. But in 2020, we were back to a box office dominated by loud and proud men. Films on women's menstrual health would be made with barely any female dialogue. Men would constantly speak for and in place of women. While Hindi film scripts were changing to feature vocal and exciting women, male characters continued to receive a much larger share of humanity and subjectivity while the ladies remained hideously objectified. The films in which women spoke freely and frequently were often those without male superstars. When women's words were central to the storyline, their characters were usually concepts or causes, rarely complex, fully formed people. They were what Paromita Vohra called 'a new catalogue of [female] types—badass, ditzy, heroic, victims'. A woman on celluloid is always the Beauty, the Bitch or the Bechari, never even our own muddled desi Bridget Jones.

At the same time, sophisticated multiplex films have relaxed the need for men in the movies to be as charismatic as Shah Rukh or as muscled as Salman. Their plots help an audience appreciate male characters beyond the metric of sexual attractiveness, masculine strength or wealth. They accord a rich interiority to capitalism's male losers with sympathetic stories about corporate burnouts, elderly men, balding men, unemployed-youth-turned-sperm-donors, coal mafias, gangsters and psychopaths. The new heroes of the multiplex are hardly matinee idols, they're terrific scripts about the men-next-door. Women, though, are still objects, their sex lives seemingly the only arc of interest. They remain physically present, whether they are wrestling, dancing, performing jauhar, or looking painfully glamorous, but are nearly always silent. At the close of this book amidst a pandemic, I measured how many lines of dialogue women spoke in some of Hindi cinema's biggest hits. The results were depressing. At the movies, most women remain gorgeous and mute.

Before the pandemic closed down cinema theatres, the highest-grossing Hindi film in 2019 was *War*, starring Hrithik Roshan and Tiger Shroff. Its contribution to Hindi cinema is surely the mainstreaming of homoerotica. The camera pays lingering tribute to these men, their muscles, their moves and their beauty. Women are incidental to this worshipful tribute to the male physique, which pretends to be a stylish action film with a fleeting interest in the Indian Muslim identity. One woman does appear for a brief post-interval bikini-clad scene and song, dying soon after. Another plays a crucial role in the plot but says almost nothing. Compare this with Shah Rukh's final release before the pandemic, *Zero*, which boasted two powerhouse female performances—Katrina Kaif playing a fiercely charismatic, troubled actress and Anushka Sharma playing a scientist. The film has no interest in male heroics and is full of scenes in which these strong women ridicule Shah Rukh's character for not being able to match up to them. The contrast is made literal by the fact that Shah Rukh's character is a dwarf. Of course, Khan will always keep us guessing, never allowing me or anyone else to cage him with clichés. His post-pandemic release is being made by the same team that created *War*.

Shah Rukh isn't a feminist icon. The overwhelming power of men to dictate the commercial fate of a film will never allow that. As you probably know, or as you'll discover through the course of this book, he has stalked too many women on-screen and said too many toxic things in his filmography. But when measuring screen time and dialogue of his biggest hits relative to his contemporaries, Shah Rukh's films are found to have more time and space for women's words. Female characters tend to play a more equal part in his oeuvre, perhaps because establishing romantic love or familial harmony requires women to participate more than, say, in a testosterone-laden action drama or a gritty gangster story. Although even in films where he plays criminals or robots, women's words are central to the plot. And women have much to say about Shah Rukh, from Mumbai to Morocco. He isn't a feminist icon, but certainly a female one.

Being Shah Rukh means being an important icon for women across vast regions, religions and classes. Someone who unites many women in admiration, anger, and anger's parent: expectations.

3

Engineering Shah Rukh

My critics complain that I do only love stories. You can't generically dismiss me off as a lover boy. If mothers like me as an ideal son and women want to marry me, it is because they see the subtleties of Shah Rukh Khan, not just the caricature who has his arms widespread.

—*Shah Rukh Khan, 2016*

I met Vidya Shekhar at a Sunday matinee screening of *Ae Dil Hai Mushkil* (*ADHM*) in 2016. The film was director-producer Karan Johar's attempt to explore unrequited love among an impossibly good-looking group of wealthy south Asian migrants living between London and Vienna. Only half an hour of the three-hour-long film is spent in India for a wedding sequence. Shah Rukh Khan had a five-minute cameo. I was determined not to miss it.

The Diwali release of *Ae Dil Hai Mushkil* had been thrown into jeopardy. Big budget Hindi films tend to jostle for release dates centred around festivals and public holidays. But right-wing nationalist groups had threatened to vandalize cinema halls that would screen the film. Why? Because the cast of *ADHM* included the Pakistani dreamboat Fawad Khan. Politicians, once fringe but now just as likely to be mainstream, declared that the film's use of Pakistani talent disrespected Indian soldiers fighting cross-border insurgents in India. A month before the film's release, relations between India and Pakistan had soured significantly following a terrorist attack that resulted in the deaths of seventeen Indian army personnel in conflict-ridden Kashmir. Indian authorities claimed that the attack was sponsored by Pakistan. Eventually, the Indian Motion Pictures Producers Association issued a statement declaring they would not employ Pakistani artists in the future. The Film & Television Producers Guild of India expressed solidarity with the government's counter-terrorism efforts.

At the peak of the controversy, Karan Johar released an emotional statement on video: 'I have always felt that the best way to express your patriotism is to spread love. And that's what I have always tried to portray through my work and my cinema. When I shot my film *ADHM* from September to December last year, the climate was completely different. The circumstances were completely different. There were efforts made by our government for a peaceful relationship with the neighbouring country. And I respected those endeavours, those efforts then. I also respect the sentiment today. I understand the sentiment because I feel the same. Going forward, I would like to say that of course, I will not engage with talent from the neighbouring country, given the circumstances. But with that same energy, I beseech you to know one thing—that over 300 Indian people in my crew have put their blood, sweat and tears into making my film. I don't think it's fair to them to face any kind of turbulence on account of other fellow Indians.' The film-maker offered homage to the Indian defence forces in the opening credits. The production house contributed fifty million rupees to an army welfare fund. These statements and concessions paved the way for the film's peaceful release on 22 October 2016.

Karan Johar's plea on behalf of hundreds of employees hints at the size and economic might of India's $2.8 billion film industry, one of the largest in the world. It employed nearly a quarter of a million people in 2017, according to data website Statista. Each year, around 2,000 films are made in India in more than twenty languages. As per the Federation of Indian Chambers of Commerce and Industry (FICCI), in 2019, the film industry outperformed expectations amidst an economic slump and grew at ten per cent. The Indian film industry is dominated by Bollywood, which contributes forty-four per cent of revenue. Within India, the number of cinema footfalls increased to a billion in 2019, of which 340 million were for Hindi films, reveals the Ormax Box Office report for that year. Unsurprisingly, gross box-office collections for Hindi films reached a historic all-time high in 2019 at ₹49.5 billion.

A week ahead of *ADHM*'s October release, the moment tickets were available online, I booked one of the best seats in my preferred movie theatre in Delhi. The seat had extra legroom, located in a row parallel to a section break. There were no seats immediately in front, allowing an uninterrupted view of the screen. I was a veteran of single-seat selection for this cinema hall. As, it turned out, was Vidya.

The cinema hall, with about a hundred seats, was packed. The film went on to be a mega-success at the box office in India and the UK. I had managed to settle down early and started scanning my surroundings, noticing families and twenty-something couples wearing their casual Sunday best. Large groups of female college students arrived, excited to see Fawad Khan. 'Pakistani men are way hotter than Indian men, yaar,' I heard a young woman announce to her group. Her friend giggled and said sarcastically, 'Don't be such an anti-national.' The gang of girlfriends erupted in laughter.

Behind me, an army of south Delhi's ubiquitous designer-labelled aunties assembled themselves. They'd arrived with their shimmering honey-golden hair and shimmering honey-golden bags, mildly drunk from wealth and brunch. There's probably a higher concentration of bleached blonde hair in some south Delhi neighbourhoods than in many American suburbs. The brunch club was eager to see the film's lead actor Ranbir Kapoor. They sang his praises: 'Sona munda hai.' The boy is beautiful, the boy is golden. I tuned into their conversation out of habit. The female gaze on the male body has always piqued my interest.

As the advertisements started, I noticed Vidya with one hand in her pocket, walking into the hall alone. She approached her assigned seat only to discover that a couple with intertwined hands and legs had occupied her place. Vidya was tall and toned, one of the few women without blow-dried silky straight hair in the hall, wearing her curls and her kurta with an easy confidence. She was the kind of woman who strikes you as sexy because she appears so relaxed. Vidya had booked a seat in the best row as well, eight places away from mine, also hoping for legroom and comfort. The couple did not budge. She looked displeased—the impending negotiation on seating arrangements would cost her the opportunity to watch the trailers in peace.

'We arrived late, most of the tickets were gone. They could not find two seats together for us. So, we had to buy tickets in separate rows. Could you exchange with us?' the Boyfriend said. The Girlfriend in the pair-bond also requested Vidya to trade seats with her boyfriend. I observed Vidya consider their proposal, quickly scanning the seat they suggested and rejecting it for limited legroom. She turned her eyes back at the couple and politely refused. She had spent effort and additional money to book her assigned seat, and it was far superior to the seat being offered to her. Vidya shrugged her shoulders and smiled, asking the Boyfriend to return to his allotted place. The young man remained seated and expressed surprise that Vidya wouldn't relent. 'But you are alone, ma'am, so we thought you could adjust,' the pair pleaded. They thought Vidya would privilege their coupledom over her own comfort. Everyone in our row was enjoying the spectacle. The Delhi aunties were paying attention as well. I heard one of them sigh and tell another, 'Why is the girl being so difficult, they're such a sweet couple and they asked nicely; it's just a seat.'

Vidya remained polite and firm, she said no. The couple left the cinema hall. Their goal was to watch the film as a social activity, a public celebration of their togetherness. Vidya wanted to stargaze in relaxed solitude. As she placed her purse and popcorn on the seat, we caught each other's eye. She was pleased that she'd been able to stand up for herself. But her pleasure was marred by guilt for having to eject the couple out of their cinematic experience. Sensing that she felt singled out, I smiled at her. We were the only two women in this crowd who had decided to watch the film on our own, the only women in the hall without any company. She smiled back. The silent solidarity of solitary women. Several sympathetic glances later, we became friends through the course of the film without exchanging a word.

It was not our shared singleness that forged our friendship in that dark hall. It was Shah Rukh. We cheered in unison when he appeared on-screen for his cameo. We hooted when he was thanked in the credits. Acknowledging our naked enthusiasm, we radiated approval towards each other. The film began by thanking the Indian army and ended with a black backdrop and the words: 'We love you, Shah Rukh.' Vidya and I *loved* Shah Rukh, and we were goofy and loud in expressing our adoration. The Delhi aunties, the gang of college girlfriends and the other people sitting beside us cast looks of judgement. They felt embarrassed for us. We were clearly uncool and odd. Neither Vidya nor I cared. Because our fandom in this posh and safe cinema hall was a place of no apologies, a place where we retired from the male gaze, a place where we sought no permission to be ourselves, where no other being's presence mattered. It was one of those fleeting moments in a dark hall where we did not care about being pretty, pleasant and proper. Vidya and I were mild and meek in regular life but reported shared histories of yelling at people who conducted phone conversations during a film screening. A cinema hall allowed us to abandon what others thought of us, to unabashedly claim our comfort, fun and freedom.

Meet-Cute

I tried and tried when I was younger to learn something about love, and since it wasn't taught in school, I turned to the movies for some clues about what love is and what to do about it.

— *Andy Warhol, 1975*

As we waded through the crowd exiting the movie theatre, Vidya made the first move and asked me what I thought of the film. While I had enjoyed it, I made a series of complaints against the lead male character in the movie. She nodded her head in agreement. One scene had bothered both of us tremendously.

In *ADHM*, Ranbir Kapoor plays Ayan Sanger, a musician and the son of a wealthy businessman. Through the first half, we watch Ayan's youthful heart grow cynical and cold after being romantically rejected by his best friend. Kapoor is an astonishingly gifted actor, he transmits Ayan's pain and longing to you like currents in your cinema seats. The music and direction obviously amplify the film's charge. Romantic rejection and loneliness unleash a period of musical creativity for Ayan. Simultaneously, to rebound and recuperate, he initiates a relationship with the successful, self-possessed and galactically gorgeous poetess Saba, played by Aishwarya Rai Bachchan. After they hook up at Saba's Art Deco flat in Vienna for the first time, the film does something big-budget mainstream Hindi movies almost never do. The couple doesn't automatically fall in love. Nor do they wake up feeling confusion, guilt and shame. Neither one dashes out of the door in horror. Nor is the woman's body objectified to titillate the viewer. They don't play cool and casual, pretending that the sex was meaningless. Instead, the audience sees two people assessing the implications of their intimate interaction in a calm, collected and mature way.

If India's employment rate helps us track our economic transformation, popular Hindi film extravaganzas track our moral transformation. Because Hindi cinema reaches more people than theatre or literature, these images tell us something significant about what is permissible to depict and imagine at any given moment. Johar's hyper-sentimental romantic dramas, in particular, are important as barometers of how mores are shifting. For all the sorrows and joys of love depicted in Hindi cinema, men and women are rarely seen *talking* to each other about the terms of their love and intimacy. They recite poetic praise for their beloved, sing songs, dance in coordination, hold hands and perform soft porn, but remain comically squeamish when it comes to conversing about sex.

Depicting sex is no longer taboo in Hindi cinema. Many contemporary films try and cram at least one 'hot scene' or 'item song' into the storyline because sex drums up viewership. Historically, villains in Hindi films divorce sex from love; they are depicted as rapists or immoral users of the female body. Of late, a subgenre of thrillers uses consensual sex as a means for men and women to manipulate each other for profit or revenge. Another subgenre attempts to portray the corporate or creative workplace as highly sexed, where women are mere pawns in the power games of men, suggesting sex as the only way a careerist woman can get ahead. Bollywood sex comedies show men being punished for seeking sexual satisfaction outside marriage. A few films use casual sex to suggest that characters are living in sin and have drifted away from their cultural and moral moorings. In a shameful, frankly racist scene, the 2008 film *Fashion* shows how a supermodel only realizes her ethical compass is broken after she wakes up in bed with a black man. And, finally, a nascent development: films like *Cocktail*, released in 2012, which use a woman's inclination for premarital sex as shorthand to signal how unapologetically modern and cool she is. Of course, she is eventually punished by romantic rejection and a car crash.

Big-budget romantic Hindi films rarely accede that a sexual encounter between decent people may simply be for pleasure or play, that sex may never lead to love or marriage. The traditional trope in modern Hindi romances is that you'll only have sex with someone you love, and sex is the apotheosis of love. If you have sex with someone and don't bother to love or marry them, you're worthy of punishment or the audience's judgement. Hindi movies rarely show how ordinary people struggle to make meaning of their sexual encounters. In doing so, these films conform to supposedly traditional Indian values in which any *talk* of sex remains taboo.

Despite the intensity of their passions, you'll never truly understand why people in Hindi film love each other as much as they do. Love is youthful and naïve in popular Hindi cinema. It becomes an attribute or a noun, not an action or verb, in these images. It is an innate immutable feeling *within* a person catalysed by another, not a series of ever-changing interactions *between* two ever-changing people. In the standard Hindi film format, love usually leads to marriage and sex. Shah Rukh's films from the late 1990s epitomize this ideal. Other than a recent 2017 film, I cannot recall a single movie in which Shah Rukh plays a character indulging in casual sex. The audience has only seen him perform 'sex scenes' in four films, where the actor is seen in bed with a woman—always someone his character whole-heartedly loves—without any graphic displays.

Shah Rukh's films and song sequences are immensely sexy, but passion is rarely consummated before marriage. He has only portrayed sex outside marriage in *Maya Memsaab* (1993) and *Kabhi Alvida Naa Kehna* in 2006. The former is a film based on *Madame Bovary*, where Shah Rukh plays one of the lead character's several lovers. The latter, a Karan Johar film, shows Shah Rukh's character explore an extramarital affair, only for the cheating spouses to be penalized by a three-year-long separation before they can be reunited. In all his romantic films, true love must translate into the union of marriage. It is marriage that generally grants legitimacy to the sex. Lovers may also unite in death.

Few Hindi movies divert from this mode; even fewer capture conversations between two consenting adults the morning after their first sexual encounter. But as the script of sex, relationships and marriage changes in pockets of India, the movies are changing as well. The scene that annoyed Vidya and me in *ADHM* starts to signal the messy nature of this change, and how Indian modernity imagines caddish tendencies to be charming. It is shot in an open-plan kitchen, an increasingly popular feature of elite Indian homes.

Ayan sips his morning coffee. He requests Saba's permission to use her poetry for his songs, which she grants. They begin to negotiate the meaning of their sexual encounter. Saba, a divorcee, says she isn't looking for a serious relationship. Ayan suggests they continue seeing each other casually. She asks about the rules of engagement. 'Rules,' he says, 'that can be easily broken.' Saba considers this no-strings-attached arrangement. She turns to Ayan and asks, not unreasonably: 'So, you get my poetry for your music, you get a chance to forget your lost love and broken heart, what do I get by being with you?' Ayan pulls Saba towards himself and says, 'Am I not enough?'

They embrace, and the camera zooms in on Saba's look of pure contentment. Ayan's mere physical presence and embrace are enough to satisfy this savvy and independent woman. The film never reveals any redeemable qualities that make Ayan adequate, let alone 'enough', to meet Saba's relational needs. He seems selfish and emotionally stunted, boorish and silly at times. And magically, the women in this film think his selfishness is charming. Saba is totally out of Ayan's league. I imagine he's phenomenal in bed.

Vidya, who had turned thirty-four a few months before the release of ADHM, agreed with my theory over a post-movie coffee. 'That must be it,' she said. 'It's his sexual prowess. They don't show us anything else that he can offer; he's just a messed-up rich kid. Honestly, a guy like that is no match for a woman like that. But look around us in Delhi—the ugliest men are with the loveliest women, and the women are insecure. The men think they've done these women a huge favour by being with them. At least Ranbir is handsome.'

We were giddy at the random nature of our meeting and our serendipitous connection, aware that we lived in a city where people in their thirties tend to already be ensconced in cliques. Delhi is not designed for random encounters with strangers. It is not easy to meet new people occupying different worlds from yours. If you are white, you earn extra social interest. But among Indians, you don't randomly smile at strangers on the street and in parks; the city is not built for pedestrian life. The footpaths are crumbling, and even before masks, the heat and pollution rendered us spiritless with limited smiles to offer. For women, the city is unfriendly as well; we are forever frowning or resting our bitch faces. Most of us hesitate to start talking to strangers at bars or restaurants—it is considered deviant and not culturally acceptable. And there are serious risks of bumping into a posh Delhi gunda. Vidya recalled how she was once followed by a group of men in a car as she drove home one evening after a friend-date. They whistled and screamed abusive taunts. It was only when the men saw that Vidya was driving towards a police van stationed further up the road that they sped past her. Vidya recognized one of the young men in the car; they had exchanged smiles at the restaurant where she had met her friend.

If New York is the city for epic encounters with strangers, New Delhi is the city where one avoids them in drawing rooms. Life in Delhi can feel like living in a Victorian novel, hoping to be announced and introduced to another. New spiritual practices and businesses are tapping into the city's market failure for connection by allowing people to 'network' and mingle through apps, chanting groups and paid membership clubs. Fortunately, Shah Rukh introduced Vidya to me.

My encounter with Vidya was an anomaly. We had not been to the same school or university, we did not work together and our parents did not know each other. In the capital city of India, networks formed at school and college remain preeminent. Past the age of thirty, you socialize based on what you do with your own labour and time. Lawyers drink with lawyers, journalists with journalists, new mothers with others in their 'Hot Mom' WhatsApp groups. People who own farmhouses spend time with others who own farmhouses. For couples, socializing occurs within an extended group of other couples. Our interactions with people outside our social bracket are limited to our employees—who drive us around, clean our floors, do our dirty dishes and look after our children—or those who perform one or the other quotidian service. Delhi, with its million floating social bubbles, can feel provincial. For elites, a city of twenty million people becomes a guarded citadel of twenty.

Fandom forged my bond with Vidya. It opened us up. We talked about our families, boyfriends and résumés. She was a product of three prestigious institutions—an Indian Institute of Technology, an Indian Institute of Management and a partial scholarship to study at an Ivy League policy school. After 'enduring the corporate boys' club for five years' at a multinational firm, she took a pay cut to branch into sustainable energy at a well-regarded private foundation. Her new employers respected weekends. As with her consulting job, though, Vidya still felt like she needed the support of a senior male to gain credibility for her ideas. However, her new office was less hierarchical than her previous place of work. 'At least here I can ask my male boss to send an email supporting my argument if he buys it. At my previous firm, those doors were guarded by men who would go drinking with each other and were often awkward with women.' She enjoyed her job and had hopes of starting her own renewables business. Coffee turned into dinner. Vidya continued to make her acid observations about Ranbir Kapoor's character. 'But Shah Rukh made it worth the time, even if he was only in it for five minutes.'

As she sipped her gin in contemplation, Vidya said of Shah Rukh: 'I'm so glad he endorses as many random brands as he does. I like driving past a billboard with his photo, it makes me smile to myself. Somewhere, we've travelled together, you know. It's nostalgia but something more. He is so different from typical Indian men—he doesn't preach, and he doesn't only build muscle and show strength. He is so comfortable being weak. Even if it's an act, I appreciate it. In fact, I've grown to admire him much more as I've grown older. He seems considerate and thoughtful when he talks about women. It's rare to see that in our country where every man can come to seem like an asshole or a predator or someone fundamentally unable to talk to women.'

Vidya's long-term boyfriend of nine years had broken up with her on the phone after he cheated on her. 'My first year back in Delhi from the US in 2013, we fought a lot and he called me arrogant because of my credentials. He himself had not been accepted when he applied to study abroad. My mother said it was clear that he was uncomfortable with my success. I did not believe her then. But looking back, it's obvious that he was punishing me. I don't think he did it on purpose, he was very nice and progressive, but it just happened.' Following the end of her relationship, Vidya became increasingly shocked at the cavalier attitude of the men with whom she pursued relationships. She gave me a summary of the brutishness on display—'The guy who ghosts after three months of wonderful dates; the guy who starts chasing after another girl at a party you take him to; the guy who says he needs to be with a north Indian girl only after we've had sex; the guy who ignores all women he doesn't find attractive and can't talk to your female friends with respect; the guy who tells me that I should stop working if things have to become serious ... there are all kinds of morons out there. My experience of trying to find a partner tells me that most men in Delhi can't date or marry women who are more successful than them. They need a girl who depends on them completely, who will look at them the way I look at Shah Rukh. Some guys do this without realizing it. And others will pretend to be liberal initially, but it won't last.'

A recent survey of Indian urban millennials—those born between 1981 and 1996—found that an overwhelming majority could not imagine a life without marriage and parenthood. Vidya was defiant, in no rush to find a husband. She held no desire for motherhood either. According to the Census of India, she was a demographic anomaly, part of a minority of just eleven per cent of adult Indian women who had never been married. At her age and in her class, the vast majority of Indian women were wives with at least two children.

In India, our families and our popular culture prepare a woman to think of marriage as the most important thing she can do with herself. They teach her that a life can only be concretized and legitimized through a stable marriage. And most Indian women learn to love the men they marry. Families coach young women to temper their expectations from conjugal partnerships, teaching them to settle and adjust. Some of this counsel can be helpful, but the socialization of Indian women aims to stymie female sexuality and ambitions for an equally rewarding intimacy. Vidya's relatives and friends, for instance, feared that she was 'being too picky,' that she should settle for a sensible boy. 'Sensible,' Vidya joked, 'usually means someone I'll find unattractive. But I just can't be with someone I don't admire or find appealing. Blame the Shah Rukh movies, the books I've read, but I just won't do it! I'd rather be alone than settle down with someone who I'm not drawn to! My standards are as high as Shah Rukh!'

Vidya's Inheritance

As an engineer and a Tamil Brahmin, Vidya was right at the top of India's modern caste-class system. Her mother Lalitha, a physics teacher with graduate degrees in sciences and teaching, married the third man she was introduced to. Vidya's parents met on multiple occasions before marriage, and this in 1978 was considered 'too much', too progressive, for small-town Tamil Nadu. Vidya's maternal grandmother was the first woman in her family to take up a job as a teacher at a prestigious private school near her home in Salem. And her great-grandmother was the first woman in the family to complete a college education before marriage. Each step required effort and calibration, none of these freedoms and achievements came easily. 'Yes,' she told me, 'families in south India are more focussed towards education, but it wasn't at all obvious that women would be allowed to go that far in their studies back then. Once my great-grandmother received an extensive education, she was keen to support my grandmother's choices and so on, all the way down the line to me. The women in our family have helped each other.'

Lalitha opted out of employment (as a schoolteacher) after Vidya's birth in 1982 to become the primary caregiver for her daughter. She was the first woman in her family to find contentment in giving birth to a single girl child. Lalitha resisted the pressure from her own parents to have a male child, telling them that she did not have the desire or capacity to give birth again. When her in-laws began to insist, arguing that she 'would need a son to take care of her in Delhi,' Lalitha became livid. Both she and her husband argued that a preference for male children was primitive and not befitting of an educated Tamil family such as theirs.

The decision to have a single daughter remains unusual in India, more so in the 1980s when Vidya was born. Even in 2016, only five per cent of Indian women above the age of forty had stopped giving birth after just one girl child. In Vidya's case, her parents made a joint decision driven by pragmatism as well as their progressivism. They were the first in their families to move to Delhi and it was an expensive city. In their own home, free of external influence, the Shekhars refused to accept that Vidya could only earn success and upward social mobility through marriage. Her parents invested heavily in her education, hoping that she would do well for herself and eventually for them. They encouraged her to be independent and to find meaningful work.

Because of her parents' beliefs and her own perseverance, Vidya became part of a highly privileged minority of Indian women. On that October evening in 2016, as Vidya and I ate and drank and fangirled on our own dime, we were among less than seven per cent of women our age in the whole country who held a steady, salaried job. Even in wealthy, urban metropolitan Delhi in 2017, a mere 13.7 per cent of women between the ages of fifteen and fifty-nine said they were employed for *any* paid job, compared to 71.4 per cent of men of their cohort. The average monthly earnings of an urban female salaried worker in Delhi were roughly between ₹14,000 and ₹25,000. Out of every ten urban women with salaried jobs in 2017, only three had written contracts with their employers. Only four per cent of *all* Indians with regular salaried jobs earned more than ₹50,000 per month. Vidya, with her two postgraduate degrees, earned four times as much after deducting taxes and enjoyed excellent social security benefits. And so, through generations of accumulated capital and care, Vidya found herself able to afford tickets to watch any film she wished at any time, all on her own. Her economic success allowed her to find love on her own terms, she did not need a man to support her family or herself. It allowed her to indulge herself, Shah Rukh and her fandom.

Vidya described Shah Rukh as a bundle of all things virtuous in her world of cisgender romance. We talked about how being a teenage

Shah Rukh fan was culturally on-point in the late '90s, albeit uncool among our more anglicized classmates. Persisting with fandom into one's thirties was troublesome. It wasn't easy to come out and reveal oneself as an adult female who still swooned over a movie star. *Being a fan* was a problematic admission amongst our friends. We were expected to have grown up by now. Part of maturing as an adult involved being steady and rational. An adult temperament required us to be stingy and cynical in our admiration of mass culture and popular icons. No sensible woman was expected to giggle uncontrollably the moment she saw Shah Rukh on a billboard. Fandom betrayed our lack of self-possession. It hinted at us being women not adequately in control of our hormones, feelings and actions. It was an act of wilful silliness, one that did not adhere to what was expected of serious well-educated thirty-something women like us.

The Student and the Fan

Don't ever take yourself seriously enough to be so clear about your own ideas that you stop respecting other people.

—*Shah Rukh Khan, 2015*

What did fandom mean for Vidya? She did not conform to any prototypical notions of a 'fan'. Even as a teenager in the 1990s, there were no Shah Rukh posters in her room, she had never acquired much memorabilia. Her mother wouldn't allow it. Vidya would often tell me that her love for Shah Rukh needed no material objects, only access to his movies. She found Shah Rukh in 1993, a year after his film debut. As an eleven-year-old, she came across one of his movies on cable and was hooked. Since then, she tried to make a point of watching all his films, even if she had to wait till they were shown on television. Her parents and close friends weren't all that interested in watching Hindi films in a movie hall. In middle school, she pleaded with her parents to buy her soundtracks and video recordings of Shah Rukh. Vidya's parents would agree, so long as she did well at school and finished her household chores.

Vidya told funny stories about how her parents worried that her growing obsession with Shah Rukh would make her a poor student. How she would jettison homework and even friends on days that a Shah Rukh film would play on television. It was impossible to contain her teenage enthusiasm. By the time she entered her mid-twenties, video clips of Shah Rukh were easily accessible on the internet. For her, Shah Rukh represented what many cultural anthropologists would call the 'sublime'—something that can only be experienced and cannot be clearly articulated or expressed. In her book on Bollywood and post-modernism, Neelam Sidhar Wright writes about popular Hindi cinema as 'being unique for its persistence in trying to present the unpresentable and summon the sublime on-screen—particularly intense emotions such as love'.

For Vidya, Shah Rukh was not an actor or an icon, he was a feeling that she floated towards. She lacked the words to describe how his imagery made her feel. Words like grit, ambition, warm, safe, nostalgic and loved were options she used and discarded as inadequate. Between the ages of twelve and sixteen, she maintained a private and inner shrine for Shah Rukh. 'It wasn't cool to like Hindi films and actors in my family or my school. My mother would look at me strangely if she caught me grinning foolishly at a Shah Rukh movie. I felt shame, so I kept the extent of my fandom quiet.'

As Vidya saw more of the world, Shah Rukh's images gave form and shape to everyday anxieties and longings. Eventually, she came out as a fan. She said her public declaration of fandom was, in part, catalysed by a longstanding rivalry with a frenemy from school. In the first year that I knew Vidya, it was impossible to talk to her about Shah Rukh without also talking about her batchmate. We labelled her 'the Student'.

Vidya and the Student had been close friends from kindergarten to middle school. They spent long afternoons on the phone exchanging the names of boys and books they liked and complaining about their parents. They bestowed the label of 'best friends' on each other. Then, as they turned sixteen, Vidya was dumped, ghosted. Her best friend stopped returning her phone calls. The Student had gained new admirers and friends from her extended family network and tuition classes. Vidya had spent a few evenings with the Student's new circle and knew she did not belong. 'I could not really pinpoint it, back then. I thought I wasn't cool enough or something silly like that. But now, I can explain it. They were just more Westernized and sophisticated than me. The books they read, the music they knew, I felt so out of place. Now I also know that my feeling of being a misfit was because they came from better-connected and richer families than mine. It was that simple. We could no longer relate to each other's worlds. She did not even try. We grew apart.'

The Student knew how much Vidya loved Shah Rukh. And following their break-up as best friends, she used this knowledge as a tactic in classic teenage warfare. Vidya's enduring love for a Hindi film icon, despite her access to Western media, became a weapon to humiliate her for bad taste. At school, during lunch breaks and free periods, the Student would loudly mock Vidya in front of their shared friends. Vidya barely defended herself, unable to match the Student's quickness, wit and social clout. Still, she missed her friend and ached for the old times. She hoped her silence would elicit some sympathy from her former best friend. It never happened. The Student was too busy discovering the world, enjoying the perks of teenage cool and confidence. In their final year at school together, the Student shamed Vidya for her 'nerdy, cookie-cutter' decision to take engineering exams. To keep things interesting, some taunts related to Vidya's unwaxed 'hairy' legs were added. Even in her thirties, Vidya could recount each rebuke she had filed away in an extensive catalogue.

Never a 'popular' girl in school, without the Student's patronage, teenage Vidya found herself on the social fringes. Despite her obvious intelligence and affinity for maths and science, she was not a 'topper', unable to conquer the rote knowledge required to do well in the ruthless Indian exam system. India's prestigious schools produce what Rabindranath Tagore once called 'a community of qualified candidates,' compelling young students to become 'victims of the mania of success in examinations'. Beyond tremendous psychological stress, the impact of such curricula is more insidious, converting a creative student body into orderly subjects of comparison and competition, perfect units of productivity. Each day, Vidya's teachers and parents would remind her that there weren't *enough* options out there. Good exam results became the ultimate exaltation. Vidya reflected, 'So many girls I knew at school gave up on a career or studying further because they believed that a bad score meant they were bad people. They were so scared of the academic competition that they decided to marry quickly and never pursued any other options; they lost heart.'

The Student's circle and Vidya's close friends did not feature in the academic merit list either. However, they seemed to be doing well in other fields—debating, drama clubs or the boyfriend Olympics. Vidya did not receive as much male attention. She was unable to talk about these troubles with her mother or her friends.

Instead, she became sarcastic and withdrawn, convinced that she lacked the beauty and skills required to socially succeed in the world. At this juncture, she turned to books, television and Shah Rukh Khan. 'Looking back, I know that watching some of his late '90s movies did more harm than good. He was the winner who would always have women interested in him, everything would go his way. Those movies should have come with a health warning like the ones for cigarettes. I loved those movies because I loved him, but I know better now.'

Through four years of conversations, I came to understand Vidya's grievance. Being attacked and rejected by a close confidante spurred in her the need to be among the winners of the great Indian rat race. Unable to battle the Student through conversation, she would fight her through achievement. She turned with renewed vigour to her textbooks. Perhaps conventional scholastic success, measured through marks and entrance exam results, would give her the confidence with which to finally overcome the Student and the void left by her rejection. Vidya locked herself into a lifelong competitive struggle with the Student. An endless exam.

Finishing school in 1999, Vidya wasn't aware of career options beyond the usual engineering, medicine, law or management. Diligently, she prepared for the engineering entrance exam with military precision, surprising herself and nearly everyone at her school by gaining admission to an Indian Institute of Technology (IIT). Having struggled mightily to make it to the right engineering school, she then struggled to keep up her grade point average. 'There were barely any women in my class,' she said. 'And none of them were friendly with me. I was too different from them. I spent my time with the boys. It was fun but very hard.'

For Vidya, jostling through the cramped corridors of Indian academic life, somewhere, subconsciously, Shah Rukh and his success became synonymous with confidence. At college she met many young men from small towns who loved Shah Rukh as much as she did. To them, loving Hindi movies and movie stars was natural. Indeed, many of these men came from families so poor that watching a film in a cinema hall was a treat, an extravagance. For many of Vidya's classmates, Shah Rukh represented a '90s fairy tale—manifest proof that tenacity and talent would earn social mobility. One of her closest campus friends would go on to join the elite Indian Administrative Service (IAS). On the day he called to tell Vidya the good news, he said, '*Ab main toh Shah Rukh ban gaya.*' Now, I have become Shah Rukh.

Vidya's time at IIT helped her grasp the contemporary engineering of Indian society. She studied her batchmates like an anthropologist discovering a new tribe. In the first six months, she grew grateful for her enthusiasm for Hindi films as it offered one of the few common experiences she shared with her small-town classmates. Her interest in music and books helped as well. Suddenly, she was popular and cool, loaning and recommending albums and authors to her new friends, able to talk knowledgeably about both Shah Rukh and Bob Dylan. The boot was firmly on the other foot. Observing how several of her friends struggled to buy books or fancy meals, she felt guilty about her wealth and good fortune.

Back in south Delhi, she had not felt rich. In the Shekhar home, scarcity had announced itself. Her father had sold off his birthright so that they could buy a modest Delhi home. He had abandoned his roots and source of socio-economic support in Tamil Nadu, all in the hopes of joining the atomistic metropolitan elites of India. But Vidya's father never abandoned his extended family. He loaned his sister's financially flailing family a large portion of his savings. Eventually, Vidya's parents sold their flat in Delhi to be able to buy a home in Chennai, where her aunt and widowed grandmother could stay near a good hospital and fellow cousins. As the male head of the family, her father needed to take responsibility for his female relatives. Neither woman had any income or employment of her own. But the expenses mounted and he found himself in the deepest debt. At the time, she was in the second year of her engineering programme and recalled how hollowed-out and sad her parents seemed. 'They really lost something when they had to sell the house; they felt like all their life's work had been in vain. My mother was so worried that my father could not retire with any peace of mind, given that we had no savings left. I knew I had to do well both to help them and to avoid a similar future.' Property, income and network wealth became the prism through which Vidya saw the world.

At the age of twenty, in her third year at engineering school, absorbing the financial insecurities of her parents, bolstered by new friendships with a far more diverse group of men, loving Shah Rukh became an important assertion of Vidya's will, social rank and preferences. Vidya had escaped school. But she could not yet escape the Student. They would continue to be part of the same set of friends. All through the summer holidays, spent largely with the old school gang, Vidya began to talk incessantly about Shah Rukh films and the interviews he had given. She was declaring her fandom. She was advertising a new-found confidence in herself and wanted the Student to know they could now feud as equals. Both women enjoyed quibbling with each other. As the years progressed, their fights became rather stylish.

After finishing her engineering degree in 2003, Vidya toyed with the idea of pursuing a PhD abroad. However, business school in India followed by a high-paying job seemed like the more pragmatic path. I sensed that Vidya had wanted a life in the arts or academy, a life devoted to research and writing. She had the aptitude and the scores to do well in the social sciences. Sadly, she had inherited debt from her parents, not a surplus of savings. She also developed desires for a 'good life and to see the world'. Her father was never a philosophical man. But he did cling to one script of certainty: that children of the 'new middle classes' should know their place and stick to jobs for the new middle classes; that the world of Indian intellect and academia was only available to children of intellect and academia.

Each night during her final semester at IIT, Vidya's father would lecture her on how success in the arts and the arts of academia required one to spend years with low pay and uncertain contracts that a family like hers could not subsidize. To him, the Indian private sector was a far safer route, one which economic liberalization had made accessible to salaried families like his. Earlier, only a government job could be described as secure. Suddenly, with India's economy opening up, there were better options with private firms and multinationals. He knew this was a formulaic path, that Vidya might have wanted something different, but at least these options were open to his daughter. She could make money first and pursue her creative aspirations later. She could build her own safety net. Vidya's parents had joined forces to make the jump from provincial Tamil Nadu to the professional, salaried class in Delhi. Now she was poised to make the next step, to climb the corporate ladder and consolidate family welfare.

All through her years in business school and after she'd got her first corporate job, Vidya kept tabs on the Student. All reports nourished her envy. She heard that the Student was working with a Planning Commission member, a family friend. The Student was paid a pittance, particularly in comparison to Vidya, but she was earning considerable social capital before she departed for her doctoral studies in the United States where that capital would be further burnished. Later, as Vidya struggled with being forever sidelined at her first job, she heard that the Student had dived off the post-modern deep end, uttering 'ethno-gobbledygook everywhere' after reading important French thinkers and subaltern studies.

Vidya became animated when she told stories about her nemesis. 'She said something,' Vidya told me once, referring to the Student, 'about how she could never buy a designer dress because it cost too much. She said this while wearing these incredibly intricate pieces of gold jewellery, which she said her grandmother had passed on to her. So, if I spend my own money on buying something nice for myself, while paying the required taxes, that's flashy and spendthrift. But she is fully moral and pro-proletariat because all her expensive things have been inherited. I've been to her house when we were younger. Her parents had live-in help when some of us did not even have a part-time maid back then. They also have the most famous people's paintings on the walls. It's money beyond what anyone of us can dream of or aspire to. She pretends that she has lesser wealth than me and my friends who work in the corporate sector. It makes me so angry.' Over a glass of wine, Vidya would work herself up into a fit of mock outrage: 'She once told a mutual friend that she did not believe in money, that it was a construct. That's right, money is a construct for those who have plenty of it.'

In 2010, Vidya turned twenty-eight and had completed five years in her corporate job. Having cleared up a significant part of her family debt and built some savings, she applied to a public policy course at a prestigious American university. An American policy programme would help with skills and networks. Vidya complained that debt followed her everywhere. Although she received a partial scholarship, she needed to organize a student loan to finance the rest of her education. After a period of non-stop applications and interviews, in 2012, she returned to India with a plum job offer. It wasn't her dream job but paid enough to tackle her outstanding student debt and build savings towards buying a home.

By 2013, the Student was settled in a post-doctoral position at a famous American university. The position allowed her to spend time doing archival work in India. The Student had grown up to become a serious woman with serious pursuits. She had inherited opinions, property and connections from her entrenched Delhi establishment family stuffed full of foreign-educated bureaucrats and university professors, and its extended network of artists and intellectuals. Vidya said the Student was prone to fits of high-minded moral outrage, feeling little compunction about subjecting people to harangues about her supposed feminism and empathy with the poor and downtrodden. 'She likes the poor,' Vidya would tell me, still exercised by residual resentment about the Student's privileges, 'as some romantic idea you discuss, it's not like she will ever have to compete with them or even middle-class people for opportunities in her field. That way, engineers and management students are different. I do not buy into all this "merit" nonsense. I see how wealthier kids can be better coached to enter an IIT or an IIM. But even then, we have competed and studied with a far larger section of India than her. Somehow, her American university income allows her a clean conscience, while everyone with a good private sector salary is a stooge of neo-liberal capitalism who needs to constantly feel shame.'

From Vidya, I grew to understand that the Student's life's desire was to be acknowledged as a serious public intellectual. Her ambitions were heavily influenced by the interventions made by Arundhati Roy and Ramachandra Guha in the 2000s. She craved their talent and celebrity; she wanted her words to matter as theirs did. In her thirties, she was an extraordinarily intelligent and engaging conversationalist. At school get-togethers, all through their twenties and early thirties, Vidya tried to engage with her childhood best friend. In nearly each of their perfunctory exchanges, Vidya persistently felt that the Student appeared more interested in correcting her, or calling her out, as opposed to understanding her.

'You'd always walk away feeling like *you* were the sole reason tribal communities in India were being persecuted. One night, she asked me how I could look at myself in the mirror because I was working at a multinational. I felt like asking her if she was paying off any student loans on her own or if she had to support her parents. To remind her that some of us did not have the luxury of pure ideological positions like her. To help her register that I needed to save for my old age all on my own, that I had no land I could rent or sell, that I had financial needs that her family will never have,' Vidya said.

'A feminist on paper,' Vidya complained about the Student, theorizing that her frenemy could only provide unsolicited counsel to women of her own class or compete with them. All her feminist consideration and kindness were reserved for the children of established Delhi families she grew up with. At a school reunion party in 2015, the Student looked aghast at Vidya's persistent self-declared fandom as a thirty-something adult. 'I thought you were a serious person,' the Student said to Vidya in her haughty Received Pronunciation English, heard only in central Delhi drawing rooms and BBC archival footage. The Student had spent the rest of the evening criticizing Vidya for being a fan of an actor whose films were filled with toxic imagery and whose numerous endorsements fuelled consumer capitalism in India.

To Vidya, this vociferous dismissal of Shah Rukh seemed to reflect nothing but the Student's unexamined privilege. 'Doesn't seem like she wanted to understand you or your point of view anyway,' I suggested gently.

'Perhaps,' Vidya replied. 'Maybe she was looking for any excuse to shame me. It's the typical bitchy thing that happens among women sometimes. Some women fight over boys, some make fun of each other's purses, she and I poke holes in each other's interests and politics. I can't be a Shah Rukh fan and a feminist, apparently. I can't watch a Yash Raj film and appreciate Bergman. Strange how people obsessed with talking about removing class divisions keep using all kinds of cultural markers to suggest how gauche others are, to keep them down. Her attack on Shah Rukh bugged me.'

'Why does he mean so much to you?' I asked.

'He is self-made,' she replied without a moment's pause. 'The films may not be the best. But he was a boy from Rajinder Nagar who rose to the top, he was an outsider who made it on his own, without any family connections in an insider-club industry where he knew no one. He came from nowhere. I admire that more than anything else.'

Nowhere Man

*I'm not here to compete, I am here to rule. A simple middle-class boy gets up in
the morning, has dreams in his eyes. When he comes to Mumbai, he says: 'You
know what—I am going to rule this, I am going to rule it over the people
who have existed here.' In all goodness, in all niceness, I don't have a father or
a grandfather, I don't have a mother who can give me an extra push here in
Mumbai. But I am going to be a star who is self-made. And if I am
going to be self-made, I am going to create a category for myself that
did not exist before and will never exist after.*

—Shah Rukh Khan, 2011

No one comes from nowhere. Shah Rukh came from a post-Partition
Muslim family that worked hard to afford their son a first-rate
education at a renowned Catholic school in Delhi. His high-quality
schooling allowed him to access the finest government-subsidized
higher education in India, at both Delhi University and Jamia Millia
Islamia. This education in the 1980s distinguished him economically
in India, at a time when most young men lacked access to a decent
school. He did not come from 'nowhere', he came from the neo middle
class of Delhi.

For years, Vidya and I would argue about just how 'self-made' Shah
Rukh really was. She would present his success as a purely ahistorical
phenomenon of sheer hard work and individual genius. I believed,
much like all the authors I had read, that achievement was socially
manufactured. This was particularly true in countries as unequal
as India, where caste determined your starting place in the world.
Vidya would admonish me for my 'Bengali liberal lefty' beliefs, which
delegitimized the success of anyone with even a modicum of caste or
class privilege. While she acknowledged that the benefits conferred by
caste enabled individual accomplishments, she'd contend that these no
longer applied within the social gatherings and offices she occupied

as a working adult where 'everyone was nearly the same because our parents had done financially well'. She insisted that wider access to better schools and high-quality education in Delhi had flattened out differences based on caste or religion. The only thing that created distinctions within the well-educated elites were social connections and family wealth.

To her, Shah Rukh's success was symbolic of 'a man going far beyond what anyone expected from him given where he came from'. I knew she wasn't talking about his religion, his success as a Muslim man. India had several Muslim superstars before his screen debut. She was talking about networks. The apple doesn't fall far from the tree in India. The latest round of data released in 2020 shows that India has one of the lowest rates of social mobility in the world. Your life path and career are often entirely dependent on what your parents do, who they know and how much capital you inherit. Economists highlight the role of kinship networks and caste-based communities in mediating access to information and training for jobs, and providing financial support while workers explore their prospects. In a 2019 survey completed by the business-connections company Linkedin, 76 per cent of Indians said that 'contacts' were the most important factor in determining if they found a good job. Vidya herself complained bitterly and at length that 'interesting careers in arts and letters or policy' in India were only available to people with enough family money to take risks and serve long and underpaid apprenticeships. It is precisely this perception of her own victimhood, motivated by her inability to access creative careers beyond a corporate desk job, that made Shah Rukh's success feel so politically charged and seductive.

Shah Rukh's meteoric rise in an industry often regarded as nepotistic and insular is legend in India. It's a fascinating and peculiarly '90s narrative, given that prior to Shah Rukh's entry into film, the majority of male and female superstars in Hindi cinema were 'self-made', claiming no help or inheritance from a family in the film business. One of India's first matinee idols, Dilip Kumar, was discovered in the 1940s working in his father's dry-fruit shop. The legendary Dev Anand was the son of an advocate and worked as a clerk in an accounting firm before being cast in his first film. Icons such as Amitabh Bachchan and Guru Dutt, although hailing from families in the arts, were not to the screen born. Sridevi was the daughter of a lawyer, Madhuri Dixit hailed from the Marathi salaried middle class and the angelic Madhubala, a superstar in the 1950s, was the daughter of a poor man who had lost his job at the Imperial Tobacco Company. Dharmendra's father was a school headmaster and Rajesh Khanna was an acclaimed sportsman. Perhaps Raj Kapoor was the first Indian superstar to emerge from a strictly film background, being the son of the great Prithviraj Kapoor. His grandfather, though, had been a policeman in Peshawar. Waheeda Rehman's father was an administrator, while Meena Kumari and Nargis were introduced to films through parents who were musicians and artists. Even when someone did have a film background—such as Rekha, the daughter of the actors Gemini Ganeshan and Pushpavalli—it did not appear to cushion your path through an entire career.

Clearly, Shah Rukh was not the only or first 'self-made' star in Indian film. You might even argue that some of his '90s contemporaries such as Akshay Kumar were also outsiders. Why then was his professional success viscerally special to Vidya? Why was his rise cherished as stronger evidence of social mobility than the journeys of many other self-made stars of the past? The answer might lie not only in how Bollywood was changing to become increasingly incestuous and nepotistic, but how the aspirations and composition of India's elites were changing as well.

At the time of Vidya's introduction to Shah Rukh, the film landscape was dominated by actors and actresses who were children of the industry. The men ruling the '90s were Govinda, Anil Kapoor, Salman Khan, Sunny Deol and Aamir Khan. All these stars, except

Govinda, came from film families. Several of Shah Rukh's female co-stars, such as Kajol, Rani Mukerji and Karisma Kapoor, also hailed from established film families. The media played this distinction up, appraising Shah Rukh's rise through a sociological lens, always reminding us how the likelihood of entry and success in fields such as acting was transferred as an inheritance as opposed to being earned by merit. Intriguing that no media outlet at the time bothered to report on the reigning actresses of Bollywood the same way—after all, like Shah Rukh, Sridevi, Madhuri Dixit, Juhi Chawla and Urmila Matondkar had never inherited acting as a career through family. We never heard journalists or audiences in rapture of women who made it on their own. Most reportage on these women was restricted to their beauty and love affairs. When I asked Vidya about this anomaly, her response was phlegmatic: 'It's because women's achievements aren't seen in the same way as men. And his success was far more electric.'

The more I probed Vidya's admiration of Shah Rukh's career, the more she parried and deflected until one day she just came out with it: 'I think his success is important to me as he is a lot like me. I am a lot like Shah Rukh.' Incredulous, I asked what she meant. 'It's not a direct comparison of our personalities but I feel like we're from the same social group, we come from the same place. We are Delhi people, our concern is to own a home and have savings, we want more than what our parents had. Shah Rukh represents that desire. I do not think his grandparents lived in the city before his parents moved here, just like mine. And I knew boys like him. He was similar to many of the boys I went to school and IIT with, middle class but not super wealthy or connected. He had to take his solid education and use it to create his own networks, to find work for himself and succeed. It felt like he had to make compromises and do jobs he may not have liked to earn more money. I can relate to that. He danced at weddings; he was one of the first actors to start endorsing brands. Earning well and doing well were important to him. He cared about money and making it, he knew how important it was to find security. People like me and him, without anyone to rely on, need to work to make a good living. We have limits. For people like us to pursue an artistic path is tough, we do not have the profile for it.'

She paused and drew a link to which we would invariably return: 'But you know, *this* is why I don't expect these kids from established propertied Delhi families to like Shah Rukh the way I do. I mean, take the Student. We went to school together. She liked Shah Rukh just as much as me when we were kids. Then, she started complaining about Hindi films and claiming she was too evolved for them.'

The pain in her voice was sharp. 'She and I are very similar—our parents were able to send us to the best schools in India, we speak English. But there is a difference between this girl and me. And it's an important one. Just like Shah Rukh, my parents could only give me a good education, but I had to use it to make my own way. I don't work in my parents' fields. They don't know many people in Delhi, they can't call in any favours for me and they can't connect me with anyone for work. I can't make a casual call to the friend of a friend who can give me a job or help me draft an application essay or furnish a recommendation to an Ivy League college. No one in my immediate family or their group of friends has even left the country. For women like the Student, her family has lived far longer in Delhi and have made the right contacts. They own their homes and there is far less pressure to make money. They grew up very differently from people like me.'

Of course, there is nothing new in Vidya's feelings of envy and relative deprivation. Differences of network wealth have existed for generations in a caste-based society like India. If Vidya feels scorn about the privileges the Student has enjoyed, most of India would abhor Vidya for the privilege of her Brahmin surname. Vidya's family, being upper-caste Tamilian Brahmins, courted tremendous sociopolitical wealth. But she was convinced that these did not translate into the same welfare gains as those accruing to the Saraswat Brahmin Student in Delhi. She claimed that her caste privilege meant nothing in a world in which the Student's parents could call in favours from an old college gang of high-ranking buddies.

Vidya was the first 'full Delhiite' in her family. She was born in Salem and moved to India's capital city at the age of five. Her parents had gone to school in small, sleepy towns, ensconced in a tight network of cousins and family friends, surrounded by people just like them. The Student's parents went to Delhi University and met at Oxford, mingling in a far more diverse and cosmopolitan crowd. While the diversity of Vidya's peer group, compared to that of her parents, created spaces for new friendships, they also offered spaces for new rivalries. 'How can she be the same middle class as me?' Vidya wondered about her frenemy.

Through all our conversations between 2016 and 2020, Vidya always described herself as 'middle class.' It was her way of signalling that she lacked financial privilege and needed to strive for economic security. In his late twenties, Shah Rukh's success in films meant he became a member of India's economic hyper-elite. What about Vidya? Could thirty-something Vidya, with her lucrative salary, lay claim to being middle class? And the Student? Where did they belong in the economic map of India?

The Six Maps of India

Social scientists use six methods to map hierarchies of privilege and class in India. The first is caste. Vidya's Hindu Brahmin surname disqualified her from any claims of being in the social middle. Second, political scientists such as Devesh Kapur have suggested that we use college degrees and a person's ability to pay income tax as measures to define the middle class. Based on Kapur's definitions, Vidya and the Student would qualify, but the middle class they constitute would be an advantaged sliver of the Indian population—just over eight per cent of Indians have college degrees and under five per cent file income tax. A third broader method that economic sociologists such as Maryam Aslany use combines the nature of a person's job, income, lifestyle, education, social ties, aspirations and attitudes to identify the middle class. Deploying such an expansive definition, in 2011, she found that twenty-eight per cent of India belongs to the middle class, of which about three per cent are upper middle class and fourteen per cent are in the lower middle. Vidya and the Student would certainly be part of Aslany's upper middle class as both are highly educated, hold well-paying, stable jobs, are eager and able to get ahead while saving for their future.

Of course, we can always rely on economists to be neatly reductive. It's a methodological streak that proves helpful in categorizing people, if not understanding them. A fourth method to map privilege in India, favoured by economists, is to simply use a person's 'consumption expenditure'—their ability to buy goods such as food and smartphones. Spending is a useful measure of a person's disposable income. If we use purchasing power to ascertain class, Vidya would never qualify as middle class. Nor would the Student. As per the most recently available data, the average Delhiite spends ₹3,298 per month. Vidya and the Student might easily spend ₹3,000 on one meal in Khan Market. Earning on par with the global upper middle class, they comprise the top five per cent of spenders in rich Delhi, let alone the rest of India.

A fifth map uses some standardized metric of personal income to classify humans. In 2015, a Pew Global Research study defined 'middle income' populations as those that earned between US$10 to US$20 per day. In India, this means anyone earning a monthly salary roughly between ₹20,000 and ₹40,000. Based on this definition, only three per cent of India's population was in the middle-income bracket, a population of nearly thirty-two million. Between 2001 and

2011, India added seventeen million people to this middle-income category. In the same time period, over two hundred million people became middle-income in China, while Brazil added about twenty-four million. Vidya and the Student would be 'high income', part of a group of a little over one million Indians who earn more than US$50 a day. The majority of India—at seventy-seven per cent—earns a 'low income,' between US$ 2 and US$ 10, or approximately between ₹4,000 and ₹20,000 per month. This low-income group, estimated to be 938 million people, largely comprises India's vast casual labour force with ad-hoc earnings and no written contracts. It includes construction workers, agricultural labour, street vendors and waste-pickers. They have recently escaped chronic poverty and live precariously close to the poverty line. The pandemic and the absence of an adequate livelihoods stimulus has battered these workers.

Thus far, any socio-economic map of India would place both Vidya and the Student in a tiny, hyper-privileged class, members of the top five per cent of their country. However, income alone is an inadequate measure of wealth—it doesn't always account for earnings from rent, stocks or financial shares. People also lie about how much they earn. We might exaggerate, for example, to impress a prospective father-in-law. Or we may under-report to avoid taxes or efface ourselves. Incomes also need to be adjusted for debts; nearly half of Vidya's substantial monthly salary would be eaten up by servicing loans and family creditors. The super-wealthy, likely, don't even need an income. They own 'assets'. As a result, a sixth map of India is needed. This map relies on measuring 'wealth holdings'. Wealth or a person's net worth is tough to estimate. The government does not transparently release all tax and income data. However, statisticians approximate by adding up the value of land, buildings, vehicles and financial assets owned by an individual, and deducting their debts and loans. Economists Ishan Anand and Anjana Thampi meticulously analysed such data between 1991 and 2012, providing us one of the most insightful comments on the wealth distribution of modern India. They found that the average wealth of an urban Indian increased from ₹26,204 in 1991 to ₹145,773 in 2012, largely propelled by the increasing value of land.

Vidya owned no properties or land, but she did hold valuable stocks and an expensive car. With this information, I could still comfortably place her in the top ten per cent of India's wealth distribution. The Student would probably qualify for the top five per cent, given that she would inherit multiple properties from her parents. Her family owned two houses in smart south Delhi colonies, one in which they lived and one that they rented for certainly more than ₹100,000 per month. Her mother came from a family of esteemed foreign service officers and some trickles of old money, a fact Vidya knew and often repeated. The booming real estate market in India and the social value conferred on owning property made the Student's family psychologically, socially and financially far more affluent than Vidya's could ever hope to be. In their paper, Anand and Thampi underpin Vidya's obsession with the Student's home-owner status in a simple, declarative sentence: 'Land was, and remains, the most important asset.'

The Student was lucky to be able to claim her father's property as an unmarried daughter. In the late 1940s, the Indian Parliament opposed Ambedkar's Hindu Code Bill which contained clauses to ensure equal property rights for Hindu women. In 1956, the Hindu Succession Act was approved, whereby property would pass through men; only divorced or widowed daughters could claim rights to their ancestral property. Nearly half a century later, in 2005, Manmohan Singh's government amended the Hindu Succession Act to allow property to be inherited by women. Amidst the pandemic, in August 2020, the Indian Supreme Court further clarified that women could claim these property rights even if they were born before the 2005 amendment. These legal changes allowed the Student to access her father's property directly. Data from 2018 suggests that women hold barely twenty per cent of the country's household wealth, far behind the global average of nearly forty per cent.

Combining tax data, survey data and national accounts statistics, economists Thomas Piketty and Lucas Chancel try to create a sharper measure of national income in India. Using these methods, with all their limitations, they find that the top ten per cent owned fifty-six per cent of national income in 2015, increasing from thirty-five per cent in 1992. However, these numbers hide significant gradations within the top ten per cent, a slice of society that includes senior government officials, billionaire real-estate tycoons-turned-politicians, landowning farmers with barely any English, socialites who speak nothing but English, government clerks with cushy dowries, high-minded families like that of the Student, Vidya with her stock portfolio, a businessman counting crores and Shah Rukh himself. In fact, amongst India's economic elite, concentration of wealth has amplified. The wealthiest one per cent of Indians owned twenty-one per cent of all income in the country in 2015, up from just ten per cent in 1992.

Vidya and the Student probably belong to the next nine per cent which has consistently owned a third of Indian wealth since 1991. Statistically, the Gini Index amongst India's top ten per cent—a measure of the degree of wealth inequality with 0 representing total equality and 100 representing total inequality—increased from 37 in 1991 to 49 in 2012.

As India became more unequal in the decades between the 1990s and 2010s, not only did inequalities *between* the poorest and wealthiest increase exponentially, the inequalities *within* the wealthiest have also grown. In 2015, the average income of an adult in the top ten per cent was five times the income of an average Indian. Simultaneously, the average income of those in the top 0.1 per cent was fifteen times the income enjoyed by an Indian in the top ten per cent. Anand and Thampi find that wealth correlates well with caste. In 2012, the average wealth of a 'General' caste person—a statistical term to indicate upper castes—was four times that of a Scheduled Caste person. And despite the growing inequality across castes, in 2012, the Gini Index of wealth inequality *amongst* urban upper-caste people (77) was as high as the wealth inequality across all Indians (74). The Credit Suisse Wealth Report of 2018 estimated that the wealth share of the top ten percenters in India had increased to nearly 77.4 per cent, where the constituent share of the top one per cent alone was 51.5 per cent. Such extrapolations would suggest that not only is India becoming more unequal, but inequality between the mega-rich and the merely rich continues to grow.

This data helps us understand Vidya's irrational sense of relative deprivation, even if we don't necessarily feel all that sorry for her. It also explains her insistence that she is part of a nebulous 'middle class,' despite being in the top ten per cent of the country's wealth and income distribution. Vidya was no fool or neocon: she knew her own privilege, she knew the gap between herself and the rest of the country had grown unimaginably. She supported affirmative action for underprivileged and historically disadvantaged communities. Yet, she viscerally *felt* the growing inequalities between her segment of society and those who were like her in theory but were, in reality, leagues apart. She knew the gap between her and the Student had grown giant as well; that her high-paying job would never accord the same prestige or financial freedom as the Student's access to powerful people and prime real estate in Delhi. She didn't measure herself against the average Indian, she measured herself against the Student. Vidya felt victimized by her own lack of culture, clubs and connections. She saw how those with property and old money were always more sure-footed members of the elite. That they would always help each other out, while rolling their eyes at economic wannabes like her. Vidya witnessed how a new generation of intellectuals and 'influencers' usually came from families that owned land and had industrial-strength money or important connections; how the public display and transmission of old networks and pre-existing privileges was the sole point of high-society culture; how the Student's family used all their entrenched might to ensure their daughter amassed more success. Vidya craved the safety net she believed the Student had. It was Vidya's pursuit of success, without being embedded in powerful networks, that she believed made her 'a lot like Shah Rukh'.

Vidya met no struggle or strife, she thrived, making the most of her own privileged position on the Indian totem pole. But her envy of those 'with mummy-papa's homes and powerful connections' coloured her politics and world view forever. She knew her grievances were petty, knowing fully well that you could not hate someone for what their parents gave them. Unable to express her feelings openly or adequately, she found Shah Rukh as a talisman, his triumph over 'pedigreed' actors symbolic of her own struggle. A man who could call himself the King of Bollywood without irony. He escaped the curse of connectedness and scaled heights unknown.

Eventually, Vidya's grievances and status-anxiety found political expression in Narendra Modi's biting contempt for Rahul Gandhi. Well into her twenties, even her thirties, she had translated her envy of the Student into her devotion to Shah Rukh. In 2014, she poured all her hate for the Student into a vote against Gandhi. She opted for the BJP because she thought the Congress was a party that 'aimed to preserve the privileges of these networked types only'. Five years later, unable to ignore mob-lynching episodes and a tanking economy, she voted for the opposing Aam Aadmi Party (AAP) in the national elections. She liked Arvind Kejriwal, leader of the AAP, an activist-engineer with experience in the civil service and no connections to Delhi's Lutyens' elite.

When the 2019 election results were announced, she had mixed feelings, disappointed that the BJP had won another term but relieved 'that people like the Student continue to be irrelevant to the country'. Vidya espoused the need to 'take India back' from 'lazy liberals' who she believed could 'only criticize without building anything'. In January 2020, she called me to report the latest episode in her conflict with the Student. It had begun as an argument on a school WhatsApp group and degenerated into yet another squabble involving Shah Rukh.

The argument was triggered by nationwide protests in late December 2019 against the efforts of the national government to implement a National Register of Citizens, and the subsequent attacks on students in universities. The Student had found a tenured academic position at a strong state university in the US. She was also considering a temporary return to teach in India and was a voluble online presence, expressing support for the protests. Vidya had attended a protest in Gurgaon. She felt the cause was just, she told me, 'But it makes me feel weird to stand with people like the Student. I see her smug self-righteous social media posts and feel no solidarity with her. I stand with people suffering from the impact of such laws and, I suppose, given the times we're in, I must set some of my personal issues aside. But this girl makes it impossible.'

On seeing Vidya's photos from the protest on their school WhatsApp group, the Student started complaining about why 'Vidya's Shah Rukh' was not coming out and supporting the anti-CAA-NRC protests. The Student was full of praise for actress Deepika Padukone who had joined a protest meeting by students at the Jawaharlal Nehru University. Vidya tried to explain that Shah Rukh had been very outspoken on intolerance in the past and paid a heavy price. Vidya described the Student's reaction: 'She just refused to see it, she can't see grey, everything with her is black or white. With us or against us, you're a moral coward or a moral saint. But life is lived in the middle.

It was so frustrating. Not everyone can speak out in the way she can. That doesn't mean they're silent.'

Despite how national politics had forced Vidya and the Student to share a moment of allegiance at the 2020 protests, they would always be spiritually divided. A few weeks into the national lockdown, Vidya mocked the Student's praise for an Arundhati Roy piece on the pandemic on their school WhatsApp group. 'I did not realize Ms Roy was a public health expert,' she said.

'Perhaps not, but we need her voice more than you data types who have created this problem by not seeing human costs of our development model,' was the Student's response. 'How', barbed Vidya, 'can you survive this crisis without expertise or data? Can you write articles which make vaccines and money magically available to people?'

This type of sparring was everywhere. The pandemic had triggered panic in Vidya, the Student and all upper-class people with cushy lives. We saw the plight of our fellow countrymen from our comfortable homes and knew we were somehow implicated. Many of us came together to donate, crowd-fund or feed the hungry. But all along, we knew these were band-aids for a fracture. Yet, none of us knew how to forge a way forward. There was no politics possible, we were all locked up, busy protecting the lives of those near us. When the uncertainty and pain became impossible to bear, we needed to look away. The Student wrote angry liberal posts and read her favourite intellectuals. Vidya obsessively followed Shah Rukh and technocrats.

For Vidya, the Student would always remain an empty shell of propertied privileged woke-ness. Never having met the Student, I had no way of knowing if she felt the same level of animus and competition towards Vidya. She never talked much about how she imagined the Student perceived her. Having spent a fair share of my own Delhi life with folks like the Student, I conjectured that she did not take Vidya seriously enough as an intellectual opponent. Instead, she probably looked down on Vidya for being earnest. To the Student, Vidya's earnestness was probably best captured by her decision to unambiguously think well of Shah Rukh—a man whose interest in making money and escapist films made him hideously capitalist and terribly apolitical, the anti-thesis to an outspoken feminist hero. It seemed to me that these two ambitious women would perpetually play what philosopher Agnes Callard deftly defined as the 'Importance Game,' which works through 'casual references to wealth, talent, accomplishments or connections'. In each other's company, they would perform nonchalance without feeling an ounce of it. The moves would be exhausting and endless.

The Student might be infinitely poorer than Shah Rukh now, infinitely less influential and connected, but for Vidya it was the superstar actor who had scrapped and worked for everything he had. And it was the Student who was cosseted by luxury and privilege. Vidya's conclusion only had the effect of drawing her closer to her idol and the fantasy he represented.

Chennai Express

Vidya's first solo film outing was to see Shah Rukh's *Chennai Express* in August 2013. She celebrated her single ticket and struggled to celebrate the movie. That year, morale amongst many fangirls had plummeted to an all-time low as Shah Rukh's box-office collections reached an all-time high. *Chennai Express* was box-office gold, earning US$63 million worldwide. An 'action-comedy' in which the comedy involved caricatures of Tamil people, the film broke business records. Vidya considered herself too much of a Delhiite to let the exaggerated Tamil accents bother her. But she winced through most of the film. The hero seemed more boorish than the men Shah Rukh usually played, the film more testosterone laden. She was convinced that her hero mirrored her discomfort, refusing to grow up, even as he played a man in his forties.

I shared most of Vidya's misgivings but I'll admit that there were parts of the film I enjoyed. Fans are rarely immune. There were still glimpses of the Shah Rukh I loved, scenes in which he appears utterly *devoted* to his love interest. And this act of male *devotion*, where a man will worship a woman before marriage or motherhood, is what makes each of his films unique. Salman protects women, Aamir teaches us, Shah Rukh *sees us*. At the time, I needed Shah Rukh more than ever. I needed to be seen. Such was the sorry state of my personal affairs.

4

An Actor and an Aristoprat

A man said to the universe:
'Sir, I exist!'
'However,' replied the universe,
'The fact has not created in me
A sense of obligation.'

—*Stephen Crane*

An eternal obstacle in the path of romantic success has been my choice of men, especially those brought up in the city I call home. Of course, I am implicated in choosing to pursue romantic partnerships prone to excessive trauma-drama, but I share the blame with Delhi. Like a stoic and strict parent, Delhi absorbs all my accusations without much of an embrace. The perils I face because of my expertise in making distinctly terrible personal decisions are only exacerbated by the way this city constructs my romantic choices. Most of us are expected to couple up early—find our life partner from a network of school, college or colony friends, long-term family acquaintances or parental intervention. But if you blossom late, or prioritize your education, or come to the city as a single woman and find yourself looking for a mate in your late twenties and thirties, Delhi closes itself on you. The 'good ones' are all gone, making other women happy. The nice, sensible boys don't do much for your loins, while some surprise you with affectations of the worst type of alpha male. You smile and suffer through the mounting indignities, believing this will all end with the advent of Love. You cry, read, watch old Shah Rukh romances, pick yourself up and attempt to sift through the remains of the city's romantic detritus. Films and friends fuel hope—if this city managed to manufacture Shah Rukh Khan, there *must* be someone out there. But reality launches multiple missile strikes on your faith.

In the national capital of India, the winter air has become as toxic as the tactics deployed by many of its bachelors. This is a city where I've watched a stout, portly man give a petite beauty queen a hard time for her weight. A friend told me about a man standing at five feet two inches who abruptly ended a first date, three minutes into it, following a three-month-long exchange. His excuse was simple: He knew that in a 'market' controlled by and favourable to men, he could find a woman who would add several inches to his social standing. It was why he felt no embarrassment admitting that he predominantly dated 'modelly' girls. A man with multiple failed businesses laughs at his date's successful ventures. And on countless occasions I've giggled at a certain young global-leader-type man (who has sadly conflated achievement with being photographed attending important meetings): he'll lecture women on 'leadership,' only to eventually suggest that these women quit well-paying jobs because there is 'no growth or future in it for [them]'. At times, he will consume too much vodka and confess that women use their gender as an excuse for their general professional incompetence. You sigh and dream endlessly of Shah Rukh.

For all the single women I know, dating in Delhi feels like an incessant confrontation with one's worst insecurities and inadequacies.

For those yet to find happiness in solitude, lamenting about romantic mishaps becomes a part-time job in this city. Those who don't complain have capitulated to its conjugal circus—many are worn out, others have given up, a few have struck gold. In my case, the first two decades of life were spent being socialized to find 'The One'; I wasted the third searching for him and I anticipate that my fourth decade will be spent recovering from my quest.

In the early 2010s, the Indian army and I could have been accused of perpetuating a similar form of discrimination: favouring Jats and Rajputs above all others. While my dearest friends borrowed language from *Friends* to suggest I was dating the 'who's who of human crap', a petitioner in the Supreme Court highlighted the same caste-bias in the Indian Army's recruitment policies for the Presidential Body Guards (PBG). Unsurprisingly, the army defended itself on physical grounds—the PBG was a small ceremonial unit which demanded tall officers (over six feet) with common build and appearance to ensure adequate 'pomp and projection' during events at Rashtrapati Bhavan. Thus, only martial castes would suffice.

Despite the trivial nature of my love affairs compared to lofty affairs of state, I found parallels between the army's defence and mine. For me, too, a partner had become an accessory in the performance art that was my social life in Delhi. Unable to bear the weight of being on my own or being myself, I chose to burrow into one of Delhi's feudal landed gentry. Determined to break away from the nerd herd at university, I was mesmerized by this man's quiet confidence. His self-possession born of privilege, so redolent of the financial freedom arising from successful 'investments', seduced my anxious salaried soul. He also looked like Shashi Kapoor. While his frame was many standard deviations away from the average men who populated my life, I ignored the fact that his intellect did asymptote to zero.

In the early days of our year-long tryst, I became a cringeworthy participant of patriarchy, unwilling to find a moment, or myself, interesting without him. He became The One; I became possessed by his past, convinced that his interest in me was some fleeting mistake. His attention became the only worthwhile form of validation. My sense of self fluctuated with The One, his moods and his libido. Ensnaring him into a monogamous relationship became my sole spiritual pursuit.

Roland Barthes, the great philosopher on the architecture of love, once said, 'The scene consecrates the object I am going to love.' In Delhi, that *scene* which frames our choices in love—the set design and furniture inside our heads—is arranged by an aggressive patriarchy.

As my friends and I started our respective forays into heterosexual adult romance, we quickly theorized that the upper-class mating market seemed neatly divided between males with unwarranted self-confidence and females with unwarranted self-doubt. Most of the men we encountered believed that without much grooming or grace, love and belonging were spiritual guarantees. Whereas women folk—despite our salon visits and virtues—were instructed to think of love and belonging as quests rife with competitive struggle. As a student of implementation, I've always thought this cultural transmission of confidence and anxieties to be fascinating. It is not good enough, though, to simply declare that unlike women, elite men expect to easily find love because of entitlement and patriarchy. The remarkable aspect of our social structure is how we keep fortifying male entitlement and patriarchy, how we sustain similar terms of engagement between men and women, despite myriad changes ushered by the law and time.

In a country where the state struggles to convince us to treat each other fairly, or even to use a toilet, we have achieved a sophisticated form of social engineering when it comes to safeguarding gender roles. Our institutions, so ad hoc and dysfunctional when it counts, have displayed a surpassing efficiency at reinforcing gender identity. Somehow, we ensure that men and women inhale what society expects of them, and magically, most of us play out our respective gender identities and idioms. Men must earn money and women must earn love.

Statistical Straitjackets

Earning love is, of course, far more laborious than earning money. In India, the support offered by men and government agencies when it comes to household chores and care ranks amongst the lowest in the world. Women bear the overwhelming burden of being the sole providers of care for children, nourishing the future workforce, while also caring for the elderly. Love motivates us to take on back-breaking gestures of care with good cheer. Even with plentiful domestic help, love ensures that women enthusiastically keep house. Feminists have long argued that women's unpaid, unappreciated role as caregivers is a form of 'domestic slavery' which we are socialized into accepting. At the same time, they recognize that women undertake care for family members and loved ones for all kinds of reasons, including to consolidate their position within relationships, to express love and to feel loved in return. But men are rarely expected to perform the effort-intensive parts of caring and loving. As the scholar and writer bell hooks has pointed out, 'Sexism decrees emotional care and love is the task of women and men come home too tired to deliver emotional goods.'

For women, love is hard work. Beyond the drudgery of domestic chores, the responsibility for keeping track of other people's feelings and needs has by default been devolved to women. In our society, it is women who must display consideration and patience, who must respond with equanimity when, as is the norm, love's labours are neither recognized nor duly rewarded. At the office or factory, you are paid money to accept the frustrating invisibility of your efforts. Love, as expected of women, is similarly invisible, intensive work without any clear norms of remuneration. Love needs time, skills and effort.

Earning money in the world outside, though hideously stressful, is far more straightforward.

The edifice of India's economy is built by the money men make and trade held together by the invisible love and unpaid care women offer. A 2017 World Economic Forum report found that sixty-six per cent of Indian women's labour goes unpaid. Only twelve per cent of men's labours were unpaid. Oxfam has found that Indian women put in 3.26 billion hours of unpaid care work every day, estimated to be a contribution of nearly ₹19 trillion to the Indian economy. In 2017, nearly six out of ten Indian women aged fifteen and older spent all their time exclusively on unpaid housework. By contrast, seven out of ten men aged fifteen and older were employed or actively looking for employment. Despite sharp increases in the numbers of educated women, this distribution of labour has remained the same for the past two decades. As India's economy grew at an average of seven per cent between 2004 and 2011, the share of women in the labour force fell to 32.6 per cent before plunging even further between 2011 and 2017 to a historic low of 23.3 per cent.

In 2017, amongst urban youth between the ages of fifteen and twenty-nine, women reported the highest ever unemployment rate in independent India at 27.2 per cent, compared to 18.7 per cent for men. Commenting on India's high unemployment rates in the *Economic and Political Weekly* (*EPW*), two leading labour economists noted that 'job-loss growth has not affected men, but only women in net terms'. While the 2018 government labour survey offered the small mercy of reporting no further decline in female employment shares, the pandemic has only made the Indian workforce more masculine, particularly in cities. According to the government's quarterly Periodic Labour Force Survey, between April and June 2020, the period of India's national lockdown, nearly fifty-seven per cent of urban men above the age of fifteen were employed. The same share for urban women was 15.5 per cent. By the end of 2020, as per a report published by economists at Azim Premji University using nation-wide survey data collected by the Centre for Monitoring Indian Economy (CMIE), ninety per cent of male workers, those who had jobs in the period before the pandemic in December 2019, were able to hold on to some form of employment while seven per cent were unable to return to the workforce. For women with jobs prior to the pandemic, between April and December in 2020, only forty-three per cent were able to continue working while nearly half never returned to paid work. This implies that five out of ten working women lost employment following the first wave of the pandemic. While the COVID-19 crisis pushed many Indian men from good jobs towards precarious self-employment, women simply exited the workforce.

These facts have been well documented and disseminated. Somehow, their implications haven't been fully absorbed. In a republic of 'hurt sentiments' where innocuous web series, tweets, stand-up comedy routines or food cultures trigger legal cases and public protests, there is hardly any mass outrage about women being erased from the workforce. Posh men will read articles in the international and Indian news media bemoaning the abysmal levels of female employment and the economic imbalance between men and women. Then they will go on to forcefully counter the data with 'nuance' and claims of how 'things are more complex, let me explain the ground realities to you'. Talking about the data on women's employment with 'Ground Reality Uncles' has become one of my preferred pastimes at Delhi society events. It's my sole party trick: I don't have much to say to people that doesn't involve graphs or numbers.

At the one party I attended in 2020, before the pandemic forced us to shun the company of other people, I tried to impress a popular chronicler of Indian history with evidence on gender gaps in India's jobs landscape. Unlike Ground Reality Uncles, the historian engaged on the facts with a series of questions. Where did the data come from? 'The Indian government's National Sample Survey or the NSS,' I replied.

'Is it reliable?' he followed up. Acknowledging the epistemic bravery of trying to collapse people's experiences into numbers, I nonetheless explained that the data provided a powerful signal of how economic opportunities were distributed across gender, locations and social cleavages. A dear journalist friend joined us. He mentioned how those who watched the Indian economy looked forward to the release of these data: 'They provide the best long-term view of the Indian labour landscape. So much so that delays in the publication of the 2017 results were finally pre-empted by a media leak and formal resignations by the government's top statisticians,' he added.

We talked about the history of India's labour surveys. The Historian was curious about how the information was collected, wondering if only upper-class professionals with formal paychecks were considered 'employed'. 'What about my maid? Is she counted?' he asked, blushing as he realized how typical that question was.

Much like film-makers, statisticians too have struggled to capture the complexity of Indian life. But the latter community has no interest in fantasy or escapism. In 1970, a Committee of Experts on Unemployment Estimates submitted a report to the Planning Commission in which it observed: 'In our complex economy, the character of the labour force, employment and unemployment, is too heterogeneous to justify aggregation into single-dimensional magnitudes.' Following the recommendations of the Expert Committee, India's first employment survey was conducted between September 1972 and October 1973. Ever since, the government's statistical machinery has consistently conducted employment surveys every five years using a more or less identical approach. Abiding by the spirit of the 1970 report, the survey questionnaires collect detailed information across a large and statistically representative swathe of every Indian state. Surveyors don't walk up to a selected home and simply ask if family members are working or not. Instead, they try to record all paid and unpaid activities each person has been involved in for the past year, week and day. This activity information is compared and used to identify tasks that occupy the majority of a person's time and effort. The aim is to ensure that multiple occupations, part-time workers and the various nuances of the world of Indian work are reflected in the data.

No one is more sceptical of statistics than statisticians. They warn us about the statistical straitjacket that employment surveys force upon the fluid and layered labours of Indians. In conversation with such worries, activists and statisticians have over the years collaborated to ensure that the informal and intermittent nature of women's work can be documented better. As a result, I told the Historian, the notion of 'employment' used by the government's survey tries to be broad and inclusive, going far beyond full-time regular salaried workers to include casual labourers, the self-employed and part-time workers. Those without written contracts or formal working arrangements are recognized as workers. Those helping family enterprises are also considered part of the working population. 'Your part-time domestic worker or the local street vendor are included and categorized as employed. Women offering tuition classes from their own homes for just a few months of the year would also be included in this broader definition,' I clarified.

So, what do these employment estimates tell us? As of January 2018, seventy-seven per cent of India's workers were male. A more recent survey conducted by the Centre for Monitoring Indian Economy (CMIE) found that women accounted for only 10.7 per cent of the workforce in 2019. For the past twenty-five years, gaps between men and women in the rural labour force have widened to historic proportions. The gap between the share of urban men and women in India's workforce has remained consistently wide. The Historian focused on unpacking the urban employment dynamics surrounding us. Between 2004 and 2017, 14.9 million new workers entered the economy in urban India. Of these, only

2.9 million were women. If we slice the urban employment numbers by age, caste, location, education or wealth, gender gaps remain substantial. Marriage and childcare in India prevent women from taking up or sticking with paid jobs. In 2017, as in 1993, nearly seventy-one per cent of urban Indian women between the ages of thirty and thirty-four were engaged solely in unpaid housework. Even amongst urban women between the ages of twenty-five and twenty-nine, close to seventy per cent (69.4) exclusively attended to domestic duties. These women were not 'unemployed'; they were too busy with housework or had simply given up on trying to find paid employment.

'What about well-educated and elite women? They must be working,' the Historian retorted, pouring himself another drink. My journalist friend sidled away, having heard this conversation play out too many times with other equally incredulous party guests.

I explained that less than a quarter of India's wealthiest urban women work for an income. Women with postgraduate degrees have the highest chance of being employed. However, the per cent share of postgraduate men with jobs is nearly double that of women with the same degree. 'Is it better in south India?' he asked.

'Yes,' I replied. 'These job gaps widen in northern states. However, gaps exist in the more progressive southern states as well. For example, in Tamil Nadu, nearly eighty-three per cent of urban men with postgraduate degrees were in the workforce compared to 46.3 per cent of women.'

Having found a captive audience, I expounded further. 'If I narrow the 2017 numbers further to exclusively focus on urban populations between the ages of fifteen and fifty-nine years of age,' I said, 'which helps us avoid counting children and the elderly, 74.2 per cent of men were employed. The same estimate for women is 19.8 per cent. Even in states reporting the highest share of women with jobs, Sikkim and Andhra Pradesh, less than a third of urban women work for an independent income.'

'What about India's largest cities? How many women in metropolitan India earn regular salaries?'

Very few, I said to my interlocutor, whose shoulders by now had slumped. The two cities reporting the highest share of women with regular paid jobs are Raipur and Coimbatore. Raipur makes me scratch my head. Coimbatore is easier to explain, home to one of India's largest garment zones and, closer to my heart, it is one of just three cities in the country to report more Google searches for Shah Rukh than Salman.

The hip cities of Delhi, Bengaluru, Kolkata and Mumbai report huge gaps between men and women in salaried jobs. In the busy Greater Mumbai municipal area, which includes the posh townies of Colaba and the beautiful gluten-free people of Bandra–Juhu, a mere 15.4 per cent of women hold regular salaried jobs. Men in Greater Mumbai do better, with 40.4 per cent holding stable, salaried employment. If I broaden the analysis to include those engaged in casual labour, self-employment and those looking for a job, gaps between men and women in cities remain large. In Bengaluru, for instance, only 22.2 per cent of women are in the labour force compared to over three-quarters of their male counterparts. And urban men tend to earn more than urban women too, in each bracket of class, caste and education.

As I talked about these numbers, the Historian and I were joined by a red-blooded Delhi Wonk, member of a band of clever men who 'worked in policy'. Besotted by their own potential, boring in their naked self-promotion, they spent their time at social gatherings dissecting their recent Twitter debates, choosing to only listen to those they deemed powerful. Their CVs had become their personalities. Convinced that they would save India from the ideas of those without doctoral degrees, they loved their own voices far too much, having received too much love from the education system and their mothers. I must begrudgingly acknowledge that this Wonk probably saw me *exactly* as I had described him—just another ruthlessly self-absorbed nerd. The Wonk tried to change the topic, to no avail. He was unhappy that the Historian refused to slide off into a corner with him, unable to understand how anyone would want to talk to a woman of no influence in a Delhi drawing room. Now, the poor Wonk was forced to join us. He entered the conversation by clumsily telling me about his lunch plans with my boss the next day. I knew this to be untrue, given that my boss was in Dhaka and I had spoken to him an hour ago. The Wonk believed the jobs data but wondered if women simply didn't want to work.

The Historian demurred: 'Most of the ambitious Indian students I encounter in doctoral programmes are women. They dominate the media too.' We spent another half hour discussing various causes of the crisis. Noticing an important editor from a foreign news publication, the Wonk vanished within ten minutes.

Given the continent-like size and heterogeneity of India, it is perfectly possible to live in a micro-milieu which feels like New York, full of ambitious and professionally successful women, without recognizing how small and statistically insignificant these spaces are. You can't imagine the number of times someone in the poshest or remotest part of India has suggested that constant female presence on TV or on the radio suggests that Indian women must be empowered and strong, that we should be hopeful. Media certainly feels like a feminine space in India. However, these are tiny enclaves, currently in decline thanks to a bad economy and a pandemic. The 2017 government employment survey tells us that the seemingly ubiquitous female faces in the media—billboard models, journalists, authors, musicians, creative professionals, performing artists and sportswomen—account for about 0.5 per cent of working women in urban India.

I told the Historian about Ground Reality Uncles, those who denied India's female job crisis. We wondered if they felt implicated in the dipping female employment numbers. Drawing on the work of Ambedkar, feminists argue that even with the strongest infrastructure and best reforms, families that can afford to rely exclusively on men for money will continue to guard women's access to jobs because of an obsession with protecting their sexual purity. In 2016, a survey by the Centre for the Study of Developing Societies (CSDS) amongst Indians aged fifteen to thirty-four reported that eighty-four per cent of their marriages were arranged. Nine out of ten of these weddings were within the same caste. According to another survey by scholars at the Research Institute of Compassionate Economics, the results of which were published in the *EPW* in January 2018, around sixty per cent of non-Dalits in rural Rajasthan and forty per cent in Delhi supported legislating against inter-caste marriages to protect endogamy. Even in 2021, a well-designed Pew survey on social attitudes found that more than sixty per cent of all Indians wanted to ensure women did not marry outside their respective caste groups. Using such data, activists argue that caste and patriarchy are married. They highlight how families desire control over women's bodies and mobility to maintain the purity of their caste networks. Such control is a key reason why women's employment opportunities are minimized; the ultimate goal is to reduce any chance of boyfriends or workplace romances from taboo communities.

In fact, a key theory explaining the decline in female employment in India centres on how economic growth has made it possible for millions of families to practise conservative values by withdrawing women from paid jobs. Sociologists call this the 'Sanskritization' effect. Higher incomes allow family members to perform puritanical upper-caste social rituals where women's bodily honour is guarded strictly within the home. As incomes increase, families no longer need more members to work in order to stay afloat and women are discouraged from working outside. This phenomenon has contributed to India being the only middle-income country where a phase of rapid economic growth and poverty reduction has not resulted in more women working outside the home.

Another effect of Sanskritization is that improvements in the economic well-being of historically disadvantaged castes have not triggered improvements in the job opportunities of women within these groups. While Other Backward Castes (OBC) and some segment of Scheduled Castes (SC) have made economic gains over the past three decades, employment gaps between men and women within these communities have only increased. For the past fifteen years, half of all OBC or SC men have always been employed. Female employment rates within these groups have halved in the same period. Sociologists posit that these gaps are not only due to discrimination, but also because communities want to emulate the puritanical practices of the upper caste, among whom female employment is the lowest. Many also say that with increasing incomes, even working-class women are happier to avoid jobs outside the home as a choice. Dropping out of employment allows women to be flexible in how they allocate their energies—between raising their children, offering ad-hoc unpaid services to family enterprises when needed and enjoying some free time.

Is sustained urban employment inequality because of Ground Reality Uncles? A demonstration of purity? Or is it a decline in jobs that have historically employed women? Perhaps women find more fulfillment at home? Or they risk losing love if they build careers? Is it simply the lack of political enthusiasm for women's economic concerns? While caste-based politics has come to dominate the Indian electoral landscape, feminists highlight how the political discourse aimed at empowering women is often 'steeped in the patriarchy it is claiming to fight'. It's frustrating and clichéd, but in a diverse country like India, all of these are robust and inadequate explanations at the same time.

What has always been clear is that any talk of these numbers is certain to embarrass Indian elites, who like to project themselves as modern members of a modern country, with modern independent women. But the cold hard evidence shows us the shocking inequality of economic opportunity between men and women in the country. Despite rapidly increasing educational attainment for girls and declining fertility, a 2020 World Economic Forum report on gender gaps in economic participation and opportunity placed India in the bottom five countries of the world, with Pakistan, Syria, Yemen and Iraq.

It's not necessary that all women must find jobs. However, various studies show that many of the young women engaged in 'domestic duties' would like the opportunity to earn on their own. Their aspirations are curtailed by norms and an unfriendly public space. Jobs, even with poor pay and uncertain contracts, can allow new solidarities and personhoods to emerge. Work opens new spaces and connections outside the home. We can fall for someone we meet through work; we can love who we are at work; we can cling to our work when we feel unloved elsewhere. One can turn to relationships at the workplace for fun, reprieve or meaning. We can become daughter-bureaucrats, mother-embroiderers or wife-musicians. Men access such diversified and hyphenated personhoods with far greater ease. Women who wish to cultivate professional identities, who don't enjoy motherhood or the act of loving exclusively within families or being full-time caregivers, generally suffer in India. Love, ideally secured through marriage and caregiving, remains fundamental to Indian female life.

'Unsurprisingly, a minority of Indian women earn an independent income. Women's dominant role as caregivers with men as breadwinners is an enduring characteristic of India's urban employment landscape,' I argued, as the Wonk approached us again and asked me to 'Stop lecturing.' He turned to the Historian with a smile and added, 'The data is not that interesting.'

Lutyens' Laboratory

With the socio-economic stage set in their favour, men with pedigree, property and potential can sense their comparative advantage in the mating market and thus exert power. And somewhere within this advantage lie the seeds for male deification, and the production and preservation of an infantile male ego—manufactured and nourished by protective parenting and privilege, scarred by a disciplining father and a doting mother, propped up by culture, easily bruised and eager to lash out.

Of course, all my theories on love and masculinity were tested in the romantic laboratories offered by The One. We met at a party back in 2012. You rarely encounter men like The One on dating apps in Delhi. If your profile conforms to an algorithm of attractiveness, you're likely to encounter their poorer cousins who've fallen on tough times. Unlike The One and his crowd, poorer feudals hold no Gymkhana memberships, political connections or thriving enterprises, but are in possession of guns, crumbling estates, irregular incomes and a mountain of despair and debt. You've seen them zipping past your car or staring at white women in bars, men with 'Rajpoot Boys' stamped on their metal-hued chariots. But despite their varying feudal fates, the landed gentry's male progeny seem united in their quest for escape— hoping that speed, an air of entitlement, smug self-satisfaction and ritualistic casual sex will compensate for the toll that history and the economy have extracted from their moustached manhood.

Misogyny is not a monopoly of the elite. Alpha males are found across class distinctions. We've all suffered through these men—the clumsy Casanovas, the fat-shamers, the gaslighters, the bullies, those who deify tradition and family honour, all the while celebrating the treatment of people as products. The feudal men I survived would wax eloquent on the complexities and social gradations within their own caste groups. But my romance and heartbreak experienced none of this nuance. My love affair dwelled in a strictly small social milieu.

Accustomed to reading statistics about how the top 20 per cent of Indian families account for 45 per cent of the country's total disposable income, I understood the economics of inequality. Notwithstanding our claims of middle-classdom, I knew that the economic middle was largely rural and uneducated. Just by virtue of living in urban Delhi and being high-school graduates, nearly everyone around me was in the top-two economic tiers of the country. But I also knew that the richest one per cent of India earned twenty-one per cent of its income, up from six per cent in 1982. The One would joke that he was part of the '0.1 per cent'. He was probably right. These 0.1 percenters, the elites within the elites, steadily lost wealth after World War II till 1983. Since the mid-1980s, their share of Indian income grew to 8 per cent by 2015, nearly the same level as they held before India gained independence.

The social texture of this wealth ladder revealed itself to me during my days and evenings spent in love with The One. Despite being neighbours on the economic spectrum, an invisible partition divided this man's world and mine. This partition was discriminating; it allowed sex and flirtation but prohibited authenticity and camaraderie. He hated talking about work, considering it a low form of culture. From his mother to his family friends, glamorous, unemployed women for whom marriage was an insurance policy were the norm in his social circle. The men, meanwhile, were a gallery of competitive anxieties, hanging by the skin of their teeth to their family legacies. The modern laws of Manu divided the world into three clans: his family, his boarding-school buddies and The Rest. For The One, The Rest were not people but functions to satiate multiple appetites: X for jokes, Y for clean shirts, Z for sex.

I was Z100. He was extractive, blissfully at peace with the everyday exploitation underpinning his pleasures. His boarding-school buddies often suggested that the Indian caste system had historically kept civil strife in check, as people internalized their rank in the world. It was liberalization that created the muddle, as everyone wanted more. Any discussion of social stratification would yield long, pedantic lectures on how I needed to 'calm down and stop overthinking' and accept that some people come from more than others.

Surveying The One and his friend circle, I quickly realized that there was nothing particularly unusual about Delhi's elite bachelor-playboys. They seemed to be standard-issue assholes of global shapes and sizes. The One's upbringing had taught him charm, not sincerity. And I was far too earnest. The fact that I was an economist-in-training studying labour, welfare and inequality made matters much worse. When the magnificent sex-haze of our initial months started to wear off, I noticed how clueless he was about his privilege, unwilling to acknowledge how status preserved his life of consistent gratification. His world views were frozen in time—none of the information from his past translated into any insight on how to navigate the present. It seemed his people had indoctrinated themselves against change, against any introspection or investigation of one's own experiences. Self-criticism was a disease, best vaccinated by humour and substances. None demonstrated the willingness to update their priors based on evidence or encounters. Such blindness was acute when it came to matters of sex and love. Terms like 'player' and 'bad boy' were glorified, divorced from all the pain that said players and bad boys caused. None of that past pain, witnessing lovers becoming a puddle of tears in front of him, implied any change in his treatment of women. It was all castigated as the 'usual female drama'. Aligned with my hopes to secure him, ignoring my own privilege, I risked his ire and tried to educate him on his past and place in life, on how unfairly he conducted his love life, how his wealth subsidized the value of human dignity in his personal exchanges. Bearing this Bayesian burden proved impossible. Economists are taught to torture data; I ended up torturing myself. In these moments, I became too unappealing. I was far from seductive, I was being serious and shrill.

His social gatherings were anchored on the notion of 'talking shit'. These evenings always followed a predictable pattern: after entry and a stream of greetings, the men and women would segregate. The men would talk of their days at school or college, the women would talk of their children's days at school or college. Basic chatter on travel, TV shows, business dealings, politics, gossip, nannies, schools and fashion served as lubricants. Contact details and reviews of caregivers, caterers and trainers were often exchanged. Male–female conversation was limited, often cast as flirtatious banter. The One policed my social moves at these events. Once, when I was amidst a conversation on the dynamics of property prices with one of his friends, he felt compelled to come up to me and whisper, 'You're taken and not really his type, remember that.'

I was hardly a picture of poise and calm, convinced he was sleeping with everyone. He laughed at my anxiety. 'It'll take a man thrice my strength to conduct as many affairs as you think I'm capable of.'

We rarely ventured into his terrain together as a couple. But I yearned for encounters with these ethnographic specimens, to see men in their forties refer to each other as Bugs or Donks, preserving their pickled adolescences in the brine of the other. Their sole currency was peer approval. Metaphysical backslapping. Soon, I recognized that love affairs were merely the heteronormative icing on a dreary homosocial cake. The men and women shared close ties from their previous incarnations as single people: everyone had been with everyone; everyone tailed a history like a string of rusted cans. Lust, avarice and the anxieties of marriage were a second atmosphere. The single men often cycled through a series of strivers before settling on a woman of their own 'temperament'. Temperament was code for a woman who would give up her job after marriage and came from the same caste group. The social environment often felt like full contact sport. 'Dating' seemed like a ridiculous euphemism.

The women merely served as paeans to male sexuality. The One and his friends would parade their partners, as if to say, 'Look at what I've acquired.' He had several single friends—kinsmen who seemed bruised by the conjugal market—although his married friends led far more single lives. One such married member of the brotherhood asserted that his girlfriends often looked like members of a Victoria's Secret catalogue, while his Indian wife was a great mother and successful businesswoman. The men loved Salman Khan, whisky and spending time with each other. Berating Shah Rukh Khan as a 'sissy' of epic proportions was also a favourite pastime, one that nauseated the fangirl in me. The men often looked bloated and ill. They loved hunting, describing life as one long, big hunt. Garden-variety sexism was rampant; women who were unknown entities were often accused of being gold-diggers or 'operators'. I heard murmurs of an elite swingers' club. This was hard to believe; these men seemed incapable of finding women attractive, given their clear love for each other.

So what if his society was repressive? He looked like Shashi Kapoor. The drinks were great and the women were well-dressed and slender. Beautiful, intelligent and bored, these ladies had invested their entire lives in priming and perfecting their minds and bodies. Now they waited to be desired at social gatherings, while their husbands were drunk on the past. The One never expected much from me. Stay slim and smile, he would joke. And never discuss your job, never ask anyone about their work.

In a country with rapidly shrinking numbers of women in the workforce, I wore my employment as a badge of honour. But this was a sensitive issue. Being a working woman who paid her own bills made me an oddity and I was thus instructed to lie low. In our first month together, I recall asking one of his friends' wives about what she did with her time. She smiled and said she was a princess. I earnestly asked if her role as princess was her profession, indicating that managing properties, homes and old estates must be a tough job. She scowled and said, 'We have servants for that. I focus on public relations when I get time. You mean, you go to office *every day*?' I nodded, moving away as she sipped her vodka tonic.

My conversations with the other women would usually degenerate into both parties feeling assaulted. I was assaulted by their perfection, while they felt assaulted by my ambitions. At the time, I was interviewing for a job I'd always dreamed of—it paid well and would ensure I could support housing and healthcare for my parents and rent my own flat. The job offered an opportunity to work with colleagues who were some of the best technicians and guides in my field. 'This job is like a husband,' said The One, when I described what the position meant to me. In the run-up to my application deadline and interview, I was a nervous wreck. The selection process was extremely competitive and I was possessed by possibilities. Days and evenings were spent doing mock interviews, constantly grasping at my future. One night, while I was preparing interview essays, The One suggested we attend a dinner at his friend's. My clueless self, draped in a saree and social anxiety, committed one party faux pas after another. All I wanted was reassurance as I insisted on discussing interviewing techniques with the ladies and his friends. But all I did was display occupational desire and nervousness. This was interpreted as crass and arrogant: the table felt I was 'showing off'.

As we drove back from his friend's concrete central Delhi mansion, The One said, 'I need to have a word with you.' We parked and walked up to his living room. He maintained a stony silence. I wondered if it was the whisky or the wonders of my company. The One's manservant was asked to pour us a drink and depart for the evening. Drinks were poured in beautiful cut-glass tumblers; The One played an old concert recording of a Hindi-film musician that I could not recognize. His stare oscillated between the ceiling and myself. I was suddenly paranoid. Was he breaking up with me? Was I being ousted from his hallowed harem? A part of me was itching to leave as well. A million thoughts muddled my mind—*I need to send out that application essay. I need to find all my academic transcripts. I wish he would put me out of my misery soon. But how will I manage without him?* As he maintained his silence, a question from one of my application essays came back to me: *What motivated you to apply for this position?* My answer: *For the past few years, I have worked at the intersection of activism, administration and academia …*

'You behaved very badly today,' The One suddenly announced. 'This kind of behaviour just won't do.' And then, for forty-five minutes, he proceeded to dissect my performance for the evening. I had never felt uglier. It appeared that I'd rambled on about my interview and upset all the unemployed housewives in attendance. 'These are business owners, a few were single-haveli royals, do you think they care or know much about what you do?' he continued. 'It was embarrassing and insulting for everyone. No one is impressed by your degrees and education here, nor by your interview. I wish you'd just calm down and stop being so frantic. Learn to talk about other things. Or sip your drink quietly.'

I lashed out. I wasn't responsible for the labour-market insecurities of his dinner-party audience, nor was I responsible for their feelings. And I had obviously never meant to hurt anyone. I stormed out of his house, angry and humiliated. Back at home, I realized that this was a pattern. To The One, all my achievements became a sour source of embarrassment. When I did receive my coveted job offer, The One never bothered to congratulate me. He could not feign any interest or enthusiasm. My closest friend organized a celebration; the invitation was declined.

A few weeks passed, and I finally summoned his company. After rejecting the party invite, he had tried contacting me a few times, but I could never bring myself to return his calls or messages. It was amidst the machinations of moving into my new apartment that I yearned to outsource all of life's logistical decisions to someone else. There, all alone in a three-bedroom flat, flooded with packing boxes, I needed him more than ever. I needed him to cloak and shield me from social judgement for abandoning my parents, to distract me from my own guilt and loneliness, to divert my mind from my own migration.

In 2013, when I decided to move out of Chittaranjan Park, a Bengali-dominated former refugee colony in south Delhi, and find my own place in Nizamuddin East, my family felt betrayed. Not because I was living alone, but because I chose to live in a neighbourhood closer to power. My mother remarked, 'Why don't you live in Defence Colony or someplace nearby?' For her, Khan Market was the epicentre of a five-kilometre radius of sycophancy. 'IAS officers and rich Congress types live there. It's green and lovely, but never forget that your parents live on the other side of the Ring Road, stuck in jams at Savitri Cinema.'

Where you live has historically served as a credible signal of your place in the social map of India. Economists write about location premiums—where you are often predicts who you become. In cities, your ward number and its municipal grade suggest how much rent you pay. Delhi is acutely stratified: living in Bharti Nagar means your family works in tax administration, living in Sunder Nagar hints at old money. The new wave of labour migration into Delhi settled on the outskirts of east Delhi, most of the city being too expensive. Data shows that place is an effective and statistically significant predictor of urban poverty; governments usually use residential address to target welfare programmes effectively.

Growing up, I'd never been able to fully settle into Delhi. When people ask me where I am from, I find my own answer to be a complete fabrication. I mutter 'Delhi,' since I've lived here for a majority of my life, but you'll always pick up on a note of my uncertainty. Close friends will attest that until my first year at work, I barely had any bearings for the city and its social or physical geography. Moving constantly back and forth between tiny towns in Jharkhand and Bengal, followed by the big move to residential areas, my daily life always felt disconnected from the display that was Delhi. From my earliest teenage years, I knew that I lived in a peripheral universe far away from the Great Parts of the Greater National Capital Territory.

With this final move, two kilometres from Khan Market, I had arrived into the heart of independence and luxury.

'You're exactly like us now,' The One said. And he was right. But it wasn't the house or its location that made me like him—I was no property owner. No, it was my freedom. I had acquired some of his freedom. If we wish to define a line to divide women across the social spectrum into the haves and have-nots, the ability to find free time or independently 'buy leisure'—drink, smoke cigarettes, watch movies, go to the beauty parlour, attempt self-care or do absolutely nothing—emerges as one of the strongest statistical and sociological definitions in all of south Asia. The poverty of choice plagues our women.

National data shows that women's physical movements in India, and certainly in the north, are constantly policed. Most need permission to visit any public place, and hardly exercise control over their daily routines. Marrying an educated man does not alter this landscape of surveillance. Wealth can't help either. In fact, nearly every wealthy Indian woman I know has experienced some nice-guy-turned-control-freak episode.

Naila Kabeer, a leading scholar of women's work who teaches at the London School of Economics, worries that families use their instincts to protect daughters or wives as a means to shackle them. 'It's because these concepts of honour and shame are yet to change radically, and wherever these concepts exist as a cultural motif, they are very bound up with women's sexuality', she says. 'We still live in a world where family and male standing depends on how women and their bodies behave. What families are trying to do in their unintendedly coercive ways is to protect themselves and their own daughters. And this discourse of sexuality pervades how women are expected to be outside private spaces. Women are constantly worried—what bits are showing? Did I smile too much? The honour of the family revolves around the virtuous woman. When a woman becomes a wife, there are new dynamics around jealousy and men's ownership of their wives' bodies. The moment a woman steps out, you are signalling something to the world, that you have broken with tradition. And in such highly sexually segregated societies, I find this preoccupation with women's bodies just astounding and unchanging. In a way, there is no similar obsession with men's bodies. Men's bodies are supposed to be healthy and productive, but no one polices them the same way.' Privileged women are often those who exercise complete control over their bodies and how they spend their time. And so, in this house, with my new job, no longer patrolled by family, free to do what I wished, I was gifted the ultimate female privilege.

I was free to make terrible choices.

Following a late-night message, he immediately landed up with a bottle of wine, congratulating me on the space, suggesting cushion designs and seating plans. And without much conversation or conflict, we resumed our dance. Of course, there was no offer of commitment, no apology attached—all my anger was relegated to the school of 'overthinking' and 'bad behaviour'. And so, I continued playing it cool and casual, fearful of assaulting him with my expectations.

Tell us again: *Why have you applied for this position?*

That night, I realized I was a hypocrite. Despite my lectures on class and feminism, I was embarrassingly proud of my dalliance with The One. He, with all his preordained wealth and confidence, represented the kind of man a woman like me wasn't supposed to get. And yet I had managed to seduce him. In associating status and welfare with a powerful male, I was no different from the unemployed princesses his friends had married, the ones I judged so harshly as my feminist enemies. No one in my social circle could relate to the world I currently occupied. *You are with the anti-Shah Rukh*, my best friends surmised. In those days, I returned to the actor's interviews and imagery repeatedly. Shah Rukh's distant icon felt more emotionally available than the real-life man I was involved with.

I should have known better; most women do. In Delhi, it is a truth universally acknowledged that a single man in possession of a good fortune must be busy building his harem. The natural corollary is that single women in possession of independent incomes must run in the opposite direction. Why elite bachelors chose to remain toxic bachelors is a boring question with an obvious answer: it's a predictable misogynistic power trip masquerading as a good time. No, the more interesting question is: Why do elite women give in? Why do independent women end up indulging toxic males in romantic pursuits? Why had I applied to this position? As some of my wisest friends asked, 'What was this compulsion of The One?'

For women, Delhi leaves little recourse. Dipping female employment, tilted property rights, unequal division of housework and relentless hostility towards women who seek to engage more with the world beyond their home make monogamous marriage so much more than a relationship. In the absence of a supportive state, through love and matrimony, many women hope to secure a safe and profitable human arrangement. A man is no longer a man, he becomes a source of identity, survival and sustenance. He becomes a symbol of lost opportunities—if you're going to give up your career for a man, he'd better be the best bet. Anthropologists say that the northern parts of India are part of a 'classical' patriarchy belt. Women transact in the 'patriarchal bargain'—putting up with all kinds of indignities imposed on them by men and family life, because the gains from cooperation seem vital. Economists use dull and precise language—a women's bargaining power is weak as her exit options are limited. No one sits you down and instructs you in game theory or patriarchy, you gradually learn the rules of the game. Soon, you become complicit in your own discrimination, looking for a man to help you trade upwards in the world.

I belong to a small minority of elite, employed Indian women; most of us don't come from socio-political capital, family property or old money, but we are part of the hyper-privileged set of Indians with regular salaried jobs and social security benefits. Wealth ought to obfuscate any need for us to seek out or pine for the beneficence of a posh man. Marketing campaigns are often targeted at my purchasing power. We are part of a new generation of women—the first in our families to experience what sociologist Anthony Giddens called a 'pure relationship ... where a social relation is entered into for its own sake, for what can be derived by each person from a sustained association with another; and which is continued only insofar as it is thought by both parties to deliver enough satisfactions for each individual to stay within it'. In a country where only five per cent of women exercise exclusive control over who they marry, we belong to an empowered minority.

Most of our mothers never had the luxury of love outside marriage; many never had the chance to date or marry a man of their own choosing. For my grandmother, growing up between West Bengal and Jharkhand, family was the entirety of one's world. The idea of forging friendships outside the family unit was a concept my mother introduced to my grandmother. The idea of trying on relationships before finding someone you wanted to marry was a concept I introduced to my mother. Through a combination of some male support, many female sacrifices and sheer grit, my tribe has gained the spirit and skills for freedom. And yet, time after time, in churches, cafes and bars, I keep hearing the same tale: of strong-willed women falling for some silly, elite alpha male, and feeling empty and defeated by the mating market.

Women who feel frustrated by their freedom are tethered to tradition. Your own success ought to obscure any need to derive meaning from a man's social or financial station. Your experiences outside the home ought to provide some sense and succour. Independence ought to bolster an appetite for resistance and rebellion. But strange things happen to the grammar of women's expectations here. An unfriendly and taxing public sphere loads women's intimate interactions with heavy and unspeakable burdens. The puzzle in Delhi is perhaps not why some independent women fall for toxic bachelors, but why they resign their love lives to the trappings of male power and prestige. Why do so many successful women acquire a taste and tolerance for inequality in their private lives? The latter question, and my own complicity, remain the root of all my romantic struggle and rage. I check my anger often; it oozes out as nervous cocktail-party chatter on occasion.

Up until encountering The One, my love life was dull. Much like Vidya, I had failed to find the right man but had miraculously found the right work. Suddenly, I'd become a sum of my professional competencies. And just as suddenly, my competencies seemed like disabilities in the dating pool. Men explained my job to me, finding my obsession with it an ungainly, unattractive attribute for a woman. My passion for what I did and my ferocious attachment to it became a deficiency that no cosmetic product could hide.

In my early thirties, I finally understood that many of the straight men my age, those who operated outside the arranged-marriage market, had been socialized into desiring women who were cheerleaders or status symbols. I stopped blaming these men for their romantic choices, realizing that we were all victims of our unequal society and circumstances. The Delhi scene, where feudalism wore Prada and pretended to be a market economy, only made matters worse. Each of us wanted our private lives to require minimal effort.

The young men I met, who were my equals, were, like me, obsessed with fulfilling their potential, constantly in conversation with their glorious future. Our drive was exhausting, days and evenings were spent navigating the labyrinth of Delhi's opportunities. Energies were channelled to decipher this city's professional codes and patronage networks. Thanks to the economic boom of the mid '90s, which had survived even the 2008 global financial crisis, young English-speaking metropolitan Indians had more options in the early 2010s than ever before in the country's history. Money was available for those who knew how to get it. New magazines were being set up, new companies were hiring people, new books on India needed to be written, new scholarships were announced for studies abroad. And we threw ourselves into the ring. Competition was our raison d'etre. The 2010s made eager arrivistes out of us all. And a part of success was being invited to the right places and showing up with the right person.

The One wasn't trained to pursue professional competition or social goals—he only possessed a sex drive—nor was he trained to romance economic equals. He was trained to romance the idea of himself. And so, I returned to him. I knew that most conversations between us served to confirm my inferiority. But in those long, lazy, languorous afternoons and evenings, I found a man who was completely at peace with himself because he never needed more in life. In my time with him, I occupied a place far removed from the Status Olympics of Delhi's drawing rooms. He did not care about my plans or my parents. The One distinguished himself from the alpha men I encountered in my own milieu, those who espoused revolutionary anarchist sentiment when it came to the country's industrial and political landscape, and yet subscribed to the most vanilla-conformist masculinity in their love lives. He did not hide his preference to avoid emotional labour, seek multiple partners and thin youthful bodies behind lectures on liberalism. There was a strange kind of honesty in the sex he was having. Our attraction guaranteed entry into parts of Delhi I'd never dreamed I could go. I admit I feasted on the envy of other women when they saw us together. I wore the best sarees, drank the best wine, was whisked off to laps of luxury on simple whims. I became greedy.

Before reuniting with The One, my romantic life had fallen into this anxious slumber, waiting to be jolted awake. The days in office were rewarding, the nights were spent stalking him on social media, surveying the sexual competition, all the while longing for love. But finding a replacement was impossible. If this were not the case, I'd have moved on to another male and forgotten all about him. But I could never forget. The One and his elusive seal of approval started to define me. His absence held me captive to a primordial sadness, one I could not relinquish through tears.

Life in Delhi felt incomplete without The One and his friends. I missed the martinis he made, missed my muscular body pillow. I missed walking into rooms with him. Soon, I realized that all men above six feet knew each other in the city, and circulated within their own glamorous cocoons, ensconced from the regular world of meet-cutes, app dates and Defence Colony patrakar (journalist) parties. So when the time came, my desperation and sexual dissatisfaction drove me right back to the feudal circus. A few months after our reunion, I met one of his childhood friends, a Harvard undergrad, who was allowed to discuss his time at school and his business ventures endlessly. In fact, I witnessed The One host parties to celebrate his male friend's professional achievements. Some even received a Facebook nod. And soon I learned that for The One, men carried Ivy League degrees, factoids on finance and plush jobs with more dignity than women. Womankind was best suited to careers as supplicants—earning ad-hoc incomes in fashion blogging and social-media influencing.

In that second phase of our relationship, accusations of 'overthinking' became his anthem. Holding The One to account on any expectations of dignified reciprocity was quickly cast as an act of attention-seeking and overthinking. Being angry at the prospect of an hour's wait was overthinking. Very often, we'd attend events with complete strangers. The One would often dislodge me at these gatherings, suddenly treating me as an invisible party trick. Expressing any feelings of abandonment—rational or irrational—was always a sign of overthinking. Expressing irritation at last-minute plans, given the constraints imposed by work deadlines, was overthinking. Once, I turned to The One and complained about a friend who made creepy and obvious advances towards me. In response, he offered, 'Really? In a classy place like this? He's just drunk, you're overthinking again.'

Fortunately, this emphasis on overthinking allowed one strand of common interest with the ladies at his congregations to emerge. Each one had been accused of overthinking as well. Each had her own tale of woe. We swapped stories, like soldiers in a battlefield. Seeking separation after discovering your husband's infidelity was a salient category of overthinking. Most female speech involving the disclosure of private emotions was typically classified as an act of overthinking. Intimacy was overthinking. I was never able to forge strong friendships with these women, I was too busy marking myself as distinct from them. We were made of different social materials. But condemned as female overthinkers, we found common ground, a moment of sisterhood and solidarity. Things between The One and me started to hit rock-bottom. Asserting intellectual dominance, worldly wisdom and sexual will became central to our connection, every exchange morphed into a boarding-school debate.

The thread of solidarity between us ladies unravelled on the issue of beauty. A friend of his suggested that I was far more 'shapely' than any of The One's ex-girlfriends. The ladies all agreed vehemently. Many suggested trainers, dermatologists and maintenance routines. Blind to the hidden compliment, paralysed by sexual competition and body dysmorphia, my life became an endless series of gluten-free chilas.

One night, I landed in Delhi from a trip to Patna. It was cold, the rain smacking everyone in the face. We were to attend a small dinner party, our second as companions. My obsession with The One had morphed into an obsession with my waistline. No one could accuse me of originality. Through chronic dieting, I had finally achieved my goal weight. The plane food tasted like dust and I was starving. As I rushed towards the dinner table for my first cheat meal after becoming a feudal pet, I found all six feet three inches of The One blocking my path. He gently held my wrist and placed my empty plate down on the table. 'You can't eat here,' he said, his eyes widening with horror. Puzzled, I asked why. He looked from the deserted table to the glittering crowd and said, 'Only dogs eat in public. Put the plate down, you don't need the food.'

At that moment, I wondered if eating was too intimate an act for these buttoned-up, polo-playing sociopaths. But I noticed his cousin's wife shovelling kebabs into her mouth. I stared at the biryani and my empty plate. I ate. He glared. I called myself a taxi. The next day I suggested we break up. He smiled and agreed. I never did fit in, he said. 'You're too serious, you take everything too seriously.' I could never separate the Church from the State. And I needed to attend finishing school.

Following our separation, when the days collapsed under a deluge of uncertainties, I would walk to central Delhi's Amrita Shergill Marg to flirt with real estate. Only bungalows worth ₹220 crore enveloped by ancient amaltas trees would soothe my soul. I know many who wander this street, marvelling at its elements. All of us united in our strange, psychosexual obsession with the hyper elite, ogling at their excesses. Nothing elicits greater desire and derision from your average 'middle-class' Indian than Lutyens' Delhi. The area, spanning nearly 3,000 acres, holds a thousand bungalows; most remain reserved for ministers and senior government officials, with seventy properties for private use. Unsurprisingly, the private residents of these enclaves are some of the richest Indians alive.

Despite Amrita Shergill Marg's popularity as a museum of elite excess, on my walks interrogating class and heartbreak, I was certain to see no one I knew, if I saw anybody at all. Delhi is often described as a capital city in search of its own country. But the residents of Amrita Shergill Marg seemed superhuman, able to teleport to their own planet. How else could you explain the silence and solace? No one is ever spotted running errands in the neighbourhood, and the gardens and guards look impossibly bored and manicured. I had heard rumours of Halloween parties and awkward dinner conversations, but possessed no evidence to corroborate these claims.

On one such day, animated by a state of stress, I found myself wide-eyed at the Marg again. It was a windy autumn evening. I was trailing behind a young man and woman as they walked towards the Lodi Gardens bus stop. They were arguing in Bengali. The event marked my first experience of pedestrian human activity in this realm, a major rupture in the bubble. I was alert, at attention. She reprimanded him, 'You're too distracted. Look down, do your work and avoid looking at madam directly. These people don't like it. I brought you here to do work, not indulge in nonsense.'

His response was muted; I was unable to hear him. After muttering a few lines, he shrugged his frail shoulders, suggesting a reluctant acceptance of her feedback. Several weeks later, I spotted her again, clinging to a mobile phone. She wore the same yellow saree—her uniform perhaps. I sped up, hoping to eavesdrop. Her voice gained greater momentum as we walked past Goa Sadan, a state-government guesthouse that served as a halfway marker to the bus terminal. I heard her frustration and amusement as she yelled into her device, 'Didi, we need older men to work in these houses as part-time help. These young boys have no control and can't manage. They stare and slow down work. They have never seen women like this in Medinipur or in Delhi. Our madams here are top-class beauties, they spend hours at the gym, wear expensive things and eat nothing. I send all new boys to work in houses in Defence Colony or CR Park. That colony life suits them better. The madams are not the same. He can work for a Bengali family with children. He can do work properly there.'

We reached the bus stop. This guide to top-class beauties halted and noticed my interest in her conversation. She returned to her phone. 'Didi, I'll call later,' she said, disappearing into the 522 CL Delhi Transport Corporation bus. And I ambled towards perspective.

Once I started to *see* the dynamics within my past romance, unseeing was no longer an option. I bumped into two male members of The One's crew on a flight from Mumbai to Delhi. After take-off, they gestured furiously at me, suggesting I join them in business class as they had a vacant seat nearby. I was seated in 'premium economy,' three rows behind them. I suggested that they join me on my seat, as the row was empty. One of his friends came up to me, smiled and said I was silly. 'You were always such a strange girl. Why are you refusing such comfort, yaar?' Why, indeed?

I walked into business class and immediately felt uncomfortable. The gaze of the flight attendant and other passengers burned into me. I entered some mild state of paranoia. In premium economy, I was entitled to ask for a coffee. Here, I was mute. The One's friends ordered me a cup and went on chatting about their previous conquests and holidays. After forty-five minutes of sheer discomfort, I walked back to my seat and breathed a sigh of relief. In business class, I was dependent on the good graces and kindness of my powerful friends. I kept wondering—what if the flight attendant asked me to leave? Would these men support my stay or kick me out immediately? There were no such existential questions in row 4A. I knew where I belonged. The view from premium economy was the same. Business class felt excessive.

But, of course, it was excess that interested me.

The final phase of my break-up with The One required divine intervention from Bollywood—a source of endless wisdom. A close friend and I were drinking at a trendy bar when one of India's hottest young actors walked in with his giant entourage. There weren't many people in the bar but once he arrived, the staff basically closed down the place. But all was not well. At some point, in the middle of all the revelry and madness, the man started to shed tears. He vanished with his friends, returning with puffy eyes after being consoled and counselled. I knew this man: he was charming, beautiful beyond belief, incredibly gifted; his first film remains one of my all-time favourites. Back then, in July of 2013, before he hit the big time, the man had all the obvious ingredients to become a bona fide megastar. And yet

I'll never forget his social posture that night, sad and alone. In my drunk, heartbreak-fuelled stupor, I walked up to him, gave him a hug and asked why he was crying. I could not understand how a man with so much—talent, success, fame and beauty—could feel anxious. Bewildered by my curiosity, he offered some glib nonsense about his upcoming film. He tried to divert my questions by offering premiere passes, compliments and jokes. I kissed him on the cheek—my closest Bollywood encounter—and said goodbye to him and my expedition for an Indian male demigod.

Meeting this actor felt like an act of metaphysical healing. Here was a man, thoroughly blessed and rewarded by our patriarchal society, who nonetheless felt able to publicly display his weakness and vulnerability. In that moment, this shiny Bollywood product became a full-blown person. And soon, I acknowledged that The One was never a person to me, he had become some silly prize. A beautiful bauble that would bestow meaning on my person. And I saw my fervent yearning for what it truly was—a distraction from the hard work of finding meaning and belonging as an ordinary working woman on my own terms. Even today, I smile when I see photos and hoardings of the actor, grateful for his humanity and our trivial exchange. I'll never forget, as I was walking away that night, his director friend whispered to the superstar, 'What did she want?'

In his meditation on why we are so interested in those who live lives of excess, psychoanalyst Adam Phillips argues that they 'disturb us, get us worked up, because they reveal something important to us about ourselves, about our own fears and longings'. He emphasizes the role of culture in navigating a conversation on excess and offers: 'Because we are nothing special—on par with ants and daffodils—it is the work of culture to make us feel special; just as parents need to make their children feel special to help them bear and bear with—and hopefully enjoy—their insignificance in the larger scheme of things.'

Many months later, I spotted The One and his clan at Khan Market. They were accompanied by an impressive panoply of sexy young women. But I was ignored. One of his friends waved a cheerful hello as they departed. My heart and sense of self-regard sank. I'm used to the host of childlike behavioural patterns following break-ups: but the sting of sexual slights from The One would always feel important and potent. A reminder that I had dared to journey into business class on a premium-economy ticket. And while this brief interlude was wildly fun, no finishing school, academic degree or waistline measurement would ever make this man treat me the way he treated his family or his friends: as a fellow human being. Watching The One and his surrounding cast of friends and admirers, I realized that I no longer yearned for romance or sexual validation from these men—I desired only an honourable fellowship.

To me, The One and his buddies were a collection of Delhi's antiquities. Wealth had fortified their personal narratives of specialness, but its ability to guarantee insulation from any feeling of insignificance was waning. Excess, sustained by old money in a poor country with a politically ascendant middle class, is a lonely and loathsome place. But The One always seemed in control. *That propertied blood*, I thought, *forever in control. Forever hiding any anxieties in buddy-hood, land parcels and whisky.* And there I was, in the great tradition of weak-willed women, attempting to cloak all my feminine anxieties under the farcical shroud woven by male control. I remember looking closer at the gang of women surrounding The One. They displayed an amicable servility that I'm certain I exhibited during our time together—proof that silliness is an all-gender and top-ten-per-cent disorder. *Serves us right for being elitists in love.* In India, stupidity is our greatest luxury good.

—⚏—

I've spent a good part of the last few years trying to understand my preoccupation with The One by searching other friends' romantic and sexual relationships for answers. I realized how popular culture had made us lightweights for love. Each of us ached for it—the way heroines in Shah Rukh Khan films did. The way Shah Rukh did. And suddenly, I had a plan. Muddled by the lack of romance in film and life, I decided then to collect and write stories about us fangirls. These stories would be a private ode to silly girls in ordinary places who dreamt of a more equal and dignified kind of love. Stories to escape the tiring and hopeless race to find the One.

Over the years, I became a node in a large sisterhood of Shah Rukh fangirls. Some of these women were close friends, others were colleagues, clients and mentors. I met fans at airports and malls, befriending them through swapping fan-tales. Others I pursued as research subjects to better understand their fandom. Their stories comforted me. And I collected them, meticulously writing up life histories and episodes as diary notes. In 2013, when Shah Rukh transitioned into macho-land, I decided to rely on the fellowship of women fans to resurrect our hero. The plan was to collate and assuage our collective despair.

5

An Elite Composite

You can only learn when you have leisure.

—*Jiddu Krishnamurti, 1977*

I've developed a simple test to detect misogyny in any Indian, Bangladeshi or Pakistani man. If a man likes Shah Rukh, he is usually progressive. If a man likes Salman, he is bad news. If a man likes Aamir, he's often a bearded liberal who likes his own voice too much. My test rarely fails.

—*Fan interviewed in 2016*

I started with the ladies I knew best, those born in the 1980s into socio-economic privilege, those just like Vidya and me. This was an easy place to begin. I typed up a survey questionnaire seeking anonymous interviews with Shah Rukh fans. It sought basic demographic information and a willingness to participate in a series of conversations.

Through coffee runs and catch-up sessions between 2013 and 2017, I discovered that the fandom of elite thirty-something women took a similar shape. We were very different people, but it seemed we saw Shah Rukh with the same pair of eyes. Ours was the last generation of Indians to navigate adolescence and early adulthood without apps, the internet or a smartphone. Prannoy Roy relayed the news of the world to us and we could never stalk our high school crushes on Instagram or Facebook. In the 1990s, we discovered Shah Rukh. We were his *first* set of fans, the first generation of women to claim him. We made him a superstar.

Each fan I interviewed was adamant that she had grown up to abhor films where Shah Rukh's characters stalked or harmed women, choosing to deify his romantic on-screen persona instead. But as we entered our twenties and thirties, our love for Shah Rukh started to change. We began to prefer his exchanges with the media and his public appearances to his movies. Interviews and lectures became a core part of Shah Rukh's oeuvre. At the time of my interactions with fans in 2013, each of us was drawn to his off-screen media persona more than his films. In their thirties, these women would gush about his interviews like teenagers.

As fangirls grew up to become fan-women, many stopped following Shah Rukh's movies but continued to obsess over him. One frazzled thirty-four-year-old fan-woman met me after three failed attempts to schedule an interview. She was juggling home and employment and found it impossible to find time for herself, let alone my questions. 'I have a new cook at home and I need to supervise her. Can't leave her alone to cook,' she said to me after cancelling our first appointment. The day we met, she had emerged from a twelve-hour day between office and household errands. Straightening her hair with her fingers, she explained: 'It's nice when Shah Rukh has a new film coming out. I'll go see the film, of course. I go to support him and to see what he is doing. I enjoy watching him. But the best part is that his release requires him to do many media interactions and interviews as well. That's always a treat to watch! It's part of his big performance. I need it, just to know that there are thoughtful men like this in India. And he always says something important or interesting.' She illustrated her point with a recent interview Khan had given to a journalist: 'He said something like how he can dignify a woman so much that she will fall in love with him. Which other icon or star talks like that about women in India?'

In 2018, a young Bengali fan complained that the romance in Shah Rukh's films had 'ruined her for life'. She accused Shah Rukh of making her a hopeless romantic, forever expecting the 'perfect proposal' from a man, one where he would emulate her hero's on-screen romantic routines. Eventually, she upended gender roles by proposing marriage to her boyfriend through song and poetry. Abandoning all expectations of the man behaving like Shah Rukh's romantic avatar, she took on the role of Shah Rukh in the proposal, going down on her knees as she romanced her beloved and asked him to marry her.

The women who responded to my call for interviews felt romantically ruined by Shah Rukh as well. They were a diverse group that I traced through a technique called snowballing, where one fan would connect me to another and so on until what started as a snowball became an avalanche. Tired of being statistically rigorous in my regular work life, I decided to follow a curated selection of fangirls instead of using rigid sampling rules to select the women I interviewed. Most of the women interested in talking to me were approaching their mid-thirties. They were thoughtful about their fandom. Marital status was an organizing principle of their selfhood— it was often the first thing they wrote about themselves in messages or conversations.

Everyone used English to talk about sex, love and marriage. The women I met believed they had more in common with characters on American TV shows than heroines in Hindi films. About half of the fan-women were married, a quarter was in what they described as happy relationships and the remaining quarter was single. Everyone was straight. Two out of every five married women I interviewed said they had married for love without any family involvement. Most were pleased with their marriages but wanted their husbands to spend more time with them. One fan-woman said, 'It's strange, the difference between men and women. When I've had a long day, I want to talk about it. He just vanishes into his TV. I think this is why many women like Shah Rukh's films—he goes on talking to women about his feelings and everything. My husband jokes that Shah Rukh talks too much.'

Of the women who had found their partners through arranged marriages, a majority had met their husbands several times before accepting the proposal. A small minority of the women had eloped, as their partners were from different castes or religious communities. Love of Shah Rukh wasn't the only common trait shared by married fan-women—a majority of them did not work outside the home. Several women dropped out of the workforce during the four years we knew each other. These choices were always deemed 'natural', typically triggered by pregnancy and childbirth. Nearly everyone I interviewed struggled to piece together a coherent timeline or narrative of how they became full-time housewives. *It just happened.* I heard that phrase a lot. A sense of social persecution, confusion and guilt loomed large when we talked about their employment decisions. After four years of difficult conversations, I traced three distinct groups within the married pool of fan-women. Each group felt judged by the other.

The first group comprised women who did not see paid employment or financial independence as central to the way they defined themselves as people. They had never cultivated a career-minded sense of self. Much like their mothers, this group did not desire to work outside the home and retreated from the professional or corporate world after marriage. They felt that motherhood and family were their calling, offering them a source of meaning and purpose. A thirty-six-year-old fan said, 'I did not enjoy working and did not have the background to get a well-paying job. There was no point in doing something you did not care about and you did not enjoy, or wouldn't do well in, especially when I did not need to work to survive. I love being a mother and a good wife. I have a great time at home, my in-laws let me go and do whatever I want. I have freedom. My husband loves me and makes good money. He gives me all I ever need. None of my close friends work either and we spend a lot of time with each other. I have a good life. But I do feel judgement from working women and society towards housewives and women who don't work. Nowadays, among the higher strata of society, a career has become a status symbol for women. I know women who ask their husbands to help them set up some small business, not because they care about the work but because they want the label of being a career woman. I don't care and don't really need to impress anyone other than my family.'

Another fan was married to a successful real-estate agent. She said, 'I think many men would also stop working if they had a choice and society did not pressure them. Very few of them do work that they like.'

A second group of women felt their professional identities were vital to their personhood. However, they gradually gave up these careerist ambitions after childbirth. Divided by their impulses towards both motherhood and their careers, they were encouraged to delay their return to employment by the meaning they suddenly discovered in caregiving. In any case, there are few incentives in India for women to return to work after motherhood. Women continue to face a severe 'motherhood penalty' in the Indian job market. The ability of upper-class homes to secure domestic workers does not alter how motherhood tends to push women out of the workforce. In a survey of Delhi, we found that forty-seven per cent of adult women said they quit work after giving birth. As per data from CMIE for 2019, only ten per cent of mothers from the wealthiest segment of urban India, those between the ages of twenty and fifty-five, held a paid job. Even with expanded maternity leave following an important legislation in 2017, employers offer little flexibility to handle jobs and childcare. Women often receive less pay than men to do the same jobs and have fewer opportunities to get ahead. Urban Indian men are also arguably world champions at shrugging off their childcare and housework duties.

While some of the women I interviewed had felt pressure from their husbands and in-laws to focus on children and the home, the decision to leave paid work was rarely framed as having been coerced. Most claimed they were happy to have left what they now saw as 'soul-sucking jobs' and 'male chauvinist pig office environments'. They felt great pride at being good mothers. But beneath this front, I sensed some regret. One woman said she felt 'judged by some close friends who work. But being a mother is a full-time job. Doing well in the corporate world takes too many hours and too much energy. You need to be driven. Being a mother changed that for me. And you can only give a hundred per cent to one goal in life'.

Another woman reflected, 'My husband is soft and funny, like Shah Rukh. He never told me to stop working, but it felt like the sensible thing to do. A child needs his mother and I did not want to miss out on spending time with my baby boy. And it's not like work was great or very meaningful for me. My husband was doing very well in his job and we could afford to be a single-earner home. I hope I'll return to work after my son is older, but it seems tougher each year. I'm not an artist or a businesswoman, I can't work for myself. I did well in the office environment, but I know that the kinds of jobs I enjoyed need dedication and I need flexibility. Those are incompatible.'

Sociologists call it the 'discouraged workers effect', where women feel discouraged to work as their husbands make significantly more money than them and the workplace does not treat women fairly. Weighing the pros and cons of returning to paid work, many women find greater love, social recognition and self-worth in being caregivers, thereby steadily withdrawing from the world of paid employment. According to data collected by the International Labour Organization (ILO) between April and June 2018, an urban Indian woman spends five hours on household chores every day, while an urban man spends twenty-nine minutes on housework. India ranks in the bottom five countries of the world when it comes to the share of men helping in housework, alongside Pakistan, Mali, Cambodia and South Korea.

The married mothers I interviewed felt balancing work and care was too difficult. Wives left jobs as their husbands rarely showed any aptitude for childcare and household management. One of the women I spoke to said that she and her husband had been at business school together: 'But once I was pregnant, we decided that I would leave work as his skills as a father could not substitute for my skills as a mother. It was a practical decision.' Another said, 'Somedays, I am so angry that I want to shout at everyone. The only words my husband and in-laws will exchange with me are about food and clothes. Nothing else. I had to quit work and take care of my son, and it's been tough finding the right job again. There are fewer opportunities and too many candidates. I keep telling my husband that he should pay me a salary for all the work I do at home!'

A third group comprised a minority of married fans who attempted, in the Indian context, to be superwomen. They continued to work outside the home after marriage. The ILO's data highlights their time poverty: the average employed Indian woman works 44.4 hours per week, far more than her sisters in other developing countries who average thirty-six hours. Overworked and stressed, this group was the most annoyed about the amount of housework it was still doing. Despite employing cooks, cleaners and nannies, these women said they felt disproportionately responsible for the care of children and elders in their homes. One woman explained, 'People think life is so much easier if you have staff. But it really depends on the kind of help you get. I have a maid who comes for shifts, she doesn't live with us. It takes effort to coordinate all the lists of things to do, to buy groceries, to help the children with homework. I like to run a good home and want my family to eat well and live well. That makes me happy. It requires energy. My husband doesn't care as much about these things. Getting him to care or do his share would make me a nag and need even more effort, so I silently do it all.'

I asked each of the married Shah Rukh fan-women I interviewed to measure the hours they spent doing chores or organizing housework, compared to their husbands. They did so for one random Friday. The results—married working women would often finish an eight-hour shift at the office and spend another four hours managing or doing housework. Their husbands would spend nine hours at the office and less than half an hour on chores, which mostly amounted to giving the driver instructions. When I shared these results with all the women, not one expressed any surprise. One respondent said, 'You know, I offer prasad each time my husband decides to help me clear the dishes. I've only managed to make the offering ten times in the last year. And my friends say I'm better off than most!' Another added, 'It's not that my husband is not supportive or progressive. I think he would do more if I asked him for help. But I feel guilty to ask as well. I know it's strange and not very feminist, but I feel like I'm failing if I ask him to do my job.'

As our conversations progressed, a few more women would confess that quitting their jobs had left them feeling resentful. They felt betrayed by their husband's lack of interest in their careers. As one thirty-something ex-human resources manager told me, 'I was very upset that my in-laws and husband suggested that I leave work after our daughter was born. But I was equally angry at myself for not being able to fight more. I had always believed that marrying a good man would mean that my husband would always support my goals. But after I was pregnant, I realized that even the best men prefer it if women stay home.' She laughed and said, 'In real life, there is no Shah Rukh. All men are like Salman. Women have to fight with tradition and have to accept losing the fight. I had to accept being at home because my husband would never be able to take care of the house and children the way I can. My daughter is five now, and my in-laws are keen that we try for a son. I have refused, but my husband doesn't draw the line with his parents. Each time I say I want to go back to work and that we could manage with a nanny and our in-laws being home, my husband says my work would be pointless as he earns so much more than I could. He feels I should stay at home and enjoy it as other women do. But I can't, I miss my job and office life. Somehow, in India, women are automatically expected to give up work. It's considered natural, and I don't think it is. I won't teach my daughter that.'

For these married women, Shah Rukh had become a symbol of their youth, a time of optimism, a time when they believed it was possible to find a man who would love them as they were and always stand up for their choices. Real life required far more bargaining. A man could love you, he could be persuaded to marry you, he could be a terrific father, but he wouldn't necessarily champion your freedom. 'Sometimes, I watch those romance films of Shah Rukh's with my teenage daughter and warn her,' a woman said to me. 'I tell her that there are no men like that in real life, no man will fight for you. You'll have to fight for yourself. She laughs at me and can't believe that I like such soppy films. She is far more sensible than I was at her age.'

While the married women I interviewed were largely out of the workforce, most of the single women continued to work outside the home. This pattern in my interviews mirrors trends found in national surveys. Analysis of CMIE employment data for 2019 shows that even amongst the wealthiest top twenty per cent of urban Indians between the ages of twenty and fifty-five, only about six per cent of married women were employed while fifteen per cent of unmarried women reported working for an independent income. Employment rates were the highest for divorced and separated women—67.8 per cent.

The unmarried working women were independent but made unhappy by the great Indian conjugal circus. Each had a harrowing story or two from the trenches of singledom. 'Unattached or divorced men, who may not even be as successful as me, find far more acceptance and dating success here,' one said. For most of these single women, marriage and monogamy were constant preoccupations. They felt like baggage on an airport carousel, waiting to be claimed by the One. Countless nights of agony were masked by the 'I have very high expectations' refrain. Despite their dreams of Shah Rukh, many of the women said that they'd developed a pathology to fall for the wrong type of man: impossible organisms who could never treat their partners as human beings. Others felt that there was no suitable candidate in sight: Liberal women slept with a combination of married men and non-committal single men. Conservative women sang the song of 'compromise,' capitulating and marrying bores.

The tone and texture of these chats left me feeling uncomfortable. Women who had quit their jobs appeared, broadly speaking, to have better relationships with their families and partners and even themselves. There was less bargaining in their equations with loved ones, and fewer frustrations. Once I stopped looking down on these women from my feminist high horse, I wondered if they were more clear-eyed, having made their peace with the disappointments and sacrifices inherent in love and marriage in a patriarchal society. Working women, whether married or unmarried, complained to me about the lack of reciprocity and equality in the affection, housework and sexual satisfaction offered by straight men. When I'd ask any of the single women to describe their ideal partner, the answer was simple. If only he could be an iota of Shah Rukh. When I asked married women about Shah Rukh, they sang praises of his love for wife and family. As I write this, I laugh at our romantic plight. How did films configure the template of our desire? How did Shah Rukh become *the* ideal man?

How You Invented the Ideal Man

Shah Rukh, my research convinced me, has the coolest female fans. My interviews not only fortified my love for Khan, I fell for his fans too. We talked endlessly; one fan anecdote led to another. The actor's shadow loomed large over our intimate lives. Each one of us actively followed Western icons. However, we relied on Mr Khan to help shape a more indigenous ideal man. Based on eighty in-depth interviews across Delhi, Bhopal, Chandigarh, Lucknow, Raipur, Mumbai, Kolkata and Patna, let me create a composite picture of the typical upper-middle-class Shah Rukh fan and her quest for love. If you are such a woman, you have my love and my sympathies. Here is your map of impossible expectations. Here is how you invented your ideal man.

Initially, the notion of the ideal man emerges as a silly crush on a good-looking actor in a darkened theatre or family living room. The ideal man is conjured up while watching films beyond a pre-teen's comprehension. Cinema is the glue that holds your family together, especially as you have nothing else in common with your relatives. You probably look and sound like a firangi to your grandparents. You call yourself 'upper middle class' to signal that your family has moved up the socio-economic pecking order, but you are not from India's old-moneyed English-speaking elite. Your parents might have been the first college graduates in their families, pioneers who established comfort with the English language and escaped their modest hometowns for higher studies or well-paid jobs. They met financial success in the 1980s, finding work that allowed a leap into India's fledgling metropolitan life.

But your parents will hold on to their humble roots. Your father is not rich enough to plan exciting summer holidays, nor is he wise with investments. Your mother is exhausted much of the time. In June, you are banished to the small towns where your grandparents live, just so your mother can have some space, some time to breathe. You grow up noticing how awkwardly your parents wear their success, distinguishing them from some of your friends and their families. Farmhouses and foreign holiday trips are rarely part of an upper-middle-class fangirl's memory of summers in the '90s. Discussions of acquiring good air conditioners, good jobs, good husbands and good properties are ubiquitous.

In June 1992, thanks to your mother being a Rishi Kapoor fan, you watch Shah Rukh's debut in *Deewana* as the disgruntled son of a wealthy industrialist. His character casually stalks the woman he loves, eventually winning her heart and walking away from his family money to become a mechanic. His first Hindi film song, also his first scene in the film, follows him on a joyride along the streets of Mumbai. Taking in the sights, he looks at the camera, raises his arms to the sky, and offers his opening salvo, '*Koi na koi chahiye, pyar karne wala.*' I need someone to love me.

You see him. And, for the first time, you encounter your hormones. You've never seen genetic material like this before. You ache for him and for the possibilities he represents. A fan is born. In the mid-'90s, you start calling your local cable bhaiya, urging him to play pirated prints of Shah Rukh films. Your parents are embarrassed and reprimand you. In November 1992, you encounter him in Aziz Mirza's wonderful *Raju Ban Gaya Gentleman*, playing an ambitious young civil engineer from a small hill-town, hustling to get ahead in brash Mumbai, but still able to sing a song about 'Loveria'. You hum that tune all through 1992 and 1993, much to your mother's chagrin. '*Love, love, love, loveria hua.*' Love love love, I have loveria.'

A year later, in the months of November and December in 1993, you are stunned by his negative turn in *Baazigar* and *Darr*. You watch these films on the colony cable channel without parental guidance. You are probably a latchkey kid, left to your own devices while mom and dad are at work. The next year, Shah Rukh offers two major releases—in the first, *Kabhi Haan Kabhi Naa*, he plays a polite loser in love. The second, *Anjaam*, sees him return as a deranged, near-psychopathic stalker, unable to bear romantic rejection. The characters Shah Rukh played in these films, in his own words, gave the 'Hindi movie creep a whole new dimension'. The gendered implications will only occur to you much later. At the time, you will be hooked. Your teenage hormones are unaware of morals or feminism, so you shamelessly sing '*Yeh kaali kaali aankhen*', besotted by Shah Rukh's confidence, on-screen charm and good looks. And slowly you start to sculpt your imagined ideal man, mould him from the raw material of these pictures and your fantasies. The first rule: an ideal man must look like Shah Rukh, the pre-six-pack version.

India's action heroes of the time hold little appeal for you. How can bulging biceps and pelvic thrusts convey talent? Your parents suggest that Shah Rukh lacks virtue, that other actors don't play villainous roles that encourage young men to scare women. In protest, you stomp your feet and proclaim your undying faith in Shah Rukh. 'No other hero can make heroines so happy,' is your childish defence. Awed by how the women in all his song sequences *glow*, you start to realize that *this* is what you want: a man who can make a woman feel radiant. You believe that the love of an ideal man, like *him*, will make you as beautiful as a Bollywood actress.

During the Diwali holidays in October 1995, you watch *DDLJ* with your family in a cinema hall. Your mother, aunts and sisters will have made sure your dad bought tickets well in advance. For you, it will be love at first scene. Back home, your twelve-year-old avatar will wear a frilly pink dress and pretend to attend a dance with Shah Rukh while '*Ae kaash ke hum*' from *Kabhi Haan Kabhi Naa* plays in the background. Soon, you'll graduate to wearing a white dress and dancing to '*Mere khwabon mein jo aaye*' from *DDLJ*. Mustard fields, London and 'Europe' will become synonymous with good husbands. Love will mean extending a helping hand on a train. Love will mean marriage. Love will be a monogamous fairy tale.

Millions of young women walked out of cinema halls after watching *DDLJ*, desperate to find the right man. The idea was not planted by Shah Rukh. It was sown by the luminous Kajol who played the female lead, Simran. She was astonishingly beautiful yet relatable, a combination that feels impossible in our current era of vegan film stars. Simran starts the film by reciting a poem for her mother, one she has written herself. She writes about her fantasies of meeting an unknown man—andekha anjana sa. Shah Rukh's performance as her lover, Raj, concretizes these fantasies. The ideal man would be a foreigner to oppressive patriarchy by believing in the freedom to love and being able to shower his beloved with unabashed affection. Paradoxically, he would also remain an ally of tradition, emulating Raj from *DDLJ* who risks losing his lover as he refuses to elope, determined instead to win her father's approval for her hand in marriage. In *DDLJ*, after an hour of being a hostile brat who harasses Simran, the empathetic Raj Malhotra whom female Shah Rukh fans so vividly recall emerges. Suddenly, he worries about Simran's welfare—from her coffee order to her decision to accept an arranged marriage with a stranger to her prayers.

In the second half of the film, he attempts to endear himself to the women of Simran's family by helping with housework. 'It was the first time I'd seen the hero peel a carrot in a film and spend so much time with the women of the household,' said one fangirl's mother to me. The film equates romance with doing the dishes and considerate domesticity without an ounce of sex. *DDLJ* concludes on a railway platform in rural Punjab. Simran receives her father's blessings and runs to join Raj on a train speeding out of the station. How magical it would be, you think, to be pulled onto the Marriage Express by the man of your dreams, a train ride that will transport you to bliss.

In 1996, Shah Rukh plays the object of a woman's mad obsession in *Chaahat*, followed by an NRI who falls for a bar dancer in Mumbai (*English Babu Desi Mem*). The films are not your favourites. But the subsequent year is good: Shah Rukh has four releases, starting with him playing a mute servant who revolts against his feudal lord in *Koyla*. In *Yes Boss*, he portrays a middle-class wannabe who revolts against his entitled rich boss and India's feudal workplace culture. The resistance is triggered by love—his character falls for his powerful employer's mistress. *Pardes* has him portraying another NRI who falls for a woman he is not supposed to. All these men are revolting for love without rejecting tradition, though they are torn by its whims and strictures. The year closes with one of his greatest musical-romances, *Dil To Pagal Hai*.

Back in the late '90s, urban India started experiencing the joys of satellite television and dozens of channels offering entertainment all day and all night. You discover Shah Rukh's engaging facility for interviews with his unique brand of self-deprecating-self-aggrandizement. You can't believe your luck. Here you are, alone at home after school, and you can switch on the TV to find your favourite star talking directly to you. Each English-speaking fan I've met recalls these early interviews. Shah Rukh was part of the first generation of celebrities who benefitted from India's telecom revolution. The proliferation of satellite television networks led to many more shows about the film world being broadcast into Indian homes. New TV channels required new content. The burgeoning media industry in India found a profitable partner in Hindi cinema and transmitted news of celebrities every day. You could watch an actor being interviewed each night on one television network or another, while whole newspaper supplements were dedicated to gossip about film. Media houses relayed Shah Rukh's icon and interviews consistently. Your hero, articulate and friendly, was inescapable.

These televised conversations marked the beginnings of the actor's best performance till date: his version of the unapologetic middle-class superstar. Chain-smoking, self-aware, clever, brazen and hilarious—your devotion will be fortified. He displays a charming contempt for the interviewer, the film industry and his own celebrity. Acting is a business, he emphasizes. 'With that kind of exposure, even a doorknob can become a star,' he says with a wink. There are self-deprecating jokes about his 'five standard expressions' and limited skill as an actor. He keeps describing himself as an outsider to the industry. Shah Rukh's interviews usher the phrase 'middle class' into your dictionary. In his interviews, the actor talks about freedom and secularism; he makes you cry with tales of financial insecurities and how he worked endless hours to make sure he could look after his sister and wife. And so, you glean: an ideal man will diligently battle his constraints. He will take care of you, offer you a good home, serving as the best breadwinner and the safest bet. He will be the One and the One ought to be Enough.

What a contrast Shah Rukh is to the men your teenage self will encounter on the streets, out in the world. Slowly, you recognize how the creep following you from a bus stop or crank-calling your number seems to mimic the stalker your hero played in his early films. You grow angry at Shah Rukh. You start policing yourself; you walk in groups; you believe you need protection from the world at large. You occupy public spaces with an attitude of sustained vigilance. You shrink. You watch Shah Rukh in his interviews and love stories, wondering why the men harassing you cannot learn from the more loving parts of his icon. Soon, you compartmentalize. You despise Shah Rukh as the stalker. Instead, you choose to see the best in your hero. He reciprocates your good faith in him, ceasing to portray the obvious creep.

Your adolescent belief in marital fidelity will mirror the national media's adolescent interest in Shah Rukh's monogamous monkhood. You read, captivated, the *Filmfare* articles that laud Shah Rukh's prowess at being a faithful husband. To the shock of your parents, all this feeds into TV interviews intended for the whole family over dinner. You remember those scandalous evenings very well. There you were with your prudish family: dal, sabzi and sex. Three interviews are always cited.

First, an interaction in 1996 on India's buttoned-up public broadcasting network, Doordarshan, with journalist Rajeev Shukla. 'Everyone says they love their wife,' Shukla says to Shah Rukh, 'but in the film business, every day, we hear of some affair between some actor and some actress. How come there is no such news about you?' Shah Rukh jokes about hiding his affairs in the same place he hides his tax returns. Then he says, winningly, 'I am happily married. I love my wife immensely. I love all the actresses I work with. They are my friends. And in the kind of society we live in these days, it isn't necessary that you have to romance the girl you work with.' A second discussion, around the same time, of Shah Rukh's fidelity, takes place on Star Plus, one of India's first private TV channels, with journalist Tavleen Singh on her weekly show *Ek Din Ek Jeevan*. She follows Shah Rukh through a working day as he shoots for the film *Duplicate* (1998). Singh suggests, in a voiceover, that most well-known Indian actors tend to become romantically involved with multiple actresses, as if an extramarital affair is a status symbol for married men in the film industry. She goes on to describe Shah Rukh as unusual and 'not spoiled' by his fame, since he has yet to be sullied by scandal. She asks him about his fidelity on a national television show in a country as conservative as India. You giggle and remember how bored he looked. Khan has grown accustomed to being the poster boy for marital monogamy.

He grins and replies, arms outstretched and hands interlocked, 'I think I'm gay. Everybody keeps asking and saying this: Why isn't your name linked to any other actress? But they're friends. I participate in their happiness and sadness. I was always under the impression that the heroines I work with, that I'm supposed to work with them, I'm not supposed to make love to them. So, I decided that I'll work with them.' Decades later, when the writer of this book will interview you in your thirties, you'll express cynicism about all that eulogizing of monogamous marriage. Instead, you'll admire how Shah Rukh treated women as colleagues and comrades, that he travelled from interview to interview reminding us that women in the workplace were professionals, not sexual objects for male pleasure and conquest.

Another televised interview with Simi Garewal in 1997, filmed shortly after the birth of his first son, will further burnish Shah Rukh's image as a devoted husband and evolved man. Not only does he announce, 'I think I have a lot of woman in me,' the man talks about idolizing womanhood. When asked about his wife, Shah Rukh's face will light up. 'I am an actor,' he says, 'because I don't like being Shah Rukh. She is Gauri because she loves being Gauri. She brings such a sense of calm and peace to my life. And I don't want to do anything to destroy her peace with herself.' And so, Shah Rukh The Star will persuade your adolescent self into believing: Being a man's wife means being something truly special. A husband will value and honour your inner integrity; he will co-sponsor your emotional well-being.

You'll review his films. You'll hear him talk on TV. And you will believe that an ideal man is destined for every woman; that true love is instinctive and will always end in marriage; that every woman can find her happily ever after on a railway platform. Love will become supreme, the ultimate acclamation for a woman. This belief in love becomes a certainty, as sure as the result of arithmetic calculations. As one fangirl said, 'I walked out of his romance films and just knew that there was this kind of love in the world. Like two plus two is four—if you met a man like this, you would melt and fall in love. It was the easiest concept to accept.' Another fangirl said, 'I watched that Simi interview and learned one thing: that my parents' marriage was not like his. And that I wanted what Gauri and Shah Rukh had.'

August 1998 brings the thrill of *Dil Se* into the lives of Shah Rukh fans. He plays Amarkant Verma, an All India Radio executive. Cinematographer Santosh Sivan makes his eyes sparkle. All us female fans will remain forever indebted to Farah Khan for choreographing the songs of *Dil Se*, for getting him to do *that* dance on *that* train. You dream of running your fingers through Shah Rukh's aerodynamic hair. His character, Amarkant, falls obsessively in love with a terrorist and dies in her arms, preventing her from self-detonating at the Republic Day parade. He dies for love of woman and country. As one Shah Rukh fan said to me, 'No wonder our generation of women is fucked when it comes to love. We saw this beautiful man dance on top of a train, romance women in the most beautiful settings and do it all with such conviction that we all bought the dream of love that he sold us. That love, we decided, was what we needed in our lives.' Shah Rukh was always marketing love. Seeing the actor dancing on top of a train will forever make you smile; the image of him wearing a lungi amidst Kerala's backwaters will forever flame your lust.

October sees the first of Shah Rukh's many Karan Johar romantic hits, where churlish handsome men are undeservingly gifted the kindness and love of wonderful women.

As more cash flows into the country through the end of the 1990s, you watch Shah Rukh's characters abandon their early stalkerish desperation and start looking for love in plush mansions. He looks shinier. As do his female co-actors. In 1998, Shah Rukh stands on top of a bus for an iconic soft drink advertisement and proclaims, '*Yeh Dil Maange More.*' The heart wants more. Our new national anthem.

At the turn of the millennium, this first generation of Shah Rukh fans are amid the emotionally tumultuous adolescent years. One day, after receiving the highest grades on a math exam, you return to your desk to find a note from an anonymous classmate saying, 'You'll do well in math, you're really ugly.' And you discover a woman's market worth. Attention from a desirable male becomes the only currency that matters. If you meet great sexual success and social validation in your youth, you are unlikely to remain a faithful fangirl. You'll become sensible and treat Shah Rukh as mere entertainment, since you no longer need a distraction from reality. But, if your teenage years remain harsh with little fun or friendship, Shah Rukh will remain an important source of social nourishment.

Very few of your high-school crushes yield positive returns. Many will insist on being friends. The word 'friend' will become a slight, a chronic consolation prize. You recall thinking that someone like you would have no chance of befriending a man like Shah Rukh. Even the 'friend' in those dubious Shah Rukh love triangles looked like Karisma Kapoor or Kajol. And Shah Rukh was the star, the cynosure of all attention. In your late teens, you surmise: an ideal man is also the *best* man, the one who consumes the limelight and will always be better than you, better than most, coveted by all. The love of such a man can make you powerful, because you will bask in his reflected promise and potential. To secure the love of such a powerful ideal man, you will need to be as perfect as possible. The elite fangirl will be consumed by the culture of Oprah's marvellous makeovers. She will resolve to transform, the way Kajol did in *Kuch Kuch Hota Hai (KKHH)*, into a thin, graceful, perfect creature with threaded eyebrows and straight hair. Cultivating beauty will emerge as your permanent and primary job, a guaranteed pathway to love.

As you approach adulthood, the race for college admissions begins. You abandon all attempts to be pretty. Board exams will always remain a blur. You'll remember tears and stress, listening to Shah Rukh songs during short breaks from studying calculus.

Your world exponentially expands after you leave school. Your mother has never heard of Marx or Freud. You're always catching up on literature or pretending to have read books you barely know, rapaciously consuming every bit of culture available to you in the college library and the baby-internet of the early 2000s. At this time, being a Shah Rukh fan will take on a political dimension. You are not only supporting the only Indian icon who seems properly sexy—a man who studied at Hansraj College instead of St Stephen's—you are also expressing disapproval for unearned privilege.

In your final years of undergraduate studies, financial stability and independence become paramount. At home, observing how your aunts complain about having to ask their husbands or sons for money, surrounded by discussions of loan instalments, monthly rent and credit card payments, you realize that work can subsidize Shah Rukh and the various pleasures of life. It'll pay for your movie tickets. Some of you form a fierce attachment to the idea of a salary that is your own singular possession. If you have a job, you won't need your parents' money or permission. But you'll always need a man.

Many fans described their youthful attempts to meet Shah Rukh, waiting forlornly outside 'Mannat', his Mumbai mansion. As a college student in Delhi, I read about a visit to the local PVR for a promotional event related to *Devdas*, his 2002 spectacular, at the time the most expensive Hindi film ever made. My best friend in college, Taneia, agreed to join me on my quest to meet Shah Rukh. We arrived at the cinema hall, where huge crowds had already gathered and policemen were blocking people from entering. Taneia suggested we try the fire exit, where we found a Haryanvi security guard standing impassively in our way. I begged for us to be allowed entry. He laughed and said, 'All you silly girls these days; leave him alone, he is only an actor.' We continued to plead until he shrugged his shoulders and gave way. I got close enough to stand about an arm's length from Shah Rukh while he was being interviewed by a journalist.

A ring of bodyguards surrounded the actor. He smiled benignly at dozens of us jostling for an autograph. 'Next time,' he said. I called out to him despondently, 'But there will never be a next time!' He flashed me a wicked grin, said, 'Inshallah, there will be a next time,' and escaped through some hidden exit. Several fans reported similar stories of near-misses. Each fan seemed to have met her own 'Inshallah' moment. She would go home and report to an unimpressed sibling or friend. They would roll their eyes. 'You need a real boyfriend, what were you hoping to achieve?'

What were we trying to achieve? We were chasing fantasies. And it was that inch between fantasy and reality, between securing that autograph and having Shah Rukh disappear with his entourage, that made life so exciting and frustrating. Unable to trust God to arrange another meeting, each one of us resolved to manufacture the Next Time on our own. Some waited for decades, some gave up, others could only manage to sit still for a day.

Looking back, it's clear that crazed fandom was a way to transfer pent-up desire. In youthful times, it was a diversion from the usual discomforts of growing up, brutal academic competition, the sting of sexual slights and dipping grades. Fandom was a way to cultivate a self. Socially awkward, you escaped into fantasy. But fantasy extracts its toll. Through the years, all those Shah Rukh films and interviews cultivate a temperament to get carried away. You build a fragile femininity, always wanting to be the fangirl in relationships, seeking men whom you can place on a plump patriarchal pedestal. You'll tell me how you usually demonize and deify the men in your life, they'll never be real people to you. When the reality of their humanity strikes, it'll leave you bitterly disappointed.

For single fans, no man, we were beginning to find, fits our fantasies, comes close to that shimmering Shah Rukh mirage. For married women, too, their marriages are often reminders of the unattainability of the ideal. Sexual romance never survives a shaadi. 'That's not what marriage is,' one of you will say. Marriages become spaces of undulating power struggles, some thrive, and others silently collapse under the weight of domestic ritual and childcare. In April 2020, as the world fought a virus, married fans with whom I maintained a correspondence would tell me how unfair marriages felt, how the male thumb was pressing down on the scales. Despite husbands making token offers to help, there was little most of them could actually do without the housework becoming even more onerous. Wives without live-in help felt they had 'stopped thinking'; they were busy chasing children and one-pot recipes. Many tried to steal as much private time away from their families as they could manage. For one woman, this meant losing herself in the Shah Rukh filmography when everyone else was asleep. 'Watching his films while in lockdown,' she said to me, 'was a reminder that this was not the way love ever actually goes. I remember watching these love stories with my husband when we were young. We were so into each other. Now those people we once were are gone. I still love him, and he loves me. We're used to each other, and we're building something, but it's not the love Shah Rukh sold us. No one ever tells you what kind of husband Raj would make for Simran.'

In your late thirties and forties, you see Shah Rukh's romance films from the '90s very differently. None of these candyfloss lovers seem like stellar men. In the first half of the movies, they appear self-indulgent with a tremendous appetite for negging. You note that

Shah Rukh's Amarkant forcibly kisses his love interest in *Dil Se*, that Raj does not fully respect Simran's dignity or consent on that train. Yet, these troublesome episodes do not dent your enthusiasm for the films. Much like Simran and Meghna in the movies, you are inured to bad male behaviour.

You allow Shah Rukh to rise above the men he essays. The songs and interviews help. So does his on-screen talent to depict love and longing. Each of these films holds one—or several—pivotal psychological moments when a deeply flawed male places a woman— her world view, her needs, her politics—above his narrow self-interest. In film after film, you will see him sacrifice his ice cream (*Kabhi Haan Kabhi Naa*), his job (*Yes Boss*), his prestige (*Deewana*), the patriarch's approval (*Pardes*), his chance of easily getting the girl (*Kabhi Haan Kabhi Naa*) and even his life (*Dil Se*). Khan's intense portrayal of steadfast commitment to the woman he loves eclipses your memory of his '90s romances. You fully acknowledge the triggering aspects of these films, and yet choose to celebrate the love Shah Rukh offered women in them. You are eager to suspend disbelief for your hero.

Nowadays, navigating post-pandemic life, you don't think of Shah Rukh as often as your teenage self. He has become part of a landscape you admire and take for granted, like the clouds or trees. You hope to see him play a sexy older man in a web series. On terrible days, when you are exhausted or heartbroken, you invoke Shah Rukh. You smile at the sexiest being alive. Your vision is usually one of him in that iconic *DDLJ* red-and-white jersey, waving and grinning, suggesting you leave your troubles behind. A scene memorized in your soul. A romantic con artist. You look up his social media feed and wonder if he is helping in the kitchen.

Separate Spheres

You meet me in one of the few five-star hotel cafés of Raipur, wearing a chiffon saree encased in dust. You've told your family that I'm the friend of a cousin staying at the Hyatt hotel. We bumped into each other at a party in Delhi a few months ago. I had dismissed you as a princess, floating on your tall heels, discussing wellness and Ayurvedic routines, your nose turned up. But then you told me that you were a Shah Rukh fan. 'I'm a big-time Shah Rukh nut,' you had said apropos of nothing. 'But I have lots of problems with him too.' I remember being confused and disarmed by your admission. I could no longer categorize and file you away. Instead, I found myself warming to you. As you left the party, you gave me your phone number and suggested we talk.

Your Rajput husband comes from centuries of money and is worshipped in your home town. Each day, your mother reminds you of your good luck. On this day, I'm in Raipur for work, and we decide to meet. I watch you glide into the hotel lobby, accepting the fawning formal salutes of the guards and staff. The manager appears to escort you to my table. You remove your bug-eyed Chanel sunglasses and order a lime soda. The waiter is suddenly servile, keen to impress you. 'This is all because of my husband,' you say. 'Without him, no one would care. There are plenty of poor Rajput girls these days.' Your first memory of Shah Rukh, you tell me, was when your family watched *Chamatkar* in the early 1990s at a private screening. Small-town royals, you say, with a wry shake of the head, did not go to the movies until pretty much the turn of the century. You take me back to those early days of your life when you were introduced to your favourite film star.

You are a preteen. Your older fashionable cousin is a Shah Rukh fan and gets everyone together to watch *Chamatkar*. Your parents admire actor Naseeruddin Shah, and join the screening. However, your focus is on Khan. You instantly fall in love with this man who is happy to play the buffoon, who is a tad effeminate, who does not take himself seriously, unlike every man you know in real life. 'He was so sweet and kind. And so good looking,' you tell me. 'There was something different about him. After that, we watched all his films. I forced my brothers to bring all his movies home. They weren't too happy. They were Salman fans and my father preferred English films.'

Soon, you start reading Shah Rukh's interviews (your aunts and cousins ferry film magazines from Delhi) and following him on TV. You recall feeling manipulated, like he's selling himself. But even his approach to self-marketing is refreshing. 'It was so unusual for a man to sell himself as a good husband. No one else seemed to be doing that.' You tell me that you've grown up around men with large chests and larger egos. That these men think crying is weakness and often drink themselves to death. They laugh at Shah Rukh, whereas you feel safe and warm when you see the actor weep on screen. It was the first time you'd seen a man cry like that, 'like he meant it'. This feeling of safety when a man is fragile and vulnerable has stayed with you. 'All these years later, I still love him. Just the way I did when I was a kid. Even now, he is so different from the hyper macho nonsense we see in our country. And I think he's become sexier with age!'

You grow up completely unaware of your limits in a gloomy dilapidated home. Your family members are erstwhile royals in a corner of feudal north India we agree to call Obscurabad. Your father proves to be a disastrous landowner, businessman and politician. But he loves you and lets you run free. In the company of a large group of cousins and aunts, you drive jeeps as a teenager, climb trees and read undisturbed for hours. Your favourite family member is a sophisticated aunt who is said to have known the royal women of Jaipur. She is a highly literate widow, introducing you to Jane Austen, the Brontë sisters and Doris Lessing. You smoke your first cigarette with her. You learn to love the act of thinking. You watch French and Japanese cinema with your Delhi cousins. As you finish middle-school exams with many distinctions, you imagine you are preparing yourself to live the life of an intellectual forever dressed in black.

You live in a harmonious home, but it's a struggle for you to assert yourself. You refuse to be lost among your brothers and sisters. Finally, the Class 10 Board board exams offer you your chance to fly. Your mother suggests that you need to join a reputable boarding school to prepare better for the exams. Your father agrees. Your mother mutters something about marriage.

At school, you rise as an intellectual of stunning beauty and grace. People find you a little unnerving. Your teachers tell your parents you have great potential. Your mother mutters something about marriage again. You dread marriage, defining it as a bottomless dark ditch from which no Rajput woman has ever emerged. Behind those young eyes, you are shrewd and wise. You've studied marriage, observed its internal logic, you know it damages women. The force of the husband's family consumes the wife. Marriage, in your world, excommunicates a woman from herself.

You finish school and gain admission into one of the best undergraduate colleges in the country. It is in Delhi and your parents ask a cousin to take you on as a lodger. You think you're finally leaving Obscurabad behind. You study philosophy and hope to become a postgraduate student at the University of Chicago so you can meet Martha Nussbaum, whose photo you have pinned up in your room, next to your Shah Rukh poster.

You take to Delhi like a duck to water, at home in your role as an ingénue at the city's poshest dinner parties, at home at the Gymkhana or as a bargain shopper in Sarojini Nagar. You're most at home, though, in your college library. You save your crushes for long-dead thinkers and their equally long-dead theories. Your friends call you 'asexual' because you ignore the many men who are in love with you. But men don't excite you. Nussbaum's essays do. You are thirsty for knowledge, for culture. There is so much to learn.

You hear of your impending marriage from your mother. This happens a few weeks after you return to Obscurabad for the summer. You've just graduated, and your head is full of plans and strategies to apply for further studies abroad. You lock yourself in your room when your mother gives you the news and swear you'll run away. But you know you won't. Your favourite aunt explains the inevitability of it all. Your father is in debt and your marriage is his way out. You are told to be a good Rajput woman, strong and unsentimental. You euthanize your expectations of freedom through a Shah Rukh movie marathon.

Tears well in your eyes as you sip your lime soda and say, 'I don't think men can grasp how sad so many of us women are to marry them. If they knew, I don't think they would want to go through with it. I don't think I've ever cried that much. I tried to read. The books didn't help. Watching Shah Rukh movies did, but only a little. Till date, though, when I watch *Kal Ho Naa Ho*, it's like I'm back in my bedroom trying to come to terms with my upcoming marriage. I always feel like I'm dying along with Shah Rukh in that movie.'

Your husband touches you during the two years of the marriage. Once you produce two sons, he leaves you alone. Your cousin says she sees him in Mumbai, going to parties with a B-grade starlet. You don't care. Sex is not central to your idea of intimacy, conversation is. Your marriage is as wordless as it is sexless. Your husband speaks English poorly. He dislikes how sophisticated and posh you are, although he married you for precisely these attributes. But your manners and social success dwarf his sense of superiority. There has been violence in the marriage. You left for Obscurabad the night it happened and threatened to call the police. Your cousins have friends in the media, and you're sure the case will be reported in the local papers. But your families settle the matter. Your brothers stand by you. They promise to take you home if you feel unsafe or insecure. You don't fear your husband, you feel he is a weak man. You know he won't hurt you, but you don't ever feel safe enough to be yourself with him.

You tell me that he's probably hired a detective to follow you the afternoon we meet. You yearn for monthly trips to Delhi to meet family and old college friends. You discover a hidden appetite for sex five years into your marriage. Your body's urges surprise you. You've fostered a 'sex friend' in Delhi, a man you tumbled into bed with as an experiment. He is too dull to entertain you with conversation. But the sex is satisfactory and secretive.

If your marriage doesn't make you happy, at least your children do. You're glad you have sons; they won't be burdened by marriage like girls are. You promise to raise them to be progressive. 'So they know that good men can cry, and they make their wives feel like Shah Rukh makes us feel, safe and loved,' you tell me. Your in-laws won't allow women to study or work outside the home. But you've brought work and study into the home. You're taking a correspondence course in philosophy and have built an extensive library. The library, a flat you rent in south Delhi and a monthly allowance were the conditions for returning to Raipur with your children. You have crafted what economists who study power and bargaining within families call a 'separate sphere', where spouses live as separate units within a marriage. Your husband cares about his reputation more than he cares about you, but you know he loves the children. He coughs up whatever you need to make sure there is no scandal. You're planning to ask your husband to fund a private art collection.

Next year, you will move to Delhi to help your sons settle into a prestigious private school. Every afternoon, at three, when the house is quiet, you close the door to your room, light up a cigarette and read or watch old Shah Rukh films. Through these idle afternoons, you've watched *Paheli* the greatest number of times. A remake of the film *Duvidha* by Mani Kaul, it was released in 2005. Set in pre-modern India, its plot centres on the marital dilemma faced by a young woman, Lacchi, in conservative Rajasthan. She is keen to find love through her arranged marriage. Lacchi marries neglectful Kishan, played by Shah Rukh, who spends their wedding night working on his accounts and leaves for a business trip the morning after. However, a ghost falls in love with Lacchi and takes the shape of her husband to seduce her. He confesses the truth of his identity and Lacchi falls for the ghost and his romantic overtures. Here, in this spectral avatar of Kishan, Shah Rukh personifies female desire—sexual and emotional. Eventually, the authentic husband returns from his trip. The rest of the film follows a cast of characters as they try to resolve the riddle of two Kishans. Romance eventually wins, as does Lacchi's fantasy of finding true love.

In your thirties, you are finally able to articulate why you love 'Shah Rukh's romances and silly song sequences'. In these songs, the leading man pays whole-hearted attention to the woman he claims to love. Khan can conjure up a gaze of romantic devotion unlike any other human on celluloid. With all his romantic might, he gazes at the magnificence of his lover, his eyes tearful with joy and spiritual satisfaction. Shah Rukh's gaze is soppy and ridiculous to the rational sensibility, but you don't care. Because that look is not one of condescension, not where a woman is seen as a troublesome burden or a debt-recovery instrument or an object of lust, a silent, uncomplaining outlet for male carnality. In all his films, even when he plays it cool or attacks female dignity, he spares a moment in the song sequences to unleash that trademark gaze. He looks at his lovers with a remarkable register of adulation and admiration, a spiritual and bodily embrace you've never actually experienced.

You desperately want that gaze, you want those arms to hold you with that look, the look of a man who worships a woman for her spirit and self. In real life, your options are limited. Considering the constraints of your Rajputana reality, you're happy to vanish from your husband's gaze and revel in your hard-won singledom within marriage. You spend your days humming and contemplating those Shah Rukh songs, reading and making notes from books suggested by Maria Popova's blog, thrilled that your husband no longer pays any attention to you or your beautiful thoughts.

—◆—

Many of the elite and upper-middle-class Shah Rukh fangirls I surveyed felt shackled by the pillars that organized their lives. Workplaces, families and men are yet to fully adapt to the recognition, love and freedom these women expect. No wonder fangirls cling to their fantasy of Shah Rukh as if to driftwood in a raging sea.

In talking to me about Shah Rukh's persona, film critic Mayank Shekhar highlighted that he was a star largely for Indian expatriates and big-city people. He said that Shah Rukh's 'Bollywood escapism, centred on NRIs, befuddled ordinary people in small towns'. It's an important point—elite women have usually represented a key segment of Shah Rukh's multiplex audience. But we were clearly not alone. A mass-market star of Shah Rukh's wattage must have legions of working class and middle-class female fans, both urban and rural.

Since the mid-1980s, the traditional male-breadwinner model of Indian family life has found itself under duress. An eclectic set of forces have cast millions of young women out into the world to find new ways of being and doing. Through my encounters with Shah Rukh fans, I'd dipped in and out, over a decade, into the lives of several such women—all members of the tiny and shrinking Indian female workforce—divided by caste and class but united by paid employment and their fandom. Surveying Shah Rukh's digitally savvy multiplex fan base was easy enough. Tracing the 'masses' was going to be a tougher ask. While I had phone numbers and contact details, the women in question had no time to waste on my project.

I read through old notes and stories, trying to convert information into insight. Every fan-woman I had met—from Lutyens' Delhi to rural Uttar Pradesh—would offer stories of how a man had compromised her selfhood, how her family would treat her like a ticking time bomb, how the marriage market made her feel worthless, how they were underpaid and how public space remained unfriendly. Each Shah Rukh fan had a common source of frustration: few experienced emotional equality or domestic parity in their relationships with men. Each turned to Shah Rukh iconography for consolation or diversion. But wealth and the comforts of caste and class made for heartbreaking divisions—while all our freedoms were tightly ring-fenced by patriarchy, the choice enjoyed by women in the upper strata of society was far wider.

Elite women, like Vidya or the Rajput Philosopher, had choices, no matter how constrained. They enjoyed the perks of a good education and, as a consequence, gained access to new possibilities and ideas.

They could choose to work or withdraw from work. They could delegate some of the tedium of motherhood to hired help. They could throw money at their problems and mitigate if not erase them. They could hold out for butterflies or settle for staid security. They could even live alone. But this language of choice escaped working-class women. Poverty and precarity dictated their decisions to work. Marriage and motherhood were not lifestyle decisions, they were the only path to love, status and security. Their power to manoeuvre was severely restricted. Being without a man was simply not pragmatic or permissible.

Amidst these suffocations, I still encountered women who felt entitled to have fun, who aspired to greater control over their bodies and hearts. They believed in a woman's unequivocal right to choose her own life. Some simply opted out of the lives their country and culture had set out for them and forged new paths. They used the money they earned to rent accommodation and VCD players. Their hard-won independence allowed them to possess their own mobile phones, bank accounts and email addresses.

Before venturing into the lives of the Shah Rukh fans I met from India's villages and working-class communities, I will start with women from the middle class. With the stories I heard from the daughters of shopkeepers and small business owners, women who were on the cusp of adulthood when the world entered a new century. As India's economy opened up, they were expected to stay indoors and marry well. Instead, they chose to become government clerks or flight attendants, finding stable well-paid employment, earning and travelling far more than anyone in their families. They dared to gamble away the safety of family and arranged marriage in favour of sexual adventure and professional ambition. I decided, for reasons of interest and logistical convenience, to call on these rogue women, these cultural outlaws, first.

II

Baazigar
(Gambler)

6

Adventures in Accounting

Our lives are spent offering accounts for everything—where we went, what we ate, what we can cook, who we met ... everything must be counted and explained. Women make the best accountants—we have answers for everything, we expect to be probed, our lives are audited. Men have no such thinking; once they finish school, they are free to do as they please. Who asks them questions? Only their wives and mothers, who are usually ignored.

—Accountant–Fanwoman, 2016

I started by calling on a fangirl who worked in the bureaucracy. She lived in Delhi and accessed emails regularly. When I sought permission to write her story, she suggested we call her the Accountant. No ordinary accountant, her lament was that she could never complete her chartered accountancy training. Instead, she was a 'gazetted accountant', she would often emphasize. She exuded pride in her profession, in her hard-earned skills and status. Her training in accountancy, albeit incomplete, had changed her life. She often remarked that women made the best accountants—all their lives were spent keeping records. According to her, Indian men were immune to cultivating a temperament of compromise and fastidiousness. Women were well suited to constant scrutiny and numbers.

Nobody thinks of accounting as a radical profession. Whoever heard of a banker or accountant leading a revolution, my liberal friends sometimes joke. But Indian female accountants are radicals, joining men in competitive, technically demanding jobs that earn good money and often require long hours. Women have historically been a feeble presence in the accounting profession in India. However, the accounts are changing. In 2015, India had about 300,000 qualified chartered accountants, of whom twenty-one per cent were women. The number of women enrolling to take the accountancy proficiency test doubled between 2012 and 2014. This is well behind the United States, where nearly sixty-two per cent of accountants and auditors are women, or Europe, where women make up sixty-three per cent of accountants. Globally, accounting is a popular profession amongst women because they have the flexibility to register their own small practices and work from home. Moreover, many large accounting firms also offer flexible timings for staff.

The Accountant was well versed in the history of women in Indian accounting. There was her favourite, 'the mother of all female Indian accountants,' R. Sivabhogam, who in 1933 became the first Indian woman to qualify as a chartered accountant. She was the sister of the acclaimed Indian educationist and social reformer R.S. Subbalakshmi. The Accountant knew Sivabhogam's story by heart. At just twenty-three, Sivabhogam had already been jailed for participating in the civil disobedience movement. Marriage proposals were scarce—the Accountant believed that conservative families did not want a daughter-in-law who had been a jailed Gandhian female freedom fighter. 'Her family in Madras was sending marriage proposals but I guess no one accepted,' the Accountant said. Unfazed by her plummeting value in the marriage market, Sivabhogam decided to become, of all things, an accountant. The Accountant's interest in

Sivabhogam was piqued because 'the female topper in the chartered accountancy exam gets a prize named after her'. She went online and combed the dusty stacks of the college library to find everything she could about Sivabhogam.

In 1937, Sivabhogam set up her own independent practice after winning an appeal against British laws that disbarred erstwhile prisoners from registering themselves as accountants. In 1955, she became the chairperson of the Southern India Regional Council of the Institute of Chartered Accountants of India (then the Madras Council). Till date, she remains the only woman to have ever held the position. Sivabhogam practised for almost three decades. She expended considerable effort on trying to motivate young women to take up accountancy, offering coaching classes and prizes. Busy and increasingly prominent, Sivabhogam never did get around to finding a husband. She made the choice to avoid falling in line with marriage, a choice with which, absurdly, aspiring female accountants in our own time still grapple. 'Girls have higher pass percentages than boys,' said an auditor I spoke to, 'but many drop out along the way. You need to clear three phases of exams and there is a period of work experience needed. This is a long-term investment. Many of the girls give up after taking the second intermediate exam. The process is very tough and competitive, it requires great focus and, I'm sorry to say, but I feel most girls are under too much pressure to look good and focus on marriage and settling down. Exam preparation is rarely their top priority.'

The Accountant had modern-age heroines too. She would gush about Satyavati Berera of PricewaterhouseCoopers (PwC) India. In 2016, Berera became the first woman chief operating officer of a Big Four accounting firm in India. When the news of her promotion broke, the Accountant emailed an interview Berera had given to the national press. 'When I joined the profession in the 1980s,' Berera said, 'there were a few women at the entry level but rarely any women at the managerial level. I can even recall that there were clients who insisted their projects should not be assigned to women, probably because they felt it (the job) was not conducive for women. I am happy to see we have come a long way from there. Working at firms like PwC, EY [Ernst & Young], Deloitte and KPMG—the Big Four—can be challenging for women as it entails long hours and extensive travelling, at times even to remote areas. My family initially used to be concerned about my working late hours. But soon they grew out of that. PwC provided a robust support system. This, coupled with support on my home front, enabled me to overcome the challenges.' In the Accountant's email to me, she asked: 'How many of us are lucky enough to have such support from an office or our families?'

We met in 2009. At the time, I had been hired by an international development agency as a consultant working with the state government of Delhi, attempting to complete research on how welfare programmes were functioning in city slums. After spending a fair share of my first job organizing student-led surveys in the slums and colonies of Delhi to understand employment patterns of urban women, this new assignment felt like a natural extension. It offered a higher salary and improved prospects. Excited by this new phase of my career, I had an upgraded life plan. The Accountant, though, was unimpressed by the way I was managing my professional life.

She *was* impressed with my organized labyrinth of data files and careful notes. These were meant to serve as inputs towards the final report I would submit to the government and my employer. 'You can't hide a good education,' she remarked. Amused by well-off well-intentioned creatures like me, she was convinced that my interest in the urban poor was a fad, a passing phase. She felt I should focus on a corporate career and not waste my energies on local administrators and activists. The Accountant understood Delhi to be a waiting room for women like me, one I was expected to depart. An American husband and an American job, she would tell me, ought to be my goal: 'I suppose your consulting can lead to a full-time job with this agency, and then you can leave and go abroad. It will work out, provided you work very hard.'

Our first encounter came soon after she had passed an exam to join one of Delhi's least glamorous subordinate services. Her job was to assist a junior accounts functionary in a government department. Buried under a rigid hierarchy, with too many sirs and madams from higher-ranking administrative cadres above her, she undertook the thankless invisible clerical labours that made governments visible.

Her path to the Delhi Secretariat was paved by too many exams, too many nerves and much apprehension. 'Men in government act like they were born to be here,' she told me. 'Even the most useless contract staff is sure of his promotion or of becoming permanent. They are surprised when things don't go their way. We women are the opposite—all our successes, however small, surprise us. I remember on my first day, I kept wondering if my work was okay. The men around me would make fun of how unsure I felt, joking that I was constantly seeking praise. It was my first time working in government as a full-time officer, so I needed to build my confidence. The men around me always looked confident. Give an Indian man a good exam score, a good degree and a good job and he thinks he is God (*apne aap ko sakshat bhagwan samajhtein hain*).'

After the untimely death of the Accountant's grandfather, her father's family sold land in Meerut to set up a small store in Delhi during the 1950s. As Delhi urbanized and the economy opened, business was good. Consumer companies were becoming more professional about pricing and managing supplies. People seemed to have more money in their hands. Their neighbourhood of Rohtas Nagar in east Delhi started to change, new apartments were built. New families were moving in. Each needed bread and bought branded soaps and powders. The Accountant was an only child born in 1981. Her mother had been unable to conceive a second. All her cousins were boys. A few of the young men in the Accountant's extended family and immediate neighbourhood became the sons her father and mother wished they could have had. She felt they were more feted and celebrated by her family, invited for elaborate meals and sweets every weekend after puja at the local temple. Her parents, like everyone else, laughed extra hard at the things these men did. They were pampered. The Accountant enjoyed the company of her male cousins and colony bhaiyas but grew resentful of how her elaborate network of Aunty jis and Uncle jis would ignore her and fawn over the boys. She refused to dissolve into her gender, unwilling to become just another sweet obedient girl who deified and praised boys. Her refusal found voice in her school report card. If she could not be the sweetest or funniest, she would be the most studious. Exam-based excellence was her retaliation for the male worship she perceived in her world.

She was the first woman in her family to finish college, work outside the home and that too in government. 'My father was well respected in our neighbourhood. Now, everyone looks at me the same way,' she said. The odds of becoming a government officer in India are probably as impossible as becoming Shah Rukh. Almost any government post attracts hundreds of thousands, if not millions, of applicants. The Accountant was undaunted. She had an affinity for numbers, memorizing answers, study plans and organized thought.

Shah Rukh archived her academic slog. She usually remembered his film release dates based on the exams she was studying for at the time. He was her reward and diversion from exam anxiety and a torturous study routine. As an eight-year-old, she watched him on national TV in *Fauji* (1989), following each episode with religious fervour. 'He was so handsome and such fun to watch. I don't remember the show very well, I was young, but everyone in our colony would talk about it. He was a star for us even back then. We would all finish our homework and sit together to watch.' Reflecting on the TV series and his fame, in an interview with *India Today*, Shah Rukh said, 'In six-and-a-half hours I became the nation's heart-throb.'

The Accountant watched *DDLJ* at the age of fourteen on a blotchy bootleg video at her friend's home. Before *DDLJ*, she had seen similarly poor prints of *Maine Pyar Kiya, 100 Days, Baazigar, Lamhe, Chandni* and 'some Govinda movie' on the local cable movie network. In 1993, her father bought a satellite subscription to keep himself informed and entertained during his long days at the shop. When he closed up for the night, the Accountant would ferry the TV upstairs where her friends would join her for movies and celebrity gossip. 'All the older girls in my colony liked Salman Khan after watching *Maine Pyar Kiya*,' she told me. 'But I liked the actress more. Then we saw an hour-long show on *Doordarshan* about the making of *DDLJ*, and all anyone in the colony and at school could talk about was going to see that movie. The songs were always on TV. One by one, during Diwali, all my friends at school had seen it. My mother insisted that we watch the film, but Papa did not feel comfortable. We watched *DDLJ* in the colony as Papa did not want to see it in the hall.'

Growing up in an ordinary residential corner of east Delhi, the Accountant described how *DDLJ* helped frame the idiom of love for an entire generation of teenage girls in the late '90s. Accustomed to arranged marriages and a life of dull domesticity, none of the women, she said, had ever seen a man like Shah Rukh's romantic avatar before. 'That movie changed something for all of us. We talked about it at family gatherings, during school lunch breaks and sports periods. I can't explain it, but there was something special. His kind eyes … my mother liked him too. We'd never seen a man talk to women with such respect and love (izzat aur pyaar se), never seen a man pay this kind of attention (dhyaan) to a woman. He was in the kitchen talking to the ladies. The way he talked to the heroine's sister and mother! Our entire block was in love with him. After that, he kept doing love stories and I tried to watch as many as I could. Sometimes, a few of us friends would go to the cable bhaiya's house and request him to play the latest Shah Rukh film on the local video channel. Our fathers did not approve. We borrowed money from our mothers or brothers to buy cassettes and magazines secretly from the local market. My friends and I would share these.'

As a child, the Accountant would wander the streets and parks of her neighbourhood all day; it was too unsafe to be out at night. In her last year in school, she won a sizeable cash prize for being an outstanding student. She used some of the money to buy a Walkman. As a school topper, she had finally won the attention and admiration that she wanted from her family. So, the Accountant was spoilt with her gadget of choice.

Once enrolled in a commerce degree at Delhi University thanks to her excellent board exam scores, her world did not immediately expand. She needed to help out in her father's shop and could spare little time to mingle with her college cohort. In those early months in North Campus, when her friends would eat momos and drink lemon tea after class, she took the lonely bus back. The Accountant was livid with her father, certain that his sudden helplessness was a ploy to prevent her adventures in the world outside. She began to take deliberately long and circuitous bus routes to return home from Delhi University. She would use DTC stops the way soldiers used bridges, monuments and landscapes for reconnaissance: to locate herself in an unknown landscape, to chart her path in the world. Shah Rukh songs were her music of choice aboard these DTC adventures. She would always carry extra batteries for her Walkman. The Accountant would also travel armed with safety pins to punish 'perverted types', men who molest women on buses, a painfully common phenomenon in the city.

She would usually wait for an empty bus or a 'ladies only' service. Amnesty from the male gaze was necessary, as these bus rides were her time to contemplate the world. If the bus wasn't too crowded, she would hum her tunes. She was happy with her life in Rohtas Nagar, but on these DTC buses she yearned. From her earliest days in college, she was convinced that there was a wonderful world hovering out of her reach somewhere near Connaught Place. On her favourite bus route, touring the full circle of the Central Secretariat, she would stare at the bored bodies emerging from government offices. Later, she would take buses that took her past Khan Market and Prithviraj Road. Such excursions into the city became a treasured routine, time to daydream about the future. She could hardly wait for her real life to begin.

'My father,' the Accountant said, 'was very strict about me going anywhere. The city was unsafe. My friends were even touched inappropriately while waiting in a crowded line to submit their exam fees at the university office! Back home, the boys on the street used to heckle and catcall and I needed his permission to step out of the house. He wasn't even sure if I should go to college; the school principal, my mother and I had to fight to convince him. When I started college, he was nervous and used to drop me off himself to the bus stop.' Very rarely, the reins would loosen. 'After I finished my first-year college finals in June, I went and saw *Josh* with my closest friend. Her brother had bought tickets for us. A few months later, near Diwali, after I was in my second year, we saw *Mohabbatein*. I paid for the tickets myself with money I had won in a college academic competition. My friend's brother had picked her up from the movie hall and they gave me a ride home. My parents saw him driving up to the house. Though my friend was also in the car, my mother slapped me. It was the only time she struck me. She said the cinema hall was no place for a girl to be by herself, or even with another girl. My parents were also angry that I had spent the money I won on expensive tickets instead of giving it to them for safekeeping. My mother said that the films would play on cable, so there was no need to watch in a hall. My father said that these Shah Rukh films were too Western. I was not allowed to go to college for a week as punishment.'

Following this showdown, the Accountant's plans to watch films were shrouded in secrecy and shame. She made clandestine visits to the cinema halls near Delhi University with friends on the pretext of 'extra classes'. While she was able to conceal her ticket stubs, at home she could scarcely contain her enthusiasm when Shah Rukh was on TV. She would sing and swoon. Unable to resist the actor's lures, as long as it was contained within the home, her mother joined in the singing. Mother and daughter would also make time to watch his many interviews. But her father's disapproval only grew, convinced that his family had entered a crisis of enthusiasm. He complained that Shah Rukh was a fake, that he talked too much, that his films were for NRIs and south Delhi types, not middle-class people like them who lived across the Yamuna. He lectured his daughter about the need to have better sense (samajh). There was something about Khan that the Accountant's father found intensely troubling.

The Accountant maintained a diary, her own motivational scrapbook. A work of faith carried forth since her thirteenth birthday, she would paste Shah Rukh photos and write down the things her hero said that she found inspirational. She said her English improved because of how obsessively she would follow Shah Rukh's interviews; her desperate attempts to mimic and understand his words ensured she perfected her grammar. She used the diary to plan her study routines and journal as well.

In her second year of college, she began frequenting the colony cyber café. She would pay to surf for an hour, searching for both part-time jobs and the latest Shah Rukh interview. The place was full of men staring at pictures of blondes. For her though, the internet, like staring out of the window in a DTC bus, was a portal to other worlds. Her parents, perhaps sensing her desire to make a life for herself, began to talk about her marriage prospects. That night she turned to her diary and found comfort in something Shah Rukh once said: 'Whatever it is that's holding you back, it's not going away unless you stand up and start forging your own path with all your might. Stop whining and start moving.' Once, her career advice to me was another Shah Rukh quote. 'Don't become a philosopher before you become rich.' These scraps of Shah Rukh wisdom were a haven, full of self-compassion when the world was full of woes and worries. 'It's okay to be confused,' she would say to herself to dissolve some momentary pain, quoting from an interview he gave to a film magazine. 'Confusion is the route to all clarity in the world.'

'Papa's discomfort' was perhaps the phrase the Accountant would use most often in our conversations. Listening to her describe how her father spoke of Shah Rukh, it was as if he thought the actor's films and images were pollutants harming the atmosphere of their home. He felt he had to regulate his daughter's fandom for her own good. It was a strange experience for the Accountant—to hear a man she loved exude such open loathing and suspicion for another man she loved. Her fanhood was under surveillance, her father started interrupting her closed-door study sessions to check if she was studying or fangirling. On occasion, he would catch her red-handed, writing or pasting cutouts she had collected into her diary. She would be suitably scolded. It seemed as if her father feared his daughter's budding sexuality. That diary petrified him. He worried about how the words and quotes his daughter wrote in her diary removed her from Rohtas Nagar and from his grasp. That journal allowed her to cross-examine the world—a space that made her seem dangerous, odd and elusive.

Looking back, the Accountant felt that Shah Rukh was the first axis of inequality within her home that she found spiritually unacceptable. 'When my father wanted to know where I was going or would ask me to be near the house,' she once told me, 'I understood he wanted me to be safe. I was never angry at him for long. And no woman will complain about doing housework and the other duties of a daughter. I wanted to help my mother. But he made me feel guilty about something so simple, about liking an actor and watching his films. He would never tell my male cousins to not watch cricket. My friends told similar stories. We were all so angry because we knew that the boys in our families and in the colony watched films by themselves all the time. No one would shout at them or hit them for going to the movies as long as they did okay at school. But some of us girls were top students and we had to lie when we went to watch movies.'

'When my mother slapped me that time for going to a movie,' she added, 'even though she liked Shah Rukh as much as me, that's when I knew what I wanted in life. I wanted to be like the men around us. I wanted to watch films without having to take permission or feel guilt. Learning to speak English and becoming an accountant were the only way to get a job and be free.' The Accountant equated freedom with cinema tickets.

In her final year of college, the Accountant decided to tutor colony children in English and mathematics to bring in some extra money. The classes were conducted at home and earned her a little under ₹2,000 every month. She saved the money with care. Her father was unhappy that she did not hand over the money to her mother. I imagined he feared what this new money would bring into his home. After complaining once or twice, he stopped, as the idea of asking money of a daughter mortified him. 'My father,' the Accountant explained, 'thought it was the job of a man to take care of his family, to provide. Men would never talk to women about money where we come from. But he knew I was doing a good thing bringing in money for myself, so he never stopped me.' Soon, the Accountant was earning enough to buy her family Diwali presents. She sought help from a cousin to secretly open a bank account for herself.

Her days were packed, going to college, helping her mother with household chores, working for two hours at her father's shop between four and six while he prayed and napped, teaching her classes in the evenings and making time to study for four hours at nights. She barely

slept, she told me, surviving on instant coffee and her determination
to get out of Rohtas Nagar. On weekends, she would use a little of the
money she earned to go to a Barista or watch a film without telling
her parents. It was a taste of the future she wanted to make for herself.
Life was exciting with some cash in her hands.

After she graduated from college, in 2002, she continued to tutor
neighbourhood kids and persuaded her parents to let her take the
accountancy foundation and intermediate tests. She knew she was
starting on a long, arduous journey. Becoming a chartered accountant
would require five or six years, including multiple exams and a
three-year work experience requirement. She would need to enrol
in a coaching centre to prepare for the exams but the fees were too
expensive for her to afford on her own income. Her father said he
could only pay for a year's worth of classes. It was enough. Her mother
was certain that she would never be able to navigate the rigours of
accountancy training. The Accountant survived the foundation exam
in 2003 and found herself in a classroom full of boys. She befriended
Tarun in her first week at the coaching institute and they became
study partners. She helped with his homework and assignments. In
return, he held her hand and showered her with compliments. They
watched films at a theatre nearby. This was Love. The first movie she
watched with Tarun was *Veer-Zaara* (2004), an epic Indo-Pak love
story, released without much protest during the festive Diwali season
of November 2004. The Accountant longed to be touched the way
Shah Rukh's Veer touched Preity Zinta's Zaara.

Tarun suggested she join a study group with him to prepare for
government exams. His parents had advised him to keep other options
open, they had told him that the government was the country's best
employer. All the men she knew were planning to try for government
jobs. Tarun had joined a famous coaching institute to prepare for
these exams and his study group comprised the friends he had made
there. If she joined this group, he told her, they could spend more time

together and she could help him study for the exam. The Accountant needed little convincing; she could try for government jobs as well and joining Tarun's group would give her free access to study material without having to pay for another expensive coaching class. She would meet new people. And the more hours she spent away from Rohtas Nagar and with Tarun, the better. She told her parents that her new study group was all female. 'If I had told them it was mostly boys, they would have never let me do it. They thought all these exams and classes were hobbies before they got me married.'

Her new study group, impressed by her aptitude and her ability to retain vast amounts of information, encouraged her to consider government jobs seriously. In 2004, the Accountant qualified for a subsidy offered by the institute at which she had been taking chartered accountancy classes. As her work became more impressive, Tarun began to change. He began to tease her, gently at first and then more belligerently, that she was the beneficiary of the women's quota. 'Everyone,' he would say, 'is partial to female candidates.' The quotas, of course, were a fiction. The procedures for the Accountant to pass exams and get a job were just as rigorous as those Tarun faced. But he continued to make passive-aggressive jokes about the hard work and effort men needed to exert to support their families. Every study session would end in an argument. She began to feel guilty about her success, about making him feel bad, about reacting angrily to his taunts. She was convinced that she had become a terrible girlfriend. Terrible for exploring opportunities India accorded to a tiny minority of female commerce and accountancy students.

Before their first major preparatory exam at the CA coaching institute, Tarun asked to borrow her notes. She obliged. He photocopied those notes and sold them to other students. Furious, the Accountant confronted Tarun. How could he treat his girlfriend this way? Tarun told her that she had never been his girlfriend. They were not from the same community, he said. There was hardly anything serious between them, he declared. Anyway, his parents were trying to find a wife for him. After the exam, her non-boyfriend became openly hostile. Tarun began to make fun of her in the company of other male students. In her earshot, he joked that he only spent time with her for her notes. 'It made him feel good, making me feel small,' she told me.

The taunts took their toll. The Accountant began to struggle academically, failing her first attempt at the CA intermediate exam. Her once-enthusiastic teachers suggested that she stay at home as girls made better home economists or 'gharelu' (family) accountants. They said they had seen this pattern before—bright women who did not fare well in competitive exams. Her father too began to discourage her, reminding her that they weren't financially well-placed to find her an articleship with a chartered accountant. Nor could they afford for her to keep retaking the test. But they could find a boy for her to marry. She wept and turned once again to Shah Rukh for comfort and inspiration.

'Success is a poor teacher,' he had once said. 'Failure makes you humble.'

Romance and accountancy had failed her. She decided to retire from both. Acknowledging her limitations, she resolved to return to the grind of India's competitive exam culture. She accepted her parents' offer to introduce her to men, as long as she could study and apply for suitable government positions. Her parents would not allow her to consider private sector jobs as the value of her income would be dwarfed by the value of her marrying into a good family. They were also fearful of late nights at a faraway office. A government job carried a whiff of assurance because of its stability and status. It was a more familiar and accessible idea. After days of bargaining, a peace agreement was broached—they indulged her sarkari dreams and she indulged their shaadi obsession.

Her neighbours gossiped: 'Of course she has to study and find work. No one will marry her.' She never spoke to Tarun again. Boys became just another leisure pursuit meant for other women. She had only Shah Rukh. The world of young men became invisible, she lost interest in being sexually successful and coveted. Her parents had attempted to organize a few matches, but she was rejected each time. She was too tall. Or too educated. Another potential match suggested that when they were married, she could use her accounting skills to help his business from home. He felt it was important for women to use their education without neglecting their domestic duties. Feeling patronized by this would-be benevolent patriarch, the Accountant told him, in front of both their families, that she planned on continuing to work outside the home after marriage. Accountants did not bargain.

The Accountant realized that the pleasures of sexism appealed tremendously to insecure men, and that most men she encountered in Delhi were insecure. 'Boys are like this (*Bande aise hi hain*),' she told me. 'They can't control our performance in jobs or exams, so they make us feel bad about ourselves.' She gave up on marriage and romance in real life, convinced that progressive men belonged to a milieu she could not access. A good job was a better bet. For the Accountant, to disappear from regular life into serious study of job advertisements and her course material was to seek a momentary yet essential fantasy, a place where she hoped to find fairness and freedom.

The Sarkar Notes Everything

Notes from a meeting in 2010, Delhi Secretariat

I am attending a meeting where some discussion needs to be further discussed. The Accountant has been asked to take notes. The next 180 minutes must be recorded with agility and diligence. In Mission Mode, it is customary for junior staff to clean Excel sheets and prepare minutes. She must follow tradition and apply herself. 'I wonder if they train you for this in Mussoorie or the state service academies,' she jokes while we're waiting to use the ladies' toilet designated for us non-IAS officers. She has many serious complaints about the poor quality of training provided to 'lower-level officers' like herself. They never prepare you for the pain from persistent scribbling. They never train the state cadres to consume copious amounts of chai and stay awake through policy babble they barely care to understand. They never teach you the grammar of government files—where to use active or passive voice, what to omit or submit. No upwardly mobile officer is expected to spend too much time hunched over prehistoric sarkari stationery, capturing the policy-wallah's dance of Deep Thoughts and Statistics. Very few are even expected to listen. It is well acknowledged along the corridors connecting New and Ancient wings of the Secretariat: an officer who wishes to become a respected babu must survive the production of notes and manipulation of minutes. Learning to create files from meetings is the lot of ambitious lower-grade bureaucrats.

Relentless record-keeping must be part of a young bureaucrat's oeuvre. 'There is no meeting if there are no minutes. There are no minutes if you don't take proper notes,' Director Sahib had emphasized while staring at her breasts. Eleven months at the Secretariat have taught her three things. And she has taught me well.

1. The sarkar notes everything. Especially breasts.
2. To avoid trouble, it is best to file and forget.
3. The most valuable meetings have reams of notes, which say nothing.

The divas and devis of the development industry bless the occasion with their practiced smiles and sarees. Even the wicked white men of the West emerge from their Lodhi Road offices. The air hangs heavy with agenda items. Discussions need discussing. Policies need peddling. Breasts need noting.

As the audience settles, Raju ji—The Perennial Peon, An Officer Going Nowhere, He Who Makes Files Disappear and Smells of Cutlets—grins and says to the Accountant, 'All these ladies, all these firangis, they look like film stars, just like the people in your Shah Rukh films.' He means people like you, she tells me. My own kind: Delhi's new breed of techno-optimistic policy care-bears—forever seeking impact; overeager faces fumbling for data and a foothold, we mask our insignificance with postgraduate degrees from Harvard. As an astute member of the Delhi bureaucracy and the Indian middle class, the Accountant recognizes the self-assured fragrance of New Delhi's old-fashioned intellect, endowed and entrenched.

'Raju is right,' she says with acid economy. 'All you NGO ladies always smell good, like fresh jasmine amidst the stench of urine.' She starts to complain: her Kota Doria saree feels crumpled; she stinks of multiple bus rides to ITO.

And then the babus arrive. Crisp safari suits saunter in with faulty fountain pens. Gazetted smells of gazetted officers.

The joint secretary and his directors take their seats at the head of the table. A few files float by, and an army of support staff congregates. She knows this meeting will be short. JS Sahib cannot be expected to engage with every agenda item at every meeting. He is a busy babu. Busy and Buzzed. He had just been at a marathon meeting, where he was a mute spectator to a spirited screaming match between Mantri ji (the minister), legislators and their real-estate buddies.

Dinkar ji, the deputy director, assumes control of the meeting. Everyone in the office admires Dinkar ji. He wears his balding head and bulging belly with Brahminical élan. Unlike other state service officers in the department, he is never soaked in sweat. His body is fortified with Bhringraj oil; no hint of paan, chicken tikkas or cheap rum in his diet. He prays every evening in his office as he routinely works overtime. He seems perfectly in control. It's that Brahmin blood, the Accountant says, always dignified. Brahmin officers have infinite virtue, she thinks; no decent pandit would be tempted by money, alcohol or flesh. But these beastly Bihari directors can never be trusted. The Accountant's laws of Manu divide the Steel Frame of the Secretariat into three clans—the Bihari IAS officers who preside at conference tables, the Delhi state cadre officials ('often Brahmins and Baniyas') who manage their affairs and the contract workers ('usually Balmikis') who clean up after.

She occupies a rickety chair at the outer periphery of the meeting. This distance ensures that plebeian administrators such as herself don't perturb the delicate sensibilities of senior officials and the bigwigs of the development junta. Also, the ability to gracefully crane one's neck while attempting to decipher discussions demonstrates an officer's guile. The conversation is full of vacant buzzwords. Someone urges the government to consider efficiency, another suggests inclusiveness. The Information Technology Department representative requests the government to 'table a simple approach'. His name is 'Bakul, IAS'. He is a bureaucratic rock star. What is it about some men and their unabashed confidence? Looking at Bakul Sir, you can tell that here is a man of poise and calm, anchored to the notion of his past and impending glory. The Accountant pins the blame on the Indian Institute of Technology. The Indian Institute of Infinite Confidence.

Bakul Sir suggests simple solutions. He has usually thought of *everything*: nothing you say will be novel for Bakul. His comments garner gazetted enthusiasm. Soon after, non-sarkari participants coo in their soothing jargon. Hands flail and manicured fingers point effortlessly at papers. She tells me that Bakul is handsome. Her glances at Bakul's hands have gone unacknowledged. His fingers seem bored and disinterested. They are wrapped around a teacup on the conference table. The table bears a government stamp with its age. It is a seventeen-year-old relic, host to a panoply of platitudes and prideful misdemeanours. It looks bored as well.

I imagine the table speaks to her. It laments the loss of a bygone era—when babus were upright, or pretended to be; when files and fingers weren't fickle with memories. Sarkari laments linger in long winding corridors and oppressive conference rooms, hovering over meetings and agenda items. A good officer files everything, she thinks. A great accounts officer learns to forget. The Accountant stares at her dry nails, the notepad and its brimming contents. She softly hums to herself, '*Jiya jale*', a popular song from Shah Rukh's wonderful *Dil Se*. It's her favourite Shah Rukh song. She is proud of how far she has come from Rohtas Nagar, beaming at her notes and files. They cure a broken heart, she will proclaim. As we exit the committee room, she points at the IT department representative and says he reminds her of an 'anti-middle-class' ex. At lunch, I ask her to explain. This is a clever ploy. She loves to explain.

Bade Bade Deshon ki Choti Choti Baatein

Once upon a time there was a Planning Commission, where young consultants joined different teams while waiting for government exam results. The Planning Commission was rumoured to be a great place to find a distraction. The bureaucrats were polite and extremely well educated. There were various specialists who would join projects or meetings. The discussions were wide-ranging—on skills training, water technologies, subsidy reforms and soil erosion.

The Accountant thought places like the Planning Commission served as a refuge for the glamorous, over-educated and under-employed. It was a public works programme for the elite—a hundred days of guaranteed employment for the idle Indian intellectual. But the Accountant knew she was lucky to have such a stamp on her résumé. It was 2008 and she was in a contractual clerical role, helping in accounts and administration for a short-term UN agency project. She had been working at an NGO and her employer had recommended her CV to a friend at the UN. Her ex-boss encouraged her to explore the position, explaining that such experience would help the Accountant in her quest for a government job. The workload would also be light. To tackle her parental reluctance, cleverly, she solicited support from her oldest male cousin. The family favourite. During negotiations, she told her parents that the new offer was close to a government job, given that it required travelling frequently to the Planning Commission. Her cousin emphasized that this was a very prestigious placement, and it would only last a year.

Securing the job had been a coup. It came with a secondhand laptop that impressed her parents and friends at home. On her first day at work, a jaded peon to the stars of the planning galaxy said, 'The poor must dig ditches; the rich must write reports worrying about them. All this worrying needs strong tea, clean toilets and tasty snacks. That's how generations of cleaners and peons have found work. It's been like this for the past thirty years. *Humari dukaan aise hi chalti hai.*'

On her fourth day, she noticed the man who would eventually break her heart. He stood quietly, content and cautious, surveying the scene and avoiding eye contact. On her fifth day, she noticed him again, his handsome face buried in a computer.

He was Prakash. He was a lecturer on sabbatical, he was a husband on his marriage break, he was an absent yet loving father, he was an academic waiting to write a decent paper. He smirked at conferences, he frequented deserted ministry meetings. He was resolute in recording every event in an Excel sheet. Teaching, as an occupation, had its moments of drama. He was held hostage by his citation index, torn apart by academic acrobatics. However, for most of his time at university, Prakash's mathematical eloquence ensured he was carefree—happily loitering on the peripheries of his own lived life, content to publish or perish in academia. Free to evade his teaching duties, empowered to explore the campus and its corridors without limitations. By following his mentor and taking up a short policy consultancy within government, he diluted his own freedom. Now, no longer peripheral, he had to mark his presence. He was forced to be a planner; he was forced to give gyaan.

Their tepid romance started and ended with immense simplicity. He asked for a 'plain Nescafé' in the canteen. He asked her name, and how to pronounce it. For their first date, he took her to the India Habitat Centre on Lodhi Road. The beautiful and sustainable red-brick building was a multipurpose and multicultural city hub, blossoming as an important site for food, arts and letters. Habitat was a place to see and to be seen.

When the Accountant walked into the All American Diner restaurant, she'd never been anywhere more glamorous. The waiter found her a nice booth in the corner. As she waited for Prakash, a handsome white man was seated at a table across from her. He made small talk with her about the city, enquiring if the Qutub Minar could be seen on a Sunday. She wasn't sure but nodded in the affirmative. The 'hot gora' paid his bill and left our Accountant with a giant grin on her face. This was her first interaction with a foreigner. Prakash arrived, fifteen minutes late. The Accountant had worn a pink saree and blow-dried her hair at a salon. Feeling extravagant, she had paid extra for an air-conditioned taxi to arrive, aiming to avoid any sweat. That weekend, the year she turned twenty-seven, she drank her first cocktail.

Going to Habitat after work became routine, even after her assignment at the Planning Commission ended. Sometimes, after drinks, they'd walk into performances being staged in the vicinity. A month later, they watched *Dil Se* together at his home. She experienced a small prickle of doubt when Prakash did not join her in tearfully mourning the death of Shah Rukh's character. Till then everything had seemed simple. Prakash lived in a small Delhi flat. They found it easy to talk; when they had sex, she found it easy to orgasm. She knew he had a wife, though they were 'basically separated'. When she suggested that he formally leave his wife, he laughed at her 'middle-class morality,' urging her to grow up and move past the world of 'silly Shah Rukh films'. A tearful separation ensued. She attempted to contact him. Silence. More tears. Within a month, the Accountant learned that she had passed her exam for a job at the Delhi Secretariat. Soon, time to pine for Prakash was scarce. She would assist the accounts. The sarkari management of heartbreak was clinical and efficient.

The Accountant told me this story right after our 2010 meeting with Bakul IAS. She said it didn't take her too long to get over Prakash but that 'comment about my class was hurtful. What does asking a man if he is serious about a relationship have to do with being middle class?' I asked her to explain what being middle class meant to her. She scoffed and cited ten Shah Rukh interviews from the late 1990s and 2000s.

She quoted the actor's self-proclaimed need to buy a home to ensure financial security for his family. How he accepted roles which other actors refused. Shah Rukh did things people born with money would not because he prioritized providing for his family above personal pride, she said. 'That is what it means to be middle class.' She ended with a discussion of how his family was unable to afford cinema tickets, expensive health treatments or shoes. Being middle class was a state of mind, a series of moral choices.

'I was such a fool to fall for a married man,' she said. 'This would never happen to any of the other girls in my school or colony. They all studied Arts and are married.' She laughed, nearly choking on her cutlet. She sipped her plain Nescafé and added: 'When women become accountants and work outside the home, all kinds of mistakes happen.' She winked and quoted that famous Shah Rukh line from *DDLJ*. '*Bade bade deshon main aisi choti choti baatein hoti rehti hain.*' In large countries, people will always make small mistakes.

Om Shanti Om

Between 2006 and 2009, the Accountant had spent three arduous years preparing for three government entrance exams. What made matters worse were the 'marriage exams' she was forced to endure. During those days, every Shah Rukh interview or film release became a seasonal time of healing, a psychological break from the general nuisance of her immediate society. A place where she could forget the taunts from her cousins, aunts, parents and friends about how her government exam-scouting and studies were merely a 'part-time' effort while she concentrated full-time on matrimony. A place where no one could find her. A place where she could ignore the fact that her male cousins never faced the same level of scrutiny in marriage or work. A place where there was no recordkeeping, no score to settle. A place where she would never be asked to account. On tough days, and there were many, she would cry into her scrapbook. An endless loop of tears and tests constituted a significant part of her late twenties. 'Even after I got such a good job, people never allowed me to fully enjoy it. Everyone was only interested in when I was marrying.'

After joining the Delhi Secretariat in early 2009, she found herself in a peculiar place in the marriage market. Her job had all the status, stability and prospects of a lower-grade government officer. She planned to compete for the position of assistant accounts officer within the government, exclusively open to internal candidates through exams, and move upwards. Her current subordinate service job, though prestigious to an ordinary Indian, was not as high-ranking or well-paying as the elite IAS or the Delhi, Andaman and Nicobar Islands Civil (DANIC) services. Thanks to the private sector boom at the time, all her prospective grooms through arranged marriage proposals earned significantly more money than she did.

As a result, in all her interactions with matchmakers and interested families, she was expected to give up her job, despite its stability and relative prestige. 'After they check on our plans to work outside the home,' the Accountant would tell me about the questions posed by prospective in-laws, 'they always ask us how well we can cook. One of my friends was asked if she could make continental cuisine as the boy was very fond of foreign food. She was worried that no other proposals would come for her and decided to get married. Her twelve years of marriage have been spent being a cook and cleaner. She loves her children, but she says she would leave him if she had a place to go, and if she could support her kids.' Everything the Accountant said about marriage was in the form of a cautionary tale. 'I have another friend from college,' she once told me. 'A girl like you, English-speaking and from a good school. She married a man from IIM-Bangalore and moved to London. She says that her husband barely talks to her, other than telling her what he wants for dinner. Can you imagine a world in which we refuse to marry men who can't cook for themselves? If we asked the boy's family if *he* could cook! If men were tested as much as women are. Very few people would get married, or maybe boys would learn to take care of themselves! It's happening with the IT programmers from the south, my friend says that those boys are better able to cook and clean as they have lived on their own in other countries. But those stories are rare. And who'll let a Baniya girl marry a boy from the south anyway? Who'll let us move to the south?'

The Accountant was tired of being perpetually evaluated and assessed. Shah Rukh wasn't an antidote to loneliness; he represented a space where she felt unquestioned, where she could pay attention to herself and her desires. Accounts were the antidote. Her love for numbers, orders and files. Her pride in her job. 'Perhaps if I had found love, I wouldn't care as much about accounts and finding a good job,' she said. 'Sivabhogam was also single. Maybe if I was married and happily settled, I would have given up and focused on my home as everyone else does. Women find love and leave work behind. Keeping a husband and family happy is a full-time job. I talk to my married friends, and managing a man is tougher than managing files.'

Shah Rukh became a map through which the Accountant navigated and made sense of the world. He also assumed the role of a personal life coach and self-help guru, one she would summon whenever she needed encouragement to pursue her independence. In particular, she repeatedly watched *Om Shanti Om*, his hilarious and heart-warming 2007 release. The film features Shah Rukh reciting a set of iconic dialogues on how our lives are similar to the stories of Hindi cinema. He suggests that the universe conspires to ensure we all find our respective happy endings. If our current circumstances are unhappy, his character says, we should know that the film is far from over. *Picture abhi baaki hai mere dost.* These lines, like so many others her favourite actor enacted, offered hope and consolation. They became her sole source of sustenance and repair during the dreadful years preparing for endless exams, when she realized that high marks were her only path to feel superior to her male cousins, that test results were the only way for her to live the life she wanted to, that families like hers could not afford for their only child to join an accounting firm as a poorly paid intern, when she struggled to find a job between plush offices and dingy government buildings. His films, interviews and imagery sheltered her when she had nowhere else to go. She turned to him when her parents disappointed, when self-doubt dominated her days, when her closest friends vanished into a routine of manicures and men, when she felt she could not be employed or loved or deemed herself too worthless to be employed or loved, when her heart could not stop hurting or when her brain carried the deep and privileged agony of learning too many life lessons.

In 2015, as the Accountant inched past the age of thirty-four, she told me that her mother and father had given up looking for a match. 'They've grown tired and realize that no one is looking for someone as old as me who wants to continue to work. They once thought that a government job would improve my marital prospects. But the opposite happened.'

Much before young female actors and pop stars from the West advocated self-partnering and it became hip to be your own soulmate, women like the Accountant opted out of the meat market and decided to embrace themselves. 'One day,' she said, 'a family had come to see me and made some nasty comment about my complexion. They said that all that hard work and travel to office was making me look dark and tired. They left, and I felt horrible. Usually, I would cry alone in my room. This day, control nahi ho paya and I started to cry on my mother's shoulder. I think that was the day they decided to stop looking for a groom. They saw how these matches were always insulting my hard work and everything I had done in life. My parents loved me too much to watch me suffer. Something changed that day. Things became better with my father and mother. We decided that akele rehna theek hai.'

The Accountant was never anti-marriage or against love, she would be happy to find someone. She watched Shah Rukh as a substitute for the real thing, refusing to abandon her workplace as a price for love and conformity. In doing so, she defied a social narrative which assumes that a woman's commitment to her career is like some fast-fashion piece of clothing, one that can be easily jettisoned at the turn of the season.

India is busy modernizing for its men. Women occupy a different experience. As per the India Human Development Survey in 2012, eighty per cent of Indian women need approval from a family member to go outside the home to visit a health centre. Three out of five women need permission to visit the local grocery store. In 2015, only forty-seven per cent of urban women could go unchaperoned to a public space. Even within loving families, women are always made to account for what they do, where they go, what they eat and who they see. Men's lives continue relatively account-less and free. When young men are surveyed about why they migrate away from home for jobs, many say they moved out of a sense of adventure. In her own way, the Accountant was an adventurer and a rebel—boldly going where no girl from Rohtas Nagar had ever gone before.

Loveless in the Labour Force

The Accountant felt pride about this lowkey rebellion. Yet, her joy was always inhibited. Society, it seemed, had robbed her of the ability to wholeheartedly enjoy her achievements. Her friends and extended family gave her the perfunctory compliments about her job and breadwinner status that they were expected to, but no one evinced any real interest in how she lived in the world. They asked her male cousins about their salaries, office politics and career growth, all questions they failed to ask her. Her prestigious government job offer was a glass full of giddy thrill, served with a dash of disappointment. She was surprised that there was no 'dhamaka' among her neighbours when she got her coveted government job. 'Boys getting any salary-wali job would always result in a party. My parents and I would go with gifts, strangers would eat sweets. There was nothing for me. My parents were very proud. I knew that. My father called all his brothers and cousins to inform them. A few friends invited me to celebrate with lunches or coffees. But there was no party. They would have organized one if I had asked, but I expected them to do so on their own. If I was getting married, then there would have been a big explosion of joy. I guess a good job is not seen in the same way, but I really think it should be.'

Her friends celebrated their children being able to walk and speak, the promotions their husbands received. She participated in each of these celebrations as a proud and supportive friend. No one ever celebrated the small projects she finished at government. I knew that she desperately needed someone to mirror her sense of achievement, to recognize how far she had come, to see merit in the choices she had made, to acknowledge that her way of participating in the world wasn't menial or meaningless. But each time she tried to talk to her friends and family about her work, she got a blank stare. 'It's my fault. I do work that none of my close friends from the colony or my family can understand. The men are used to money talk and the women discuss children, gods and TV. My father and cousins will not discuss politics with me, even though I know more than them! My college friends don't have jobs, and I worry they'll think I am showing off if I start talking about the Secretariat. At least we can still talk about Shah Rukh.'

Once, she helped a maternal cousin in Ghaziabad buy a motorcycle. Her aunt had called personally to ask for help. The Accountant earned more than most in her family and bought the bike as a gift. The day it was brought home and blessed by a pundit, all of the Accountant's maternal family were present. Later, at a family gathering following the ceremony, everyone complimented her male cousin for doing well enough to buy such an expensive bike. No one in the family set the record straight. The male cousin never said a word. All she received was a private second-hand thanks from her aunt, routed through her mother. When the Accountant asked why everyone seemed so unwilling to acknowledge her contribution, her mother said, '*Theek nahin lagega, samjha karo.*' The Accountant looked at me, still bemused all these years later. 'It was as if they were ashamed of my salary. If a man in the family would have bought that bike as a gift, they would have never hidden that fact.'

Economists would say that the world was extracting emotional rents from the Accountant. As an unmarried successful thirty-something working woman living in Delhi, she was navigating a world designed to impose what economist Sendhil Mullainathan calls a 'hidden tax'. Writing in the *New York Times*, he says: 'The working world is unfair to many women, yet even when they succeed, they must confront another series of challenges. Their hard-won successes are taxed in ways that men's are not. The taxes I'm talking about aren't paid in dollars and cents or imposed by the government. They take the form of annoyance and misery and are levied by individuals, very often by loved ones. I call these impositions taxes because they take away some of what an individual earns, diminishing the joys of success.'

Of late, it has become trendy for technocrats to talk about the 'women-in-the-Indian-workforce problem'. International agencies and philanthropic foundations have identified increasing women's employment in India as core to global development goals. A large community of wonks earns profit and prestige by testing and scaling 'interventions' to remedy gender-based employment gaps.

In July 2018, I met the Accountant for the last time. A few years away from her forties, she had recently been selected as an assistant accounts officer after an examination in 2017. This was an exciting time for her, she had actuated her plans of moving upwards within government. She talked about her training being conducted by national government officers, a matter of great esteem. I asked her about the female employment crisis in India. She placed all the blame on Indian families and unsafe public spaces. 'I am happy that life worked out this way for me. My friends' husbands don't even take them to the movies after the first few years of marriage. They look tired all the time.'

She argued for material resources and cultural change. 'I think we need lots of safe hostels and scholarships for women and to find ways to reduce the money families have to spend if a girl wants to study and pursue a career,' she said. 'For me, I needed course material, coaching, travel: all that is expensive, and most families don't want to spend on more than a simple government college degree for a girl. Families won't even allow a girl to get a part-time job so she can help pay for herself. I also think all reserved seats should only be for girls within every community—they need it more and parents may change their attitudes if they see that a girl has a better chance of a good job than a boy. In India, families are prepared to spend on a boy's studies and on a girl's marriage. That mentality has to change. Even with scholarships, hostels and reserved jobs, if men, parents and in-laws don't feel happy about women wanting to study and work, nothing will ever improve.'

As the Accountant instructs us, there are no easy technocratic solutions. We need intimate revolutions at home. We need families and loved ones to stop imposing taxes on women's desires for achievement outside the home. There is no policy fix for feeling that your achievements as a professional woman will never be as rewarded as your achievements as a beauty, wife or mother. Unless women feel safe and confident about pursuing their ambitions—be it work, family or both—unless families and loved ones celebrate and support their work outside the home as much as what they do inside, increased female employment shall probably fuel greater conflict and stress for working women.

At the close of our conversation, the Accountant said that films needed to help too. She worried about how female characters in popular films conditioned women to avoid thinking about their careers. 'Even in Shah Rukh's films, we never know if the girl has a job. And can you remember any film that tells young girls that they need to find pride not in the man they are with but in being financially independent? The films have changed, they have loud girls who are free to smoke, drink, even have sex before marriage, but rarely do they show women feeling proud of their work. Honestly, I feel every actress who does an item song should donate to a scholarship fund for girls to offset the harm she is doing. Among the films I've seen, only in *Luck by Chance* (2009; Shah Rukh has a cameo in this feminist Bollywood epic) we see how the heroine stands alone. In *KANK*, his successful wife says she had to work as the man could not earn enough. Also, in *Dear Zindagi* (2016), the film with Shah Rukh and Alia Bhatt, you see how a girl struggles to make her career and believes it matters.'

The Accountant continues to live with her parents. Living alone would be a heresy too far. But after her promotion, she decided to buy a home. The idea made her proud and sad. When she was young, as a teenager or a twenty-something, she could never imagine herself purchasing accommodation on her own. She would most certainly need a man. Maybe someone like Tarun or Prakash. Buying a house was a perilous journey. Real-estate companies were collapsing, banks were reluctant to extend housing loans to single women with single incomes. Fortunately, she had a government job and a healthy bank balance. She was seeking investment options to save for the future. At this pinnacle of her success as a single woman, the culture continued to remind her that what she had done was more worthy of suspicion than unalloyed praise. 'Everywhere I go, they assume I have a husband, and the paperwork is arranged in that way. Each time I must explain I am unmarried. Why should my marital status come up all the time?'

Shah Rukh remains the man in her life and her easy access to him is a symbol of her independence. 'His interviews and lectures have become better with age. He still looks so good. I'm happy that I can watch him without needing anyone's permission. *Shah Rukh tak pahuchne main maine bahut mehnat kari hai.*'

All through the multiple lockdowns in Delhi, the Accountant diligently helped pay the government's bills. Yes, she did have a corona scare. She recovered and promptly returned to work. Each time I think of her, I imagine her desk full of organized government files. Her elegant scribbles described the affairs of accountants, planners and participants—simply. The notes were incomplete. There was no mention of anxious single women, unacknowledged gifts, lost tuition notes, fangirl-accountants, lamenting tables, puritan pundits, heartbroken officers, loan payments or power-drunk men. No Issues. Nothing complicated or contrived. Simple files for simple folk. The transcripts of their trysts and troubles lurked on the margins.

7

A Girl Called Gold

Udi udi jaye / Udi udi jaye / Dil ki patang dekho udi udi jaye
(It's flying away / It's flying away/ Look; my heart is flying away)

—*Raees (2017)*

2017, Chanakyapuri, Delhi

'Do you think I can eat popcorn before my procedure day after?'
Gold asked as we emerged from our security check at the mall.
She was excited about her upcoming surgery and what she would
look like after recovery. We were early for our show and decided to
caffeinate. She continued: 'Have you ever noticed that all the heroines
have such clean skin everywhere? It's not just make-up or airbrushing.
When I was working, this TV actress was flying on my sector and she
was wearing a slip dress. Very exposed. But she can show whatever
she likes, she had no breasts! Clothes never look indecent on flat girls.
They have nothing to hide (laughs). But seriously, she had no scars,
perfect skin, nothing wrong on her anywhere. She was perfect—the
back, the face, the navel, arms, legs, *everywhere*.'

Gold marched on, leading her parade of praises for the physical perfections of famously beautiful women. We placed our coffee order. I had barely registered what she said, finding myself too distracted by the evidence of change in our city. It's hard to avoid spouting cliches like a foreign correspondent about the chaos of change in India, impossible to remain analytically ambivalent to the headiness of the cultural shifts in cities like Delhi. Everything had changed. There we were, at a PVR cinema hall, watching kids from a nearby school buy mochas at Starbucks. An ordinary scene of elite urban consumption that could have been, and indeed was, replayed anywhere in the world. No big deal. But there we were—watching kids spend money that their parents never had as school students, at a Starbucks that did not exist five years ago, inside a mall that was built on top of the demolished dust of one of India's first cinema halls, once a thrilling symbol of modernity itself.

A school student, still in his uniform, started shouting at the barista, a young woman with limited English, who looked like a frightened squirrel. The students were impatient and unwilling to accept that making coffee for the four families who'd ordered before them might require them to wait for their own orders. The barista attempted to be conciliatory through this onslaught of nouveau-riche insolence. In these glittering new temples of Indian consumerism, old tensions of caste and class are still rife. Teenage entitlement remains eternal. I suppose *everything* cannot change.

But questions of what had changed and what remained the same did not interest Gold. Shah Rukh, beauty and clear skin did. It was 2017, and *Jab Harry Met Sejal* had recently released to no real acclaim. The film, which bore no connection beyond its title to the 1989 Hollywood romantic comedy *When Harry Met Sally*, starred Anushka Sharma and Shah Rukh. I was thrilled that Shah Rukh had returned to this genre after a series of action films. Sadly, most Indian viewers disagreed. The film was torn to shreds on Twitter, panned by critics and made little money. But old-school female fans such as Gold and myself were ecstatic. Here was our hero, once more staring so ardently into a woman's eyes, seeming to discover himself as he discovers her. Here was Shah Rukh, once again in conversation with an intelligent woman, a man for whom communication was intrinsic to connection and love. 'There's a full lip kiss also,' my friend told me, 'probably his second in a film, very rare,' Gold offered as we collected our order.

In his role as the titular Harry, Shah Rukh was more chiselled than in his early films. His character was the proverbial toxic male, hardened by the woes of migrant life. But still, he remained vulnerable, working to undermine and subvert the steroid-laden cocksure masculinity of his contemporaries. In the film, Shah Rukh plays a man who has run away from his village in Punjab to become a tour guide in Europe. He falls for a Gujarati girl, wealthy and spunky. Unsure about his place in life, the precarious nature of his status in Europe, he is a bundle of masculine self-doubt. He feels unworthy of this woman as he has lived a life of debauchery without accumulating much money or dignity. Shah Rukh is spectacular in his portrayal of Harry's weaknesses. An unforgettable scene captures his character crying uncontrollably in a corner, talking to himself as he tries to soothe his broken homesick heart.

The wonderful Phoebe Waller-Bridge, creator of *Fleabag*, talked to *The Guardian* newspaper about being asked to help write a James Bond film and how she took the film's treatment of gender seriously. Bond is, of course, famously promiscuous and cavalier in his attitude towards women. But, Waller-Bridge said, 'The important thing is that the film treats the women properly. *He* doesn't have to. He needs to be true to this character.' For some unfathomable reason, the writers of *Jab Harry Met Sejal* make the spirited female lead behave contrary to her character. They make her needy, addicted to male approval. She keeps worrying about being the 'sweet sister type' and is forever asking Shah Rukh's character if he thinks she has sex appeal.

Once debauched and prone to casual sexism, Shah Rukh's character lashes out. Harry may treat Sejal badly, given that Harry is a deeply flawed person, but the writers treat Sejal worse. Sharma, an amazing actor, is poorly served by a character who is badly written, whose motivations and actions are entirely inconsistent with who she is meant to be. Despite all these troubles, even in its cringe-inducing moments, there are flecks of vulnerability in the leading man's eyes. What glorious relief.

Gold was relieved and happy for various reasons. After years of turbulent singlehood, her marriage was peaceful and wonderful. The scars from those lonely years were healing and now she was in India to remove the scars from her back acne as well. 'Soon, my skin will be absolutely clean. I finally saved enough for that Fraxel procedure I told you about. Doing it here is cheaper and becomes a spa holiday. The acne marks peel off very quickly.'

As we entered the hall, Gold complained about Anushka Sharma's recent advertisements for a global deodorant brand that claimed to help whiten the armpits of Indian women. Since 2012, these commercials had been everywhere, with Sharma proudly showing off her fair, unblemished face, only to smile and reveal her fair, unblemished armpits. 'Next,' Gold said, 'it'll be our elbows that have to be smooth and fair.' Her frustration wasn't ironic or humorous, it was the frustration of a student discovering surprise sections on an exam she had to ace.

Because beauty and bodily perfection were the ultimate exams for Gold. Beauty had tested Gold all through her twenties and early thirties in the most strenuous ways, teased her with its new mathematical riddles, posing problems which seemed impossible to solve. How do you maintain perfect armpits while holding on to a sweaty laborious job in a warm country? Perfect hair while clearing food trays and dishes? Perfect complexion while mid-air, collecting trash and unclogging toilets? Perfect smile when dealing with boorish customers? Clear skin despite being caked in make-up all day? Sweat without stench? Wellness and fitness when you suffer from a chronic lack of sleep and time? Look like a movie star without the accompanying army of helpers and hangers-on?

Beauty defied any easy resolution for a hard-working woman like Gold. She thought of beauty as a clear marker of a cultivated sense of self. A sign that a girl found time for herself, that she appreciated herself. Seen from her perspective, beauty was not a genetic blessing but a form of self-acknowledgement that she considered an achievement. She frequently reprimanded me for looking shabby or not eating properly. After my painful break-up with The One, her advice was that I needed to find myself a trainer and lose seven kilos. 'If you don't take care of yourself, you can't expect a boy to want to take care of you,' she said with irrefutable, infuriating logic.

The manufacturing of beauty genuinely made Gold so very happy. As a young woman growing up in the state of Rajasthan, which reports some of India's worst gender equity indicators, her control over her external environment was so limited as to be irrelevant. Unable to edit the world outside, she edited herself. She made her body the locus of her control. When I first met her, I struggled to understand how she held on to her busy job. Her appearance—blow-dried hair, designer dresses, perfect nails—suggested an abundance of energy, wealth and time that you might not immediately associate with a young woman who had fled an arranged marriage to make a life of her own.

The First to Fly

In January 2018, India became the world's third-largest civil aviation market. The sector has been an important employer of young women as flight crew since the 1960s. Till the early 1990s, air hostesses, as they were once called, embodied the mystique of flying, an act few Indians either needed or could afford. Flying seemed impossibly glamorous and the flight crew had to reflect this world of beautiful people doing beautiful things. Airlines hired out-of-work models, beauty queens and aspiring actresses who needed to make some cash until they got their big break—all personable young women not averse to hard work in exchange for travelling the world for adventure and financial freedom.

While women have been working the skies as flight crew since the birth of Indian aviation, most media interest and national pride has been focused on the women who become pilots, intruding on an overwhelmingly male-dominated profession. Indeed, with 1,092 female pilots in 2018, twelve per cent of all commercial pilots in India are female, the highest proportion anywhere in the world and twice as high as Western countries such as the US and Australia, which generally have far more women in paid jobs. Globally, fewer than five per cent of pilots are women.

Women doing jobs that are traditionally deemed male always fascinates. These women wear the haloes of those who succeed in specialized, technical and therefore masculine fields of achievement. No one thinks of celebrating the accomplishments of the female in-flight crew unless they fight terrorists and serve national honour, despite them being the first generation of Indian women flying in the skies, possibly the first generation of women working outside their homes. This is because care-oriented service jobs which require dealing with the demands of people are not considered *as* technically demanding as flying a plane. Men who perform this 'feminine' role are also unsung, though usually given positions of greater responsibility or considered necessary for 'security' when passengers become unruly. But no pilot, scientist or academic I know could manage Gold's job. None could wade into the messy world of public dealing with as much grace and beauty. The scientists are ensconced in their labs, the pilots are ensconced in their cockpits. Gold had to manage the expectations, annoyances and attitudes of hundreds of people every day.

Pay for pilots is based on seniority and flying hours under strong union agreements; it is one of the rare professions in India where there is no gender pay gap. Those gaps—favouring men in terms of salary, career longevity and promotions—were reserved for cabin crew. Only in 2006 did a woman become the first flight in-charge at Air India, three years before she retired. That too, after Air India changed its rules to allow women to become in-flight supervisors. This reform was challenged by male cabin crew through a legal case and finally upheld by the Supreme Court in 2011.

Before the mid-1980s, women taking up jobs in the aviation sector were primarily from Christian and Parsi families. These communities have historically reported better education and employment outcomes for women. They also have fewer restrictions on female mobility. 'Many of the Hindu girls who came for air-hostess interviews in the 1960s and early 1970s either had to fight with their parents or lie to them,' said a retired flight attendant, who had joined Air India in 1969, in an interview to journalist Aarefa Johari.

Given the long participation of women in the Indian aviation sector, the industry has much to reveal about how the role of women in the workforce is imagined in a patriarchal society—with the female employee forever expected to be dutiful and beautiful, an item on display as opposed to a valued professional. It is a remarkable history of the battle women have waged for basic personal freedoms such as working past a certain, absurdly youthful age, or the right to gain a few extra kilos or get married without drawing censure or suspicion. News reports from the 1970s show how female crew members were scrutinized and evaluated in ways their male contemporaries did not have to endure. In 1981, a group of women employed as cabin crew at Air India took their case to the Supreme Court, which struck down such archaic practices as requiring air hostesses to retire upon their marriage, first pregnancy or at the age of thirty-five, whichever came first. In September 2003, though, the same court allowed the female retirement age at Air India to be reduced to fifty, while men could retire at fifty-eight. Bizarrely, the Air India Cabin Crew Association felt this was a positive judgment which accommodated the wish of women employees to lead a 'tension-free life at home'.

The emerging Indian middle class began to take to the skies in large numbers in the late 1990s. Annual passenger air traffic grew ten-fold from over seven million domestic passengers in 1993 to eighty-one million domestic passengers in 2015. The social composition of flights completely changed. 'It was not common like it is now,' an ex-Air India employee told the newspaper *Mint* about the transition from the more exclusive, glamorous nature of flying to the democratized era of 'low-cost' airlines and no-frills flights.

While the backgrounds of passengers, pilots and service staff changed in the '90s, women's battles for ethical treatment and dignity of labour continued. Air India fired ten female flight attendants for being overweight in 2009 and six years later grounded 130 women for weight again. Unlike men, who are not subjected to any medical exams, women crew members for Air India are required to take an internal gynecological examination. Private airlines such as SpiceJet required women to be unmarried to be eligible for cabin crew jobs. And there are countless stories of passengers misbehaving with cabin attendants. In 2018, the minister for women and child development asked Air India to 'sensitize' male staff, following a series of letters from female cabin crew complaining of sexual harassment at the senior-management level.

As flights became cheaper and more accessible for ordinary Indians and the industry mushroomed, there were plenty of jobs going for girls like Gold. She was the first female member of her family to take up work outside the home; the first to live in Delhi. Certainly, she was the first in her family to fly.

Gold clarified, 'It's not like my mother did not work. She had so many jobs in the house. She took care of my father, she helped manage our money and constantly checked our colony's water supply. All these jobs would take a lot from her—she was never paid for any of this work she did, and she barely got any sleep. I remember her late at night, sitting in our courtyard, staring at the stars. She said this was the only time she had to herself. I'm sure she was dreaming of being in a better place. I used to have a tough time sleeping as well. But at least it wasn't because of money or water. And now that I am married, I don't lose sleep over a husband either. I feel sad for my mother as I think about how different my life is to hers, but I suppose I have been sad in ways she never had to experience. She never had to be sexy! She did not have to find a husband on her own!'

Dard-e-Disco
The Disco of Pain (2008–2010)

Gold Mendiratta wore the tightest dress on the most blessed body in *all* of the club. The first time I heard her voice, she was a lioness, roaring at a Ralph-Lauren-shirted business scion, 'How can you be this fucking cruel, chutiya. Don't ever talk to me again!' It was 2008. Gold, twenty-four, was in a rage over this young man's attempts to grind with her on the dance floor. The man walked away, unabashed and amused, he and his friends grinning widely at each other without any sense of shame or compromise. Gold's wrath grew. 'Go back to your Russian whores. I bet you can't even get hard for any of them.' The final salvo. The lethal limp-dick attack.

It was a violent rupture of an otherwise sedate Delhi night. I was part of another entourage and stunned into silence. Back then, Gold and her friends loved to party with India's rich, young and feckless. There was a rhythm and routine to a typical night-out—make-up supplied by her flatmates, faux-Prada dresses supplied by a friend who was a student at the Pearl Academy of Fashion, tequila shots supplied by her friends' boyfriends or hers. The girls would huddle together in a cab and meet one of these men at a posh restaurant for dinner. Gold and her friends were pursued by men—at airports, hotels, clubs and marketing parties. At their fancy dinners, they would barely touch their elaborate meals. 'We're competing with square, flat white girls, can't afford any flab,' explained Gold's girlfriend chorus. Clubbing would follow. It was a time of plenty, and Gold's community of single people was in the mood for sexual accumulation.

Collect, collect, collect and then select.

Gold Mendiratta was never a night owl. But for two years, between 2008 and 2010, she could not sleep. Her fatigue and chronic sleeplessness had started to bore her. But her state was not tiresome enough to tire her into a restful slumber. Gold wasn't exactly an insomniac—she would eventually doze off. But falling asleep was a wrestling match, a twisting, turning bout with restlessness. Each night repeated itself. She would get home from work, quickly undress and eat her calorie-controlled dinner while watching TV. Her flatmate often travelled for work, and Gold found herself alone for large stretches after flights. Having cleaned her solitary dish, she would make plans to party with friends. If they were at a hotel outside Delhi, the usual clubs would suffice. If they were back in Delhi, their favourites were Shalom, or the Hospitality Employees Love to Party (HELP) gatherings. After a big night-out, they would eat late-night kebabs or parathas and having barely touched these to maintain her trim figure, Gold would come home to think about all that had transpired.

Her preferences in men operated by privileging sexual experience and a strong belief in the laws of transitivity. If a man had slept with several beautiful women, it meant he knew what he was doing in bed. If this sexually experienced male expressed a desire to sleep with you, it meant you triumphed over the women in his past. As a result, Gold was often interested in men with an affinity for sexual conquest and multiple sex partners. The gynecological perils of such practices were clear. Also, it was inevitable that said man would eventually want to sleep with a new woman. If he acted on his desire, which he invariably would, it meant that this New Woman would hold more sexual power than Gold. 'It means she is better than me, period. It sounds stupid but everyone works this way,' she said to me once, explaining the framework.

It was common for young men and women in the aviation and hospitality industry to mingle and marry; they were part of a new satellite service community following the boom in both sectors. India's new service jobs—hotels and flights—needed workers who were willing to migrate far from home and keep odd hours. In those days, Gold's sleeplessness was triggered and sustained by the mechanics of her relentless shifts and party schedule. And she spent much of her two sleepless years falling in and out of one doomed romantic dyad after another.

She would come back home from a club, stare at herself in the mirror for an hour, wondering how her face and outfit worked that evening, scanning and enjoying the youth and beauty of her body. If an attractive young man had expressed an interest in her, the heady euphoria would be tempered by doing internet fact-checks on him. The high of being beautiful would last for an hour, followed by a concomitant hour-long low brought on by obsessive, jealous comparisons with other girls she'd seen and met at the club. 'I keep staring at myself and photos of other girls,' Gold told me, 'and I wonder—am I pretty? How do I actually look?'

If she was with boyfriend at the time, the worrying was more acute. 'These boys, they all come from small towns and suddenly become players. In Punjab or UP, they would only meet girls from their towns or schools. They reach Delhi, and they have girls from Kerala, Himachal, Rajasthan, Bengal, Mizoram, everywhere. They can also meet foreigners! And they can go out with as many girls as they like, it's cool. And they're always looking for someone better. It worries me that he'll leave me, and I think all that worrying keeps me awake. If I'm single, I worry about when I'll find someone. If I had stayed on in Jaisalmer and never left to work, I wouldn't have to worry about these kinds of things as much,' she said.

This pattern of anxiety repeated itself—abetted by the types of men Gold pursued sex and relationships with. I noticed how a very small subset of men held her interest. 'Very few are good looking, yaar,' Gold would explain. One evening, scanning the scene at an upscale restaurant, she said, 'The problem is also with us girls. We only want boys who don't want us. Those who we think are above us, better than us. You won't admit it, but that's your problem also. You want someone higher. It's not your fault, I know it's probably tough for you to find many men interesting or attractive. It's the same for me. My friends find nice boys who work in hotels or other airlines. Like here, so many of the boys who work for other companies in ground-staff management like me. And they are nice, polite and doing well. But I just don't find them interesting. I am always looking for the worst kind of men, and I can't seem to stop although I know they won't make me happy. We girls are screwed, yaar.'

The most coveted men knew their value and worth, they would treat women as collectable items. And Gold wished to be collected by these sought-after men. I hear economists in India complain of the lack of free markets in the country. They worry about how ordinary consumers of electricity, water and food rarely ever face market prices as the government intervenes in how these commodities are priced and distributed. I only wish they'd study the brutal free markets of love constructed by young men and women like Gold and her friends. Heartbreak, paranoia and unintended pregnancies surrounded them. Men would abandon contact at any mention of an abortion. Women were responsible for all sexual hygiene and contraceptive measures. There was no equality in the sex being had.

In public, you had to play it cool all the time. In private, women like Gold were confused. She revelled in a paradox no woman in her family had ever faced. On the one hand, she loved her new freedom to date and fuck as she pleased. In the same breath, she bemoaned the pitfalls of her own freedom, sad that she had jettisoned traditional protections offered by finding love through arranged marriages and community ties. Psychoanalyst Carl Jung once described a paradox as a human being's ultimate spiritual possession. For him, a sense of paradox was essential to 'comprehending the fullness of life'. Gold struggled with comprehension.

Jaisalmer–Jaipur–Delhi
(1984–2006)

Born in 1984, Gold thought she would live in Jaisalmer forever. It was common to see her, between the ages of nine and thirteen, dancing and belting out the latest Shah Rukh love songs to her heart's content in the courtyard of the family house. At fourteen, soon after her period started, her mother insisted the dancing happen in private and the singing stop. At fifteen, she would dance in closed rooms, humming Shah Rukh songs while helping in the kitchen. In 2003, at the age of nineteen, she ran away from Jaisalmer.

Ms Mendiratta was a runaway; she chose to forsake the safety net offered by her business-owning family in favour of trying to make her own life. She credited competitive sport for her gumption. It had enabled her to build vast amounts of emotional stamina and physical strength. Sports also allowed her to run free from the strangulating courtesies and politeness of everyday life in her household. 'I was such a bitch on the field,' Gold said proudly. She often gloated about how she had once tackled a Delhi Sikh girl with such ferocity during a school hockey match that her opponent was reduced to tears: 'I made a Sardarni cry, can you imagine! I was that tough.' Playing against other school teams outside Rajasthan and participating in cultural events allowed her to collect friends, admirers and connections beyond the oppressive preordained set of her Khatri khandaan.

With her growing taste for freedom and achievement, arguments between Gold and her father grew so loud they became legendary among the neighbours, eventually floating as folklore in her colony. Their fights were formulaic—her father would obstruct her freedom in one way or another, she would scream insults at him, then run away to a friend's house for the night. The next day, her eldest sister would appear at school to collect her. Gold never missed a day of school, she enjoyed her English classes and extracurricular activities too much. She would scowl at her sister's attempts at appeasement. Eventually, she would follow her sister home. All memory of the familial dispute would vapourize by the time they reached. Her mother would hug Gold. And there would always be kheer.

Gold described Jaisalmer as 'ajeeb' or strange. The old part of the city near Hanuman Chowk was bustling, but the residential areas were eerie and quiet. It wasn't that Gold lacked company or excitement—there were friends, foreign tourists and Shah Rukh on TV. As she entered her late teens, new coffee shops sprung up around the city. These were not aimed at foreign tourists alone but also fashionable young locals. Boys and girls would meet in groups, much to the discomfort of family elders. 'One day,' Gold said, 'my father took my cousins and me to a café in Jaipur. We were there for a wedding. He did not mind the place but could not understand what we were doing. My father had never heard of cappuccino or mocha. This idea of people sitting at a table inside a rich-looking shop, spending ₹100 and drinking from cups amongst strangers—he thought it was something tourists did, not families like ours. He'd never even had a milkshake! If I order a soya milk latte anywhere, I think of him.'

She hated her parents and loved them in equal measure. She hated her small-town life but found comfort in its routines and provincial familiarity. Once, while talking of Jaisalmer, she said, 'With more money coming to Indian families, more Indian families started coming here. My father says that earlier, mostly Bengali tourists visited the area, thanks to that Feluda movie. But sometime after 1995, we started getting many more foreigners and Indians from different parts of the country. For us, growing up as school students, that was our idea of fun. After school, we would go to the old city and spend time in the tourist parts. My favourite thing was to watch Shah Rukh films at Ramesh Talkies.'

She continued, 'The cinema hall was in the old city area near the fort and far away from our homes. I had to convince the girls to join. Boys were more confident about going anywhere. The cinema hall was not a proper place for a girl without her family. Girls in my group of friends were scared that something may happen, or their relatives would see us. That tourist part of town was always crowded during the winters, and we could go see a Shah Rukh film if it played, meet friends and just spend time away from home. I did not think about it so seriously back then, but as you start to ask me these questions, I realize that our way of doing things was very new in Jaisalmer. Earlier, only the Rajput boys would be out and having fun when they'd be back home from boarding school. The young people of the town did not really go out that much. But things changed, and I don't know exactly when. There were younger people going out after school for films or food. My sister agrees with me as well. Old buildings, old ways of doing things were changing in front of us. Funny that you don't notice it when it's right before your eyes!'

Gold's father ran a successful logistics business. He planned for his daughter to marry within the community. Gold was convinced that her father wanted a son-in-law to help control her temperament. Her manner, her interests, her blatant disregard for seeking permission needed constant management. Her siblings were not as truculent. 'My older sisters and brothers have never left Jaisalmer. They married who my family suggested and they live life exactly as my parents do. They've never been interested in anything different. They shop at the same place for groceries, they meet the same people, no change. But I knew I wanted something else,' she said.

The first time Gold ran away from her parents' home for more than one night was to compete in a state dance competition in Jaipur. She was gone a week—just enough time to make it through three rounds of the contest and experience the pleasures of living without family in a new city before she took the train back home. In her last year of school, the dance competition was Gold's final tryst with fun before the competitive panic of board exams. Her father wouldn't allow her to participate. No decent Khatri girl, he would thunder, 'could dance for strangers. It was obscene'. He stopped talking to Gold, other than to say: '*Kuch sharm karo, humare baare main socho.*' Have some shame, think about us, think, in other words, what the neighbours will say.

Hoping to assuage his fears, Gold invited her father to watch a dance rehearsal at her school. She expected him to applaud. Her best friend, the daughter of a public works department contractor, choreographed the performance with twelve dancers from the school. They were a gang of Shah Rukh fans and decided to dance to three of his popular songs—'*Ye kali kali aankhein*', '*Koi mil gaya*' and '*Chaiyya chaiyya*'. 'You should have seen his face after he saw us rehearse. It was completely red. I had never seen him like that before. He wasn't angry, he was sad. He looked so disappointed, I felt awful. I knew I had hurt his feelings.'

As she uttered her words, and through the many conversations we would have, I sensed that she revisited that rehearsal hall often, a space painted with her father's shame and disappointment. That hall, where she realized that all her fandom, her freedom, all her hopes to pursue her own interests and desires would be irreconcilable with her father's demand that she be a dignified young lady, that she conform to his gaze and maintain honour, which precluded dancing to her favourite songs.

After completing school, Gold enrolled in a local college. Her board exam results were strong, but her parents were unwilling to let her migrate and study in Jaipur or Delhi. This was a brutal blow to Gold's already fractious relationship with her parents. 'I did not understand how my mother did not support me. They refused to let me leave Jaisalmer. My sisters had never done as well as me in the exam. I had ninety-two per cent in English in my board exams, those were the best marks in those days. I could have easily enrolled in a BA Pass degree outside Jaisalmer. My eldest brother had studied engineering outside Rajasthan. They never said it clearly, but I knew that my family thought that a girl's only job was to marry well.'

College was a bore for Gold. The course material was boring, the teachers were boring, her classmates were boring. In her first year, her parents became a frenetic matchmaking machine. Gold was seventeen and they hoped to have her engaged by the time she was an adult. They introduced her to a new boy every quarter. 'In my first year of college, I met three boys with their families. Some were a bit more modern and suggested we meet more than once. For one reason or another, the proposals did not work. It had nothing to do with my preferences. We weren't the right profile of family for them, or vice versa. I used to feel bad; some of the men were nice. My mother and sister explained that the match wasn't just between the man and me—it was a business deal between two families. It taught me that my father thought of my education as a hobby, and marriage was my main occupation.'

Gold's most significant heartbreak was the failure of her third arranged suitor to step up and profess his marital interest. He was a Khatri boy from Jaipur and planned to settle in Delhi. An attractive and well-mannered young man, Gold was impressed with his English and soft-spoken ways. 'He helped my mother carry the cups and plates back to the kitchen. No boy ever did that when he came to meet us. They usually behaved like they were doing us a huge favour by drinking our tea and eating our food.' The young man suggested they meet for coffee with her cousins. As was custom, the cousins vanished into a shop while Gold and her suitor ate lunch at a five-star restaurant. 'I was so impressed that he took me to a nice place and that he was so confident in the way he ordered the food. It was Italian, and I'd never had non-Indian food before. But he asked me what I would like and explained the menu to me, without making any fun,' she said. The lunch was great. They talked about their plans and families. The young man said he preferred Gold to many of the girls he was introduced to. Gold felt her body sway, 'I was carried away, like a fool. Back then I remember thinking, just like the film, kuch kuch hota hai.'

The young man vanished. His extended family sent a message that the Mendiratta family was not a suitable match. 'I think it had something to do with dowry. The boy was gold, they kept saying. As if I was worthless,' she emphasized. Gold was engulfed by tears and self-pity for a few months. Fortunately, Shah Rukh's film *Kabhi Khushi Kabhie Gham* was out and helped to ease her pain. Her brothers bought first-day-first-show tickets and took her to see the movie twice. 'It reminded me that there was a world outside Jaisalmer, that there was London and decent men out there. I loved Kareena. Shah Rukh made me smile. He was so hot in that film.' Gold eventually conspired with Shah Rukh to wreak havoc on her own marital prospects in the second year of college. In 2002, the year Gold turned eighteen, her parents heard that their neighbour, Mr Arora, was telling people he had spotted Gold Mendiratta at Rakesh Talkies. She was watching *Devdas* with a foreigner!

'I am sure Mr Arora added as much masala as possible,' Gold told me. 'All I did was take a tourist to watch an Indian film, and I was trying to make new friends.' When Gold was confronted with Mr Arora's accusations, she laughed. 'I told my parents that I had made a new friend. He was a German first-year college student who was volunteering for the summer with a heritage preservation organization. They behaved like I had murdered someone.' Gold's mother asked why she could not watch movies with her sisters on TV. Her father wondered why she needed to be out in that old part of town at all. How did she meet this foreigner? Gold explained that they met at college and they were only friends. 'Yes, of course I was interested in him, but I wasn't going to tell my parents. My parents asked me to avoid him, but I said I wouldn't.' Of course, her parents prevailed.

Gold's brothers were tasked to escort her everywhere. She was grounded. Sports stopped, as did any extracurricular activities. Gold was unafraid of confrontation. She revelled in screaming harsh truths at her relatives. A house-bound activist. 'I think I'd started giving up on my family at that time. I realized that I could not convince them with my words or tears, that I could not expect them to give me my freedom.' In those days, she would stare at the television screen, hoping to find Shah Rukh. She would read books her sisters brought back from the library. Guarded and secured inside her home, she struggled to comprehend her crime. 'I could not understand, it was just a movie. Then my sister told me that Mr Arora told Papa that he should be careful because I was too free.' His exacts words were '*Gold bahut free hoti chali ja rahi hai.*' Gold is becoming too free.

Years later, in 2016, when I asked Gold to reflect on those days, she said she felt she had been censured and punished not for being out with a white man but for being unashamed of being out with a white man. 'I looked too comfortable,' she told me. 'Girls being comfortable in cinema halls, girls being comfortable in the company of men was crossing some line. If I had looked meek, if I had covered my face, or had been looking down at the ground, they would have felt bad for me and been kinder. I am sure of it.'

Even in the early 2000s, though girls were free to go to school or hang out with their friends at markets, being in the company of a man in a cinema hall in Jaisalmer town was considered dangerous and sinister. Girls could not be trusted in the company of men. The cinema hall was a place where men took their need for lust and leisure, no place for a woman without her husband or family. Gold should have carried an air of remorse—having fun and being too comfortable in public was considered obscene.

Claiming comfort in public space, being at ease with one's body in the company of strangers, remains an everlasting hurdle for Indian women. According to a large-scale survey by Save the Children in 2018, three in every five adolescent girls felt unsafe in crowded spaces. One in four feared being abducted, physically assaulted or even raped if she ventured outside her home. Two out of three adolescent girls were worried about being verbally abused, stalked or being inappropriately touched in public. In urban areas, forty-one per cent of adolescent girls felt unsafe in local markets, while nearly half feared using public transport. Only a third of urban women 'dared' to venture out to local markets alone. Most families and men felt young women could be kept safe by simply abdicating their right to enjoy public space. The study observed, 'As many as half of the young men and parents of adolescent girls surveyed felt that the best way for girls to be safe was that they avoid certain public spaces altogether, or that they should simply avoid going out after dark.' According to the study, a quarter of young urban women felt unsafe in cinema halls.

For Gold's father, his youngest daughter's penchant for Shah Rukh, films and the company of foreigners had caused irreparable damage to her marital prospects. After the *Devdas* episode of July 2002, through Gold's second year of college, only one suitor had appeared. 'They were upset that the boy did not have his own business or an engineering degree,' Gold smirked. Despite the boy's own lack of appeal in the marriage market, his family decided against the match, claiming that they wanted a 'simple girl' who would be comfortable with cooking and domestic duties. 'My father,' Gold told me, 'was worried that very few families were contacting us with matches because Mr Arora's stories had reached everyone.'

Finally, in 2003, the third year of college, Gold found a match in Bikaner. 'My father never asked for my opinion. It wasn't that he did not love me, he loved me too much. That's why he wanted me to marry. Because for my parents, a girl's only guardian is her husband. If I married well, I would be safe. Then my father's own financial problems wouldn't hurt me.'

Gold was willing to play along. 'I was never attracted to my prospective groom. When I saw him for the first time, I said to myself, "Really? They're expecting you to marry this man?" But I wanted to leave my father's home. I wanted my mother and sisters to be happy and I knew that this was the way we women were expected to live. Those were tough days for my father's business, and I told myself to make peace and find happiness where I was. So, what if I did not want to touch him? That would only be a few times, I thought back then. He seemed like a good man. Let's give this a try.'

That trial period was disastrous, a phase of unbearable discoveries. Over a series of lunch dates and festival events during the run-up to their wedding, Gold discovered that her future husband did not share her enthusiasm for Shah Rukh or his films. He watched English films and socialized with his male friends only. On her part, she could not bring herself to care for her prospective in-laws or the awful company they kept. She also discovered that her prospective groom had a foul temper and a habit of shouting abuse at waiters in hotels. He expected his wife to be demure, domestic, forever asking his permission to use money or to meet friends. He was an only son and was used to being waited upon and fawned over. His wife was meant to be a cheerful housekeeper.

As the wedding date drew closer, Gold began to panic. 'I'll never forget—a *DDLJ* song was playing on TV at home and I burst out crying. My mother and sister immediately understood. They consoled me, telling me how love like that was for films and wealthy people. They knew I was crying because there would be no love or travel in my life. I began to avoid Shah Rukh songs and movies, except I was so sad that I was always thinking of him!'

She thought having her own mobile phone could cheer her up, help her keep track of the world and her friends. After her father decided against gifting her a phone for Diwali in 2003, though each of her younger brothers had phones, she decided to ask her prospective bridegroom. He was reluctant: a phone would be dangerous, she would contact too much of the world. 'Phone kyun chaiye?' Why do you need a phone?

As Gold explained her need for phone conversations with friends and access to entertainment, her husband-to-be looked alarmed. He bought her jewels instead. Her eldest brother proved a lifeline, giving her a phone along with a cash gift. These were enough raw materials for her to plot an escape, to elope with her expectations of a better life. An old school friend was a hospitality trainee at a posh hotel in Jaipur. She offered Gold a place to stay.

Gold carried a few pieces of gold jewellery she had inherited from her mother, crying as she quietly crept past her childhood courtyard. After reaching the train station, she called her eldest brother. 'He did not seem surprised or angry, I think he saw it coming. He knew that life in Jaisalmer and Bikaner would make me sad. He said there was no point coming back home as Papa would not forgive me if I didn't go through with the marriage. He said he would tell my father himself that night and told me to stay in Jaipur and open a bank account. He sent me some money through a friend and suggested I study something useful. I think he was hoping my father and I would reconcile, and I could move back soon. But that never happened.' Her brother helped Gold find paying guest accommodation with family friends. This was tougher than finding a husband.

And so, with the help of her friend and a brother, Gold walked away from her family when she decided to walk away from the man her family chose for her. She was tall and lean, and Anglocentric notions of attractiveness were being exported and assimilated through Indian popular culture, much to her benefit. In Jaisalmer, Gold felt admired, but she was never the prettiest girl around. This was not the case in Jaipur. 'I met event organizers through my friend in Jaipur. They told me I should model. I was like Karisma Kapoor and in Jaisalmer everyone liked Madhuri Dixit. Does that make sense? In Delhi and Jaipur, everyone wanted girls like Karisma,' she said referencing the body types of the two leading women in Shah Rukh's *Dil To Pagal Hai (DTPH)*. An entire issue of *India Today* in 2011 was dedicated to the new Westernized ideal body type, in which our natural curves were deemed too squashy, less attractive than the toned, athletic physique that was now deified. 'Just look at Shah Rukh or his heroines, from Kajol to Deepika. What's considered beautiful has changed to fitter boys and girls,' Gold once told me, while mocking my flabby stomach.

Gold bounced from gig to gig, modelling soap and helping at local automobile expos for a year. Her friends in Jaipur suggested she enrol in a training programme for flight attendants. Her combination of fluent English, physical fitness, beauty and a firm way with men would make her an ideal candidate. Indian airline companies did not require cabin crew to complete post-graduation degrees and preferred women who were 'well groomed' and 'confident'. Her brother, embarrassed at the idea of her modelling, stumped up her training fees. In 2006, after a year of preparation and competitive applications, at the age of twenty-two, Gold moved to Delhi. The city served as her airline hub. She started earning good money from her job as an in-flight attendant and asked her brother to inform her family. 'I was hoping Papa would be proud. But he never reacted.'

All That Glitters

In 2008, at that club where we first met, I'd never seen a woman look more fierce. Shaking, Gold had erupted. She kept roaring at the young man as he left with his gang and a blonde escort. Her friends stopped Gold from following the group out of the club. It wasn't drugs or alcohol. She barely touched booze: 'I like my waistline too much,' she would say. Having tried pot at a party, she knew it would make her slow at work, slow at the gym—a lack of alert speed was a luxury her profession would never allow her to afford.

It was simple unruly behaviour. Gold was possessed by raw and raucous rage—ready to vomit insults and blasphemy at any man who approached her. This desperate rage at being ignored, of being sidelined, trumped any upset at being mildly manhandled. She stepped out in tears to smoke a cigarette, and I followed. 'What happened back there? Are you okay?' I asked. 'It's fine, I can handle boys trying to get close. I'm good at taking care of myself. But I can't understand these boys and how they treat us. I know that guy, he's been going out with me. He has taken me on dates to cafés, restaurants and clubs. For the past six months, we've been messaging and talking nearly every night. I thought we had something. He messaged saying he would be at the club tonight and shows up with some white girl draped all over him and then tries to grind with me. I'm so sick of these men and how all this works. Shouldn't they have some manners, some consideration for how we feel? It hurts and makes me want to scream.' I suggested she watch a Shah Rukh film when she got home. It was a cure-all, I said. Gold giggled. She was a fan, she said, and watched clips online 'every night, yaar. I watch his songs online every night. But his films are all lies, there are no men like that in the world. He is not like that himself. But he calms me down'. And as we started to talk about Shah Rukh, we started talking about her anger.

Gold ko gussa kyun aata hai? Why was Gold angry? She was a young woman forever flirting with fury. Her anger was not directed at her employers, she was fortunate to work for an airline awarded for strong human resource management policies with decent pay and benefits. They respected work-shifts with mandatory hours of rest. Her pay would regularly increase, and the job helped introduce her to her future best friends. Instead, she described her anger as 'economy-class problems'. She was angry that she had to serve cookies to unknown men during Diwali holidays. She had been angry at the grotesque unfairness of the world, of how men buying flight tickets thought staring shamelessly at her breasts was part of the flying experience, enraged by male passengers who would casually watch porn on their phones even on a flight. She was angry that her job required her to smile through it all. Gold saw this combination of male arrogance and entitlement play out in every facet of life, including her search for love. For it was Delhi's romantic scene that triggered her—how it was designed and who it humiliated.

The young man who had made her so angry that night was living off family real-estate money. In keeping with the new rentier classes of Delhi, he wore a uniform of expensive Ralph Lauren shirts. He had casually mentioned his plans of going clubbing that night, not expecting to actually see Gold. She had decided to surprise him. Our Ralph-Laurened prince surprised her instead; she was shocked at the sight of him with his foreign ex-girlfriend. She had tried to talk to him about it. Embarrassed at the sight of Gold, the young man deflected, trying to grind with her and his gori partner at the same time. 'He'd told me that we were never exclusive. But we'd been talking as if we were. If he had just told me that he was seeing other people, I would have walked away. But see, these men, they know this. Which is why they hide and lie. They have no courage to tell the truth. They want to be players, but don't want to face the consequences either. They want it all. I am not weak. I can live without him. I may be sad about it, but it wouldn't make me this angry. And if I know he is seeing other people on the side, I can take my own decision whether I still want to spend any time with him. But he won't allow that because he fears losing how much I worship him. He knows that if he tells all the girls he's seeing about each other, many of us might leave him and he doesn't want to risk that sort of blow to his ego.'

Her chronic complaint was the lack of emotional hygiene in relationships with Delhi men. '*Yeh saaf-sutre tareeke se nahi kheltein. Khelne main koi galat baat nahin hai, lekin jhut bolna or chupana bahut galat hai yaar.*' Gold was no sexual puritan. Playing is fine, she was arguing, but these men were not playing fairly, they were not being upfront about exploring multiple possibilities. We exchanged numbers that night. A few weeks later, we met for coffee at the Delhi airport before she went home for the evening. I was catching a flight. She looked exhausted after her shift, make-up lines cracking up her lovely face. She sat down and asked after my sex life and was unimpressed by my answers. At the time, I was obsessing over some man who wasn't interested in me beyond sex. 'At least your fellow doesn't lie to you. He is being honest and straight. Now you decide what you want. If the sex is good, it's tough to walk away. Because sex is so important, yaar. It's the only good kind of attention men can give women. But most boys in India don't know what to do, and most girls I know don't know how to enjoy it. No one tells us about it, we can only learn from porn, and that doesn't show what we women like. It's made for boys mostly, and I think it's just teaching them to keep attacking our bodies in bed! I wish they would take some lessons from Shah Rukh—have you seen how he kisses women on the neck so often in his films? No other actor does that. Shah Rukh could teach these men. Instead they learn from God knows where.'

She continued her sermon, telling me how the guy from the club was great in bed, a good combination of gentle and strong, and yet a terrible human outside the bedroom. 'Us girls in India have this problem. You sleep once with someone and, suddenly, you fall in love with him. I know better, I've read books and articles which taught me that this is all about hormones, not feelings. I can control it.'

The morning after the fracas at the club, Gold had called her Ralph-Lauren prince. He wasn't in the mood to listen, offering her a monologue instead of a conversation. Before hanging up, he told her to learn some manners and to stop embarrassing herself. Gold called him again. She reminded him that he had proclaimed love for her, that she thought they were 'serious'. If he was seeing other people, he simply needed to disclose the facts to her. Instead of apologizing, her ex was obnoxious. 'He said,' she told me, laughing, 'that he did not owe me anything as I wasn't his wife. He said that if he had mentioned marriage, then it was serious. But saying "I love you" meant he was half-serious. Yaar, I think we need a map to understand how serious a man is about you. So, you see, now only if a boy asks you to be his wife, only then do you have any right on him. Us single women can be treated like garbage.' She started to tear up. I had little wisdom to offer, only a flavoured latte.

Of course, we were all responsible for our own emotions. This young man wasn't responsible for micro-managing Gold's feelings. But where was his humanity? Where was the empathy? Gold would shower him with compliments and attention, he would reciprocate in full force. Gold showed me the long messages where he professed his love and adoration. Reading the everyday accounts he shared of his activities, his goodnight messages, hearing of the great sex, the long dinners and his consistent interest in spending time with her, you would be pardoned to think that the young man was seriously interested in establishing a committed relationship with her. Perhaps he was not in love with her, for who knows what that means. Certainly, he signalled enough interest to warrant her surprise at his parallel relationships.

A culturally sanctioned sociopathy had become mainstream among the sorts of young men with whom Gold attempted to forge romantic connections. Several of these men lived in neatly divided and self-contained emotional compartments. Where it was perfectly acceptable for a young man to deploy the grammar of love and romantic commitment to three women at the same time, yet withhold the offer of marriage, and eventually use the lack of said offer to suggest that he was never 'serious' in the first place. These men were partaking in deception, lying about their whereabouts and what they did. Continuously hiding or obfuscating who they were spending time with. Marriage offered a social shield against any guilt or emotional accountability.

Various forces propelled this sociopathy. As Gold moved to Delhi in 2006, a generation of young globalized Indians had become accustomed to using and (mis)understanding the language of sex and mating from the West. American sitcoms such as *Friends* had beamed new modes of being and doing to young people in the early 'noughties'. Gold herself had improved her English by watching American soap operas and TV sitcoms. Now, spending her early twenties between Jaipur and Delhi, she watched *Ally McBeal*, *Sex and the City* and *Kyunki Saas Bhi Kabhi Bahu Thi*. Ambiguous, shape-shifting words like 'dating' had made the move from elite parlance (although I'm not sure Indian elites ever dated) to the vocabulary of new speakers of English.

'I am certainly the first person in my family to date, like the Americans say,' Gold told me. 'It's the same for most girls who work with me. It is because of changing times but also because there are actual places to go on dates to. Earlier, Delhi had a few cafés, and everyone went there. And you had to be very rich to go to five-star hotels. But that's changed now. There are so many more places for young people to meet. And if you go far away from where you live, no one will even see you with a boy.'

A decade after India's economy liberalized, women like Gold liberalized their desires; it was their time to disco. They had taken up jobs far away from home and the rules of traditional Indian family life, opting for new ways of buying groceries and finding love. Shah Rukh films reflected these changes, with men and women in his movies choosing their own partners and drawing on and adapting Western mores and styles of urban living. His films called for people to fall in love. Indeed, the epic *DDLJ* ends with that exact line in English, a clarion call for a new generation: 'Come, Fall in Love.' As with the foreign magazines, movies and TV shows in which Gold was immersed, Shah Rukh's films constructed romantic love as a strictly *personal* choice made by individuals. Tweaking the individuality of the West to suit Indian values, families in Shah Rukh's films would remain critical to a couple's happiness. But their involvement and blessings would be sought only after the two individuals had already fallen in love and decided to marry. Sociologists who study love, such as Eva Illouz, would say that Gold and her community of migrant professionals in big cities experienced love in a 'self-regulated market' of interactions or sexual encounters. Strictly enforced arranged marriages, where families held more power than individuals, were no longer palatable. The arranged marriage system itself evolved, accommodating the individual's need for a greater say in their choice of partner. The language of interpersonal compatibility and even premarital sex became, if not widespread, increasingly tolerated.

Collect, collect, collect and then select.

In the 2000s, several developments helped Gold and her friends create a mating market, which was full of free agents. There was a sudden expansion in the supply of migrant single people dis-embedded from their traditional communities, working in service-sector jobs such as aviation and hospitality. These professionals often lived by themselves or with friends. We also saw a simultaneous expansion in the financial ability and social acceptability to be out and about at cafés, clubs and restaurants. Condoms became easily accessible.

For women, the market wasn't as frictionless as for men. Buying contraception required grit in the face of judgement and longstanding cultural taboos. It was common to hear Gold and her friends worry that they were being 'sluts,' that they were not being 'honourable'. Women who had more than one ex-boyfriend were described as 'wild.'

Marriage remained the ultimate social sanction, and only the offer of marriage allowed women access to a higher sense of emotional reciprocity and moral responsibility from men.

As Gold gave up on her family, she wanted desperately to make one of her own. 'I thought I had to leave my family because I did not want to marry and have children with someone they chose, but now I can't find anyone to make a new family with,' she said. 'I never thought it would be this hard. I think I'm just angry at myself.' It was an anger Gold eventually came to terms with. She befriended her rage, taking it with her to dinner and clubs. Her anger at her father had forced a departure from Jaisalmer. But Love made her angrier—the sheer inequality of the business of loving. Gold could not run away from romance. She knew that the market for love—this whole heterosexual mating game—was a profoundly unequal space, in which a young, straight, attractive and accomplished Indian man operated with the complete certainty that no matter how his body or prospects changed, there would always be a young, attractive, accomplished woman waiting to give birth to his children. It felt to Gold like men, and *only* men, were free to date as they chose, either widely and indiscriminately or by committing to a series of monogamous relationships. Men would arrive at romantic encounters, their confidence cemented in this fact, always comparing Gold to their past and future possibilities. 'Sometimes, when I'm out with a new boy or talking to him,' she told me, 'I feel like I am not just with him, but with all the other girls he could be talking to as well. I feel like I need to be better than all of them if I have to get him, you know. I am always aware that he has many options.'

I reminded Gold that she had options too, given how men would respond to her. She smiled and thanked me for the compliment. 'I know, many people are interested in me. But the thing is, I don't want to date too many boys now. Men don't like it when a girl has an ex-boyfriend because they feel they are competing with that ex of hers.

They always think girls with more than one ex are boy-crazy, and then the good men won't be interested. I don't want to go through too many options in public, the fewer the better. The more men you try to make things work with, the more of a failure you seem. Everyone is suspicious of girls like that, and our worlds are still small. Everyone knows everyone, and news of people's past relationships travels very quickly. And the more gossip about you, the lesser your chances of finding someone good. So, I must be careful. It's not like other countries where you can try as many people as you like. We have rules here, and they exist only for girls.'

A Foreign Phase
(2010–2012)

At the start of 2010, a twenty-six-year-old Gold decided to test international waters in both her career and her love life. She sought work on foreign flights and sex with foreign men. At a party, she discovered a group of European expats in Delhi. I met some of these men with her; they travelled in a small tightly knit crowd and always dressed in linen. By mid 2010, Gold managed to find work on international routes for a global airline. The work paid more; it could eventually lead to business-class assignments with 'better clientele and a better workload,' she said. Gold fell for London at first sight, remembering Shah Rukh's iconic *DDLJ* song shot in Underground trains and stations. Back in Delhi, she fell for a handsome Frenchman. 'They always have rich Indian friends whom they know through university connections,' she said. 'But he is nice and tall, and better than any of the Indian fools I've met.'

Gold embarked on a series of long dinner parties and brunches with the Frenchman and his friends. She would describe these events with scornful admiration. 'No one smiles, and everyone looks very stern. Like my school Hindi teacher. Even if you've met people multiple times, they'll never come up and say hello. Like saying hello costs money.' Art parties were her most preferred outing, where she would eventually spot a few famous models and news anchors. Gold loved taking notes on how people dressed and behaved, enchanted by the self-serious and self-certain crowd of journalists, writers and artists. They spoke in discrete lectures, offering discourses rather than conversations, while drinking the 'best drinks' and all without a hint of self-doubt. Several smoked pot as glamorously as they pontificated. Feeling clumsy and out of place, she would religiously Google the ideas, pictures and people she encountered. She looked up Foucault, Walter Benjamin and John Berger.

Beyond a crude introduction to post-modernism via Wikipedia, Gold learned more practical lessons during the months she spent with her Frenchman. She learned that she was a 'real Indian beauty'. She discovered that French people despised a heavily made-up look, only to expect women to manufacture 'natural beauty,' which invariably required expensive cosmetic and dermatological products. She discovered that Frenchmen espoused the virtues of curvaceous women but only married skinny ones. 'You have to look spontaneously beautiful. All these French women do a lot to look like they did very little.' She discovered that her journey from Jaisalmer to Delhi was her staple dinner party contribution. Otherwise, people barely talked to her. 'They think I'm some experiment, like he is testing what a relationship with a small-town Indian girl would be like. I can tell from the way the women talk to me.'

Having been reduced to a beautiful bystander at events, Gold observed and reported. She noticed how foreign-educated Indians politely ignored the small-town women who did all the invisible work to make these parties possible, how they desperately wanted white people to think they were hip, how the self-appointed 'intellectual bande (men)' only talked to women with waist sizes of twenty-eight or smaller, how the larger women without husbands usually talked to each other. She discovered that her English was better than any of the European expats in the room, although the goras were forever unable to understand what she was saying. She surmised that Europeans liked different 'types of paneer'. Her biggest battle was with charcuterie. Through that year, she was hungry all the time. Dying for a taste of kadi-chawal, only to be served cheese plates and cold cuts that intimidated her. One night, she confessed her fears of fromage to her Frenchman. He laughed and taught her all there was to know. She had never felt closer to him, yet farther away from the food she liked to eat. 'He doesn't like Indian food because it isn't subtle enough for him, our food is too spicy. We'll go out together for a few Indian meals, but the main food at his friends' houses is bland and looks tricky to eat. I cooked curry in his house once, and he spent most of the next morning complaining about the smell.'

Gold was amazed at the civilizational confidence on display. Once, she returned from dinner and called to say, 'I had to tell you. This blonde girl had just returned from Jaisalmer and was introduced to me. She said she loved the city and the fort. And then she said how I must be so proud of where I came from. And you know I realized that this is the difference between us and foreigners. I am not at all proud of the Jaisalmer fort or the city. No one I know built that fort. The town was never a free or fair place for me, so I left. But she was so proud of Paris, behaving as if she built the Louvre herself! I don't love my past as much as they love theirs.'

She introduced her Frenchman and a few of his friends to *DDLJ* and *Chak De! India*. She told them how Shah Rukh had received official French government recognition as an 'Officier dans l'Ordre des Arts et des Lettres' in 2007 and was described as an 'actor of great talent and unmatched popularity'. Previous winners included the likes of the writer Mahasweta Devi. Gold told her sceptical audience about Shah Rukh's fan following in Germany and how he was probably the world's biggest star. Later, forlorn, she said that her French boyfriend and his friends 'kept saying that our movies are so over the top, that they are ridiculous. That this was not real life. And they only liked the dance sequences. Like the films had no story or emotions. But you know, I don't think there is only one way of showing love and stories on film, we have our way and they have theirs. It irritated me because I love Shah Rukh and because I felt like they were attacking our way of life, our way of expressing ourselves. I felt that they thought Shah Rukh and Hindi films were silly because that's not how foreigners display love'. Gold met whiteness as a universal subject.

More and more, as their relationship progressed over a year and a half, she lived inside her own head. With each attempt at being engaging, she sacrificed being herself. She started to dress differently, burning her savings. 'Being his girlfriend was expensive. He always paid for meals, but I had to watch what I wore in his company. But no matter what I wore, I could never be as elegant as those women. They were not as pretty as me, but they looked so effortlessly glamorous. I felt like something was always wrong with my outfits and the way I carried them.' For Gold, elegance became something white people had invented to make brown people feel bad about themselves. Eventually, she lost all interest in being interesting. She stuck to her role as the staple Small-Town-Beauty with very few words.

The Sexy Bhakt

After Christmas of 2011, her Frenchman returned from a visit back home, only to announce that he was back with his ex-wife; that they had no future as Gold had no French. 'Now I'll need to learn a foreign language other than English to find a man? My father made me pay attention to my English to help me find a more suitable match. He should have taught me French also. I did not know whether to cry or laugh,' she said. 'I was so angry,' Gold continued. 'Can you imagine any of us breaking up with someone because they don't speak Hindi?' I couldn't. 'We are all beggars in front of foreigners,' she added, warming to her theme. 'We want white skin and to speak their language. We want what they have without any appreciation for our own selves.' It was around this time that Gold began to express admiration for Narendra Modi and the BJP. 'At least,' she would say, 'they have respect for our culture and are not wagging their tongues at white skin.'

However, planning to vote for Modi in 2014 was no cure for her heartbreak in 2012. Lying awake, she would try and distract herself from her break-up with old Shah Rukh films. Gold would wonder why she was never loved the way the women in these films were, why she was always in a state of longing, convinced that no man she was interested in had ever found himself inhabiting her state of constant inadequacy. It seemed to her that the burden of emoting, waiting, playing it cool was all hers. I asked her if this was any different from the women of her parents' generation. She insisted that the men and women of previous generations had no choice. 'Some colourful uncles would have some hidden fun on the side, but back home, if someone left me like my ex did, or if a boy was cheating on you, it would hurt his legs *and* his reputation.' I would often probe her on these themes, and she'd keep describing the pleasures and pain of young women navigating the demand and supply of romantic commitment.

Gold: It is true, girls are becoming more and more unhappy these days. It's the trouble with being independent. Boys don't face these troubles.

Me: What do you mean?

Gold: Girls expect men will keep their promises, that they will commit. But that time is gone. Men like Shah Rukh are scarce these days, that's why we all admire him.

Me: Can you explain?

Gold: I mean, I'm sure he's had affairs. People keep saying that it's impossible for men in films to not cheat. But you see the way he treats his wife and their marriage—such honour and commitment. Whatever happens in private, in his interviews and everything, he makes her the centre of his life. He never humiliates her or makes her feel small.

Me: And you think men in our lives do that?

Gold: Yes, yaar, all the time. Being a playboy is such an achievement for these guys, they feel special when they make girls feel bad. And the married men seem to have more licence to misbehave.

Me: So, what can we do about it?

Gold: We have to stop caring about what men think of us. We have to become cool. Funny thing is, then, they suddenly get interested. *Jitna kum bhaav do, utna better hai.*

Me: What do you think these guys are looking for in a girl these days?

Gold: As a wife, who knows. I think they all marry the kind of girl their parents would have picked out for them. But as a girlfriend, for fun, all men want a sexy girl. It's not her face or her brains, that doesn't really matter these days. It's her body—I think they all wonder how jealous she'd make their friends at the club. So, they want what all boys want. Small waist, good complexion, good abs, good shape. Long hair and all that. But you know this sexiness is actually an attitude. Like Deepika Padukone. When she was with Ranbir, she was lovely and she will always be beautiful. But when he left her and she stopped caring for men's attention, she became sexy. Shah Rukh's like that too. In *DDLJ* and in his romantic films, he's cute but never sexy. In *Don* and *Raees*, when he doesn't care what people think of him, he is sexy. Nahin?

Me: So not caring about people makes you sexy?

Gold: Yes, I mean it's impossible to stop caring. But you have to seem like you don't. Girls have to learn not to be needy, too chep (clingy). It's hard—there are very few boys and many pretty girls.

Me: So, even if you can't be indifferent, you must seem indifferent. This being sexy seems like a lot of hard work. (laughing)

Gold (laughs as well): It is, and girls need to work hard at it. That's why many end up asking their parents to help.

Me: How can parents help?

Gold: Parents and community are like the police. If a boy does something wrong and the girl's family find out, they intervene. If a boy who was introduced by the family of the girl for a match started two-timing the girl, or having fun with her without committing, or treating her poorly, her parents would complain to the boy's family and it would hurt his honour. They would try to make the boy act properly. There would be some punishment. Knowing all this, everyone is cautious with each other's feelings. Here, away from my parents, where my boyfriend's family will probably never meet my family till it becomes very serious, he can do as he pleases and the only people who can hold the boy accountable are the girl he's with and his friends. And that means nothing to boys. Our opinions don't hurt him or his reputation. If I lived back home and had an arranged marriage, my parents would protect me, but in exchange I would have to give up my freedom.

Me: But why can't we just talk it out with these men? Be clear on what we want and need.

Gold: Are you mad? If you seem too serious, he'll never want to be with you. *Casual toh rehna padta hain.*

While the mating market was unequal, sex gave Gold a weapon with which she could combat men. 'Guys will be very nice to you till you take your clothes off,' she would say. But sex required sexiness. Gold was first introduced to her own sexiness in 1996, back in Jaisalmer, when she learned that someone had written 'Gold Is Sexy' on the wall in the boys' toilet. She was twelve years old and cried for hours at home where no one from school could see how she felt. She saw the message as damaging to her reputation. The way she described the episode and how she felt after, it was as if being classified as sexy somehow signalled her interest in sex. 'Of course, people wondered which horrible boy would write such things, but they also wondered why he had written these things *about me.* I was named, he never was.'

Between 1996 and 1999, though, the use of 'sexy' as a compliment became normalized, especially after Shah Rukh used it with nonchalance in film. Aspiring to be called 'sexy', as Indian women dominated global beauty pageants, was no longer so spiritually and morally questionable. Satellite television and international shows helped to make being 'sexy' seem almost wholesome, a synonym of 'young' or 'healthy'. As Gold put it, 'Suddenly, being sexy was a good thing. What girls wanted to be. Even boys.' But the road to sexiness also ultimately led to sex.

Gold had sex for the first time at the age of twenty-two with her first proper boyfriend, an egregiously muscular friend of her classmate from the air hostess academy. She described their relationship as an insipid transaction. He would show her off to his male friends, and in exchange, he would pay for her extravagances and offer protection from Jaipur's male gaze. 'Too many men were deewanas, following me around,' she added. The need for masculine protection from her personal fan club was hardly paranoia. Even in 2018, eighty per cent of victims of reported kidnapping and abduction cases were women. Between 2001 and 2017, data published by the Indian National Crime Records Bureau showed that 'love' was a far more frequent reason for the murder of women than terrorism. Beyond honour killings, it remains common for us to read reports of young single women being murdered for simply rejecting the romantic overtures of men interested in them. The pandemic was unable to halt such crimes against women; amidst the chaos of mounting COVID cases in June 2021, a twenty-one-year-old was stabbed to death by a male classmate she had rejected. 'Girls want gentlemen like Shah Rukh, but society forces you to need a body-builder type, a guy who looks intimidating to thugs and Romeos,' Gold theorized.

Six months before Gold received her job offer, her body-building boyfriend left her for a girl his parents chose for him. Gold, though, wondered if the sudden break-up was triggered by her inability to please him in bed. Being sexy, she thought, was far easier than being good at sex. She knew she was too conscious of her body's flaws to be comfortable naked. Her fears amplified the frenetic discovery of her faults. Her back-acne scars, her fat thighs, her hair, her large round face, her excessively angular nose, her weight, her skin colour—simply everything about her needed to change if she was ever going to satisfy and sustain a sexual encounter, without which there was no chance of securing a man's love. She became obsessed with the idea of achieving physical perfection. And there was no hiding behind the cult of nutrition and wellness. 'People just use all this health nonsense,' she would cynically say, 'as an excuse because no one wants to sound superficial. But everyone goes to the gym to look good in bed. I intend to look as good as possible, it's the only thing boys notice.'

Fitness and cosmetics conferred sexual confidence. Make-up transformed Gold. It wasn't merely a physical transformation, she applied concealer on her spirit, hoping to camouflage all her self-doubt with sexiness and cosmetic poise. Sexiness required a rigid routine. Waking up at four in the morning for her one-hour run—no matter where she was. Almonds. Dhaniya water steeped overnight. Morning potions and lotions, heavy vitamin intake. Meticulously researched, portioned, planned and prepared salads for lunch. Buttermilk at eleven, aloe water at noon, coconut water at three, tulsi water at four, green juices for dinner. Boxing training at the gym combined with pilates. Yoga in the evenings. Nighttime lotions and potions. Turmeric-rose full body ubtan on Saturdays. Fruit masks on Sundays. Weekly salon visits. *Cosmopolitan* for sex positions. American TV and films for an education in contemporary attitudes and language. Wax strips for the soul.

City Lights

In 2012, Gold had once again lost the ability to sleep. The French break-up played on her mind. Then there was the jet lag from her long international flights. Back home, her evening rituals would embody her loneliness. She would slump against the walls of her apartment and stare at the TV. Usually, she would have returned from an evening workout. Her trainer would have complimented her strength. Once done with the cardio routine, she would stand by the giant bay windows of the gym. The city of Gurgaon would seem like a museum object—an endless stream of headlights and honking cars.

Gurgaon, a village till the late 1980s, became a city in 1992. Its architecture and fortunes changed later that decade as India became a global outsourcing hub. Multinational companies, hunting for cheap office space to house thousands of employees in call centres, alighted on Gurgaon, with its abundance of land and relaxed acquisition policies. Its proximity to Delhi and the airport were especially attractive. Real-estate millionaires and tycoons emerged seemingly overnight. Alongside the high-rise office buildings mushroomed high-rise apartment buildings. An agglomeration fairy tale.

For Gold, life in Gurgaon had become an agglomeration of heartbreak, a lonely nightmare. She was convinced that she was missing out on some grand spiritual reward, that there was a version of a happier life being lived in Paris or Delhi's farmhouses that she desperately needed. At airports, at malls, at gyms, from her apartment, she would scan everybody. She believed that not one single person was as *single* as she was: her ex was with his ex-wife, her mother was with her father, everyone had someone. During her working hours, she would stare at families flying together. They went about their boring business. Mothers trying to calm screaming babies, husbands ordering meals for their wives, cousins exchanging family gossip and movie reviews. She experienced a persistent sense of isolation amidst a crowd, described by the cultural critic Olivia Laing as the very definition of loneliness. Gold felt suffocated by her singledom. Her loneliness was made more piquant by the constant company of twenty million boisterous people who lived in and around Delhi. As relief, she would close her eyes and conjure up her childhood courtyard in Jaisalmer, her safe space, where she danced and sang and played under an open sky.

One night, she called and complained. 'The problem is this flat. It feels so dark and closed.' Gold blamed her French ex for her cramped apartment. She had decided against renewing the lease to her old flat because the Frenchman had suggested she live with him in his Gurgaon company penthouse. Following their break-up, she was forced to find this small, empty apartment. 'These white foreigners are very tough,' Gold would complain on our calls. 'They can switch their feelings off like a tap. He was so caring and attentive when we were together. But in just a few weeks, all that changed. He came back from France and barely wanted to speak to me. I wasn't even invited to his farewell party when he left Delhi. I try and give him the benefit of the doubt, that he cut me off so things wouldn't become more painful and complicated. But you can't help feeling like you were used and thrown aside.'

At the time, I was in my own lonely limbo in Boston, on an academic island of red-brick buildings, starchy WASPs and fall foliage. Through a year-long stretch of calls and messages, Gold and I meditated on being solo. We talked without resolving any of our troubles. In fact, I was convinced we were enabling each other's melancholy. She wanted so much to be aloof and uncaring. For Gold was a creature of public bravado—of the Give-No-Fucks variety. She laughed at people for investing too much in men, too much in love. Now, she was embarrassed by her sadness. She felt she was constantly letting herself down, worried that her need to be with a man and to forge a family based on marriage contradicted her fight for independence from her own family. She would cry on the phone: 'I've worked so hard and done so well. Why doesn't anyone want to be with me? It feels like I fought all those years in Jaisalmer for nothing.'

Films and books tell us that loneliness does not discriminate by race, gender, language or location. That year in Gurgaon and Boston, despite all our differences, we both felt equally marked by our romantic failure. We were failures because the men we had chosen no longer chose us. We lacked the qualities needed to make us worthy of the human affection we craved. We would measure ourselves against other people, convinced we failed to possess what they did. We were always running a deficit: we weren't posh enough, powerful enough, pretty enough, polite enough, petite enough. We experienced loneliness as a chronic absence of virtue.

Compared to my life in a sparsely populated university town, surrounded by the lofty ambitions of academic automatons, Gold occupied a far busier social space. She was flooded with friends, party invitations and admirers. But her closest friends grew sick of her constant complaining, unsure of how best to help. They tried taking her out, they tried staying in with her, they tried offering counsel.

They championed her success, telling her that she was lucky to have a flat of her own.

Yet, this easy availability of support and company was never enough to calm her sense of seclusion. Most of her girlfriends were paired up, marrying or approaching marriage. And she was appalled at how her friends' romantic successes upset her ability to appreciate their love for her. Her body wasn't absorbing any emotional nutrition coming her way, she was avoiding compliments and friends like she would avoid carbs.

Loneliness is often confused with wanton self-pity. There is no pride in asserting loneliness, there aren't too many words either. The Hindi and Urdu language traditions valorize loneliness, but their poetry and art are obsessed with the notion of reunion. Shah Rukh is alone in his romance films because he finds himself in a constant state of yearning for his beloved. The films end with union, death or romantic detachment—the hero gives up on seeking his lover. This imagery is rooted in centuries of religious and mythic writing in Hindustani, Sufi and Sanskrit devotional texts. We are all alone because we are without God or a higher purpose. The lover simply sublimates this pursuit of spiritual awakening and self-discovery.

Sanskritized Hindi doesn't dominate how we express loneliness in north India. Some of us use words with Sanskrit roots such as 'akela', which means being single, or the word 'soonapan'. The latter is etymologically linked to 'shunya' which means zero, the void within. But 'tanhai', which is Persian tends to dominate in film vocabulary, carrying with it the promise of solitude and the pain of loneliness. Gold would never say she was 'tanha'. She would laugh and say, 'That's too dramatic.' For her, 'soonapan' was better but the English 'lonely' was best. I asked her if she could recall the first time she had come across the English word. She knew straightaway—it was in middle school, when she chose to read Brontë for a summer project.

I knew, on those lonely nights, as we stalked our respective love interests on social media, that we resembled the crazy people

Shah Rukh portrayed in his crazy films. It is surreal to think that the man who championed and embodied Indian middle-class notions of romantic love and sexual success since 1995 was once equally committed to portraying the dark side of chasing romantic fulfilment.

While Shah Rukh will always be south Asia's romantic superhero, his work in the early '90s as a lonely supervillain can't be forgotten. This body of work lent cinematic credence to the criminals that continue to stalk and harm Indian women in cities and small towns alike. Indeed, none of the women I met professed much love for these early films where he played the 'anti-hero'. But during this year that represented the dark nadir of our loneliness, Gold forced me to rediscover Shah Rukh's darker films.

There was Shah Rukh in *Darr* and *Anjaam*, where lovesick longing, sexual rejection and loneliness drive him into a murderous rage. There was Shah Rukh in *Baazigar*, where a longing to avenge and rehabilitate his family's reputation and his mother's honour drives him into another murderous rage. Anger, longing and loneliness were the package—and these images were intense explorations of how angry loneliness could make us. The films were portraits of south Asian incels before we knew who they were, the men for whom women were merely objects that excited lust and, inevitably, rage. Within their universe, women had no feelings or subjectivity of their own other than their instinct for self-preservation; their sole purpose appeared to be to stimulate men, to give voice and validation to male desire. A woman's preference for another man does not mean that the rejected lover must accept her choice. Instead, he must impose his will on her through violence.

In these films, the actor's character is always shown as having an unsatiated appetite for friendship, respect, recognition, love or his fair share. A man who is in a chronic state of deficit while everyone around him enjoys abundance. Each film has one or two scenes demonstrating his spiritual scarcity through clumsy and obvious Bollywood traditions. Stuttering and stammering in front of his beloved, witnessing an elite industrialist humiliate and assault his mother. In this phase of Shah Rukh's career, his characters self-harm and wound themselves repeatedly to *show* us the pain of loneliness. Two of his films from this period feature scenes in which his character carves the name of his beloved on his body with a knife, blood streaming from his self-inflicted wounds.

After her third viewing of *Darr*, a film in which Shah Rukh's character, Rahul, kidnaps a woman he is obsessively in love with, Gold announced that she could relate to and empathize with Rahul. I was stunned. Gold herself had been subject to creepy phone calls and men who followed her around the airport and on the street. Her friends stowed hockey sticks in their cars to protect themselves on north Indian roads. How could she relate to a stalker? But she felt she could connect with Rahul's rage. 'I remember the night the Frenchman broke up with me, he wanted to talk about it because he wanted me to make him feel better about dumping me so suddenly. He knew how sad I was, but he was keen to leave on civil terms so he could feel good about himself. So that he wouldn't have to deal with how selfish he had been.' She talked about their final words to each other, and the moment when he leaned in to give her the 'European fuck-off kiss' on her two cheeks. 'I know it sounds crazy,' she told me 'but I wanted to rip the skin off his face. So, when I watch Shah Rukh in these stalker films, I get it, yaar. I mean I wouldn't kidnap someone and physically harm their partners. But these ugly feelings are a part of all of us, no point pretending to be cool about it.'

When these films got too dark, Gold turned to other avatars of Shah Rukh for light. She watched *Jab Tak Hai Jaan* (2012) with her friends. He looked delicious. For those three hours, she felt uplifted. Thoughts of his sexiness lingered through the week. She masturbated, she dreamt crazy wild dreams about the hours he devoted to her neck and shoulders. That film, Yash Chopra's final directorial venture, helped Gold recover her sex drive.

After overdosing on the films, she traced the first half of a two-part documentary titled *The Inner and Outer World of Shah Rukh Khan* (2005) on YouTube; Drawing on its title, in the first part (*Inner World of Shah Rukh Khan*), film-maker Nasreen Munni Kabir and photographer Peter Chappell followed the actor for three weeks to chronicle his 'inner world'. The film is remarkable in its portrayal of the sadness and loneliness of its superstar protagonist. Shah Rukh opens up about his sister's depression, his own depression and his struggles with pain and illness. There are long shots of him alone, receiving treatment for his excruciating back pain. I interviewed Kabir and asked her if the actor's loneliness was an unintended capture of the film.

Kabir was unsurprised by Gold's use of the film as therapy for sadness. Many viewers had reached out to her, thanking her for the many moving moments in the film. The *Inner World of Shah Rukh Khan* was a Channel Four TV UK production, filmed by a crew of four people in 2004. The documentary was unscripted and captured Khan responding to questions by Kabir as he traversed his days. There are uninhibited sequences of him talking, smoking a cigarette while he drives himself to the doctor and the film studio. The documentary is astonishing in how up-close and intimate it feels. There were moments when I wanted to look away, as they felt far too personal.

The film trails the actor as he shoots for *Main Hoon Na* and struggles with his back pain. Reflecting on the film-making process, Kabir said, 'Documentaries happen by accident. If you design them, then it's not a documentary. Everything happens because people react to each other. The more you film, the more you develop a sense of trust. In 2004, he came to trust us. He probably responded to our questions in an open way, you don't see or hear the questions as we edited those out. At that time, he was facing great physical pain, and when you're in pain, you're a bit drawn into yourself. He allowed us to see the spiritual side of him, and by that I don't mean his religious side, I mean his spirit. It did come through in parts of the movie. The loneliness you see is also because people are so insensitive when it comes to celebrities. I remember we filmed a scene when he went to his parents' grave and the people around him just did not leave him alone to pray. In fact, I was very moved by what he said. When he went there, our crew kept our distance. He turned to us and said that we weren't greedy people and how most people would have been filming in his face as he prayed. I think he noticed that we respected his space. And I was amazed he let us film his family, especially his sister and the Diwali celebration.'

Kabir and I talked for hours. 'What was unusual for a star was that he did not at all restrict us on filming. We could film him twenty-four hours, even when he was not shaved. He did not worry that we did not capture his best profile. He was not vain. He is not a vain man; he is conscious of how much he is loved and his fan following. But he is not vain. Which is why you can make a documentary that is moving. People who are vain and worried about their hair and looks don't come across as natural, and the audience can pick up on it.'

Vanity murders vulnerability, it ensures the end of all authentic feeling. In that time of chronic loneliness, Shah Rukh's unusual openness and vulnerability captured by a British film crew came to Gold's rescue. Soon, she started devouring all his interviews. The star was one of the few Indian actors to discuss his battles with depression and the lonely life openly. Gold devoured all these films and words, possessed by the desire to find comfort in her hero's past travels through loneliness. His words and images became her refuge. As she started to feel better, she decided to look for a new apartment with more sunlight.

I took Gold's frustrations with her Gurgaon apartment to Bijoy Jain, a Mumbai-based architect-artist-professor credited for 'creating a new architectural language' by the *New York Times*. His lectures are unusual, often relying on philosophical provocations on the notions of 'affection' and 'lore' to help guide an understanding of architectural sites as spaces of overlapping histories, energies and materials. Amused by the tales of fan-admiration, Jain told me that Gold's nostalgia for her Jaisalmer courtyard had less to do with aesthetics, the binaries of interior-exterior or feelings of exposure, than the need for a space of 'containment and nourishment'. That, he said, 'is what a home is. The courtyard isn't about an open or closed space, it's simply us seeking an imaginative possibility that did not exist earlier. So, based on what you're telling me, the actor became the courtyard, a holding space, a small opening postulated in a tightly confined environment.' Shah Rukh served, in Jain's reading, as a stand-in for her childhood courtyard, as an idea to expel her anguish. His imagery sheltered Gold's darkness.

In those dark days in her dark apartment in Gurgaon, a small-budget film administered the final elixir for hope. While most fan-women loved Shah Rukh's romantic preoccupations as Raj or Rahul, or his performances in interviews and 'serious films', for Gold, there was only Sunil from *Kabhi Haan Kabhi Naa*. Shah Rukh himself described Sunil as a uniquely '90s character. In an interview, he said, 'I really feel the '90s were amazing as they taught us that it was not special to be special, but special to be ordinary. Cinema reflects society, so there were movies also where it was all right for the hero to go wrong. So, I played a loser who was conventionally unsuccessful but who people could identify with.'

Heroes in Hindi films rarely lose the girl. If they do, they become drunks or, worse, become obsessive and violent. Shah Rukh's performance as Sunil taught us to lose love with self-acceptance and grace. In 1994, *Kabhi Haan Kabhi Naa* was made on a shoestring budget and became, unexpectedly, a box-office hit. The film charts the journey of Sunil, a young man in Goa. He longs for acceptance from his father and the love of his childhood friend Anna. Both pursuits lead to despair. His father will only confer approval if Sunil abandons his love for music in favour of a steady job. Meanwhile, Anna expresses her love for Sunil's posh, muscular and attractive friend Chris. Convinced he doesn't have the attributes to impress either Anna or his father, the film follows Sunil's comical struggles to lie and cheat his way into acceptability.

Due to a family feud between Anna's and Chris's family, Sunil ends up being Anna's prospective groom. But he recognizes how much Anna loves Chris and decides to step aside and help the couple resolve their troubles and marry. It's impossible not to melt into a puddle of empathy for Shah Rukh's depiction of Sunil's romantic loss. You feel sorry for Sunil, but you never think he is a sorry character. His inability to secure Anna's love is no cause for shame. This arc is different from Shah Rukh's later films where he *always* gets the girl, where he offers sexist lessons on how to get the girl ('*che din ladki in*'), and where his characters classify men who do not receive a positive response from women as 'losers'.

In *Kabhi Haan Kabhi Naa*'s closing sequence, after Anna's wedding, Sunil is seated alone on the pavement accompanied by his saxophone; a woman approaches him to enquire after an address. The audience understands that Sunil has found a companion. As the film closes, they spot a shooting star. After watching the film five times in two weeks, Gold said, 'I don't know why they brought her in. It would be fine to end the film with him alone. It felt so fake. He will be okay no matter what. It's fine to be single.'

In her exploration of loneliness in a megacity, writer Olivia Laing says, 'There is a gentrification that is happening to cities, and there is a gentrification that is happening to the emotions too, with a similar homogenizing, whitening, deadening effect.' By 2013, love and life in India had globalized and gentrified. Gurgaon's villages had redeveloped into malls and gated complexes. Rajasthan's cities reported young people drinking cappuccinos. Shah Rukh had gentrified from a lonely-crazy stalker to a Westernized-dimpled superstar. And girls like Gold were expected to globalize and gentrify their bodies and hearts. They were expected to look like white women with lean frames while preserving their 'authentic Indian beauty' and 'curves'. They were expected to endure romantic competition with French-speaking women while abandoning their favourite Bollywood romances and gatte-ki-sabzi for Euro-centric notions of high culture. They were expected to negotiate a new mating market all alone, a cost they happily bore as a price for their freedom from arranged marriages and unfair community ties. They were expected to have sex like porn stars before marriage but await a marriage proposal (like good sanskari girls) before falling fully in love. They were expected to be sexy, but not too much. To seem interested but not that interested. To date, but not date too many people.

Unlike her mother and her sisters who chose conformity in Jaisalmer over freedom in Gurgaon, Gold had no intermediary helping her navigate the world of men. She relied on her colleagues and her own good sense for decisions on how to manage her career, but her personal life had very limited resources for guidance. Her close friends had less experience of the kinds of relationships she found herself in, none had dated foreigners or playboys. They had married early. Gold could no longer rely on a Khatri pre-written rulebook on how to find romantic companionship. Unable to rely on pre-existing cultural resources, Gold relied on American talk shows and self-help books. She watched everything—from episodes of *The Bachelor*, to talks by Helen Fischer to advice from the Kardashian sisters. She desperately needed these guideposts as she was expected to continually decode and negotiate the meaning of new rituals of romance. What did the sex mean? What did the long dinners and conversations imply? Who was he checking out and should she be worried? Gold was not expected to ask tough questions directly though, scared of scaring men away.

Gold continued toiling to find the right kind of love because she expected more from marriage than any of the women in her family. She knew her parents loved each other, but it was a union sustained by obligation more than passion. 'I don't think my parents were ever in love. I mean, I know it fades, but I don't think it ever happened for them. They barely speak to each other. It's the same for my sister. They married to have stable lives as they did not work outside, and they married not only the boy but his whole family. My sister married the man she did because she liked her mother-in-law. That was important for her because she was going to live with them forever. But I wanted to love the man I married.' The husband would be a lover, friend and counsellor. A vessel to actuate her personhood.

As we befriend the shiny discos and sequined dresses of contemporary life in India, we have all tacitly decided to believe that loneliness is weakness. That feelings of inadequacy are simply personal petty faults faced by those who lack maturity or self-belief. In the wonderful *Kabhi Haan Kabhi Naa*, the remedy for our hero's loneliness did not lie in him securing his heart's desire. Nor did he forge a false sense of cool or deny his hurt. The remedy required our hero to mine his lonely heart for some self-knowledge, to sit silently on a pavement and hold himself, to embrace the romantic inequality of the world, to wish on a star for the ability to move on.

A sexless year later, as she approached the age of thirty-one, Gold met Captain America—an American pilot who was a decade older. Her elder sister and brother, who had helped her effectively escape Jaisalmer, attended the wedding. This time, she paid for their ticket fare. Captain America was smitten at first sight. Gold was reluctant, burned too often by love. She agreed to a dinner date in London on a stopover. A month later, he suggested a holiday. He kissed her neck and her back. And that was enough for Gold.

Captain America held no high-culture zeal, he was an Indophile and loved the smell of curry. He felt no urge to educate or reform her. 'Everyone is surprised that I'm with him,' Gold says, 'but it's love.' After the wedding, Gold gave up on contacting her father. He had refused to attend. She visited Delhi briefly in 2017 to remove her acne scars, watch *Jab Harry Met Sejal* and meet her loved ones. During the visit, she called her mother secretly, only to be greeted with gracious excuses to shorten the conversation. But Gold no longer cared. She had forged her own family made up of a loving husband, loyal friends and a pair of supportive siblings. On the topic of her family, she often quoted a cult line from Shah Rukh's 1993 hit, *Baazigar*. She would say, 'The person who wins after losing is called a gambler.' *Haar ke jeetne wale ko baazigar kehte hain.* She had gambled by running away from home and had, through sleeplessness and sweat, turned 'defeat' into freedom. Her grit and the love of an American husband emancipated her from the life of a single-service professional in Delhi. She lives with Captain America in their beautiful home in Denver. 'I don't have to follow anyone's orders or wake up at odd hours for shifts,' she once told me over the phone. 'It is peaceful here, away from India. Maybe, someday, I'll visit Delhi again.' I never expected her to return.

8

Lost in Liberalization

In my late twenties…all the (old) systems started to feel less reliable….By the time I was forty, I was flying…and humanity was soaring with me. We were both pretty much flying off the handle actually.

—*Shah Rukh Khan, 2017*

We keep talking about modern India, we keep talking about New India. But we'll just keep talking…

—*Shah Rukh Khan, 2015*

Once you follow fan-women, patterns start to emerge. By the late 1990s, the country's elite and neo-middle class had developed a cumulative crush on Sachin Tendulkar, the Miss India pageant and Shah Rukh Khan. Educated urban fans would borrow language from the media and tell me that Shah Rukh was India's first 'post-liberalization superstar'. But if you had limited access to the media, little awareness of Manmohan Singh's 1991 budget speech, were unable to read newspapers and did not understand terms like 'GDP' and 'reforms', Shah Rukh *was liberalization*. The actor announced India's telecom revolution and its spiffier economy.

As an uneducated working-class woman, you might not have had the words or jargon to sum up the phenomenon, but you knew something dramatic had happened in the mid '90s; the evidence was everywhere you looked. So, you wove images into a timeline of your own. You told me that your world, quite literally, started to shrink—the forests of Jharkhand, the textile factories of Gujarat, the farm yields of Bengal, the hemlines of Delhi's skirts, the certainty of a man earning a monthly income. Your world expanded too: the government gave more grains; activists, panchayat meetings, new advertising billboards and polio camps dotted the year; roads began to connect every village to the rest of the country. The patwari, effectively the local land registrar, began to wear jeans. Well-meaning women visited every month, saying they were health workers. Your children started receiving meals at the new government school. The local store offered a buffet of creams and powders, choices one only imagined available to actresses and princesses. Phone booths became ubiquitous. Your call was almost certain to connect. And, as India turned the corner into a new millennium, Shah Rukh's face was plastered everywhere.

Men started to move away from their fields and find jobs in cities, bringing artefacts and diseases from the modern world as presents. Suddenly, everyone you knew worked on a construction site. The earth smelled of cement and rubber. Royals became hoteliers. You found yourself orphaned from all the familiar routines—everything had a price, farming was no longer an ideal way of life, news from other parts of the world travelled faster than ever before.

Notebandi destroyed your chances of watching Shah Rukh's November 2016 release. Instead of the local movie theatre, you were forced to queue up for hours at the local ATM with your family. Family earnings drooped thereafter, just like your husband's shoulders. Shah Rukh's films were no longer the year's biggest hits.

Now, nearly three decades after the government unleashed the post-liberalization era of cash, communication and construction, a virus arrives. Your icon is already on a break from film, promising to return after the pandemic retreats. You know his charm will survive this calamity. You're less sure of your own survival and the fate of your cousins in Delhi. But this precarity of life and livelihoods is nothing new, you've been working from home for generations. Jobs will be lost; more debts will be incurred; daughters will eat smaller meals; the sick will die undignified deaths; new ways of life will be found. Every generation has witnessed the dance of crisis and resilience, but you complain that none of these changes have ushered a radical shift in who fetches the water, who cooks and cleans, and who feels entitled to disrespect you. And no generation of women before you had Shah Rukh Khan. Perhaps, none needed him. None have been as lost as you.

—m—

Beyond women being discouraged by culture and wage gaps, there are broadly four theories to explain why they drop out of the workforce in India in such large numbers. *An income effect*—as incomes rise, even once-cash-strapped families start to believe that they can do without women's earnings. A more hopeful theory is an *education effect*—fewer woman in the labour force as a result of more women in school. The third is an *underestimation effect*—women are working but in ways that are not captured by standard surveys. Echoing other research, my own paper with Ratna Sudarshan for the ILO in Delhi suggests that relying on student volunteers for data collection—with rigorous training on how to probe for women's economic roles—can significantly increase the female employment rate captured by surveys.

Finally, there is the theory that women are dropping out of the workforce predominantly due to *the structural transformation of the economy*. What does that mean? In plain speak, job creation over the past two decades has taken place in sectors in which women are less willing or able to work, while job opportunities have reduced in industries that usually employ women. Academics find that employment gains from growth have largely accrued to men in India, with women accessing less than nineteen per cent of jobs created in the country's ten fastest-growing sectors.

Rural India has driven the sharp drops in female employment. Between 1999 and 2017, increased access to primary education has led to married rural women leaving agriculture and becoming full-time unpaid caregivers. Economists argue that, with some amount of schooling, women's value as producers of their children's nutrition, education and human capital becomes more profitable to the family than their value as rural paid workers outside the home. Since the early years of the new millennium, rural job creation has mostly been in construction and services, which hire more men. Unlike men, women have been substantially displaced from farm-based jobs without gains in other types of work. So, what kinds of jobs occupy the dwindling Indian female workforce?

Despite the drop in rural women's employment in farming, seven out of ten rural working women continue to be engaged in agriculture compared to five out of ten rural working men. According to the government's employment data, a quarter of urban working women are engaged in manufacturing, with the majority of this work taking place within small-scale informal home-based garment enterprises with low pay and no social security. In urban India, six out of ten working women are employed by the service industry. Within services, women work across a range of occupations. A third of all urban working women are professionals within institutions, private sector jobs or government administration. This includes teachers (thirteen per cent), corporate managers (eight per cent) and nurses (2.5 per cent). Then there are domestic helpers and personal care workers (eleven per cent), housekeeping and restaurant service staff (five per cent) and salespersons at shops (five per cent).

As a research assistant at the start of my professional life, between 2006 and 2010, I spent several hours interviewing women who had fused together their work and home lives: domestic workers, for instance, and home-based workers manufacturing garments or incense sticks. These interviews were meant to help create profiles of workingwomen for scholars and advocacy. To ease into conversation or to disrupt the monotony of survey questions, I would always ask the women I met about their favourite film stars and popular culture. This recess from formal research introduced me to Shah Rukh fans from agrarian communities and India's precariat. These breaks became necessary, as the women found most of my questions about their working conditions dull and depressing. Often, I was told that poor women worked when men were no longer able to keep up the breadwinning end of the marriage contract. Women who enjoyed their financial independence said their access to jobs and wages depended on 'maryada'.

In its most common usage, maryada, or modesty, connotes social traditions and boundaries, the mores and norms a woman must abide by to earn love and respect from her family and immediate community. Being decent and dutiful makes you pure, lovable and worthy of a good man. Maryada is malleable, taking different shapes and forms across the country. In Delhi, it means women should be home before it gets dark. For migrants from Jharkhand, it means women should avoid the purchase of lipsticks and must regularly attend church. Maryada becomes a ghunghat in Gujarat or purdah in western Uttar Pradesh. Maryada means loving one's children, finding the most profound meaning and resonance in caring for one's home. Most importantly, maryada means self-discipline: don't giggle or act silly, hold yourself solely accountable for household honour or dirty dishes, don't be selfish, don't wear jeans, never make decisions independent of your family, never express desire, never buy things for yourself, never discuss your favourite actor in public or watch films alone. Maryada maps the boundaries of what is appropriate or 'normative behaviour' for a woman, what she ought to do and be, demarcating the possibilities for her spirit and self.

For the elite and middle class in India, those featured in previous parts of this book, being modern has become equated with nurturing well-educated and well-groomed girls who study the liberal arts in college and work until they're married. Young men are burdened with excelling in real estate, finance or engineering and becoming the sole providers and protectors of their family. In the past ten years, the share of women pursuing management, engineering, mathematics, science or economics remains slight. Girls often study subjects which relegate us to lightweight status in the labour market, blunting our competitiveness in the economy, priming us to give up employment as our paid labour will never match our value as the unpaid managers of our households.

Our time in the labour market can feel like extended adolescence, a purgatorial period before we enter matrimonial heaven. Whatever the work we do, adult life will only begin once we've formed our particular monogamous married unit, or so we've been told. The hyper-elite imbibe the *Sex and the City* couture and chatter, treating the Western woman's financial independence (Carrie pays her own rent) as yet another expensive elusive accessory. But we've been programmed to await marriage, willing to radically alter our careers and personal trajectories for the 'ideal' man.

None of us is a brainwashed idiot. Elite and middle-class women often join the workforce planning to continue in employment regardless of marriage or children. But pragmatism trumps our principles. We bargain with patriarchy. Managing work and family life become too heavy a burden to bear alone. The casual sexism of the office environment—its bro-codes, power cliques and alpha males—gnaws away at our professional enthusiasm. The fact that men at our workplaces are paid much more than us for doing the same jobs, while treating us as somehow less serious, less willing to work hard, only serves to make it easier for us to quit. We, willingly or grudgingly, retreat into part-time, flexible arrangements at best, or, more likely, abandon the workplace altogether. A select few find men who see a woman's work outside the home as a non-negotiable part of who she is; men who don't view helping at home as irregular favours but a non-negotiable part of who they are.

For women from low-income communities with far more precarious lives, the vagaries of the market can bring freedom in the guise of necessity. Food prices spiral out of control, farming becomes unviable, a man's factory job is no longer stable enough to manage everyday expenses, a local contractor starts helping women move to cities for domestic work, the government makes educating girls a priority and announces various livelihood schemes to hire and train women. The need to step outside the home, to learn and work, provides the freedom to make new friends, to lie about your whereabouts and never return. But these freedoms aren't free. You are taxed by tradition, bound by maryada. Families reluctantly allow women greater exposure to the world beyond what is socially palatable but wax eloquent about custom and tradition as a means to try to reassert control.

Across class and social location, working women traverse this tightrope between markets, modernity and maryada all alone. Many ordinary women are taught to internalize these trade-offs early on, charting a sense of self heavily dependent on men, family and marriage. It is foolish to say that this is a terrible or coercive act, or that all women should abandon finding meaning in married life and family. It is also facile to suggest that as women, we have no choice, or to blame 'society' and 'markets' as monolithic institutions that discriminate against us. For many of us, a life without marriage, children and a good man is deemed spiritually incomplete and socio-economically risky.

If you are to be deviant and treat work as a vocation as opposed to a pitstop en route to marriage, you must continuously produce other evidence that you are a 'good' woman. This is a price you pay for testing the boundaries of cultural permissibility. You must prove yourself in the workplace. You seek these proofs to address your own guilt for wanting *more*, not to satiate the scrutinizing public. At home, you must care, cook and clean with ease and élan—and always watch yourself. You might look to your partner for support but in vain. Despite his best intentions, he too is compelled and configured to enforce tradition. Your status as a paid worker is a constant reminder of his weakening market power. As his market worth declines, so does his self-worth. He recedes from you; there may be violence, daily annoyances or even cheating. Too often, you find yourself in tears. In these moments, you realize you expected too much from him. You are alone. And there is Shah Rukh. Offering conjugality on your terms. As real men retreat, superstars gain more glory. An ideal man is found in fantasy. You scour the landscape of everyday life, but he is nowhere to be found.

Most of the women I interviewed, those with well-paid office-based jobs, expressed a deep-seated discomfort with the everyday demands of deadlines, dishes and dignity. Their lack of free time and their perpetual exhaustion often experienced as an obvious part of *being* a working woman. Being perpetually out of breath while continually keeping track of one's appearance, home and work became the natural order of things. Men have their woes; exhaustion from performing domestic and emotional labour is rarely one of them.

But what if, one day, a woman in the slums of Delhi or the villages of western UP—a woman with little exposure to the literature, theories and icons of radical feminism—woke up and caught the undeniable stench of a patriarchal conspiracy? What if the natural order of things began to appear cosmetic? What if she felt trapped by all those unwashed utensils? What if she discovered more meaningful ways of being a person than being a good wife or a dutiful daughter? What if the world of community organizing, metropolitan gossip, cinema halls, malls, factory floors, office spaces and local bazaars held more excitement and meaning for her than she'd even begun to suspect? What if making things for strangers was more meaningful than making lentils for your children? What if she preferred being a paid manager of garment orders to being an unpaid manager of her household? And what if these forays into different ways of being and doing were actively foiled by her family and her loved ones? In a world where the state can't protect or provide, would she decide to abandon the family? What if the meaning and validation offered by 'loving one's family' started to feel empty, discounted by its resulting exhaustion and discrimination?

In the absence of organized resistance, what language would she use to describe feeling discriminated? Where would she find counsel and comfort? Could she turn to Shah Rukh? Could she spend her days daydreaming, slacking off on household chores and meditating instead on mustard fields and the Swiss Alps?

III

Work from Home

9

Surveyors

The Horror not to be surveyed.

—*Emily Dickinson on loneliness*

It all started with a survey. In 2006, one could only describe me as a devoted member of the Development Studies tribe. After completing my master's, I was earnest, eager and gifted at glibly using data to hide my smug saviour complex. All the while, I anticipated and dreaded disillusionment. Like many students of development, I was academically groomed to be a firm believer in the cult of the Survey. I could not wait to find the 'field', to produce 'rigorous research' which would urge 'policymakers' to reassess the effectiveness of various government interventions. I was possessed by words such as 'patriarchy' and 'agency'. Having studied gender and development, I found a pulpit for my inner zealot at the Institute of Social Studies Trust, a humble think-tank working with humble budgets on humble issues. One such enterprise was a research project with HomeNet, UNIFEM and SEWA Union.

SEWA, or the Self-Employed Women's Association, emerged from the activities of the women's wing of Ahmedabad's Textile

Labour Association. The organization was established by Ela Bhatt as a registered trade union in April 1972. With over two million participating members, SEWA is the largest organization of poor and informal women workers in the world. Informal workers are those who do not receive traditional office-based benefits of paid leave, medical support and employee-financed retirement pensions, usually working ad-hoc jobs without any written contracts. A sizeable proportion of jobs in India are informal. In 2018, even among women engaged in regular salaried or wage-earning jobs outside agriculture, 66.5 per cent had no written job contracts while fifty-four per cent were not eligible for social security.

Back in 2006, my first research project at ISST aimed to collect data on 'home-based workers' in the informal economy. As the name suggests, home-based work was a catch-all phrase for those engaged in paid jobs within their own homes. Our findings would be used by SEWA and its sister organization HomeNet to make the risks and working conditions of such workers more visible. ISST hoped to gain some visibility as well.

When we think of poorly protected jobs resulting from the globalization process, we imagine factory-based sweatshops serving the demands of international fashion labels. This has undoubtedly been the experience of east Asia and countries like Bangladesh, where women dominate the export-oriented manufacturing workforce, accounting for close to seventy per cent of workers in these sectors. Contrary to the data in these countries, the proportion of women working in India's Special Economic Zones (SEZs) declined from 46.5 per cent in 1981 to thirty-seven per cent in 2003, with a further drop to thirty-three per cent in 2008. In December 2019, government data revealed that nearly two million people were employed by SEZs in India. The distribution of men and women isn't available. Even if we assumed that all these workers were women, employment in factories within SEZs would be dwarfed by the 17.2 million women engaged in home-based work. Instead of factories, a dominant share of women in India participate in the economy from their own homes—be it for homestead agriculture (4.7 million women) or the home-based production of goods and services.

Working from home remains a core feature of women's jobs in manufacturing. According to a report by statistician G. Raveendran for the global NGO Women in Informal Employment: Globalizing and Organizing (WIEGO), sixty-four per cent of Indian women employed in the manufacturing sector worked from home in 2017, as opposed to fifteen per cent of men. Despite home-based work being a fairly femininized occupation, women earn ₹24 an hour, while men earn double that amount.

The home serving as the principal workplace of most of India's working women shouldn't surprise any of us. Long before 'work from home' became a public health measure, only paid employment within the home was palatable to families who feared the world outside was unsafe for their women. This form of work provided a cultural cushion for families who thought women working outside the home would bring them shame and dishonour, for whom the presence of women in the public sphere meant the invitation of male sexual attention, harassment or premarital disgrace. Working for wages within their own homes also allowed women to combine paid work with unpaid caregiving, while allowing enterprises to exploit what feminists describe as the 'nimble fingers' of women at lower cost.

Three sectors employ the largest share of home-based workers: garments, textiles and tobacco products. In the late 1990s and early 2000s, women were engaged by industries as part of subcontracted value chains. Garment manufacturers would source apparel pieces or embroidery from wholesale contractors. These contractors relied on an army of subcontractors who would pay women to stitch, dye, embroider and tailor individual pieces of textiles at home. Such jobs were by-products of India's rendezvous with global trade and modern telecommunications. Technology and transport allowed businesses to divide work between homes and factories across multiple locations. Contractors could coordinate cost-effectively with workers through phones. The opening of India's economy offered many such unstable jobs to women. However, these workers were barely visible in discussions on the economy itself.

Home-based work challenged the traditional framework used by economists and governments to understand economic activities. It defied the dominant economic and political language of the 'economic man' who negotiates selfishly with the market for work, income and personal gain. *Homo economicus*, the rational economic man, enjoys a clean separation between the home and the world. The home was conceived as a feminine domain, devoted to care, rest and recreation, far away from the pressures of pay and profit. Activists and workers had to validate home-based work as an authentic and legitimate form of labour, which required government regulation and social protection. Within the broader context of the Unorganized Social Security Bill—a piece of legislation debated in the Indian Parliament in 2005 and passed as an act in 2008—activism around the informal economy had achieved tremendous momentum. SEWA and partners were keen to make visible the contributions and concerns of India's hidden home-bound female workforce. ISST's work was meant to provide perspective on the wages and working conditions of women engaged in home-based trades. The team identified three sectors for study—incense sticks, garments and tobacco products. The plan was to use these survey findings to advocate for social security measures for such workers.

Following an initial month of writing research briefs, my mentor and employer suggested that I visit the SEWA union office to conduct interviews with workers and unionists in Ahmedabad. I showed up at the Lal Darwaja office, excited but not knowing what to expect.

—⁂—

In 2006, I met Keoliben and Zahiraben at SEWA's Ahmedabad premises. I interrupted the weekly meeting. The proceedings always started with the attendees singing prayers representing all the faiths in India. After these songs of gratitude, I was introduced to a small group of SEWA's community organizers who had helped collect data on incense-stick workers in the city. Zahira was a member of this group. The women were well known in some of Ahmedabad's poorest slums. They had acquired a giant scale of self-assurance. Within the neighbourhoods of Bapunagar and Allah Nagar, where they helped organize women workers, the group seemed to know everyone's secrets, they could even recite everyone's monthly bills. Zahira Pathan was a petite woman with perfect nails and henna-coloured hair. At five feet two inches, she was the shortest in the group, but her self-confidence helped her tower over most. Zahira Pathan was so fierce, there were stories going around of her beating up a maulana. Nobody seemed to know the truth of the matter or what exactly had happened. And no one dared to ask her. If you had lent money to someone and needed to collect, you could rely on Zahira's powers of persuasion.

'Agarbatti Colony' was a colloquial name used by the women to describe part of an upgraded slum within the larger Bapunagar settlement in Ahmedabad. The 'upgrade' meant that there was a functional, if open-air and malarial, sewage system. Named after agarbattis, or incense sticks, the production of which employed many inhabitants, the neighbourhood was sustained by industry, faith and women like Keoliben and Zahiraben. Across Bapunagar, reeling from the 2002 riots, I noticed that Hindus and Muslims frequently comingled. Yet, they were increasingly segregated, each occupying their own micro-enclaves within the settlement. Both communities remained largely self-employed, working as street vendors and running their own small informal enterprises. Some worked as wage-labourers in power-loom units or small repair shops. The area was surrounded by ten incense stick factories, which needed a steady supply of raw materials and workers.

As middle-class Indian pockets grew deeper, families had more disposable income to spend on religious rituals and the accompanying paraphernalia. Strong domestic consumer demand coupled with an increasing global taste for 'Eastern' spirituality had been a boon for the agarbatti workers of Bapunagar and India's incense-stick manufacturers. Exports grew from US$48 million in 1990 to US$130 million in 2018. In 2020, the government reported that 1,490 tonnes of incense sticks were purchased in India every day. The industry employs nearly two million people and women dominate the manufacturing of incense sticks.

Zahira was a home-based garment worker and incense-stick maker. She lived in a Muslim-dominated corner—a fifteen-minute walk from Agarbatti Colony—in Bapunagar. Every week, she would collect orders from the local tailor. Stitching and dying clothes at home constituted the larger share of her workload. She sold some wedding jewellery to buy a durable sewing machine. The machine was her lifeline, allowing her to work quickly and fulfil more orders. To augment her earnings, she started taking small orders to make incense sticks as well. This work introduced her to other home-based incense-stick workers in the neighbourhood. She would walk to Agarbatti Colony every few days to collect her wages and discuss new orders with the other women. Zahira would collect a batch of hand-slit thin bamboo sticks from her local contractor. After washing the sticks, she would prepare a paste of charcoal powder and adhesive. Eventually, the charcoal and adhesive mixture would be rolled onto the incense sticks by hand and left to dry in the sun. The rolling required her to sit on the floor and hunch over a small wooden board. The completed sticks would be collected by her subcontractor. He would deliver the finished goods to the local incense-stick factories. The factory machines would douse the sticks in a chemical mixture for fragrance. Factory labour was responsible for packaging and polishing the final product. In 2004, she was paid ₹8 for rolling a thousand agarbatti sticks at home. In a month, she would earn a maximum of ₹500 from agarbattis and nearly ₹2,000 from garment work, or less than a quarter of the minimum wage. This money, in addition to monthly support from her brother in Surat, and the subsidized grains provided by the government's food programme, helped keep her afloat.

Bapunagar was created when Ahmedabad was a booming textile centre in India. In the early '60s, the neighbourhood grew to serve as a residential area for low-income mill workers. Many of these mills closed in the late '80s, displacing factory workers and forcing them to turn to casual labour, home-based businesses and migrant work outside Ahmedabad. Men no longer held regularly paid and steady jobs. Incomes from street vending were increasingly compromised by strict city regulations prohibiting where and how workers could sell their wares. And while women in Hindu and Muslim communities have been historically far more present in public space in states such as Gujarat compared to the north of India, female employment was always low. With the onslaught of inflation and factory closures, women needed to work and earn an independent income. Like Zahira, most women in the neighbourhood started helping in the local manufacture of garments, tobacco products, boxes, incense sticks and kites. Home-based work was a shared occupation for women across religions. Muslim women were more active in home-based garment work, while Hindu women were dominant in home-based manufacturing of incense sticks. The flexible nature of the work allowed women to decide how much effort to invest based on their monthly or weekly needs for money. I had even noticed some young girls rolling incense sticks to buy a dress during dandiya season. The perfumes and raw materials used by the local incense factories along with home-based production of sticks marked the colony, the drains smelling of dirt, charcoal and devotion.

Zahira claimed that her laugh was as large as her heart. She had been a member of SEWA since 1998. In 2000, she joined a few women in her neighbourhood to become a community organizer. She was in her early twenties and played an essential part in one of India's most successful women's labour campaigns, helping SEWA deepen its mobilization of poor women who manufactured incense sticks as part of a citywide struggle to demand higher wages and welfare benefits from employers. Since the '90s, SEWA had organized home-based workers. Such mobilization had been successful, ensuring that agarbatti workers were included in the official state government schedule of minimum wages. However, translating these policies into actual practice would require sustained activism. The union would also need to grow and address occupational health hazards faced by the women. The needs of garment workers and other types of home-based trades needed to be reflected as well.

Between 2002 and 2005, Zahira was part of a group of SEWA members who convinced nearly a hundred women to join SEWA's union and agitate for more pay and social security. She would spend days and nights sitting with families, trying to explain to the women and their relatives why organizing and joining a women's group was important. In her early years, she would focus on talking to Muslim garment workers who lived near her home. However, as efforts to unionize agarbatti workers accelerated, she felt deep passion for the cause. During informal meetings with local SEWA organizers, she stressed on the importance of integrating the small share of Muslim women who undertook agarbatti work into the larger union. From her own experience, she knew that these women were usually breadwinners for precarious homes, in desperate need of solidarity and multiple jobs. The local incense-stick industries were powerful. Fighting them for increased wage rates and benefits was a daunting prospect. Through years of relentless conversations on women's labour struggles, Zahira emerged as an important organizer in her slum in Ahmedabad.

There were no flashy leaders in their labour struggle. The sisterhood had limited appetite for superstars. Through the efforts of numerous community organizers like Zahira, SEWA was able to organize nearly 10,000 agarbatti workers in Ahmedabad city. In 2006, a few months before my research started, workers were involved in annual negotiations with government labour department officials and employers. These negotiations led to an increase in piece rates paid for agarbattis by ₹1.50 for each bundle of 1,000 sticks and an agreement that these wage rates would be subject to revision every two years. During these discussions, workers had also voiced their demands for housing support, welfare funds and social protection to government and industry representatives.

Beyond activism for wages and work conditions, SEWA also helped members by connecting women to affordable financial services, such as interest-subsidized loans, health insurance and micro-savings products. These were small-money products, designed to suit families with low and irregular incomes. At the time, housing security and tenure were of utmost concern to everyone I met. Families were worried about the safety of their homes in slums and upgraded colonies. In the early 2000s, the Gujarat government was in the mood to build mega cities across the state. The pattern of urbanization pursued in Ahmedabad necessitated freeing up land for infrastructure development. Riots and urban demolitions had wrecked communities in the city, creating urban ghettos and homelessness. Many of the union members' homes in Bapunagar were plots provided by municipal authorities and the Islamic Relief Committee in the '70s and '80s following the communal riots of 1969 and 1985, and these homes were constantly under threat of demolition or damage.

SEWA and its Mahila Housing Trust helped women obtain exclusive housing loans to buy and build property nearby. But only two of the hundred or so members mobilized by Zahira's group had procured loans themselves. Both were widows. Men would usually apply for loans on behalf of their families, despite SEWA-affiliated banks offering lower interest rates for women. When I asked about the reluctance to use a viable financial product, most of the women grumbled about the unhelpful people at the bank and the interest rates. Some confessed that independently procuring loans would hurt family dynamics.

Zahira thought independent loans for women was a crazy idea. Instead, married women would counsel each other to seek loans to support their husband's businesses or apply for the loan in his name. I was puzzled—how could a labour rights activist be so conservative on matters of family finances?

One day, I worked up the courage to ask her, and she smiled. 'All this empowerment ('sashaktikaran') is good in English-language reports. I have learned these words through our meetings at the office. But in life, things are more complicated. You need peace (shanti) in families. I often quote that home and house line from *Kuch Kuch Hota Hai*. You said you were a Shah Rukh fan, haven't you seen it? You know what I'm talking about?' Though I had seen the film, the connection she made was lost on me. That evening, I spotted a VCD store and bought a copy of the film to watch on my laptop.

Kuch Kuch Hota Hai

How could a soppy Shah Rukh love triangle explain the reluctance of working-class women to take advantage of financial services intended specifically for their benefit? In the film, the lead female character, Anjali (played by Kajol), loves Rahul (played by Shah Rukh), her best friend at college. Rahul doesn't reciprocate and falls for another woman. Unable to bear the heartache, Anjali decides to drop out. Her parents find her a good match in Aman (played by Salman Khan). She accepts. After the engagement ceremony, Anjali seems unenthused by her upcoming nuptials. Noticing that Anjali is withdrawn, her mother asks if she is happy with her fiancé. Anjali smiles and says, 'Of course I am happy. I am engaged and Aman is a great man, he loves me.' Her mother asks if Anjali loves Aman. Anjali says nothing. Her mother repeats the question.

The background music reaches a crescendo, Anjali sinks into a chair. Carrying the weight of her bejewelled engagement outfit and her unrequited love for Rahul, she sighs, 'I have already loved, Mother. I have already loved. I don't think I can do it again.' She points to her engagement ring and says, 'You could think of this as a compromise (samjhauta).' Her mother responds, 'I had never thought that my daughter would not love and would settle for less. I am your mother; I only wish to see you happy and settled. But a home that's built on the foundations of a compromise and not love is not a home (ghar), it's a house (makaan). The rest is up to you.'

The dialogue in *KKHH* makes a distinction between a 'house' as a building and a 'home' as family. Only Love can convert a house into a home.

The women I encountered in Bapunagar were locked in everyday battles against the men and elders in their families as they sought to work more. They had recently emerged victorious in a fight with influential industry owners. There was no ignoring them. A twenty-three-year-old agarbatti worker involved in the struggle from Bapunagar explained the change. She said, 'It is about time and mobility (chalna-phirna). Earlier, sisters would do what was expected of them by their husbands and in-laws. Once, they joined SEWA, our sisters spent time with each other discussing problems and moved around within their communities to help bring other sisters into the movement. A few like me travelled the city and country. Such a thing was not possible earlier. This bothers some people and causes fighting within homes.'

When I interviewed Renana Jhabwala, a Padma Shri-winning activist who had held various positions of leadership within SEWA, she commented on how this public visibility was the lasting legacy of unions and workers' organizations. 'Of course, labour movements and struggles help with wages and improving work opportunities. But the biggest impact I have seen is that women become more important, more visible and better respected as community members once they start to organize themselves for worker issues successfully. Their voices and needs are heard not only outside, in factories, but also inside, within their homes. No one sees them as dependent on others.'

In writing and theorizing about how well-being is negotiated within families, economists rely on game theory. These frameworks of 'intra-household bargaining' suggest that those who are perceived to contribute more within homes often enjoy greater powers in deciding how monies, food and other material decisions are made within the family. Moreover, those with greater access to jobs and other forms of capital outside the family unit are said to have higher 'bargaining power' within homes as they can always exit the family. Feminists have relied on such frameworks to explain women's ill-treatment and undernourishment within homes in north India. Social norms ensure that women do not have any options for an exit, as they have limited control on property with compromised and insecure access to jobs and public spaces. Moreover, women's care contributions to the home are often coded as weak and thereby undervalued. Amartya Sen refers to this as the 'perceived contribution' response. Money and cash liquidity are cast as more valuable contributions than the daily labour of loving and caring for the home.

But the changing nature of the labour market was emasculating men and making women's cash contributions more powerful in places like Bapunagar. In 1996, SEWA surveyed agarbatti workers to find that half the women were married to unemployed husbands. The 2006 data revealed similar patterns—men held precarious jobs with uncertain hours and pay. The men felt as insecure as their incomes. Women were increasingly playing an essential role in bringing cash and care into the family.

The women workers in these neighbourhoods were wary of alienating their in-laws and husbands as a result of their growing economic clout. These fears were hardly tactical. Yes, these women knew that their material welfare required men. Yet, many women expressed satisfaction in their increased economic responsibility but also in their relationships with family members. They did not want to lose or upset them. Most desired a happier collaboration within homes. To cater to rising masculine anxiety, Zahira said, SEWA's activism and agitation were always cloaked under a ghungat, espousing the virtues of traditions and family. In Ahmedabad, where union members had to seek familial permission to attend rallies and protests, men often resented the idea of women congregating in solidarity. Yet, the dire need for greater economic security had catalysed men, immediate relatives and the broader community to accept the political activities of working women. Where once men would give the women in their family their wages—or at least a significant portion of their wages—for household expenses, now women were turning over their income. 'It was such a change, us giving our husbands and in-laws money. I was the first woman in my family to do that,' Rubariben said.

Female employment and union membership were radical enough; possessing sole proprietorship of a house or a bank account would take things too far. 'They think it's bad enough that women are working and asking for higher wages and benefits. That women have become such important leaders in our area. This is very difficult for many men and older people to swallow,' Zahira said. She turned again to *KKHH* to remind me: 'If a woman, say, seeks a bank loan in her name only, she will have a house, but not a home.'

Zahira's conservative views on family finance surprised me. I was equally shocked at her fandom. She struck me as a woman forever confronting the harsh truths of reality, grounded and anchored in all that needed to be negotiated and achieved. A woman firmly committed to the realm of the real. Not a woman of fantasy and fangirling. So I was surprised when I asked my usual ice-breaker question—'who is your favourite actor?'—and she smiled and said Shah Rukh. When I asked her why, she shrugged and replied, '*Meri marzi.*' That was the Zahira I knew. My wish. Shah Rukh was a local favourite among women. They were happy to list the reasons they liked him—his smile, his kindness, his dimples, his face, his tameez. Zahira was not one to offer any explanations. She thought my questions silly and had no time to explain herself or her preferences to me.

Through the first week of my stay in 2006, I met the daughters of many of the SEWA members who were participating in my research. They were painfully shy, silently gripping their mothers' hands. When I asked them about their future plans, nearly all of them said they hoped to become teachers. Except Zahira's daughter, who said she wanted a job that would enable her to travel. Her name was Meenal. She was ten years old and, like her mother, a Shah Rukh fan. Unlike her mother, she was forthcoming about how Zahira would sing and dance to Shah Rukh songs even in public functions. Meenal's description of her mother's passionate fangirling was confirmed by Rubariben, Zahira's neighbour, who said she had seen Zahira cry while listening to a Shah Rukh song. But on this point, Meenal was firm. 'No one cries in our house,' she snapped. She was a mature ten-year-old, growing up too fast. Over several years of conversations with Zahira and Meenal, I was able to piece together the story of their family and fandom.

Two weeks into my visit, Meenal joined me as I waited for her mother at the SEWA office. A ten-year-old with responsibilities, she had walked back from school to collect money from her mother to go shopping for vegetables for dinner. We started talking and she asked about my research project, if I had a husband and if my parents were comfortable with my job. She said she would love to be a journalist and be on TV but that such jobs were an impossible dream for Muslim girls from Bapunagar. 'My friends have fathers and families who do not let them go outside after they grow up. So how can we work on TV if we can't go out of our homes?' She added, 'My mother is strict (sakti) and scolds me because she knows people will think I'm giving her trouble because my father isn't around. She worries about what others will say. But even if she is difficult and wants to know what I am doing all the time, I have it easier because my mother works with SEWA and there is no man in the house.'

Liquor deprived Meenal of her father's love and paternal supervision. Her father lost Zahira to Shah Rukh a decade ago, just before Meenal was born, around the time he lost his mind to alcohol and unemployment. Despite the alcohol ban in Gujarat since 1961, no one in the colony had much trouble getting hold of booze. Most of the men drank; some, like Zahira's husband, drank too much.

Married at the age of sixteen, Zahira gave birth to Meenal within a year. Her husband's family home was a two-room house without windows in Allah Nagar, seven right turns away from where her parents lived. Another year passed, and Zahira returned to live with her own family. Both her parents had passed away by then. Her elder brother, now the head of the household, supported her decision to leave her husband. Zahira's father used to manage a small plastic sales shop which was vandalized during the 1985 riots in Gujarat. To earn a steady income, her brother trained and worked in a small power-loom textile unit. Zahira's younger sister was married and lived with her husband in Indore. It was a good marriage. Zahira's brother-in-law held a salaried job as a driver for a wealthy and well-connected family in Madhya Pradesh. His employer arranged for housing within their estate and Zahira's sister worked as a domestic worker for the same family, earning enough to save and pay her children's school fees.

Between 1997 and 2000, Zahira returned to her husband several times but eventually gave up on trying to make her marriage work. Her brother's decision to migrate to Surat, along with the prospect of safe and secure housing, brought her to Bapunagar. When we met, she lived on the first floor of a kutcha-pukka house with pink walls. She had found the house through Salim, her brother's close friend. His family's small business was also destroyed in the 1985 riots. Salim's father, though, managed to gain a small plot of land in Bapunagar, provided by a local political heavyweight who was known to a distant cousin of the family.

Salim's family felt blessed with their land. They moved to Bapunagar in 1989, after spending a year in a relief camp. In 1990, they sought another favour from their politically connected relative to build a small car-repair service in a nearby shed. But the plot and construction were hardly free. Of ten houses constructed in India, seven are built by the inhabitants themselves. Evidence shows that the majority of India's urban poor prefers to build their homes incrementally with the help of local masons and informal contractors. Salim's family did the same, accruing substantial debts for the costs of building and maintenance. In 2006, when I visited Bapunagar for the first time, they still owed money to contractors. Fortunately, everyone operated through friends. Social ties blurred the lines between creditors and debtors, between mutual aid and remunerative contracts.

Salim found a job in Surat in 2000; his uncle took the reins of their repair shop in Ahmedabad. Zahira's brother planned to join Salim in Surat too. Salim's younger brother was fourteen and would eventually take over the shop. The family needed someone to care for Salim's elderly parents, at least until his fourteen-year-old brother came of age and took a wife. The money in Surat was too lucrative to refuse. Eventually, Salim and Zahira reached an agreement. She would live in their house rent-free, and in exchange cook for the family and pay the electricity bill. Zahira considered moving to Surat with her brother but his prospects were too uncertain. She had also managed to enrol her daughter into a good government school through a SEWA contact. At the age of twenty-one, Zahira moved into Salim's family's home in Bapunagar; her daughter Meenal was four. Zahira planned to hold on in Bapunagar till Meenal was of marriageable age. The thought of seeking help or protection from her husband or her in-laws never crossed Zahira's mind. She would have to manage on her own.

We never talked about religion or riots overtly. Those themes were indirectly referenced by her, she would casually add them as we discussed SEWA's role in helping and unifying marginalized workers. It was clear that the events of 2002 were unable to break her resolve. Through that painful time, amidst curfew and violence, even as she heard stories of Muslim women being assaulted and brutalized in nearby localities, even as she saw a flood of bereaved families arriving at a relief camp close to the local mosque, she relied on her fellow home-based workers and her new family.

Women in Agarbatti Colony did not leave their husbands. You learned to tolerate your marriage, let it breathe and marinate in Ahmedabad's dull air rather than fester indoors. You learned to manage your marriage, manage being manhandled from time to time. Women would often roll and paste incense sticks together. It was a communal activity. During work hours, it was common to hear the women discuss various 'nuske' (tricks) to tackle conjugal trouble. Zahira would play Shah Rukh songs on her personal transistor as they worked. The cassette and her transistor were prized possessions, acquired through combining an Eid cash gift from her brother and her savings. 'When I moved with Meenal to Bapunagar in 2000,' Zahira told me, 'I saved and bought a used cassette player. The local paan shop would sell music very cheap and the shopkeeper made me a tape of popular film music, most were Shah Rukh songs. I had helped take his wife to a good doctor in the city. Six years later, I still use that player although Meenal says it will stop working soon. Most young people listen to songs on the TV and CD players nowadays here. But we don't have these. We have this cassette player and this old cassette.'

None of the women Zahira knew had much choice in whom they married. Some were at least allowed to see their prospective grooms more than once before accepting the match. All marriages were within the same caste and clan networks, and women would marry from one neighbourhood nearby into another. 'My father promised me on the factory floor to his friend. This is the way it worked amongst us,' one woman told me. 'I know you won't understand, but it's very different from the way our grandparents were married. In those times, the amount of land you held back in your village made all the difference in who had the best husband. But when our families had to sell all their land and move to Ahmedabad for good, that changed. Nowadays, it all depends on who has the best job and pukka house. But I really wish you could tell who drinks and who doesn't.'

The working women of Bapunagar had many theories on men and marriage. A good husband was divine intervention and sheer luck. Even the best man's character would eventually curdle and rot. Life was tough on men and they took it out on the women and children, losing interest in being devout, kind and courteous. Women were protected from the harshness of the world outside, so they remained hopeful and God-fearing.

'I wish someone could talk to me or touch me the way he does with Kajol in *Kabhi Khushi Kabhie Gham*, but that's never going to happen,' Salim's brother's young wife, a garment worker, said to me. 'My husband's moods and hands are so harsh.' It was the only time any of the women had offered a hint of what they might want sexually from their men. I wanted to ask more questions but didn't want to appear prurient or inappropriate. Fully aware that while *I* would be comfortable talking about my favourite actor to a stranger, my sex life would be an unwelcome invasion of privacy. When I mentioned my research recesses and talking with the women about Shah Rukh to my first boss and mentor, a wonderful and brilliant feminist economist, she cringed. She hated a clumsy careless curiosity, which she thought characteristic of upper-class kajal-inked kids trying to understand the Poor. 'Only ask questions that you would feel comfortable answering yourself,' she'd told me. There must be some reciprocity in our research.

Still, as '*Chaiyya chaiyya*' from the Shah Rukh movie *Dil Se* played on Zahira's portable cassette player, I did feel comfortable enough with these women to ask them about their home lives, including any violence against women in their neighbourhood. None would admit to having been on the receiving end herself, but each acknowledged that they knew women who had. Domestic violence was abstract, yet ever present. Something that always happened in someone else's home, not your own. Mapuben even suggested that encouraging a violent husband to drink a lot was a good idea, that she gave her own husband enough money out of her wages so he would pass out as soon as he got home. Next up on Zahira's mixtape was '*Yeh dil deewana*', from *Pardes*. Sonu Nigam sings that song in the register of sheer hurt; Shah Rukh, driving in the deserts of Nevada, tears up at the prospect of losing his beloved. Tahiraben said that some of the women in Bapunagar were lucky because they could rely on their sisters from work or SEWA to help them fight back if their husbands beat them. Others said that a woman could evade violence by keeping herself busy with children and housework or simply by avoiding eye contact with drunken husbands and quietly sharing wages.

At this point, Zahira offered a story about her cousin, though I was convinced she was talking about herself. This cousin lived in Allah Nagar, like Zahira once did with her husband and in-laws. It seemed Zahira's cousin was a rigid spirit—unwilling to negotiate with violence. She understood that her husband's frustrations from a failed day at wage-labour would find a way to imprint her body. 'I feel so sad now that I remember those days,' Zahira said. 'Her husband was not a bad person. They were happy in the early years when he had a job. But when money became tough, all homes in the colony faced trouble. My cousin would talk about these problems with her sisters and neighbours. But her husband didn't talk, he just took out his frustration on his wife. I wish men and women could just talk to each other. But men here never like discussing money with their wives. I think it makes them feel like they are not providing for us or doing what a man is supposed to do. So, instead, men drink and hit their wives and children.'

After putting up with consistent beatings for a while, one day, Zahira's cousin locked herself and her daughter inside their house. She had mobilized a group of women nearby, including Zahira, to ensure that her husband, already drunk and angry, would not be allowed to enter. This spurred a series of endless screams and sighs, nothing new in the neighbourhood. Family feuds often served as evening entertainment during load-shedding hours. Each morning, her husband would leave to earn his drink. Each night, he would return to conquer his home and wife. But Zahira's cousin would not relent. Her heart and home were locked. The local gang of co-workers protected her. It took a year before the husband moved on, seeing his wife and daughter once a month. Zahira said she was convinced he had another family. 'How else would he feed himself,' she asked rhetorically. 'Men can't cook, and he did not look like he was living on the streets. Men can always find women to take care of them. It's women like me and my cousin who have to look after ourselves when the men don't take care of us.'

Zahira worked longer hours than anyone I knew. She was not about to give up the fragile independence she had won for herself and Meenal. Her Shah Rukh cassette kept her going. Those songs were often the soundtrack to her protest and resolve, she would turn the volume up in the evenings to drown out her long hours on the sewing machine. Much like the cousin she invoked, separating from a drunk and economically bruised husband while dealing with familial finances became Zahira's life. She was compelled to take on too many tasks. It wasn't just the weekly worrying about managing expenses. She had to placate her brother to ensure he sent enough money to her each month. She had to smile through the indignities offered by the ration-shop dealer where she collected her subsidized grains. Not too long ago, men were reliable breadwinners in the slums of Ahmedabad; they earned steady incomes from manufacturing jobs in textile factories. But by the mid 2000s, manufacturing jobs started to move to other districts in Gujarat and become more mechanized. Local men who could not migrate or operate new machines were no longer able to earn enough to support their families. With more free time and stress, many turned to alcohol or casual labour. The decline in local manufacturing required women like Zahira to play a more prominent role in their families and communities. They were expected to pay the bills, cook the meals and battle an onslaught of joblessness, riots and demolitions.

Greatest Hits

Four weeks into my first visit, a famous Shah Rukh song was playing on the radio in our shared taxi. We were returning from a day of surveys and field visits, the song was '*Tujhe dekha to yeh jana sanam*' from *DDLJ*, Shah Rukh's great romance and one of the most successful films and soundtracks in Indian cinematic history. Composed by the duo Jatin-Lalit, the song has ascended to the ranks of Hindi film classics, alongside some of the country's most-loved popular songs. For many fans, it is the sound of Shah Rukh becoming

India's national crush. Throughout the song, the lead male character confesses to his overwhelming love for a woman. It took just *seeing* her for him to grasp the madness of love. He praises his beloved and their love. He wonders what do with himself. Where do they go from here? Perhaps it's best to die in each other's arms. His breath and his life are for her. His lover reciprocates in song. She sings that she cries his tears. Because of him her sadness has lifted, her sorrows have started to smile.

Zahira sang along. I had never seen her this happy: her body swaying, she appeared giddy, liberated. For once, I decided not to ask her any questions. To let her just enjoy her song. 'I know it seems strange that women like me with such tough lives can enjoy this kind of love song,' she volunteered. 'But I am so grateful to Allah for this little five-minute song. The wonderful things they say to each other … I don't think any of us can ever find a love like this.'

So, what is it about Shah Rukh? I asked her *the* question. Why him? 'I think you overthink (*Tum bahut zyada sochti ho*). There is no major reason, we just like him. He makes me smile. It is not because he sings songs and is rich in movies. We know it is just a film. We are not that silly (*Hum bewakoof nahin hain*). But womenfolk like him because of the way he speaks to and treats women. I feel happy when I see that. There is love and respect. You don't see much of that amongst boys these days. Just look at the way he *looks* at his heroine. And I love all the songs.'

I asked about her favourite Shah Rukh film, she did not have one. She was introduced to Shah Rukh's face around the time of Meenal's birth, a year into her marriage. Zahira was seventeen years old. The 1996 cricket World Cup was on and young boys in her old colony of Allah Nagar were being paid money to paste posters on every wall of Shah Rukh endorsing a soft drink. 'He looked good,' she told me, her face as red as a paan stain. Soon after, a few women in the neighbourhood acquired TVs, and Shah Rukh and cricket were everywhere.

'I've only seen him on TV and in songs. I don't really have a favourite. Most of us must make do with the songs or wait for *any* of his films to come on TV. I can't remember the last time anyone amongst us went to a cinema hall. I've never been. Only one of our sisters (a fellow agarbatti worker) has a TV and she can't keep it turned on for long, as the electricity will cost too much. Her husband would get angry if he saw her watching a three-hour movie with advertisement breaks. Music is easier for us.'

Since Zahira did not know many of Shah Rukh's films, we spent my final few days in Ahmedabad talking about his film songs. It's a conversation that's lasted ten years. In the early years following our meeting, I'd send her an annual Eid message wishing her well and asking about Shah Rukh's latest hits. We lost touch between 2011 and 2013. The following is a list of her favourite songs. I've tried to translate the lyrics to the best of my abilities.

—⁂—

2004: 'Main yahan hoon,' from the film *Veer-Zaara*, lyrics by Javed Akhtar

All distances between us have disappeared. I am here. There are no boundaries, no restrictions. I am here. I am a secret you can never hide; I am a style you can never recover from.

2006: 'Mitwa,' from the film *Kabhi Alvida Naa Kehna*, lyrics by Javed Akhtar

Love will find a way. Oh, my love, love will find a way. Oh, my mind, please tell me: in which direction are you heading? What did you not get? What are you looking for? Something that is unsaid, or unheard, can you tell me what is the matter? Dear Beloved: what are your heartbeats saying to you? Please don't hide from the voice of your heart.

2008: 'Haule haule,' from the film *Rab Ne Bana Di Jodi,* lyrics by
Jaideep Sahni

Slowly slowly, just as the breeze drifts. Slow slowly, just as medicine
works its magic. Slowly slowly, just as your prayers are answered.
Slowly slowly, just as a veil lifts. Slowly slowly, just as you become
intoxicated. Have some patience, my friend. Take a deep breath. Shun
all your fears and worries away. Life is too short. Slowly slowly, you
will fall in love. Slowly slowly.

—⟨⟩—

Film music is an integral part of popular culture in India. Lately,
songs help promote movies. Large tracts of Indians access Hindi
film music more than they watch the films. Much has been written
on the love and longing captured by Bollywood romantic songs. The
genre traverses the poignant and the ridiculous—much like people in
different phases of love. But the overtures in Zahira's list of romantic
rhapsodies were overwhelming. As I translate and think about these
songs: the songs that Zahira hums when she rolls her incense sticks
and stiches her garment orders, the songs she hums when she wants
to forget about the pain in her marriage, the songs she hums when she
feels uncertain or unsure of her place in life—what is their vocabulary?

The melodies *are* love. They encourage us to be fools in love. No
rational alliance-making, no proposals based on landholdings, no
marriage brokered on factory floors. Love is free, and these songs urge
a happy romantic abandon. No boundaries, no self-denial, no veil, no
chains, no shame. The beloved is omnipresent. He is everywhere, in
your sight and mind, your quests and patience. It is hardly surprising
that women like Zahira lap up this romantic feast of selflessness
offered by the hero in these songs. The music and images are a retreat
from the reality of a restricted life, a life where going to the doctor
after your husband hits you requires *his* permission. And everyone

needs a place to ignore the violence of everyday intimacies, especially poor home-based workers battling inflation, insecure housing tenure and alcoholic husbands. To forget a world of petty strategies and unfulfilled promises. To sway and swoon at Shah Rukh's on-screen spiritual generosity towards the woman he loves.

In January 2007, Manmohan Singh, the Prime Minister of India, inaugurated a national conference which aimed to advocate for social security measures for home-based workers in India. The event was organized by SEWA and a network of organizations supporting the rights of home-workers in south Asia. Through his speech, Singh acknowledged the increasing statistical invisibility of women's work. Our research report on the working conditions and wages of these workers was presented, a film was made for advocacy as well. Many of the workers involved in interviews and collecting data were present at the conference. They were proud—this was a triumph of all their lobbying and hard work. Zahira was one of the workers in the audience. After the inaugural speech, a group of women approached me wearing chikankaari kurtas and wide grins. One of the women said, 'They managed to get Manmohan Singhji, why did not you ask them for Shah Rukh also.' Zahiraben added, 'Knowing you, you must have.'

It's Time to Love

Chand ne kuch kaha /Raat ne kuch suna / Tu bhi sun bekhabar / Pyar kar
(The Moon said something/ The Night heard something/ Oh clueless one, it's
time you listened too/ Fall in love)

—*Dil To Pagal Hai* (1997)

When I returned to Agarbatti Colony and its adjacent localities in 2014, the area was far more built up and concretized. Middle-class residential complexes were being planned, discussions of evictions and construction dominated the landscape. Zahira was thirty-five and obsessed with Meenal's marital prospects. 'These younger girls have gone mad,' she told me. 'They're looking for love and heroes in real life. How can I explain it to her? There is no such man in real life. Her friends are the same. They all want jobs outside Ahmedabad because they want to meet men on their own. The only good thing the 1990s brought were television, cassettes and Shah Rukh Khan. But *he* has caused all this silliness. And now, he can only help his wife and his daughter. What can he do for us? He certainly won't find a boy for Meenal.' Laughter erupted.

Her daughter, now eighteen, was standing near me as this conversation transpired. She rolled her eyes and sang a line from Zahira's favourite Shah Rukh love song, from *Dil To Pagal Hai*:

'*Pyar kar...ohoho ammi... pyar kar.*'

Superseding all the songs in the list from the previous section, Zahira's all-time favourite was a tune titled '*Pyar kar* (Fall in love/ It's time to love)' from the successful love triangle *Dil To Pagal Hai*. The film, starring the glorious Karisma Kapoor and Madhuri Dixit alongside Shah Rukh, is a lavish urban love story in which the lead female character (played by Madhuri) is convinced that true love can be found when Valentine's Day overlaps with a full moon's night. This awkward mingling of the Hindu lunar calendar with a Western holiday inspired more by Hallmark cards than any particular tradition was, post-liberalization, typically Indian. The audience suffered no cognitive dissonance celebrating the arbitrary nature of love and Cupid's arrow while, in real life, only partaking in arranged alliances. *DTPH* was the first Shah Rukh film, indeed the first film of any kind, that Zahira had watched in its entirety.

The film's soundtrack was a huge success. Though the film is over two decades old now, its songs have clocked more than three hundred million views on YouTube. Zahira had memorized the song, scene by scene, line by line. She recalled how the neon-blue moonlight shines on Shah Rukh's face as he suggests that everyone fall in love. His character in *DTPH*, inevitably named Rahul, is a love-addled theatre director and musician. The song is his public paean to romantic love, sung at a Valentine's Day party in Mumbai. Dressed in black, brown and white, he dances with a trendy crowd. There is not a single saree or salwar-kameez in sight. Beautiful bodies are draped in cocktail dresses and everyone is paired up, except for Shah Rukh and his sexy best friend, played by Karisma Kapoor. Heart-shaped balloons fill the screen. Everyone is looking for a soulmate, everyone is merry in their search. But Rahul feels a metaphysical tug. Someone calls out to him. Shah Rukh winks at the camera and offers his standard goofy-sexy grin. He, the ultimate matinee idol, sings: *It's time to fall in love.*

Zahira told me about the time her group of garment and agarbatti workers watched *DTPH* together on television. 'Nafisaben knew that it was playing and helped organize a viewing.' They shared money to hire a generator, so that a power cut couldn't interrupt the screening. A few months later, some of the women watched *DDLJ* and *Kuch Kuch Hota Hai* together at Nafisa's house. She laughed and said, 'I don't have parents-in-law. But for other women, their in-laws and the men thought we'd gone mad! People would usually hire generators for weddings or festivities only. One of our sisters was not allowed to join us, her mother-in-law forbid it. But she made an excuse, saying we had an extra order from the seth and she needed to work late. Her husband knew she was lying but he is a good man. Why would he stop his wife from having a little bit of fun?'

As devoted as Zahira was to fun, Shah Rukh and these songs, she took the world they depicted and the romantic love they sold with a pinch of salt. It was, she knew, a make-believe world, as out of reach for her as the opulent lifestyles on display. In commenting on how films sell fantasy in India, scholars often draw links between the income poverty of the country and the on-screen displays of hyper-consumption and excessive wealth. These are meant to project

the neoliberal aspirations of a growing middle class and its desire to
at once uphold community traditions and encourage individualism.
Simultaneously, the images are intended to enchant and distract the
masses from their everyday drudgery. But listening to all the female
Shah Rukh fans I met, I began to realize that they needed these
films to serve other fantastical functions. The fantasy of love songs
on Valentine's Day, of finding the One on moonlit nights, of good-
looking men and women with prospects *choosing* and *honouring* each
other's minds and bodies, was a necessary dose of fantasy for the
romantically impoverished as well. For Zahira's generation of women
in Bapunagar, these films proved the existence of aliens who lived
on another planet, where men sang love songs as a sign of affection
rather than of streetside sexual harassment. A reprieve from the
constant bargaining, incompatibility and violence in one's own lived
experiences of love, sex and marriage.

'All these movies and songs are dreams,' Zahira would say. For her,
films were simply an act of sublimation. Men were frustrated in the
world, and so they watched movies where men beat each other up.
Women wanted to love and lead a happy family life, so they indulged
in romantic songs and love stories.

Meenal was Zahira's only child. They had forged a formidable
bond, having braved repeated crises together. At the young age of
seven, Meenal started helping her twenty-four-year-old mother with
the housework and the incense business. Meenal helped Zahira with
her SEWA union duties too, sitting in many of the meetings and
accompanying her as much as possible. She idealized her mother. She
sang all the Shah Rukh songs, watched his films on TV with Zahira
and her fellow worker-fangirls. Meenal's fandom was her inheritance.
Both women were physically alike and Meenal wore her mother's
clothes, sprucing them up herself at the local tailor's shop while
doing odd jobs for him in return. She never used her mother's sewing
machine for her own personal tailoring, saying that she did not want

to interfere with Zahira's garment orders. I suspect it was also to have a legitimate excuse to move outside the house and interact with new people. While her mother always covered her chest with a dupatta, I had never seen Meenal cover herself in the same way. The scarf, meant to cover the breasts and honour of women, had disappeared from the wardrobes of many adolescent girls in the neighbourhood.

Meenal and her mother had watched *DTPH* thrice by 2014. Each time on TV. Meenal loved the film more as she grew older. The last scene in the film shows Shah Rukh holding Madhuri Dixit. The couple are wearing white and are in focus, when the following set of lines in English pop up: 'Someone somewhere is made for you.' Zahira had not read those lines. She did not read English, but Meenal could. Zahira understood on-screen romance as a beautiful falsehood. But for Meenal, love was not an impossible aspiration, it was a full-time calling. She watched all those Shah Rukh films and walked away a convert. Meenal championed a certain kind of romantic totalitarianism, she believed in the all-encompassing hegemony of love. 'Everyone must marry someone they like,' she would protest when we talked about her mother's frantic attempts at marrying her off.

Zahira had no objections to Meenal marrying for love, as long as her daughter loved a Muslim boy who could provide for her. 'I see these young girls, they like these flashy boys with bikes and phones. The quiet, sensible ones won't do. But these boys with style are up to no good. They have no jobs, spending all their days dreaming and doing nothing. And even if the Hindu boy is nice himself, the family will never treat Meenal well.'

'But can't Meenal work and support herself as you did?' I heard myself say.

Zahira had fought hard to gain independence from her marriage. She had eventually taken up a well-paid short contract job for a donor project at SEWA. Their financial situation had improved by leaps and bounds. They had bought a new transistor, a new bed and two mobile phones. Meenal was eighteen years old and earning independently through part-time garments work and supporting various NGO projects nearby. Why was Zahira so keen to have Meenal marry before she could stand on her own two feet? Would it not be more critical for Meenal to be independent? 'Because women cannot manage alone,' Zahira said sharply. 'Do you want to be alone? Meenal needs a man's help to survive here, it's too tough being on your own. A woman will eventually starve without a family's love. Even I will go to Surat to live with my brother. Maybe we can find a good match for Meenal there. My brother says there are many good Muslim families in his complex.'

Meenal was exasperated. 'Didi, can you talk some sense into my mother? It's like she and my uncle sent me to a good school only so I could find a more educated husband. I keep telling her that there is more to life than Gujarat and looking for husbands. And that I can find someone on my own. She has to leave me alone. I have decided to stop meeting the boys she wants me to. Earlier, heroes like Amitabh Bachchan used to be coolies and work in factories but nowadays decent young men like going to big cities, like Shah Rukh. If I study and take up a job in another city, I'll find someone good. Interesting (she used the word "mazedaar") men are difficult to find in backward areas like ours. All the good men are gone.'

She was right. Educated and skilled young men left Agarbatti Colony as soon as they could in search of work and better prospects. Meenal was beautiful, well-educated and spoke English. None of the young single men in her neighbourhood matched up. Young men, raised on a diet of the post-liberalization culture of reality shows and city jobs, stewed in their own aspirations. They refused to work in factories or fields. Meenal's male school friends—she was the first in Zahira's family to have 'friends'—took and often failed government exams while hatching business plans without the benefits of seed capital. A short walk through the narrow streets of the colony would reveal gangs of male youth spending more and more time watching movies and playing games on their phones. They were dependent on their parents and odd jobs of delivery and office support. Meenal was proud of her financial freedom, telling me how she had seen *Chennai Express* with her friends recently in a 'good hall'. She had paid for the movie tickets herself, earning the money from a job helping a foreign academic's research project in Ahmedabad.

By 2016, the home-based manufacturing of garments or incense sticks were no longer a means for a sustainable livelihood. The local incense-stick industries had started using machines and sourcing supplies from new locations, reducing the amount of work available to women. Demonetization offered contractors a new excuse to delay the payment of wages. Simple transactions were full of struggle. Debts were incurred, work slowed down. 'Agarbatti Colony' felt like defunct nomenclature. Demand for garments from the local markets and tailors declined as well. A lot of apparel and textile work had shifted to factories in Bangalore, Coimbatore and Surat. Meenal had managed to evade her family's marital pressure, pleading with her uncle to support her plans to study. His elevation to the role of a factory technician paid increasingly well. The promotion also offered health insurance and retirement benefits. In late 2017, Zahira and Meenal moved out of Bapunagar to live with him and his family in Surat. The house in Bapunagar was becoming crowded. Salim's younger brother had children now. There was an episode of violence after the government announced a plan to redevelop the local playground as part of an affordable housing scheme. Zahira's brother worried about future riots. By May 2017, the neighbourhood also reported two of the three Zika cases in India, frightening him further. He urged them to come live with him.

Meenal had finished her board exams in 2015 with strong scores. She knew her mother could not support her plans to go to college, so she learned basic computer competencies by working ad-hoc jobs for a local NGO till the time they moved to Surat. With assistance from his factory manager, her uncle helped Meenal enrol in a government short-term training course to further develop her computer skills. Meenal wanted to work in an office as secretarial staff to supplement their income. However, jobs were tough to find for young inexperienced candidates like herself. After a year of searching, she found work as a surveyor in a large market-research firm based in Mumbai. An 'NGO Auntie from Ahmedabad' helped connect her with the job; the pay was flexible, depending on the number of surveys she completed accurately. The firm would offer her a travel stipend and provide accommodation for outstation work. Meenal was quick on her feet and an articulate Hindi speaker, she was excited about asking questions for a living.

Zahira was uncomfortable with the idea of Meenal leaving Surat. 'I had hoped she would find a good job nearby,' Zahira said to me on the phone. 'But, these days, finding a job is harder than finding a husband.' She had called to ask if I had any information about the survey company that had offered Meenal this job. I did know the firm to be of good repute and offered some contacts and words of reassurance. In the end, her uncle brokered a compromise—they agreed that Meenal would continue to live in Surat and travel for assignments based on how comfortable Zahira felt about every new survey offered to Meenal by the company. Each offer would involve hours of negotiation between mother, uncle and daughter.

By 2019, Meenal was in high demand at work, often spending half the year away from Surat on assignments. Much like her mother, she was charming and hard-working, able to elicit responses from survey respondents. She went frequently to Mumbai, as her firm found it cheaper to pay migrants a piece-rate than hiring local staff in the city. Meenal hoped to leave Surat behind, aspiring to become 'permanent' staff at the firm, dreaming of a permanent life in Mumbai as well. On her first night in the city, she made a pilgrimage to Shah Rukh's house.

10

The Boredom of Manju

Yeh bandar bhi nahi, bande to bilkul nahi.
(These creatures won't qualify as monkeys, let alone men.)

—Home-based worker-fangirl in Rampur, Uttar Pradesh

In 2006, I met Manju through the same ISST research project that introduced me to the agarbatti workers of Ahmedabad. She was one of thirty-four young Muslim women I interviewed in the populous and poverty-stricken state of Uttar Pradesh. The interviews were short, part of a small-scale qualitative research effort conducted in two neighbouring villages in the district of Rampur. The district is classified as a 'minority concentration' area, as Muslim families account for half the population. Rampur has made significant contributions to Indian classical music and culture; the Raza library in Rampur town holds important Persian texts, among them a 300-year-old Persian translation of the *Valmiki Ramayan* written in gold.

The women I encountered were between fourteen and thirty-five years old. None had visited the famous library, nor indeed, completed primary schooling. They produced appliqué patchwork and embroidery at home, often working together in courtyards or in each other's homes. The women we interviewed in Rampur were increasingly engaged in home-based garment work as part of larger subcontracted value chains. 'Patti-ka-kaam' and 'zari-zardosi' are forms of delicate embroidery with strong Indian and international demand. Back then, the group used English sporadically. The word 'rate' was invoked to describe the wages they received for each finished garment. They used 'quality,' 'time' and 'late', words they had learned from their employers, to explain wage cuts for defects or delays.

We arrived in Rampur on a day when the area's political representative planned to inaugurate a road. Till the late 1990s, roads were unusual in rural Uttar Pradesh. Until 2001, nearly one billion people worldwide lived more than two kilometres from a paved road, with one-third of the road-deprived living in India. Nearly half of India's 600,000 villages lacked a paved road in 2001. A year later, the Indian government began a massive construction drive through the ambitious Prime Minister's Rural Roads Project, or the Pradhan Mantri Gram Sadak Yojana (PMGSY). Between 2001 and 2015, the government spent nearly US$40 billion to construct rural roads across 200,000 villages in one of the most extensive infrastructure campaigns in global history.

These roads linked villages to national and state highways across India, ensuring transport connectivity to market centres and cities. Letters and numbers fail to describe the impact. Revolution has been forged by these rural roads. 'Before these roads,' Manju's uncle said to me, 'you would have not been able to reach us as easily as you did. It used to take an entire day to reach Lucknow, if you were lucky and managed to catch a bus on the day you needed to. Now there is a pukka road connecting the village to the bus stop for Bareilly. And if you have a motorbike, you can reach Lucknow in five hours. I never thought such a day would come.' We were discussing his daughter's wedding preparations and how the new roads had made it easier to ensure guests and goods would reach their village. Economists highlight how rural connectivity across the country made it easier for men to find jobs outside farming. Between 1977 and 2017, the share of rural men engaged in agriculture has fallen from eighty-eight per cent to fifty-five per cent.

Our research team was small—just me and a young woman from Lucknow, affiliated to a partner NGO. A day after reaching Rampur's dusty town centre, at seven in the morning, we moved out to our field sites. Manju's family hosted us through the day; they had an extra cot. Manju was our second interviewee.

Investigator: Your name?

Respondent: Manju

Investigator: Age?

Respondent: ...

Schemes and Schools

Manju was born at home, without a birth certificate. Surveyors in north India are used to this. They usually cajole the respondent to recall how old they were at the time of Indira Gandhi's assassination. Manju's mother was sure that her daughter was born long after. 'She was born after Indiraji's son died,' Manju's father added. Rajiv Gandhi was killed by a suicide bomber in May 1991. Fifteen years on, the Nehru-Gandhi calendar of tragedies was getting us nowhere.

'She was born around the time the markets started selling Pepsi. I drank one on my way back from my parents' home after I had her. My first time. We celebrated,' said Manju's mother. Pepsi entered the Indian market in June 1990.

Propelled by the Pepsi anecdote, we tried three strategies, hoping schemes and schools would help us. In keeping with the government's mood and ability to throw money and schemes at all the country's problems, local administration implemented an array of programmes to support health, education, roads and social protection. We decided to use these schemes to map Manju's age.

Manju's mother said that her youngest son was born soon after the first polio vaccination camp in her village. She recalled this because both Manju and her younger brother were vaccinated at these camps. 'Manju must have been three or four years old then. They gave us some documents with the date on the day of the camp, but we've lost them.' Despite not knowing what happened to the papers, she was proud of the vaccinations. 'Manju was the first girl in our family to be vaccinated,' she said triumphantly.

India embarked on its ambitious nationwide Pulse Polio programme in 1995, when the disease used to cripple more than 50,000 children in the country every year. By combining technological innovations like the indigenous bivalent polio vaccine, large domestic financial resources and close monitoring of vaccinations achieved, India was declared 'polio-free' by the World Health Organization (WHO) in 2012. The polio campaign was simple and effective. Vaccination camps were held on two designated National Pulse Polio Days every year. Beyond these, additional rounds of state-level Polio Days were also conducted in high-risk states. On these days, free polio drops would be administered to children between zero to five years at camps. The government health machinery worked with various partners, engaging two million polio volunteers and 150,000 supervisors dedicated to the campaign. Hindi film icons championed the cause in government 'infotainment' campaigns.

One of the biggest challenges for the polio campaign was finding takers in western Uttar Pradesh's Muslim community. According to a news report in the *Hindustan Times* on the campaign, which included interviews with ministers and administrators: 'Rumours that the polio vaccine caused infertility and impotence have prevented families—mainly poor Muslims—in Rampur, Bareilly, Aligarh, Moradabad, Sambhal and Meerut from getting their children vaccinated.' Community mobilization had to provide the required reassurance. Prominent Muslim clerics and religious organizations such as the All India Muslim Personal Law Board and the Sunni Ulema Council, despite differing ideologies, came together to form an anti-polio committee. This committee then called for all Muslim families to vaccinate their children, relaying the message at mosques during prayer times and at other congregations. The Saudi Arabian government issued orders requiring Haj pilgrims from India to provide polio vaccination certificates. All the messaging worked for families such as Manju's—her younger brothers and her extended family were all vaccinated.

Thanks to these family anecdotes and recollections triggered by Pepsi and the Pulse Polio campaign, we were able to guesstimate Manju's age. Bored by our amateur sleuthing, Manju stepped in herself: 'I must be fifteen now and will turn sixteen later this year. I stopped going to school the same year I saw my first film in Bareilly. My teacher at school told me that I was nine then. They used to keep an attendance book. The teacher is educated and knows more than us. That was the year before the world turned 2000 (*duniya ke 2000 hone se ek saal pehle*), I remember it very clearly.'

I would soon learn through my research recess that her first film featured Shah Rukh. In that moment, Manju skilfully combined the turn of the century, the year she was pulled out of school and her first interaction with film to produce her age. I opened my notepad, dusting off all our brave attempts and wrote: probably born in 1991 or 1992, turned eight or nine in 1999, says she is fifteen in 2006.

Manju had dropped out of school after spending an additional year in Class 3, failing to take her final exams because she never found time to study. She struggled to understand her lessons. Educationists have argued that children need pre-primary schooling to absorb early lessons better; pedagogists would say Manju was too young and ill-prepared for primary school curricula. Instead of making her repeat the year again, her parents decided that she didn't need more schooling. Manju, in any case, was the first girl in her family to attend school of any kind, the only one able to do basic mental arithmetic and count numbers of objects quickly. She was, for however short a period, the beneficiary of the District Primary Education Programme, a precursor to the 2005 'Sarva Shiksha Abhiyan' initiative in India that made elementary education compulsory and free for all children between the ages of six and fourteen. Eventually, in 2010, the Indian Parliament would go on to make primary education a justiciable right. The sudden growth and accessibility of government schooling infrastructure changed the face of rural Rampur. Girls could attend primary school near their home. Assessments of the government programme, led by civil-society organizations like Pratham, highlight how it dramatically increased the supply of schools for ordinary people but was unable to ensure good teaching quality within the school. By 2020, nearly all children in India attended schools, but very few displayed basic reading and mathematical competencies expected from them. Learning levels remain abysmally low. Irrespective of the poor standard of education, Manju and her friends were far more confident, literate and numerate than older women in their families.

Back in 2006, I struggled at first to grasp what five years of government schooling had done for the young women I was meeting. Sure, Manju had acquired a very basic and already rusty understanding of math. She could recognize single-digit numbers. But more than the rudimentary education, formal schooling taught Manju and her friends about their own limitations. Through sitting in rooms listening to a dull teacher drone on, through watching the boys seated in a separate classroom with a better instructor, something important began to happen within these young girls. By realizing that girls could not go to school if the separate toilet was not functional, by being unable to keep up with their lessons because of housework that was expected of them but not of boys, by being so proximate to the freedom boys enjoyed in public that was denied to girls, Manju and her friends had acquired a restlessness that was distinct from the equanimity displayed by their mothers and older sisters.

They had acquired a desire to see more of the world and a grave envy of the boys around them. Data shows that Manju's case speaks to a major shift in India. While male literacy rates continue to be higher at eighty-three per cent compared to sixty-five per cent for women, analysis of intergenerational social mobility shows that most Indian girls are far better educated than their mothers. But men could still make more of their education than young women. Thanks to the new roads and a new economy, young men were free to make expeditions into the world beyond their village, to leave and forge their own lives. Girls like Manju wanted the same freedom. These young women were unwilling to stay still and silent at home, bearing witness to their own misfortune. They too, like the boys, were vaccinated, somewhat literate, somewhat numerate and ready to explore the world.

Whisky, Wiring and Women

I returned to Rampur a few times between 2006 and 2007 for work related to the ISST project. We visited another hamlet of villages for interviews. In the years that followed our first meeting in 2006, I would often hear Manju describe Rampur and her hamlet as the 'garbage corner' (kabaar-khana) of western Uttar Pradesh. 'What you Delhi girls find useful about being here, I'll never understand,' she would say. Each time I returned for work or a personal visit, Manju found her surprise, or disgust, hard to contain. To me, Rampur was fascinating. The mouldy smell of molasses from sugar mills in nearby Moradabad, the empty Café Coffee Day stand at the petrol pump on the highway, the Salman Khan posters sold in the local markets. The Shah Rukh cutouts under Manju's mattress. It all brought me a step closer to 'real India,' my ridiculous quest to establish ties on an alien planet.

Rampur was part of the sugar-growing agrarian belt of western Uttar Pradesh and wealthier than most other parts of the state. A prominent Indian alcohol conglomerate maintained its largest factory in the district. In 1999, after India eased its tax structure for domestic liquor sales, business boomed. The distillery in Rampur, which manufactured high-grade spirits from sugarcane molasses and grains sourced from farmers nearby, was modernized and became the country's second-largest liquor manufacturer. The impact of the distillery's growth on Rampur's economic health was substantial. It ensured a stable buyer of sugarcane grown nearby and employed a few local men. Because of the distillery, the local electricity supply became more consistent. 'They improved the lights and wires,' Manju's mother told me, referring to the distillery. 'The roads also improved. It felt safer with the roads being well-lit. Also, we stitch at night after the children and men have gone to sleep. Without electricity, we could never do detailed stitching work. Once our contractor, Aslam, noticed we had electricity at night for longer hours, he started giving us more intricate orders. A few of the better homes here got new TVs. The roads also improved after the new part of the distillery was set up.'

Real Work in Rampur

Our job in Rampur was simple—to create case studies of home-based workers such as Manju and her mother. Adolescent girls such as Manju were important members of the flexible workforce engaged by contractors in Rampur. In particular, SEWA and its activist partners were keen to capture the age profiles, wages, working conditions and hours of work reported by women in the home-based garment trade. This was in response to an adamant stand taken by many labour-department bureaucrats who refused to acknowledge home-based work as a legitimate category of work. In the mid 2000s, about twenty years before much of the world would be forced to work from home thanks to a pandemic, government officers—the majority of them male—believed making textile embroidery at home was not 'real work' as it was done at home, for short durations of time and on an ad-hoc basis to shore up household income during times of shock and crisis.

Minimum wages for textile industries prepared by the government would only apply to those who worked continuous eight-hour shifts in a formal establishment. There were no minimum standards laid out for the per-piece wage rates women worked for in their homes. Any complaint these women might make about labour violations would be deemed automatically invalid as they were not working 'full time'. This conceptualization of workers as only those who served conventional eight-hour days in factories or other formal offices suited the lives of men. The government refused to acknowledge or understand the working lives of women. Labour regulations failed to consider how norms around care and mobility mediated women's paid labour. 'We want to work outside,' one home-based worker told me. 'But we cannot, as it is not allowed for women and it is not safe. Outside work pays much more, but at home, we work whenever we find the time. There is no fixed time as I do not know how the day will go and what all the children will need at home. We can do as many stitches as possible between housework and other responsibilities. If we need the money, we work long hours at night.' Seventy per cent of the women employed by the textiles and garments sector in India operate from home. The home-based textile sector was, and remains, one of the most important employers for women in India. But these women are not protected by labour laws, minimum wage specifications or social security.

What complicated matters was how women rendered their own paid work invisible, unwilling to recognize themselves as 'workers'. 'I have work (kaam) at home all the time, but don't really have a job (naukri),' said one of the women we spoke to. Manju's mother snapped at her, saying, 'What do you mean that we don't have a job? It's not a good job, but we are working for money. Aslam has given us work for piece-rates. We are working for him, working for our in-laws, working for our children and husbands. But only Aslam Bhai pays us.' Manju's mother was encouraging women to accept and publicly declare their new role as paid workers. She was the first woman in the village to work for pay in the garments trade and to go outside the home to meet contractors, undoubtedly the first woman in her family and village hamlet to earn a wage. Nationally, employment numbers have remained the lowest amongst Muslim women. From 1993 to 2005, around the time I met Manju, the share of rural Muslim women who were statistically identified as 'working' had increased marginally from sixteen per cent to eighteen per cent. After our encounter, between 2005 and 2018, the share of rural Muslim women with jobs declined to a historic low of ten per cent. And of these women, most work as household hands in agriculture and crafts.

For generations, the labours of women within the hamlets of rural Rampur were hidden. Women were engaged in farming homestead plots and animal rearing as unpaid family helpers. This was in keeping with the way agriculture was organized in western Uttar Pradesh. Jobs within farming were neatly segregated by sex. As Manju explained, 'Anything that needs looking at an animal or looking down on the ground, we women usually do. Anything that requires looking up or at strangers or going outside the village, the men do.' Weeding and the cleaning and storing of grains were exclusively female chores. The diktats of purdah meant that women would only work in their own fields, or the fields of their relatives and nearest neighbours. Men ploughed and prepared the land for cultivation; they also irrigated and sprayed the required pesticides and fertilizers.

The women's interactions with the world outside their courtyards and villages were tightly controlled. Any visits to local markets to buy or sell goods was, for example, the province of men alone. This holds true for millions of women across the country. In some cases, women would pay men to deal with the public market if they didn't have men in their own families to rely on. Despite a decline in the overall number of working women, a growing share is engaged in agriculture. This corresponds to men moving out of farming and into migrant jobs in construction, transport and retail. A 2013 Oxfam report found that eighty per cent of farm work in India was done by women. Yet the popular image of a farmer in India remains sturdily, enduringly masculine.

While Rampur had spiffy new distilleries, electrical networks and new roads, one metric of rural life remained the same: women were chronically exhausted from working all the time. They had no time for themselves, and indeed no time for our survey. Manju and her mother were always busy, giving us rushed answers. We were not entitled to their time, and I felt guilty asking Manju to spend her twenty-minute break between cutting vegetables and fetching water with me, describing her life in the Real India. No amount of academic training prepares you for these ethical dilemmas. We decided to interview women in the morning when their husbands left for work. They had, at this time, a few moments to spare before they prepared lunch for the day. The case studies took five visits and two months.

Talking to men was easier. They were busy but had routinized free time to smoke and discuss the news every evening. In 1985, Devaki Jain and Nirmala Banerjee produced one of the most significant works in Indian feminism and agrarian studies—a volume of essays that they collated and edited, called the *Tyranny of the Household*. The book taught generations of Indian feminists how existing methodologies of measuring and understanding 'work'—both the produce of women and also the distribution of effort within any family—were grossly misleading and inadequate. One of the papers, written by Jain with Malini Chand Seth, quantified the time-poverty of women in six villages by measuring how they spent their time. Their 1977 study found that women worked long, unrelenting hours between the fields and housework with barely any time for relaxation. Their findings also highlighted how women were involved in far more economic production than formal statistics recognized. Jain would go on to say, 'If women's unpaid work were properly valued, it is quite possible that women would emerge in most societies as the main breadwinners—or at least equal breadwinners—since they put in more hours of work than men.'

After a decade of feminist activism, this methodology of studying the use of time was adopted by the Indian government through a larger time-use pilot survey in 1998. The results echoed previous analyses, finding that men had eight more hours each week for sleep, leisure and recreation. These findings have been consistent across time and place in India.

In 2019, the government would eventually publish results from India's first national time-use survey, although the effort would receive severe criticism for not following standard international protocols (the Indian survey usually relied on one respondent to provide information on all family members as opposed to the recommended practice of seeking information independently from each individual within the household). Even with all its methodological troubles, the data from 2019 would continue to highlight the time-poverty of rural women. If we included employment-related activities with unpaid care work in our definition of 'working', the data showed that rural men, those between the ages of fifteen and fifty-nine years, worked ten-hour days. Rural women worked longer days, at thirteen hours—spending five and a half hours on employment-related tasks and nearly eight hours on unpaid housework.

Urban women of means, like my mother, were also exclusively responsible for housework while managing their professional duties. But they had domestic workers and, by the late 1990s, washing machines to help. Much like the women surveyed in the '70s, Manju and her mother, two decades later, continued to bear the triple burden of domestic duties, homestead farming and sewing work with little support from men or machines. The burden of care ultimately rests with women. And the women we were surveying in Rampur had no rest.

The feminization of care and agriculture sustained the feminization of exhaustion. Everywhere in Manju's village, I saw young men jetting in and out on tempos and bikes, or playing cricket and chatting, or huddled in groups discussing local politics and gossip. Women barely found time to talk to each other, never mind me. In 2006, my clueless enthusiasm never waned. I would rescue these women's labours and lives, I would peel away their statistical invisibility and direct the government's benevolent gaze towards them—with Rigour, one survey questionnaire and one case study at a time. I placed my youthful faith in Data.

Research Recess

Manju scoffed at our research attempts after we finished our final interviews. She thought girls like her needed kind and decent husbands and fathers, not a survey on wages and work. 'Can your survey turn these men into Shah Rukh?' I explained that the state needed data to support workers' rights and welfare, especially those without formal jobs and contracts. 'The government will see us and our jobs through your survey, our suffering,' she said, 'and then what? Have you met the local government officers? The post offices and police stations are full of fools and thugs. I become afraid if they even look at us.' She was confused. How would government involvement make anything better? 'Let's discuss the new Shah Rukh film instead,' she said. Manju was unlikely, though, to see it for another year. Fandom was a better use of our time together.

In late 2006, when our team returned to follow up on our original interviews, I asked Manju about Shah Rukh, how they met and why she loved him. She giggled, eyes twinkling, excited to tell her story. Her body was radiant with affection for our mythical superhero. In asking about Shah Rukh, I had triggered Manju. She was suddenly on fast-forward, hurtling through the fields towards Him. Taking deep gulps of air, giddy and full of half-smiles, she spoke without pause for forty-five minutes. This was our third meeting and first real conversation. She started with acknowledging her good fortune for having an entrepreneurial mother. 'I was lucky, girls never get to go to the city here. But my mother needed to meet Aslam Bhai for work and there was no one to help her carry the clothes.' She described her first visit to Darzi Chowk in Bareilly. In 1999, a few months before Eid, eight- or nine-year-old Manju and her twenty-something mother took a bus out of their village. The hour-long journey felt too short. This was the farthest Manju had ever travelled from her home. In Bareilly, she held her mother's hand as they took a shared auto to Aslam's house. He was an important local contractor, paying women ₹50 for each patch of appliqué embroidery.

Manju's mother was a tough negotiator. She had a business plan to grow the garments trade in Rampur. Her proposal sought additional payment from Aslam in exchange for supplying more labour while guaranteeing and supervising its quality. She had trained many of the local women and they could produce orders based on Aslam's instructions on the stitch required. Aslam happily agreed—there was heavy demand for appliqué work in Lucknow and Bareilly and more supply from Rampur would help keep his overheads low. Skilled embroidery workers for Ada and zari-zardozi work were becoming increasingly rare and very expensive. Aslam saw profit in investing more monies to train and hire other types of embroiderers through Manju's mother in Rampur. Home-based workers were cheap labour, paid based on the number of pieces produced. And if the final product was not up to scratch, Aslam would simply refuse to pay their wages.

While Aslam and her mother engaged in their business negotiation, Manju was offered a Pepsi and introduced to Aslam's daughter Najma. Manju described the house to me; it was more opulent than anything she had ever seen. Aslam's shop was also his home. The first floor served as his personal residence while the ground floor was for the shop and zari work. There were garments and order papers littered all over the two-room house. And then Manju spotted the television set. The pictures on the screen, she told me, were shinier than those she had seen on the three TVs in her village. She stared at Najma watching the TV all by herself. It felt like a dream. For a girl, having a TV to oneself in her hamlet was impossible. Najma invited Manju to join her. Together, they channel-surfed until eventually finding a matinee telecast of *DDLJ* on the local network operated by the cable-wallah.

DDLJ was the first Indian film to be shot with Dolby sound mix, the 35mm colours were vivid, and the studio had invested heavily in equipment, technicians and production quality. The director Aditya Chopra, son of the legendary film-maker Yash Chopra, said in an interview that he 'wanted to give Indian film audiences a beautiful love story and a beautiful film. We wanted to shoot Europe as best we could, as a way for ordinary Indians to experience and see countries and locations they were probably never going to visit'. The unreal and unattainable foreign landscapes matched the unreal and unattainable love affair captured in the film.

In *DDLJ*, Simran is a British girl of Indian descent who lives in London. She is engaged to a man in Punjab chosen by her father. Simran submits to the arrangement, convinced that her father would have found her a suitable match. In doing so, she has given up on her own hopes of true love. Simran requests her father to let her travel through Europe with her friends as a final hurrah before married life. She meets Raj (played, of course, by Shah Rukh Khan) during her Eurail trip, and they fall in love. King's Cross Train Station, Trafalgar

Square, the London Tube and Switzerland play host to a variety of scenes that compose Simran and Raj's love story.

Foreign tourism from India, specifically to countries where the Chopras, father and son, set their films, expanded ten-fold. According to Swiss tourism authorities, 326,454 Indians visited the country in 2017, compared to 28,834 in 1992. Wealthy young couples dominated this influx, with Indian 'honeymoon tourism' becoming big business in Europe. A search on Instagram reveals thousands of tourists who visit the places where *DDLJ* was shot, reenacting famous stills from the film. Nothing was more romantic to Indians in the '90s than honeymooning in Switzerland, and that connection has only become stronger over time, as images from *DDLJ* helped code and define romance for several generations of viewers. So influential was the Chopras' production house (Yash Raj Films) in stirring touristic sentiment that the Swiss government awarded Yash Chopra a lifetime service honour. It is iconic imagery, invoked so often in Hindi cinema (sometimes as homage to the '90s or humorous parodies) that each Yash Raj romance production starts to feel like a pastiche of itself.

For Manju in Aslam's house-shop in Bareilly, real life tasted so incredibly dull after those hours in front of Aslam's glorious TV with *DDLJ* and Najma. How was she supposed to return to Rampur and get on with regular life? Too young to give much consideration to Shah Rukh's looks, Manju loved his energy. She wanted to scream his name, dance unceasingly to the songs in the movie and repeat each line, relay all that she saw to her friends, and gossip about every scene. Manju wanted to watch the whole movie again with Najma. It was an afternoon of accidental discovery. She discovered Switzerland, she discovered London, she discovered Shah Rukh and Najma. As Manju lost herself in dreams and the Yash Raj Universe, her clear-eyed mother convinced Aslam to make her the lead subcontractor for her cluster of villages and increase the supply of garments from the area. A few years later, it would prove to be an afternoon of excessive adventure for Manju *and* her mother.

Aslam's daughter Najma was a dedicated student and a fan of all things Shah Rukh. She had audiocassettes, CDs, photos and magazine cutouts gifted by her older brother. At thirteen, Najma was a few years older than Manju and attended a private school in Bareilly. A kind girl, aware of her good fortune, she loaned items from her Shah Rukh stash to Manju, as her family could always afford new music, magazines or posters. Najma told Manju that *DDLJ* had been released four years ago, that they were able to watch it on TV only because it was so old. 'But I explained to her how we were a bit behind Bareilly in Rampur,' Manju said.

Realizing that Manju was hooked, Najma told her about Shah Rukh's other films; one set in a college was a particular favourite. And a plan was hatched. Najma promised to find videos of Shah Rukh films to show Manju whenever she visited. The local audio-video shop had started stocking VCDs in Darzi Chowk, signalling the advent of new media technologies in urbanized India. The shop was a few steps away from Aslam's home, and would rent out CD players as well. Najma convinced her older brother to rent these pirated prints every month when Manju and her mother would come to deliver orders. Aslam indulged his daughter, on the condition that Najma study hard and do well in school. Manju's mother agreed as well, on the condition that Najma help Manju with her writing and reading for half an hour on each visit. Najma loved the idea of playing teacher and threw herself into Manju's education. Najma's good grades and the CD rental shops in the markets of Bareilly allowed Manju to begin her new life lessons—all through the filmography of Shah Rukh Khan.

On occasion, as Najma and Manju watched their films, their mothers would join them. Some days, they would meet Aslam's buyers, often super-elite Muslim women who lived between the

Gulf, Lucknow and Delhi. They supplied fabrics and garments to fashion designers and ran their own private retail networks. '*Taraash ke banaya hai*,' Manju's mother would say about how carefully these women had sculpted themselves—all alabaster skin, tinkling laughter and punishingly exquisite taste. One of these buyers, a Mrs Naqvi, was married into a renowned business family. She had developed a fondness for Manju's mother, sending Eid presents through Aslam. Mrs Naqvi was a progressive patron of women's self-help groups and home-based textile workers in the region. An alumna of one of India's poshest girls' schools, she consequently had a posh and glamorous network. Manju told me that Mrs Naqvi had even met Shah Rukh at a party: 'She said he was kind to everyone who wanted a photo, but very Punjabi, not Pathan, though I did not understand what she meant.'

Everyone in Manju's home and village understood that these monthly trips to Bareilly for half a day were part of her mother's efforts to be a good woman who was trying to earn more money for her family. They thought the visits were exclusively aimed at handing over the completed textile pieces, exchanging payments, reviewing new orders and identifying defects in finished pieces. This was an accurate account of what transpired. After settling the previous month's order, Aslam and his wife would help Manju's mother understand new requirements. What Manju's mother never disclosed was that these visits were also meant for fun and education—to get away from rural routines, to make new friends and connections. They laughed, watched films, gossiped. Aslam and Najma would be notified of their visit a week in advance, enough time to organize payment for Manju's mother and a film for Manju. The arrangement lasted from 1999 till 2003, as Manju grew from nine to thirteen years old. These four years served as Manju's greatest education—the Shah Rukh Shiksha Abhiyan. Najma helped Manju improve her reading, writing and ability to do simple sums. She enjoyed playing the role of film-festival curator too. Her friends would also join. And together they saw *Kuch Kuch Hota Hai, Pardes, Kabhi Haan Kabhi Naa, Dil To Pagal Hai, Dil Se, Yes Boss, Baazigar*—the works.

Through that time, through those movies, Manju convinced herself that Love, the dangerous Yash Raj variety, was real. She knew, she told me, that Muslim women in rural UP would have a hard time finding love because they were denied the possibility of travel or going away to college. Shah Rukh's romance films demonstrated that leaving home could yield adventure and, above all, romance. Manju discovered unknown English and Hindi words, she discovered London and New York. She discovered that she wished to buy a henna-coloured kurta, just like the one Kajol wore in a film.

Discussing the films with Najma's teenage friends, Manju learned that the term 'girlfriend' was used to describe the glamorous girls who accompanied rich boys at parties. And that these rich boys rarely married their girlfriends if these women only wore Western clothes. Manju learned too that there were men who looked just like her frowning, disciplinarian uncles in London and America. She realized that Indians could run shops in faraway lands. Manju danced and whirled with Shah Rukh, made certain to learn the *'Mere khwabon mein jo aaye'* song by heart. She watched the cool college kids in *Kuch Kuch Hota Hai* and admired a life she knew she could never have.

Here was a kind, well-spoken man with dimples who lived abroad, paid attention to women and earned good money. Manju had never witnessed such masculine poetry before. There, in a tiny room in Bareilly, while her mother went about the business of earning an independent livelihood, Manju sipped her Pepsi and decided to fall in love with Shah Rukh. Her first favourite actor, her first favourite anything. Her first favourite of consequence. A man who taught her about her own desire for discovery. Just as importantly, he taught her that there were different kinds of men out there, that there was a large world beyond the torpor of traditional village life. I asked her what she thought of all these movies, and the first link she drew was with the men surrounding her. 'Each time I'd watch his films, I wondered why the boys around us were so different from him? I guess that's why he is a hero. I wish they would learn manners from him, but they keep racing bikes and building muscles like Salman.'

Manju and Najma became a duet of giggles and squeals as they watched an old *Dil Se* print in 2003. 'They'd start laughing at the mention of his name,' Manju's mother said. Najma would read Shah Rukh interviews out loud to Manju. One afternoon they even chanced upon an interview being broadcast on TV; 'Najma had to explain it as it was in English,' Manju told me, 'but even if I did not understand, I could watch him again and again.' The good times, though, were coming to an end.

Continuing in her habit of forging firsts, Manju's mother also became the first woman in her hamlet to have her own phone. In 2002, Aslam gave her a mobile phone to help coordinate deliveries and supplies. The phone became a source of murmurs and gossip in Manju's hamlet. Her mother became unpopular. 'People thought something was wrong with her, that she was not good to my father because she was outside the village a lot more than most women,' Manju would say to me years later. While small Nokia phones were increasingly common among rural families in the early 2000s, hardly any were owned by women. About a year after Manju's mother got her phone, Manju said she noticed her father grow increasingly angry at their trips to Aslam's house in Bareilly. 'One day,' Manju recalled, 'we were helping her with the embroidery and playing antakshari in the courtyard. I remember we had just put the clothes up to dry. Singing songs was fun, we had a radio nearby. I knew that the men and older people did not think this was good behaviour, but it made our work more fun. I don't know what happened, the men in the village must have said something to him, but my father came out and shouted at my mother in front of the other women. He said we were defying

Allah, and singing these songs was not good for women. I had never seen him like that. He used to be happy with my mother's work.'

After a month of bitter bickering, the resentment spilled over into a loud, angry fight. Manju's father felt his job was providing adequately. Their oldest son had managed to find well-paid work as an electrician for a factory in Bareilly. Now that the family was doing well, why did Manju's mother want to work for wages? Manju's mother argued that the work was good, supported small daily expenses and they could build savings for the future. She said it felt good for her not to have to ask her husband or her son for their money if she wanted something small for her or the children. But, Manju told me, her father said they were wasting money 'on useless ideas like movies.' The fight brought on the demise of Manju's mother's phone. 'He smashed my mother's phone; he was that angry.' She had never seen her mother more withdrawn or sad. 'You should never care so much about work outside the home; a man can take it all away from you anytime he pleases,' Manju said.

A week after the fight that claimed her phone, once the garment orders were ready, Manju's mother collected herself and called Aslam from a local shop. She apologized for not being able to make their usual monthly meeting and requested that he come to the village and collect his deliveries. Aslam didn't ask questions, he simply accepted her request. Manju's father never protested either; neither did her mother seek his permission. The episode marked the creation of a new supply chain, where Aslam would send his son or arrive personally to collect the garments. Manju's mother stopped all travel to Bareilly. It was November 2003 and though Aslam would sometimes bring Najma, the girls' friendship and Manju's blossoming romance with Shah Rukh had been interrupted.

Fortunately for Manju, by 2003, her village and its surrounding areas were no longer so rural and rustic, so cut off from urban lifestyles. Now 'rurban', a mix of village agrarian life and urbanity, nearly all the homes in the area had become pukka and televisions and phones were commonplace. Shah Rukh dominated the Eid releases for the first year of her exile from the television at Darzi Chowk.

Kal Ho Naa Ho—a grand, soppy, life-affirming Karan Johar romance—was the big Eid release in 2003. Eid was one of the only times families went to the cinema hall together. 'At other times,' Manju said, 'it is a filthy place full of bad men where no woman goes alone.' Manju, though, was not allowed to go to the movies. She faced stiff resistance from her brothers and father. 'All the men dislike Shah Rukh and his films,' she told me. 'I think it's because the women are his fans and the men don't like that. I had to beg, even give my Eid money to my brother to convince him to come with me to watch the film. It was so wrong, they had watched all the films that had released that year—bad films like *Jism*; they saw *Tere Naam* with Salman many times. But they were being so difficult about one movie for me.' Three years later, while chatting with me during my research recess in 2006, the hurt from all the bargaining for film still pinched her. She would eventually watch *Kal Ho Naa Ho*, but her viewing pleasure was adulterated by the callous cruelty she believed her brothers and father displayed for the film's Eid release in 2003.

Manju was an angry teenager, irritated that the men in her family wielded so much control over even the smallest pleasures. She did not want to bargain for Shah Rukh. Young men were free to travel in and out of Bareilly or Rampur town. It was common for adolescent boys and young men to watch movies in local halls or at a friend's house in the city. Manju spoke to her mother and her fellow home-based appliqué workers about the unfairness of it all. Many of the women agreed that they wanted to see a film together. Manju's mother's friend, Roshan, laughed about how difficult it was to 'watch films covered up: you can barely hear or enjoy the film at the theatre. They take us to watch these boring Salman or Sunny Deol pictures during Eid. I doze off behind my burqa.'

In 2004, confident that her brothers and father would not let her watch *Veer-Zaara*—another Yash Raj and Shah Rukh release timed to benefit from the Eid bonanza, and even more confident that she did not want to keep begging for small pleasures, Manju hatched a plan with her mother. The Darzi Chowk video store would charge ₹400 to bring a VCD player to their village. 'My mother talked to Aslam and helped plan it all,' Manju told me. 'We stitched clothes for more hours and organized the funds. We put a little away for Aslam Bhai to rent the CD and CD player for us. The *Veer-Zaara* print would take some time to reach the store, so Najma and my mother suggested that we rent *DDLJ*. Many women in the village had never seen it. We would watch inside the home, but it was better than not being able to watch at all.' Women in her hamlet were earning between ₹20 and ₹50 for each appliqué stitch. While most of the money was handed over to the family, Manju and her mother helped start a fund for fun.

That evening, a week after Eid celebrations in November 2004, Manju's village blossomed into a Bollywood hotspot. It was revolution. Nearly all the home-based embroidery workers fell in love with Shah Rukh. Manju had assumed the role of curator now. Portable electronic devices, the existence of TVs in rurban homes and the women's own earnings allowed a new Shah Rukh fan club to emerge. These were otherwise tough times for the women of Rampur. It had been a year of drought. Money was scarce and did not buy as much it did in other years. As prices increased, the quality of husbands declined: men who discharged their pain on their family, men who blamed their wives and children for their financial crises. So, after that filmy evening in November 2004, once every few months, the women of Manju's village came together to smile at Shah Rukh. This was precisely the kind of romance they needed. And because these screenings happened inside the premises of someone's home, within domestic spaces, the men couldn't complain too loudly. 'Older people here may have old views, but no one is a bad person. They wouldn't stop us from enjoying a small film together,' Manju's mother said. The women in Manju's village had negotiated a new entertainment equilibrium.

Inequality Is Boring

In less than seven years, it was all over. One by one, between 2004 and 2011, everything changed again. Most of Manju's mother's friends had stopped doing stitching work. Their sons had left to find work in the cities and were remitting more money back home. Many of the women said they no longer felt the need to work and preferred to spend their scarce hours of free time watching soap operas on TV instead. The adolescent girls who did stitching work were steadily being married off. The Shah Rukh fan club's screenings, Manju told me, were grinding to a halt. 'It's not okay, that girls have to leave and never find the time to come back but boys get to stay with their parents after marriage,' she complained.

By the time I returned to Rampur in 2011, 'boring' had become a popular word. Every woman I met complained of boredom. The oldest said, 'We are meant to be at home. Then we get married and stay at a different home. Purdah is boring. It's all very boring.' Others nodded in agreement. A few of the younger girls smiled and agreed: '*Sab kuch boring hain.*' Everything is boring. I asked the women how they had come to use the English word to express their feelings. The answer was prompt: 'Manju Madam!' Manju's middle brother Asif had attended an English-medium school in Bareilly. He was the first member of Manju's family to learn English and the first to be educated in a private school. He struggled with schoolteachers and the syllabus, but he loved films and sports. Asif was thrilled to discover the word 'boring' the night he watched Salman Khan host the Indian adaptation of Big Brother.

Asif was spending the night at a friend's place in Bareilly after a sports competition at school. The Jat and Muslim boys in his all-boys' school loved Salman. They dressed like him, they 'gymmed' like him, they wanted to be him. Salman used the word 'boring' for a particularly dull contestant. Asif plucked up the courage to ask his friend what 'boring' meant. His friend explained that math class was boring. He clarified that 'boring' meant 'thanda' (cold), not to be confused with 'boring wells' that some of his father's friends helped build for urban homes. Asif understood the word as '*boring woh hai jisme koi jaan nahi hain, koi baat nahin hai.*' A boring person or phenomenon is one that has no life or spirit in them, nothing special to hold our attention. Soon, Asif started using the word with his brothers, teaching them the meaning. He told his brothers about Salman's jokes and antics on the TV show, how he dressed and what he said. Manju remained unimpressed.

One afternoon, as she washed the dishes, the three brothers ganged up to lecture Manju on the virtues of Salman. They said Shah Rukh—whose pictures, now faded and tattered, she still kept under her bed—was boring. Asif explained the word. Manju thought it did not apply to Shah Rukh but summed up the lives of women in rurban Rampur. It didn't take long for her to spread the word, for it to become a mantra for her friends and co-workers, all of whom lived daily with the tedium of a heavily regulated social life. The working women's group was always keen to learn new words and ways.

Beyond learning of her own boredom in the English language, for Manju, the year 2011 distinguished itself for evoking anger. For her gang of fellow fangirls and house-bound girlfriends, 2011 marked Shah Rukh's turn towards the robotic in *Ra.One*, and his reprisal, in *Don 2* (2011), of a hyper-sexy criminal protagonist. Despite several pleas, the young women failed to receive permission to travel to Bareilly to watch these movies. Although their brothers did. For Manju's three brothers, these 2011 Shah Rukh films allowed them to rediscover Kareena Kapoor's waistline and Priyanka Chopra's lips. International pop star Akon's techno-monotonic beats on '*Chammak challo*', a hit song composed with Vishal Dadlani and Shekhar Ravjiani for the *Ra.One* soundtrack, seemed to mimic the monotone beat of Rampur's social life. The song blared on repeat at all the bus stations and functions across the district's towns and villages. Even the most avid Salman fans loved Shah Rukh's moves in the song.

In 2011, Manju's brothers started taking themselves on joyrides. They would mount their shiny new bikes and ride all along the newly paved concrete section of the old National Highway 530. The boys were on their bikes and the girls were getting married. Local weddings offered a great excuse for men to cruise along the highway. There was always something that needed to be bought or transported. The young men would race between the towns on the highway, accompanied by other boys from their village and neighbouring hamlets, all of them ferrying their cumulative angst between Rampur and Bareilly.

The bikes had been Eid presents for the men of the family after a good financial year. Families in Manju's village were once completely dependent on erstwhile jajmans or Jat landowners for their livelihood. The Jats grew sugarcane and Muslim men were carpenters, welders, repairmen and agrarian labourers. While Manju's family owned a small plot of land to cultivate for themselves, her father worked to supply iron equipment and wires to landholders, as had the generations before him. At the start of the twenty-first century, thanks to a boom in construction activities between 2004 and 2010, Manju's father and brothers started sourcing plywood and ironworks for new buildings and projects being constructed in rapidly developing Bareilly. They helped government roadworks by providing blacksmiths and labour. The windfall from these opportunities helped them upgrade their house and send Asif to his private English-medium school. More financially secure than they had ever been, it was an excellent time for the family to organize a marriage for Manju.

While the urbanizing and growing economy of Bareilly in 2011 helped the men of rural Rampur earn more, none of Manju's brothers or their friends desired a life dedicated to full-time farming or iron works. Farming had lost all lustre, being a blacksmith wasn't professional enough, it felt like a life spent in dull and undignified retirement. The young men wanted to work in Mumbai, Delhi or the Gulf.

To their dismay, much like Manju's, Rampur was only two hundred kilometres from Delhi but felt light years away from anything of interest or consequence. While Manju's dissatisfaction was contained within the walls of her home or the boundaries of her hamlet, her brothers took to the streets. These reluctant future farmers and blacksmiths of India had little else to do but go on joyrides, the speed of their bikes propelled by discontent. All along the roads connecting Rampur to Bareilly, you could see them in the evenings, hands held up to the sky, eyes fixed on an unknown horizon. They would ask the universe and any woman they saw just the one question: 'Wanna be my chammak challo?' For these joyriders from an obscure part of Rampur, 'chammak challo' meant a prize catch. The men in Manju's life were in the mood for conquest.

Manju and her friends experienced inequality very differently from their mothers and grandmothers. While her mother had made peace with restrictions on where women could go and what they could do, Manju and her friends had not. They experienced inequality as boredom—the years, months and days seemed to blend into each other, passed as they were in the same streets and the same courtyards, with so little mobility that even a joyride on a newly paved highway was not an option. Whenever I had an opportunity to watch the women get together to stitch garments or do housework, all conversation was stimulated by the energy of their boredom. Even a quick visit to a new shopping complex in Bareilly before a wedding could last weeks of hushed whispers and exaggerated retellings. The most excitement was reserved for the secondhand reports from male cousins who had managed to ride their bikes to Noida or even Delhi, bringing back news of how young city people dressed.

As with the young men, the young women yearned to see a world they only caught glimpses of on TV, or through the tales told by those who'd made it out of Rampur. Everyone was waiting for a magical joyride that could take them away from their boredom of confinement into the world of highways, malls and markets. For women, this joyride equivalent, their way out, was a good marriage to a good man. 'If you marry well,' Manju once said, 'you can do anything you want. Aslam Bhai was a good husband to his wife, he made enough money and let her watch as many movies as she liked.' All that stood between Manju's boredom and a consistent supply of Shah Rukh films was a sympathetic husband with a good job.

Manju's Marriage

In 2011, Manju was matched for marriage into a well-off family that owned a profitable small business in Bareilly. They supplied electrical equipment and electricians. Manju could not wait to escape her village. They argued again about her age. Her mother felt she was younger than twenty. Exasperated, Manju said, 'I *must* be twenty, it's the age at which all the girls marry around here these days. Plus, I am the only one in this family who is any good at math. I went to school, Najma taught me, but no one listens to me.'

'Twenty is too old for marriage,' her mother muttered.

Marrying after eighteen was a significant departure from the past, in keeping with a general trend of increasing age of marriage amongst women in India. The country continues to have the highest number of child brides in the world. However, in 2011, national surveys estimated that twenty-seven per cent of girls in India were married before their eighteenth birthday, a sharp decline from fifty per cent just over a decade before. The data, released by the Registrar General and Census Commissioner, showed that the average age of marriage for all Indians had increased from thirteen in 1901 to eighteen in 1991, climbing to an all-time high of twenty-one years old in 2011. For men, the age of marriage increased from twenty-two in 1991 to twenty-five in 2011. Manju, with her curiosity for facts and figures, knew about these numbers.

In each of my five visits to Rampur, between 2006 and 2011, Manju would ask only two things—what I thought of the new Shah Rukh film, and if I could look up answers to random questions on the census website. I was convinced that she entertained my visits because I brought easy access to the world through my laptop and dongle. Smartphones were still rare in her village. Manju, it sometimes seemed, was a fan of Shah Rukh and the Registrar General of India. So many questions for the internet. What was Shah Rukh up to these days? What share of the Indian population was married? What share was Muslim? What share owned a TV? She would write down the answers and show off her arcane knowledge at family events and with her friends. But by 2011, she had grown weary of her party trick. 'What's the point,' she would ask rhetorically. 'No one finds this stuff interesting. This place is full of boring people who don't want to know about the world.'

So, marriage happened to Manju that year, at the disputed age of twenty. Those were her words—she wasn't getting married; marriage was *happening* to her. She was simply along for the ride, a spectator with a front-row seat. In Rampur, women talked about marriage in strange ways. A happy marriage was one in which a wife produced sons quickly and could consequently hope to be left in peace for the rest of her days, as long as she did the adequate amount of cleaning and praying expected of her. Sex was just another laborious household chore—easier than washing utensils during family festivities and often described as a mild discomfort, like a lurking joint pain with which one must learn to live.

But Manju was not merely in a state of discomfort; she was displeased. The fact that she had never seen her future husband was never the source of her displeasure. *That* was business as usual. No, it was Shah Rukh—her favourite movie star, her only indulgence. Manju's father and brothers were unwilling to permit the carriage of any Shah Rukh Khan memorabilia to her new home. They planned to check her things before she left, minimizing any chance of smuggling her illicit goods. She complained about her family's bizarre restrictions to her future sisters-in-law during their visit to discuss wedding logistics and made everyone at home feel uncomfortable. Her father stopped speaking to her. No one knew what to say—so she was ignored, her request relegated to awkward smiles and samosas. Her treasure trove included the two photos cut from a magazine and a tape of the *DDLJ* soundtrack. After Manju's father halted all trips to Bareilly, Manju had requested her mother for a tape as they had no CD players in her village. One of her neighbours had an old tape player they would listen to while stitching and working. The cassette had been secured through Aslam five years ago, after much hungama at home. When he promised to procure the cassette for Manju, her grandmother was unhappy—young girls were not supposed to be listening to silly love songs, she thought. This tape was too much, she felt. It would fill Manju's head with silly notions about love and marriage, the silliness that made girls sad these days. The day the tape arrived, Manju recalled how her annoyed father had shrugged his shoulders and said to the disgruntled matriarch of the family, 'Nothing will happen, it's just a tape, he is just some hero.'

The day Manju left her village, she secretly handed over the errant tape to her younger sister, also a garment worker. Following her departure, Manju's brother Asif mailed the Shah Rukh pictures she had cut out from a magazine to me. Scribbled on the back of one of the pictures was a note: 'Didi, even after marriage, and I really hope you do get married, never stop watching Shah Rukh.' Not a scrap of

Shah Rukh memorabilia travelled with Manju as she moved into her new home. On the surface, she was cleansed of her fandom, repeatedly instructed to avoid talking about movies and actors, as it would upset her groom and in-laws.

Marriage could not cure Manju's boredom. Fifteen months after the marriage, in 2013, Manju ran away from married life—only to be chased by her fantasies. When I returned to Rampur for a visit in 2014, everyone claimed to have no idea of Manju's whereabouts. She had left her husband the year before. His family found a neatly composed note: 'I fully understand your difficulties. Life is hard these days. Please forgive me. I need to leave. This marriage did not suit me, it was a mistake.' Manju's mother said that the first six months of marriage were difficult. She had expected to live in Bareilly, where her in-laws owned a shop. Instead, her family home was a house in remote Dhaura Tanda within Rampur district. In six months, she had not conceived, leading her in-laws to worry constantly and out loud. Her husband, one of Manju's brothers told me, was a good man. But six months into the marriage, he got a job that took him to Delhi and Dubai for a year. The contract, for wiring work, was with an influential builder and lucrative. He was a pragmatic man; he knew the work would lead to more well-paid jobs which would help them raise children and build a house in Bareilly itself.

But back in Dhaura Tanda, Manju grew restless within the first few weeks of her husband's departure. While she was fond of her husband, she had nothing to say to his family and they seemed to have little to say in return. She was in her early twenties and her in-laws expected her to be a mute workhand within their home. They did not like her watching TV and did not allow her to work or leave the house. I imagined how much she must have missed her family and friends, missed those occasional movie nights she organized in her village, missed even the intricate stitching work she did. She desperately missed being the media don of Rampur, missed being meaningful. Her brother Asif asked if I had heard from her in the past year.

In December 2011, when I was in Delhi for the Christmas holidays, I had left a message for Manju with Asif. A few weeks later, she had called me from her husband's phone to ask if I had received the pictures she'd sent through her brother. She sounded deflated, as if marriage had pulled the plug on all possibilities. She talked about her husband, about how crowded her new house was, how there was no free time, no singing in the courtyard, how all spaces were always shared. 'This is a much larger family than ours. I hope we can visit their cousins in Lucknow soon. That would be nice.'

'So how *is* your husband?' I blurted out, my voice flooding with embarrassment for asking such a personal question. She was silent for some time. 'How is yours?' She knew that I was unmarried. In fact, I was reaching the end of a relationship with a wonderful Bengali man.

'It's good,' Manju said, offering some unusual counsel. 'Take your time, don't get married soon, it's really not as great as I thought.' Her husband, she said, was nice enough ('saaf aur dhang ke') but marriage itself remained frustratingly opaque. 'He will go away for a year soon. They show you love and marriage in those movies,' Manju said to me, 'but they never teach you how to be in a marriage. Najma says they show such things on TV shows now. Chalo, I'll go back to the room. He will wonder if I use up all the talk-time on the card.' And with that, she was gone.

Worried about Manju's disappearance and what had transpired, I visited Aslam Bhai after meeting Manju's family in 2014. Unsurprisingly, he knew of Manju's whereabouts. He told me he'd helped her secure work at a garment factory in Noida. It seemed her brother had lied to me. Manju's family were aware of her whereabouts, they simply could not bring themselves to admit what had happened to Manju's marriage. Her doting husband had gifted her a phone before leaving for Dubai via Delhi. Manju had wanted to spend half the year at her parents' home while her husband was away, but her in-laws were unwilling to let her go for such a long visit. Manju made a habit of fighting with her mother-in-law.

While Manju's husband was away, feeling hemmed in by his family, she invited Najma to visit. They met; Najma had recently married a young man who worked for a successful exports company in Noida. She promised to help Manju find a job near her. Najma told her father and despite Aslam's misgivings, he found Manju a job. She would be one of many women working on the factory floor for an apparel company. The factory usually preferred workers to live in hostels nearby. But he felt the factory arrangements were not too safe for women.

So Manju would live with Najma at her in-laws' place. Najma's husband would be away for work in the Gulf for the full year. This was convenient and safe. Aslam called and informed Manju's mother and brothers. 'Her mother knew,' Aslam told me, 'that Manju would never rest easy until she had her own time in Delhi. She also knew that Manju liked her husband, not her in-laws. And that she could not keep living with Najma. So, she did not stop me from helping her daughter.'

Once the job in Noida had been arranged, Najma and Aslam paid Manju another visit. Manju asked Najma to help her write the farewell note to her husband explaining her departure. They gave her a little money. Manju snuck out of her husband's house in Dhaura Tanda without a word to anyone and boarded a bus to Bareilly. From there, she travelled to Noida with Najma and her new husband.

I asked Aslam if he could give me Najma's number, and immediately called to contact Manju. She was happy to hear from me. Manju invited me to tea and looked better than ever. I returned her Shah Rukh cutouts to her. She was no longer covering her head, and the dupatta would easily fall to the ground without her noticing very much. Manju told me that the months she had spent with Najma in Noida were the happiest in her life. She would work and also help manage Najma's home as her mother-in-law stayed with them. 'It has been the best *holiday*,' she said. 'We've been watching films in the expensive cinema halls, and I saw nearly all the Shah Rukh films on TV.'

Her use of 'chutti', or holiday, struck me. Holidays had to end. How was this life a holiday? Did she plan to go back? I did not ask her immediately, considering we had not seen each other for ages, but sensed that Manju knew her time in Noida was going to end. The probabilities were stacked against her. She had, after all, always been good at this type of math. Soon enough, Manju called me to say that she planned to go back to Bareilly or Rampur. Najma was leaving Noida in a month to join her husband in Dubai and Manju did not make enough money at the factory to live on her own. She did not want to live in the factory's hostel for single women. I offered her the option of staying at my parents' house or with me. She declined. 'I need to go where I can settle down and have my own life,' she told me. 'I miss my family. You know, watching these Shah Rukh films without my mother used to make me sad. I never did tell you, but I think my mother was an even bigger fan of his than I was. That night I told you about, when my father broke her phone and wanted her to stop going to Bareilly to meet Aslam Bhai, it was *her* addiction to Shah Rukh he was complaining about, not mine. He thought she was slow with her work around the house and in the fields because she was dreaming of Shah Rukh and those songs and that I was becoming just like her.'

After leaving Noida, Manju's first move was to live with Aslam Bhai and his wife in Darzi Chowk. She planned to help with his business and earn her own embroidery money. A few months later, though, with little explanation, she returned to her husband in Dhaura Tanda. It was now 2015 and on hearing this news from Aslam, I was determined to visit Manju. I could not travel with Aslam. Manju's in-laws were in no mood to meet him or anyone involved in supporting or instigating her running away. Najma had become the villain in the story. 'It's like this now, but with time, we'll all be back to where we were. I've seen things like this happen before,' Aslam said, sounding incredibly relaxed for an outcast. I called Manju's oldest brother. He refused a few times before eventually giving in. 'Maybe if her in-laws see that such an educated person like you is writing a story about Manju, they will respect her more.' Manju had never contacted me to discuss her return. But I needed to see her. When we finally met in Tanda, after the ritual exchange of platitudes and consumption of pakoras, we managed to find twenty minutes alone with each other. I knew this would be our last meeting. She was moving on, looking gaunt but cheerful.

We talked about Shah Rukh. Manju was unhappy that he was doing more violent films than before—she had seen *Happy New Year* (2014) in Noida with Najma. 'I don't know why he is doing action films. But, you know, when he smiles, it feels like nothing else exists. I think of his films often nowadays, when I cook and clean. I think I've become like my mother. Dreaming and being slow all day long.' And then I had to ask.

'Why did you come back, Manju? You could have stayed with Aslam Bhai and his wife, worked in their business.' She shrugged her thin shoulders. 'It wouldn't have been right, the world is not good to girls on their own. What choice do we have? At least my husband was kind enough to agree to take me back. I ran away with the phone he had given me as a gift. He called me. He was angry and wanted me to come back. When I said I wouldn't, he cut the call. A few months later he called again, saying his parents were suggesting that he find a new wife. In our community, he could have done that very easily. But he told me he still wanted us to be together. He wished me well and said I could ask him for any kind of help. When I came back to him, he knew I had left because I missed my life before the wedding, doing the things I liked. He even brought me Shah Rukh CDs to cheer me up. He is a nice man, he doesn't beat me, makes a decent living, he takes care of me. That's much better than most husbands. The world outside is a dangerous place. A girl like me can't live on her own.' She started to tear up.

I knew that something terrible must have happened. Maybe someone had harmed her in Darzi Chowk. It was Manju's secret, though, and I wasn't entitled to know. Before I left, while Manju blessed the idea of the book as a diversion from my plummeting marital prospects, her in-laws gave me 'permission' to write about Manju but said I had to leave them alone. This would be my first and last visit to her marital home. Their permission has always tasted raw in my mouth, a reminder that Manju retained no rights to her own story.

Desperately Seeking Dissent?

In 2015, the year Manju returned to her marital home, *DDLJ* completed a record 1,000-week run in Mumbai's Maratha Mandir cinema hall. Several commentators in metropolitan media criticized the film as a regressive cultural text. A key argument was that it encouraged middle-class youth to avoid active rebellion against the family as an institution and helped entrench patriarchy. Why didn't Simran and Raj just dump their families and elope?

As a pre-teen in 1995, I loved *DDLJ* for indulging the fangirl in me, with Shah Rukh's arms cast open amidst pristine Swiss Alps and Indian mustard fields. I rediscovered the film while collecting survey data on home-based textile and agarbatti workers such as Manju and Zahira. During this time, many working women I encountered, from workers to business owners, cited *DDLJ* as one of their favourite films. Indeed, watching the movie itself and independently purchasing iconography with their hard-earned wages had become an assertion of their independence and personality, a mild form of protest by prodding notions of how young women ought to behave. However, when asked, women like Manju could not conceive of life without their family, however stifled and constrained they may have felt. To become truly independent was too big a leap in a country that gave women little chance or space to make their own lives.

Critics often say that *DDLJ*, with its emphasis on patriarchal permission for young love, discourages dissent. This argument narrows the space for dissent by legitimizing it only in its most blatant, combative form, demanding that dissent always be obvious and 'out there' in full view of TV cameras and Twitter. So, no act of protest short of elopement, short of the most radical rejection of family, would suffice. Demanding such all-or-nothing actions doesn't account for the costs that eloping and actively abandoning their families would impose on women from any economic strata. The way we express resistance is subject to our own personal calculus of risk and reward.

Many of *DDLJ*'s critics single out an exchange in which Raj refuses to accept Simran's plea for them to run away together. He would rather work to gain the support of her family. Is this a concession to oppressive patriarchy? I thought so, until microeconomics and the responses of women from diverse class backgrounds taught me to watch the film differently. To my surprise, Manju pointed to the same scene as a display of courage. She insisted that running away was the easier choice for men, more so when their families supported the match, as was the case in *DDLJ*.

'Women like me have seen what happens when you leave,' she told me in one of our last conversations, when she was working at the factory in Noida. 'It's tough. You can't rely on others the way you can on your own family. Unless you have a very good man. I know a girl who works with me, named Manju. She ran away from her village in Haryana to be with a boy here. Their families opposed the match because of caste and money. But she is sad now. He doesn't love her anymore and they keep fighting. I think he is also with another woman. My friend stays with him because she can never go back to her parents, they won't allow it. It's unfair, but if the boy had tried to talk to her family first, to convince them to be happy about the marriage, at least she could still visit her family when she felt unhappy with her husband. Now, she is alone. We talked about her marriage a lot during work. She told me that boys just can't be trusted these days. When financial difficulties or other women create fights and violence, we women have no money, land or people of our own to turn to. *Ladkon ka kya hai* (what is the problem for boys)? They can find jobs, other women who will take care of them and everyone lets them live alone easily.'

When I was finally allowed to write her story, my favourite survey respondent from Rampur picked 'Manju' as her pseudonym—an ode to her friend and the complicated relationship women in India have with freedom. Both Manju and 'Manju' demonstrate a clear point—eloping had made a woman's 'fallback' position in marriage weak, as economists might put it, relative to men. The police were scary, friends were far away and had their own problems. Living alone presented risks to their safety in both small towns and large cities. Regardless of their economic circumstances, moving away from husbands and in-laws created shame, turned women into pariahs. Beyond the economics of elopement, there are emotions. Parting from parents in an acrimonious fashion was considered too painful.

For Manju, the fact that Raj avoided the easy route (for a man) of running away and cared enough to stick around, compromise and fight for approval to ensure Simran wasn't cut off from her kin was a measure of his strength and maturity. In this light, Raj was radical. Where earlier all I saw was capitulation, I began to see bargains and trade-offs. I started to realize that the act of rebellion can look very different when women are rendered dependent on the family for protection and provision. Expecting a woman in this landscape to demonstrate dissent by cutting ties with her family—the only institution that provides her material security in the absence of a supportive state or an inclusive market that values her labour—is, perhaps, asking for too much.

One of Manju's favourite scenes in *DDLJ* involved Simran's mother remarking on how men never sacrifice their well-being for women, while women are expected to give up their desires without complaint. Manju would also highlight how none of the women in the film were working professionals. They relied, as the majority of women do in India, on their families and men to provide. In this context, which seems pretty and pink on the outside, striving to marry someone who loved and supported you as opposed to making the appropriate family alliance was, and remains, difficult. The film appreciated this reality (despite its Yash Raj Films gloss) and this perhaps explains why its portrayal of both romance and mother-daughter relationships touches so many women, including Manju and her mother.

Many Hindi films dramatize this essential Indian conflict, in which women express their desire to marry someone whom the family deems inappropriate. *DDLJ* was different because it took a gentle, more understanding approach to the real and complex bargains involved in following through on such radical desires. In another Bollywood film, the couple might have run away and set up a tiny home together bereft of friends and family. Or they would have committed suicide or been murdered in a brutal honour killing.

In *DDLJ*, Raj and Simran are united once the patriarch is persuaded to see the value in their relationship. Research on working women and women's collectives tell us that familial 'permission' plays an immeasurably important role in south Asia. What the film shows is that freedom is won through incremental negotiation, that dialogue amongst loved ones can be a path towards social change. The fact that we must invest significant effort to bargain for these freedoms is sad, but also reflects our social realities across class. Many women's groups and unions seek support from men in communities to help women organize. This allows for more effective mobilization. Women often only work after their husbands permit it, even if this need to take permission is a constant source of angst and marital friction. In our own families and personal relationships, we seek support for our choices. The idea is to cajole, argue, fight, convince. This is because many of us seek love and emotional support from our family in addition to freedom. This is the way we resist and express disagreement in everyday, ordinary lives. Compromise is not necessarily cowardice. *DDLJ* was not progressive. Instead, the film took a pragmatic position, showing us what dissent within families could look like. The film did mesh wooing and harassment, a common accusation against most Indian romances. But as Manju, her mother and the gang of garment workers in Rampur always pointed out—Raj did do the dishes.

After returning to her husband, Manju produced a son in early 2017. Najma informed me and I called Manju's husband to congratulate him. Surprisingly, he gave the phone to Manju. She sounded happy, telling me that her husband had decided that they would move to Bareilly for their son's schooling. They were currently living in a small unit attached to her husband's family home, allowing them some space. She had taught her husband to help her in the kitchen every morning. He would make tea for himself and pack his own tiffin. This routinized form of support made Manju as happy as the romance of Shah Rukh films once did. She said, 'After notebandi, these are tough times for women. We have to run the household. You need a person who can understand and help you in such times. It is not just about (earning) money but also about having proper thinking and manners. Many men around here start blaming their difficulties on wives and children. They drink, scream and shout. He (Shah Rukh) would never do that. That was special—it's only now that I'm married that I understand. The way he cared for women in

the films,' she told me, 'is the way all men should care for women.'
Now, Manju finished, 'I watch TV as I wish. I've even convinced my
husband to let me continue working with Aslam. My in-laws do not
like it, but my husband takes my side. He also takes me to watch the
new Shah Rukh films at the cinema in Bareilly—the expensive hall,
that's how I've seen all the new films. I'm very lucky. We go to the hall
for women and families, that's much better than before in Rampur
watching on TV and being afraid of my father,' she said. They've lived
comfortably ever since.

—⁓—

I realize that the stories here will disappoint those expecting a
clever piece of reportage on the great pace of cultural change in the
hinterlands. Nothing politically or socially radical happens in the
colonies and villages in which Zahira, Meenal or Manju live, love
and learn. That is, nothing within the rarefied realm of the obvious.
There is the persistence of patriarchy and repressive practices such as
purdah and the penetration of discriminatory labour markets, which
everybody accepts as a mundane and God-given way of life. I have
no explicit stories of woe inspired by marginalization or state-fuelled
injustice. Moreover, these women surveyed across northern India—
from Rampur to Ahmedabad—may be keen to protest for better pay
but remain reluctant to participate in any organized resistance against
patriarchy or 'pitritantra'. Many don't even know what these words
mean. They simply yearn for marital bliss and fantasize about a more
meaningful relationship with the men in their lives. They irritate
their families by going out, daydreaming, slacking off on household
chores, talking about the movies and spending their wages. Much
like the vast majority of women in the northern belt, the women I've
met over the past decade hardly vote or attend political rallies, and
often complain about the restrictions on their time and movement—
forget finding the energy and encouragement to become members

of any Morcha or Mahila Manch. They are simply too exhausted for the revolution.

Once, I told a group of Hindu women in a Lucknow slum—women who made packing boxes—about the organized resistance mounted by the Gulabi Gang, activists clad in pink saris who fight for the rights of women. Unimpressed, one of the older women in the group said that only politicians and princesses had enough security to protect them from lascivious men at a rally, even if the march was for a women's issue. For ordinary women living in what an academic might describe as 'contexts of classical patriarchy'—where alcohol-fuelled brawls and physical seclusion were considered an inevitable and unquestionable part of a woman's lot in life—the only pink saris of consequence were those adorned by the leading ladies in their favourite films.

To some observers, it may seem as if the nature of discrimination against women in the landscape studied continues unfettered, without any revolt. The norms being challenged also appear too subtle to warrant much sociological commentary or feminist enthusiasm. In 1981, the French philosopher Michel Foucault pondered how 'techniques of domination' interacted with 'techniques of the self'. These techniques implied ways through which ordinary people transformed themselves by 'conducting operations on their own bodies, souls, thoughts'. I don't hope to tell some stirring story of modernity on the margins. Instead, I can offer only a slice of how jobs and popular media have helped these 'ordinary' women fashion a sense of self.

These stories reveal the muddled cognitive maps of oppressed women, in this case rural and urban working women, a minority in north India often complicit in their own discrimination, yet indulging resistance by indulging themselves; all the while actively partaking in newer forms of womanhood. Through their stories, I hope you will come to realize that there is something spectacular happening within ordinary unexamined spaces, and that some scholars choose to re-examine gender politics in places without Protest.

Over the years, I came to understand that the actor in question, possibly due to my own obsession, was simply happenstance. Worker-fangirls such as Manju started using selected sections of his cinema and imagery as an entry point into traversing trickier terrain—talking about their unrequited expectations of reciprocity from men in spaces of marriage, money and intimacy, and challenging the predetermined trajectories of their lives.

Reading through the reams of transcripts and the notes that I've made, it's amazing to see how 'just some hero', as Manju's father dismissively described Shah Rukh, became a safe way for women to express their desire for a different reality. A reality where one can aspire and expect to meet men capable of expressing support, acknowledgement and love—aspirations which are castigated and cast as a silly girl's paradise in the present day, deemed illegitimate if expressed in an open and cogent form. In the early days of my travels, Shah Rukh was simply another superstar. Over the years, much of the indulgence in his celebrity started to create a palpable sense of awkwardness in many families. Among working-class fan-women, it became common for employers, sons, lovers, husbands and elders to publicly dissuade women from indulging fandom, buying iconography, singing songs and discussing Shah Rukh's movies. Society insisted that women tame themselves, that they stop searching for their hero on the television.

11

A Tale of Two Televisions

Unlike many countries, the TV industry in India is still massive and continues to grow. TV remains the largest revenue generator for the (media and entertainment) industry.

—*Uday Shankar, president, FICCI, 2020*

Television revenues are expected to grow at 7 per cent annually to reach INR 847 billion by 2023 driven by increased base of subscribers as households continue to get television connections and TV's price competitiveness as against OTT. [sic]

—*FICCI-EY Frames Media and Entertainment Sector Report, 2021*

There was a time, three decades ago, when families that could afford their own television sets were considered wealthy in India. In 1992, only 1.2 million homes owned a television. The number increased to eighty-three million in 2004. By 2017, 183 million homes owned a TV, that is, sixty-four per cent of all Indian homes. For all the exuberance of the internet and the excitement about online streaming platforms, access to these is confined to small urban enclaves. Recent estimates, from 2019, suggest that less than ten per cent of the country watches a few hours of streaming content every week, usually on their phones. Nearly seventy per cent of this audience is male. The overwhelmingly male viewership signals the vast digital gulf between men and women—in 2018, only forty-three per cent of women in India owned a mobile phone compared to almost eighty per cent of Indian men, the highest such gap in the world. Television content, on the other hand, remains broadly accessible to both the sexes. Seven out of ten women in the country report watching TV at least once a week.

There are three hundred million smartphone users in India, and eight hundred million television viewers. The share of families with a TV is larger in urban areas at eighty-seven per cent but nearly half of all rural homes possess a TV of their own. This is a story of two migrating TVs, moving between cities and villages, and the two migrant women who encountered Shah Rukh on them.

—⚬—

In July 2007, I found myself in Borio town, nearly four hundred kilometres from Jharkhand's state capital of Ranchi. Borio is a development block within Sahibganj district, close to the Farrakka Barrage in West Bengal, bordering Bangladesh. The area is part of the Santhal Pargana division in Jharkhand, which has reported large volumes of young women moving to Delhi to take up jobs as housecleaners, cooks, homecare providers and nannies. Borio's town centre comprised a boisterous bus stand, a bunch of buzzing food stalls and an array of shops selling farming equipment. On the day I arrived, battling the heat and humidity of the impending monsoon season and starving after a long drive from Sahibganj town, it felt like I'd landed in the galaxy of Katrina Kaif. Her photogenic face was plastered all over town. Posters of Kaif did brisk business at the haat (local market); she adorned nearly every three-wheeler that flashed by and every shop that met the eye. 'She has a Santhal nose, don't you think? Big and flat,' my translator Anna said as she pressed her stretched palm against her nose. By 2020, Anna would claim that age had transformed Ms Kaif's nose; it had become too sharp to look Santhal.

Amongst those with a proclivity for stereotypes and essentializing, the Santhal nose has long been considered distinctive. When scientists and historians felt the problematic techno-rationalist impulse to categorize tribes in India based on their distinctive anthropometric measures and facial features, they took note of the Santhal nose. Three tribal groups were broadly identified. First, the Dravidian or Negrito strain of tribes, such as the Jarawas or Kadars living in the Andamans. Anthropologists described these tribal groups as 'broad-headed people from Africa', considered the earliest inhabitants of India. The second group comprised Proto-Australoid or the Australian strain of tribes with 'broad and flat noses'. This group included the Santhal, Gond, Kurka and Munda tribes often found in the central and eastern regions of India. The third tribal group were Mongoloids living in the northeastern parts of India.

Tribal populations, also known as Adivasis, are often considered the most vulnerable and victimized groups in independent India. Data released by the United Nations' multi-dimensional poverty indicators show that fifty per cent of tribal households are poor, compared to thirty-three per cent of Muslim households. They are disproportionately impoverished, reporting double the poverty rates of the rest of the country. These communities continue to lose their land and forests to both the government and private companies. Unlike Dalits or religious minorities, disadvantaged Adivasi communities have yet to find the sort of sustained political presence necessary to bring their concerns before the legislative arms of government.

The Santhals, though, are one of the larger, more politically prominent tribes of India. The Austroasiatic Santhali language is the only tribal language notified by the Indian government. Its unique script, called Ol Chiki, was invented in 1925 by Pandit Raghunath Murmu. Art, activism, literature and film have paid attention to

Santhal life. 'The Santhal Family', considered India's first modernist sculpture, was made by Ramkinkar Baij in 1938. Created with cement and laterite gravel, the piece depicts a mother, father and child from the Santhal tribe migrating to a new future, accompanied by a stray dog. The beauty of Santhal women has been fetishized in many films, perhaps most famously Satyajit Ray's *Aranyer Din Ratri* (1970), based on a novel by Sunil Gangopadhyay. In literature and reportage, the Santhal community is represented as migrant and marginalized. Over the centuries, Santhals have remained largely agrarian. Anthropologist and activist Nitya Rao has spent two decades studying gender and land rights among Santhals in the region. She describes the community as 'continuing to be exploited by Hindu and Muslim settlers, traders and moneylenders, who control institutions of the state and the markets'. The pathos of exploitation and alienation among Santhals found expression in their successful campaign to carve out the new state of Jharkhand from Bihar in 2000. The word 'Jhar-Khand' means the land of forests. Despite these advances and concessions wrung from a recalcitrant Indian state, literacy and nutrition levels remain poor among the Santhals. New state boundaries are yet to translate into new treatment, as the community continues to rely on preserving past protections on property accorded by the state. The Santhal Parganas Tenancy Act was passed in 1949 to protect transfers and sale of tribal land, ensuring that each Santhal household owned small plots of land in the Santhal Parganas region. Land is core to a family's status and survival in the area.

Women are equally engaged in farming with men and tribal songs focus on the necessary cooperation between a man and his wife to tame their land. Still, land is inherited only by males. If a woman is an only child or does not have a brother, she must marry under the 'ghar jamai' system, wherein her husband must forego claims to his own family land and move into his wife's home, thus enabling her to inherit her father's land. If such a marriage cannot take place, the woman loses the land to other male kin. Even in 2016, a survey published in the *EPW*, of land holdings in ten villages within Jharkhand, found only four per cent of housing plots and three per cent of agricultural plots were owned solely or jointly by women, in contrast to fifty-nine per cent owned by men.

Agriculture remains rain-fed, with low productivity. Farmers cultivate rice, maize and mustard as major crops, all of which is used for subsistence. Data from the Santhal Parganas District Gazetteer shows a decline over the last century in the number of crops farmers can grow each year. Families are only able to cultivate enough to feed themselves for four to six months of the year. Subsistence farming no longer even ensures subsistence. For the rest of the year, tribal men and women take up informal employment with poor pay to make ends meet. Most Santhal women seasonally migrate to work in the rice fields of neighbouring West Bengal and Odisha, while also collecting and selling forest produce in local markets. Men undertake longer-term migration, moving towards construction sites in Andhra Pradesh or to cultivate sugarcane in Uttar Pradesh and Punjab. The army, church-related work and government schools are the dominant sources of salaried employment.

On my first evening in Sahibganj town, I recall sitting outdoors on a slim motel veranda facing a busy street. Our research partners had suggested I spend one night in Sahibganj before driving out to Borio. The motel was deemed safe for single women. I was reading notes on the veranda when Sonu, the hotel's errand boy, suggested I sit inside the room. 'Why?' I asked. 'People will think wrong things, and you'll get too much attention. Please don't be angry, madam, it will make my shift easier,' he said, turning red. Our mutual shame stalled further conversation and I removed myself from public space. In any case, the long journey had depleted my capacity for defiance. Without much talk, I locked myself in my room with fifteen cockroaches for company.

Barely able to sleep, guilty for not putting up a fight, I counted the cockroaches all night. The insects looked as embarrassed as I felt.

Anna, our translator, arrived with our taxi the next morning, and we left for Borio. I was in one of the poorest regions in the world, supporting an ethnographic research project on migrant domestic workers. The flow of young women from tribal-majority districts remains a contentious issue. Several social movements argue that a significant proportion of these women are 'trafficked', mostly for sex work, though agrarian distress and hardship also means that many of them are economic migrants, voluntarily leaving the area in search of work. Professor Nitya Rao led our research team. She tasked me with organizing a short census of a village and to follow up on a few in-depth interviews she had initiated during a previous round of research.

We travelled from Borio town to the interior and remote village of Kirkitona, our research site for the next month. During the census phase, along with the livelihood patterns in the village, I decided to investigate the Katrina posters. Lata Tudu was convinced that the first Katrina Kaif poster arrived in the village of Kirkitona at the same time when the National Rural Employment Guarantee scheme started its first public works project. 'The boys started building an irrigation well for a new government scheme and they spent some of the money on the poster.' Lata was nonplussed. 'I don't know why they like her. She is not that pretty or anything, but she is their favourite,' she said in crystal-clear Hindi. Language wasn't a significant difficulty during the census; while the elders spoke Santhali, the youth were fluent in Hindi and some Christian tribals spoke tribal dialects.

Lata recalled how her male cousins begged permission from their mother to spend a small portion of the ₹1,000 they earned from helping to build the government well to buy a Katrina poster. The work and the money were a welcome relief. The wages had allowed them to purchase oil and sugar for the home, they ate better. A small portion of ₹20 was used to buy the prized poster. She laughed and added, 'If they did not have it, they would have tried stealing coal from the moving trains on the tracks near here. That kind of work is wrong and very dangerous.'

Katrina Kaif had her big break in mainstream Hindi cinema in 2005, with *Maine Pyaar Kyun Kiya*. But she was already a prominent face, famous from her appearances in music videos and on billboards across the country. The daily newspapers devoted nearly four pages to film gossip and celebrity news, publishing multiple stories on Kaif's beauty and 'link-up', the slang for romance in such gossipy supplements, with Salman Khan. Despite no satellite television in Kirkitona village, everyone below thirty years of age knew who Katrina Kaif was and what she looked like. They might not have watched her videos or films but her pictures in the local papers, buses and on every advertisement made her ubiquitous.

In 2007, most tribal families in Kirkitona relied on agricultural work in Punjab, Uttar Pradesh and West Bengal to survive. People articulated safe and productive migration as a privilege accorded to those with land. Families with productive lands could sell smaller plots to generate money to migrate to other states for work. They would rely on entrenched community networks to settle down and find jobs in new places. Families with no land, on the other hand, were forced to migrate with no choice in the type of work they would do for money.

Kirkitona was green, lush and idyllic. There were no markers of Indian urban life. Local families were responsible for conserving ponds and fresh water. The village was divided into four major hamlets. The Hindu hamlet was separated from the tribal and Muslim hamlets by a railway track. You could walk for hours between these hamlets and not encounter another soul, never mind a paved road. As our first week ended, Anna told me that I was not alone in conducting research; I too was the subject of a study being conducted by the locals. People would grin and ask Anna as many questions about me as I did about them. How could I be from Bengal? Why was my face such a strange shape? Why wasn't I married?

Even in forested tribal Jharkhand, Delhi extended its tentacles. Not only did I meet a young man employed in a factory owned by a friend of a friend, I interviewed a migrant domestic worker who turned out to be employed by my friend's future partner. One evening, after a long day of conversations and coincidences, I was taking a walk, mesmerized by how connected the world seemed. My solitude was interrupted by one of the older men I'd interviewed earlier that day in the Muslim hamlet. He had followed me to tell me that 'women should keep the dupatta on'. That I should remain covered. He offered this advice while apologizing if he had caused any offence, scurrying away before I had worked out how best to react. I grudgingly wore a dupatta for the rest of my trip.

A week into the survey, Anna developed a high fever and had to leave to get medical attention. Lata, a fluent Hindi and Santhali speaker, stepped in to help me in exchange for a little money. I was a paying guest at a house in another hamlet that contained a phone booth in a local shop. Mobile phones didn't work in the village. Lata and I spent most of our evenings together. I'd tried my usual ice-breaking techniques, asking people about films and icons, only to be met by blank stares from the older men and women, many of whom had never watched a movie in their lives. The younger generation, in their twenties and thirties in 2007, knew film stars but had not watched many movies. 'You watch films when you leave this place,' a young man told me. The closest cinema hall, in Sahibganj town, was nearly seventy kilometres away and played Bhojpuri and Tollywood hits for a largely Bihari and Bengali audience. Lata, at twenty-four, knew about Shah Rukh and his movies. She told me that she'd heard of him from her friends who were migrant workers in Delhi. 'Most don't have that much free time, they're always working. Only one or two of them know about movies,' she said.

Once the census in Kirkitona were complete, my research lead required follow-up interviews with a few domestic workers who had migrated to Delhi. This had proven to be tough. While the women's families would share their contact details and encourage us to get in touch, these workers were kept so busy it proved impossible to schedule an interview. Most migrant domestic workers traced through our research lived in their employers' homes and seemed to be perpetually on call. Prof. Rao and I were also convinced that several of the women simply did not wish to be bothered by us and our questions.

Our research closed in late 2007. The role of land and family ties emerged as critical in mediating the migration experience. In 2008, several months later, my employers at ISST started a research project on live-in and live-out domestic workers in Delhi. This new assignment gave me a chance to talk to migrant workers from Jharkhand again. Finding live-in workers to interview, though, continued to be a struggle until I met a Gurgaon-based expat who suggested I speak to her house cook. And so, I was able to meet and interview forty-something Victoria Murmu. She promised to connect me with a few other domestic workers. Three months later, Victoria called me and gave me the numbers for five of her friends. Lily Soren was one of them. She was employed as a domestic worker at a wealthy home in posh Jor Bagh, a neighbourhood close to the corporate titans and old-money mavens of Amrita Shergill Marg.

I dialled at lunchtime. Lily picked up the phone. 'Victoria Didi told me that she spoke to some students and that you were planning to call me. I can't talk now. It would be easier to meet at church on Sunday,' she said. I waited outside the church on Sunday morning, having told her that I was wearing a green kurta. Lily was slim and tall; her nails were filed, and she wore her hair in a tightly controlled bun. She suggested that I join her friends inside for tea and biscuits.

Lily, from Simdega district in Jharkhand, seemed no older than twenty-five. She introduced me to the priest, who told me that many of the women in the congregation were migrant workers from Jharkhand and Odisha. Lily's friends too were employed as nannies and in various other forms of paid domestic work. That their employers gave them paid leave on Sunday mornings made them some of the most fortunate domestic workers in the city. I had read enough about the working conditions of live-in domestic workers in Delhi to grasp that paid leave was a rare occurrence. According to Lily, these generous employers were 'usually foreign, wealthy and had more than one domestic worker. So, we can help each other's work when one of us needs to be on leave. Our madams take care of us, they don't treat us like Indian families treat their help. Even NRI families are not as good to work for as foreigners'.

Of the women Victoria introduced me to, only Lily described herself as a Shah Rukh fan. She was also the most garrulous. Through our early conversations, it was clear that Lily liked talking about her past. Amused by my interest in her, she joked that almost no one cared about her life in Delhi, let alone the films she watched. We started meeting after church for short conversations. Lily moved to Delhi in 2002, soon after finishing high school. Her father's death extinguished her hopes to go to college and become a schoolteacher. At the time, her aunt, who worked on the domestic staff of a rich Delhi family, suggested Lily join her in the city. Lily came from a devout Roman Catholic tribal family; she was the middle child of three and the only girl. Her mother had studied till Class 5 while her father was a retired government schoolteacher. Her eldest brother, who was the most educated in the family, worked for the church in the Andamans. But Lily's younger brother, who had barely completed any schooling, moved to Punjab to work in the sugarcane fields while hoping to move further away to build roads for the Indian Border Roads Organization in Leh and Ladakh. However, money in casual labour was too casual. Many men left her village in Simdega district, and her educated

Catholic cousins were reluctant to farm. They needed to hire a few local farm hands to help plough and harvest their small plots of land.

During the Christmas holidays, Catholic migrants would return home. After her aunt's suggestion, she spoke to a few of these migrant women, and they also felt that she could try working for a 'foreigner family' in Delhi. Lily was excited by the prospect of going to Delhi. Her mother was reluctant to let her migrate, worried that she would not find suitable work in the city. 'But everybody told me that my good English from Church school would help me,' she said. Language and land improved her prospects in Delhi. Lily's family owned some arable land and this meant that she didn't have to take the first job she got; she had the luxury of being able to wait for the right opportunity, the right employers. Her brothers were earning for themselves, and her aunt was welcoming. They loaned her some money during her months looking for a job. Things weren't as desperate for her as for other girls, those who relied on brokers and placement agencies, she would always emphasize.

She arrived in Delhi on the Jharkhand Express, accompanied by a male cousin. Her family had heard news of girls going missing after they went to Delhi with Bihari and Bengali placement agents. At first, Lily feared the city. It felt too large, too alien. She stayed with her aunt and began helping with her work. Lily met her prospective employers about three months after she arrived in Delhi. They were an American family living a kilometre away, and friends of her aunt's employers. Her aunt fabricated Lily's experience, suggesting that she had worked for a diplomat earlier. Lily feared her aunt's lies. 'She said I could manage a house and though I thought I could,' Lily told me, 'I had no real experience. But even Aunty's madam vouched for me.'

The first week was tough, lonely and long. Her daily grind was dictated by the clock. She began her day at six in the morning, in time for her madam's pre-gym morning routine, and only clocked off after dinner. In between, she would be busy dusting and organizing the house till nine a.m., helping with cooking till lunchtime, and grocery shopping for dinner after a few hours of break. She clung to her prayers and her aunt for familiarity. While being at the beck and call of her madam was not dissimilar to waiting hand and foot on her brother and mother, she wasn't used to the mechanized nature of domestic work at her employer's home. Her aunt had explained the machines, but Lily was reluctant to use an electric kettle to heat water. She could not trust electricity as she did gas and fire. Her American madam helped relieve her distrust and encouraged her to use appliances. Eventually, she acknowledged, 'it cuts down on time, things get done so quickly. I remember thinking, if only we had electricity and a kettle like this back home.'

Her madam was a travelling spouse, and I imagined she was as lost in Delhi as Lily. Lily's employers were getting used to Delhi and liked the idea of being helpful to someone. In return, Lily was hard-working and diligent, eager to learn and contribute. While her madam was keen to befriend her, Lily wasn't sure how much truth or friendship she should offer. Her days were long, but she was paid well above the average wages of live-in domestic workers in the city.

There were other perks too. 'This was my first room to myself,' Lily told me. 'Back home, I shared with my mother, and we didn't have rooms like this. It was strange to spend so much time without talking to people.' In those early days, Lily refused to leave the house for her Sunday holiday. She was unsure of how to reach church and detested the attention she received from the local gang of guards and drivers who hovered outside her employer's home. 'In our village, the men are gone for work. In cities, they are all outside the security guard's quarters. The drivers and peons, they keep looking at us all the time. They are not okay. I don't like the way they look at us. Some men in the market say lewd things as well.'

In the early days of 2002, Lily had no phone of her own. She conscientiously planned to save enough money to buy one within six

months. One day, her aunt visited and introduced her to Delhi buses
and the Lodhi Gardens bus stop. She explained the routes, helping
Lily place herself in the transit map of the city.

Soon, through her first year, Sunday by Sunday, Lily ventured
deeper and deeper into Delhi. 'Our colony is so beautiful, so many
trees and big houses. I started enjoying going out and forgetting how
many people were watching me,' Lily said. At first, she would take
the 623 bus to the church and make no stops along the way. Within
a month, she began walking to the market with some of the women
from the church. If they felt lavish, the women would buy tea from a
small shop usually crowded by Bihari construction workers. Sunday
church was a must for migrant workers like Lily and Victoria. 'When
Victoria Didi had started working in Delhi, there was no mobile
phone and news like there is now. They would send news back home
through the church congregation. The priest or the sisters would send
news to the church near their village through the telephone. It was
very important for us to record our attendance at the congregation. If
a girl did not come for some time, her family would worry. Even now
(2009), we might have a phone, but our parents might not. And the
connection is often bad in the village. It is important to come. Not
just for prayers but so that everyone can see you are here.'

By 2010, I had left my job at ISST and was planning to study
in the US. Once, Lily asked me to join her at an office building as
she thought I'd find the meeting interesting. Her madam and other
wealthy Indian and foreigner madams had joined forces with an
NGO to organize learning events for workers. The NGO would
partner with volunteers for knowledge sessions once or twice in a
year. Many women beyond Lily's church congregation would join,
as their employers encouraged it. The previous session had focused
on how to open a bank account to help women remit safely. After
the session, Lily asked her employers and her aunt to help her open
her own account. 'I'm the first woman I know in my family who has

an account, that too in Delhi.' The paperwork for the account took six months, but Lily persevered. That bank passbook was a symbol of her pride.

When I joined the session, a group of fifty women were already gathered in a gloomy room, chatting away merrily. This lesson was going to focus on contraceptive techniques and sexual hygiene. A young NRI interning at a global health foundation was meant to deliver the training, along with a social worker. The intern spoke impeccable Hindi and had clearly worked hard to prepare the lecture.

To demonstrate the use of a condom for safe sex, the intern used a banana as a substitute for the penis. The plan was to show women how to put a condom on a man, since the latter could not be trusted to know how to wear a condom properly. I was expecting the young women to giggle or demonstrate shame and embarrassment, but they remained casual. Lily was nonchalant, not even bothering to interrupt a chat she was having about the new recipes her madam was teaching her. The intern-instructor, condom in one hand, banana in the other, asked the women if they knew 'what to do with this?'

Lily's friend Prabha, a twenty-eight-year-old nanny, raised her hand. Prabha stood up, looked at the banana and said, 'Put in my mouth' in English. The room erupted in laughter. Later, Prabha claimed that she never noticed the condom in the intern's hand, that she assumed the intern was asking if the women in the congregation knew what to do with a banana. Now it was the intern who became embarrassed, red-faced, giving up the floor to the older social worker, who continued the lesson.

Many women in that room had been sexually active since the age of sixteen. The average age of marriage among tribal women in India was seventeen. Sexual mores in tribal societies were different from that of most caste-societies in India. Men and women mingled much more freely. While the church and convent education attempted to regulate marriage and sexual encounters amongst young tribals, old customs endured. I would eventually learn that Lily's priest was furious that the women were attending classes on contraception and advised them to 'be good Christians' instead.

When I asked Lily about the banana episode, she laughed. 'We were making fun of the lady. As if we don't know about condoms and men. Why does she think we're children? This is the problem with the church as well. The sisters and priests act as if we never left our villages and came to Delhi, like we don't talk to each other or watch TV.'

Christ vs Shah Rukh

Alongside a year of attending church meetings, I completed a survey of domestic workers across hundreds of slums in Delhi and Ahmedabad. The survey data served as inputs for deliberations by the ILO and UNICEF on labour standards for domestic workers. These insights were aimed to inform and advocate for a Domestic Workers' Convention being drafted by the ILO, which would eventually be passed in 2011. Ten years later, India is yet to ratify the convention.

Through this work between 2008 and 2009, I interacted with activists across the country who were fighting for the rights of domestic workers. Unlike Lily and her friends, most of these workers had no time off and little dignity of labour. They worked erratic hours with erratic wages. Many reported suffering from both verbal and physical violence from employers and broadly tense, passive-aggressive relationships. Domestic workers were tired of being dependent on their employers' whims and fancies, on the luck of the draw when it came to being treated with basic courtesy and respect. Very few even had use of safe sanitation facilities during working hours, as employers would not allow them to use toilets in the house. Lily knew she was 'lucky': no middleman was stealing her salary and she had a steady income. Unlike most women working in India's care economy, Lily had the privilege of a few certainties. She knew her employers would pay on time every month and she had a bathroom.

She also had access to a television. There was a spare television in a guest room on which she could watch shows for an hour each day. 'I think my madam would let me watch for more time,' Lily said, 'but it doesn't look good.' Lily loved watching film songs, especially Shah Rukh songs. She used to hum them as she did her work and even taught her madam about Hindi films and Shah Rukh. Sometimes if she was slow or appeared not to be paying attention, her madam would joke that she was dreaming of Shah Rukh. I asked her why she liked Shah Rukh in particular. 'It just happened,' she said. 'I saw him and I liked him the best. I get to see many heroes and many songs when we cut vegetables in the TV room, but he is the best. He seems like a good man, you know. He makes me laugh. Not violent like other action heroes. We never find time to watch whole movies because of work but they play his love songs all the time on TV, so I get to see him a lot.'

I left for the US in August 2010. After returning to Delhi for my summer break the following year, I asked Lily if we could meet. She suggested as usual that we meet outside the church. Victoria saw me that morning while I was waiting for Lily. After asking the standard questions about my marriage plans, Victoria suddenly said, 'You won't believe what Lily has done. She's become a Delhi girl.' When Lily arrived, we walked around the colony and I told her about Victoria's remark. It had to do with Shah Rukh. All her friends in the church congregation thought her filmy interests had crossed a line.

Sometime in October 2010, during her daily hour of television, Lily learned of a Shah Rukh film bonanza in honour of his birthday. The channel advertised its plans to broadcast a film starring Shah Rukh every Sunday at noon for all of November. She wondered if her madam would allow her to watch these movies in their entirety. A week later, noticing that her employers were in a good mood, Lily asked her madam if she could watch these films every Sunday. Although her madam struggled to understand Lily's interest in a Bollywood hero, she said it was no problem. Madam didn't mind as long as Lily got her work done. The cook, who didn't live with the family, said she would come earlier on Sundays to help Lily, and they planned to try and watch the movies together.

Lily was thrilled. She had both permission and a companion. Her happiness did stumble upon a moral dilemma—the Shah Rukh film festival clashed with church on Sunday. If she did not show up dutifully each week to pray, her family and the local priests would reprimand her. A month-long absence would be a sign of extraordinary defiance. Abandoning Sunday church would make her seem too high and mighty to other women in her prayer group. It would signal that she considered both the church and their company to be optional; that she did not believe in the power of prayer. But this was too good an opportunity to miss. She was never going to have the comfort of going to the nearby theatre. The tickets were too expensive and she would feel too guilty spending her money on the movies, even if she went to a cheaper hall. No live-in domestic worker went to watch films without her employer. It was a simple choice: Shah Rukh or Jesus?

That first week in November 2010, she told me, she feigned a fever and sent a message to her aunt apologizing for missing the church service. In the afternoon, she watched *Kabhi Haan Kabhi Naa*. She laughed and cried with her hero, and it remains her favourite film. 'I loved it so much. He doesn't get what he wants and tries so hard. He lies and cheats, but in the end, he has to let go of what he wanted. And he seemed both sad and happy. It's like problems in life. It felt very real, and he was so good in all the songs.' Lily, in her early twenties, had finally managed to watch her first Hindi film from beginning to end.

During the telecast of *Kabhi Haan Kabhi Naa*, Lily's madam joined in for bits and pieces to see what all the fuss was about. 'It was better when she wasn't around, though,' Lily said. 'We can be free. You have to be careful around sir and madam.' That first Sunday with

Shah Rukh, those hours, were a taste of freedom. To compensate for her entertainment, she would wake up two hours earlier to do extra cleaning.

Lily's life was tightly regulated—by the church, by her job and by her own sense of what her community expected of her. While watching *Kabhi Haan Kabhi Naa*, she was acutely conscious of wasting time. As the month progressed, she began to relax. Those four-hour matinees gave her a chance to abandon the clock, to leave religion, routine and regimentation behind. '*Time kahan gaya, mujhe pata hi nahin chala*,' Lily told me. '*Itni achi picture thi*.' I lost track of time, that's how good the film was.

On the second of those filmy Sundays in November, Lily told her aunt that her madam had planned a luncheon for which she needed Lily's help. That afternoon she watched *Kuch Kuch Hota Hai*, but found herself less enamoured as 'there was too much style in it'. The third week, she claimed she was still recovering from the work she had to put in for a large dinner party her employers had hosted on Saturday night. That Sunday she watched *DDLJ*. The film left her mesmerized. 'I remember watching that film and thinking this is what fairy tales are like,' said Lily, expressive as ever. On the final week, she didn't bother sending her aunt an excuse. She watched *Rab Ne Bana Di Jodi*. The film is memorable for several reasons, especially for the hilarious exchanges between Shah Rukh's character and his best friend, played by actor Vinay Pathak, on love and being 'macho'. Lily's response to the picture: 'If only a real man could appreciate his wife and the tiffin she makes for him the way he does in that movie, girls would have much better lives.' *Rab Ne Bana Di Jodi* contains a popular song sequence in which Shah Rukh's character, Surinder Sahni, an ordinary government clerk, serenades his wife as she cooks and plates his meals. He is ecstatic that a woman is packing a tiffin for him to take to office. For Surinder, that lunch box is love. For Lily, a man so elated by his wife's household labours was unlike any man she knew in real life.

Looking back, Lily said that she'd never forget how much her madam and colleague poked fun at her. 'They said I would smile at the TV like a fool. That I was lost in my Shah Rukh dreams all month. It was true, though, I really loved watching him. It was after these films that I really started to like Shah Rukh.' When Lily returned to church, she had to put up with severe scoldings from both her priest and her aunt for absconding from her duty to God. She was becoming too much of a city girl, she needed more faith and discipline. Lily prayed for forgiveness, convinced that Jesus would approve of Mr Khan.

After we had a good laugh over Lily's Shah-Rukh-filled November, our talk turned to my marriage plans. I shrugged my shoulders. Lily told me she did not meet any boys and did not expect to. 'They'll find me a match in the village.' In 2014, though, her mother died. Lily's older brother vanished into missionary life and no longer sent much money home, while her younger brother took up a contract in Leh. Someone needed to take charge of their land and the farm, or risk losing it to distant cousins. When I tried to get in touch with her for Christmas in 2014, she was back in her village in Simdega and I could barely hear her. 'We have to climb to a specific spot to make and receive calls. The elders think it's a magical space blessed by the village deities. I've tried to explain that it's only the Airtel tower but who listens to me here,' she laughed.

Lily returned to Delhi after six months. Her employers were happy to have her back, but told her they were moving back to the US within a year. They had spent more than a decade in the city and sir's business needed him to move back home. When they left, Lily decided that she would return home for a few years as well, hoping to sort out the farming and property issues and consolidate her savings. Her madam gifted her the TV from the spare room: now she could watch Shah Rukh whenever she liked. With the help of a cousin, Lily boxed up the TV and took it back with her on the Jharkhand Express to Ranchi. Everyone in her family and church group thought she was mad, suggesting she sell the TV and earn some cash instead. But Lily was attached to that machine. 'Carrying that TV home was necessary for me. It was a gift, and I wanted to bring it home with me,' she said.

The television was wrapped and travelled with her along the scenic Gangetic route, from Allahabad (Prayagraj since November 2018) to Ranchi. Once she reached her state capital, Lily took a bus back home, arguing with the conductor until he allowed her to put the TV in the driver's booth to avoid damage. Her eyes were fixed on her prized package all the way to her village as a loud Salman film blared out from the tiny video player on the bus. Unfortunately, electricity travelled with greater reluctance to her village than the people and the appliances they brought back from the cities. The TV would only work for a few hours in a day, if she was lucky, and Lily was worried about the electricity bills. In 2016, she activated 4G on her mobile phone, but the network wouldn't function.

I called her again that Christmas. Lily was helping a local missionary school with odd jobs and she noted that the improved electricity supply meant the TV ran for a few more hours each day. But, she said, 'I hear you can watch everything on your phone these days in Delhi. That would be so nice here, as I have a lot of time in the evenings after the cooking is done.' She missed city life. Her thoughts were turning towards her own marriage. She hoped, she said, that she could move to Delhi with her future husband and they could find work together. Or perhaps her aunt could find her a groom already based in Delhi. 'Although,' she said, 'we'd have to plan what to do with the land here.'

She filled me in on local gossip. There had been a scandal involving Munna Marandi, the son of an elected representative from Sahibganj. He had been accused by the church and local women's groups of both sexually exploiting a girl and marrying a minor. 'His girlfriend was

Bengali,' Lily told me. 'She filed a case with the women's commission. They say his wife is just twelve. Nothing will happen but it is good his girlfriend went to the police.' Lily wasn't shocked by the Marandi affair. 'These men are like this only. With power and money, they can do what they feel like, without any decency. Always exploiting women, always doing what their families want. He must have left this Bengali girl to marry someone based on his father's wishes.'

In June 2017, Shah Rukh's *Raees* was televised for the first time. I called and asked if she managed to see it. It took several attempts to be able to hear her voice clearly. She said, 'Yes, but the TV can't show all the colours properly. We are one of the few houses here that have a satellite and TV.' I asked what she thought of the movie. She said that she didn't like the violence but loved Shah Rukh's spectacled avatar in the film. She complained that the TV display was of poor quality and could not match up to the telecast in Delhi. The connection was broken.

I asked her if she was lonely. I used the word 'akelapan'. She didn't even stop to think: 'I am not alone, though I get bored. I had thought I would help the church's social work here. But there is less money and a lot of difficulties these days for church and NGO work, so I am not as busy as I thought I would be. Most girls and aunties who have come back from Delhi remain unmarried because they have enough money saved up and can afford to wait to find a good match, which doesn't happen often. Many people in the village think that women who have returned from Delhi are not good wife material. We are older also. Anyway, I have my cousins here and there are other women who have returned from Delhi. We talk about how our mothers and grandmothers would find company and love in the birds, dogs and forests here. They did not need people all the time, and they believed in God. My mother thought that Jesu would bless all our good deeds. I don't believe that. Maybe because we went to school and made our own way in Delhi, that is our problem. We don't love the forests like our mothers did.'

Part-Timers

Sandhya first heard of Katrina Kaif when her neighbours named their daughter after the actress. 'It's such a strange name for a Bengali child,' she said. But strange names were not unusual in Nehru Camp. There were three young babies, Sandhya told me, who shared the name Hitler Mandal.

It was 2009, two years after I had visited Sahibganj in Jharkhand. I was managing a survey of two thousand live-out domestic workers across hundreds of Delhi slums. Live-out workers, as the term suggests, did not live with their employers. They earned wages based on the number and types of tasks they undertook. While workers who lived in west and east Delhi districts would usually work one shift either in the morning or evening, the women in south Delhi's Nehru Camp reported being 'full-time' workers. They started their morning shift at six and worked till noon, coming home to make lunch for their children, wash dishes and take a short nap before starting their evening shifts at five. They would return home at eight for another round of cooking and cleaning. I was managing a research team of students and surveyors and it was customary to visit some of the survey sites to make sense of the data being collected.

Nehru Camp was close to Navjeevan Camp and Bhoomihein Camp. All these neighbourhoods were examples of the bustle and squalor of a big city 'slum', or what Indian urbanists called a 'basti'. Community ties were, naturally, stronger than the barely existent public infrastructure. The drains were open, the streets were narrow, congested and sloshy with filthy waste water. It was hard to know where one house ended and another began. Many families adopted the street dogs as pets, but these 'pets' attacked the young children. The neighbourhood reported 'dog bite' and 'dog fever' as the most frequent medical complaints of the past year.

The state was nowhere to be found. Families, though, firmly believed in the power of education to deliver upward mobility, and scrimped and saved to send their children to private English-medium schools rather than government ones. Private tankers would arrive daily, and domestic workers would often be late to work because they were waiting in long queues to collect water for their homes. The municipal authorities barely noticed the camp, despite government announcements to provide services. Electricity was borrowed and shared through unregistered connections. Families spent three-quarters of their monthly earnings on power, food, water and schooling. Both men and women had to work to keep up. Fortunate families with strong social ties were able to access the government's food rations, but most ordinary people did not have the wherewithal or connections to perform the bureaucratic cartwheels needed to procure various proofs of eligibility for the programme. All government programmes required families to prove that they had spent three consecutive years as residents in Delhi. Producing paperwork to support these claims required superpowers. In 2009, the Aadhaar card had yet to come into being and Delhi's public distribution system for foodgrain had yet to be made quasi-universal. Families relied on a complex maze of letters from their local elected representatives, income proofs and caste certificates from the local district magistrate's office. The process and politics of acquiring the paperwork were so difficult and time-consuming that most families did not bother.

The survey had thrown up some interesting early results. We found that the wages of workers were closely linked to the property prices of the neighbourhoods where they worked. The Bengali workers were largely from Namasudra caste groups, Bengal's second-largest Scheduled Caste community. They worked in several nearby residential areas, one of which was Chittaranjan Park, where I lived before moving out of my parents' home. Women like Sandhya reported common labour histories. They started out working in smaller and middle-class homes before finding work in the 'better blocks or colonies'. These women were strong negotiators and helped each other in setting wage rates.

At the same time, there was intense competition among domestic workers. New migrants from other neighbourhoods, near Tughlakabad, were willing to work for reduced wages. Many women I met joked about teaching younger workers a lesson if they tried to push wage levels down. But the jokes had an edge. There were many stories of violence, where women would threaten and even have physical fights with new workers who were trying to undercut set wage rates for the colony. These workers were not formally unionized, but they formed a formidable sisterhood. Nehru Camp's care cartel. Information on new jobs at 'good homes'—implying a job that paid well and was safe, a job where employers treated their workers with dignity and concern—circulated in a small network. This network was also helpful in managing each other's personal domestic chores. Women would help each other with cooking, shopping, cleaning and childcare.

The women in Nehru Camp carried a deep sense of unease about managing work and care. Most domestic workers felt guilty about not being able to spend enough time with their own families. Sandhya and her friends worried that their long working hours prevented them from disciplining their children effectively. It was common to hear workers complain that their children did not study enough, eat well enough and kept the wrong kind of company. 'If I don't make enough time to scold and check my son, he'll become too much of a hero. There are many boys here who are like that,' Sandhya said in her interview. More than half the families surveyed removed their oldest girls from school so they could care for their younger siblings.

At the end of our interview, which took a week to complete, I asked Sandhya if she had a favourite actor and if she watched films. I had asked nearly thirty women this question before her. Most hadn't expressed any real preference. But Sandhya was emphatic: 'Shah Rukh does the best songs and has a very nice smile.' As we started talking about Shah Rukh, her body visibly relaxed. She giggled and said that her husband used to get angry at her for watching TV while cooking or cutting vegetables at home. 'He says that I don't pay attention when those Shah Rukh songs come on.' Sandhya's favourite film was *Kabhi Khushi Kabhie Gham*, and she loved the songs and clothes. Loved the way broken families came together. Loved Shah Rukh's sad and tender eyes, the way he married a poor girl whose father ran a sweet shop. 'Rich people only marry poor people in the movies. In real life, rich people don't even look at most of us. Like you, you only came here for your work.'

Sandhya's TV had arrived two years ago. Her 'didi', a long-term employer, had gifted her a broken TV before moving to Bangalore. 'It was better to give it to us than throw it away.' The display was cracked, the TV was old and used, but it made Sandhya happy. She told me how she was one of the very few women who had a TV in the settlement and how friends would come in the afternoon to watch when the men were away. The family would watch a few TV shows while preparing dinner for the evening. Her husband worked as a part-time office helper with a few other men in the locality. It was a precarious job, and she was not sure of his earnings. 'He doesn't tell me everything about the job, but I give him a share of my wages as he has to pay bills for us. But I pay for the cable myself, not my husband.'

In 2009, Sandhya earned nearly ₹15,000 every month cooking at six homes in a neighbouring colony. Her husband made ₹6,000 working at his office. Their combined earnings were enough to pay for their son Rabi's school fees and meet their monthly expenses. Sandhya was the primary breadwinner and the primary caregiver.

I saw her one last time in 2010 before leaving for Boston. It was hard to get hold of her; she had started working in four more houses and was sleeping less than five hours a night. When we met, she told me that she needed to save money for a new TV and needed to work in more houses. Her husband was not bringing home as much money as before. 'What happened to the old TV?' I asked. 'It broke,' she replied, and moved on to discussing her son's education prospects.

When I was back in Delhi on break, I called and asked her about the TV and her husband's job. She was surprised I remembered. 'He lost the office job and is doing small work here and there. I haven't bought the TV yet as it is costly and I have many more payments to make. But we should have one after a year.' By then, their son was in Class 9 at a nearby private school and their daughter was enrolled in a government school.

By the time I finished graduate school and returned to India in late 2012, Sandhya was too busy to meet. One day, I bumped into one of her friends at the local market. She was waiting for her son to finish work at a shop. I enquired after Sandhya. She replied candidly: 'I don't think she is too well. Her husband drinks and they fight. We can all hear it and have tried to make him stop. He nearly punched my husband for intervening. He has gone mad.' I called Sandhya to offer the name and number of a local NGO counsellor and the police. 'What will the police do? They are the same as him.' I suggested that she could come and stay with my mother for a few days. 'That's no help, other madams have suggested this. I have my children to think about. I cannot leave my own house. That's what he wants. I helped build that house.'

In 2013, Sandhya requested a local politically connected goon to 'talk' to her husband. A few months later, they had another brawl and Sandhya hit her husband back. He decided to leave for their village in Medinipur in West Bengal. She would visit for Durga Puja with the children. But she knew she would stay in Nehru Camp even without a husband. Her son and daughter were old enough to not need much supervision and she could rely on her neighbours for help. She started working at ten different houses and earned ₹30,000 monthly from a combination of cooking and housework. But she never cleaned bathrooms. 'Other girls can do that. I don't need to do that kind of work now.'

A new TV arrived during Durga Puja in 2014. Sandhya described the purchase as one of the most nerve-wracking things she had done. She hired a cycle-rickshaw and went alone to a shop to select the cheapest colour television available. She paid for it using some of her savings and a monthly instalment plan with help from two of her long-term employers. The TV was commemorated with a ceremony. The family went to the local Kali mandir and made an offering. 'It was a good day, the day that TV came. And now that my daughter helps with the cooking, I have more time to watch it.'

A fresh coat of paint for the house marked Durga Puja four years later. Sandhya and her children now had little interaction with the family 'patriarch'. They would spend a month in Mednipur during harvest season each year. During these visits, Sandhya exchanged as few words as possible with her husband, trying to get through the days before she could return to Nehru Camp and her TV. It now played uninterrupted through the evening. When I spoke to her in 2020, she had lost a few jobs because of the pandemic. A few of her friends were packing and heading back to Bengal. But the virus did not seem to bother her much. 'The madams with jobs cannot work without us, I'll find new houses for work if needed,' she said confidently. Instead, she had two complaints: she felt there was far too much of Prime Minister Modi on TV and not enough Shah Rukh; her other problem was that her daughter now spent too much time indulging in 'faaltu kaaj' (useless work) on her older brother's Chinese smartphone.

IV

Mannat

12

An Equilibrium of Silly Expectations

If being a feminist means equality, then I'm not one. I believe women should be more than us. If you're looking at being equal to us, your aim is too low—you're belittling yourself. From creating life to taking so much shit in your daily life and using it as your strength—the simple act of boarding a local train, being leched at, not getting a job because of your gender—it's shocking how much a woman has to take every day. As men, we should all experience what it is like and still stay strong.

—Shah Rukh Khan, 2017

With increasing access to social media through cheaper smartphones, adolescent girls in urban India are bombarded with myriad images of how women can choose to present themselves across the world, a veritable lookbook of contemporary femininity. How young women participate online is mediated by their digital literacy and social position. According to data published from the 2015 National Family Health Survey, twenty-two per cent of women from the poorest set of Indian households owned a mobile phone that they used themselves, compared to seventy-four per cent of women from the richest cohort. Unsurprisingly, research also shows that the ability to read and consume social media content increases sharply with wealth. Girls living on Nepean Sea Road mimic posts by stylists in New York and churn out hourly Insta Stories. Sandhya and her friends in the slums of Nehru Camp may prefer to watch TV, but their teenage daughters borrow their brothers' phones to cruise YouTube and public Instagram accounts. They beg for personal phones each year during the festival season, albeit most remain disappointed. They bicker and barter with their friends and brothers for phones, forever 'liking' and not 'sharing', maintaining an online reticence, always fearful of the backlash from an innocuous social media post. But there's no escaping the enthusiasm for female self-expression on the internet.

Amidst these forms of expression is a popular prototype of the 'strong' hetero woman. Her frame usually conforms to Western standards of beauty and her pose, her position towards the world is one of sexy aloofness. She holds firm political views. She talks about secularism, caste, gender fluidity and intersectionality. She reads a lot. She writes poetry. She attends fun events. She wears great outfits for free because as an influencer, her social media posts are often endorsements. Her skin appears unblemished. She is remarkably photogenic, each studiedly 'candid' shot a purported glimpse into her life and style. There are loud confessions of vulnerability, but simultaneous paeans to self-reliance. She tells you that feminism is cool and yearning for male attention is not. Her audience rolls its eyes in jealousy and admiration because she looks like the kind of woman who elicits male interest without much effort. Her thousand-word post advocating self-love will always be accompanied by photos of her perfect hair and her perfect legs. She presents herself as someone who has rational expectations from romantic love. She espouses the voguish vocabulary of self-care. Much like Shah Rukh's romantic persona, though, this internet persona is an illusion, an image—manufactured, choreographed and mythical.

The glam feminism on the internet, which often does yoga headstands, is as unreal as the love in Shah Rukh's films. Maybe it is a necessary illusion. Just as Shah Rukh introduced Sandhya to London in Nehru Camp, female social media stars conjure up new spectacles of living and loving for Sandhya's daughter. It is an introduction to possibility, potential. And perhaps, much like the love Shah Rukh performs in his films, we need the feminism that perfectly photo-framed social media stars perform online. These images, no matter how contrived, may serve an important function—to provide comfort, raise consciousness and elevate our expectations. Yes, talk is cheap. Many of us doubt the sincerity of these social media posts; the lifestyles and impossible beauty standards tend to undermine their feminist content. But each of these unreal online women offers new signposts for those far away from them. Sandhya's daughter gushed about the actress Priyanka Chopra's life in America just as her mother gushed about Shah Rukh. 'She has achieved so much, as an Indian woman all on her own,' Sandhya's daughter would say to me in Bengali (*'ekti mein, desh theke, atho kichu kore phel lo, ekla'*). She would notice and read the hurtful anonymous responses trolls made to innocuous posts influencers and actresses would put up. It reminded her of the malevolent whispers and gossip she would hear in her neighbourhood. Referencing Ms Chopra, she added, 'Anytime a girl does anything outside for work or college, people around will say bad things here. That is why she had to marry a foreigner.'

Women constantly risk being on the receiving end of vitriol from conservative voices on the internet or on the streets. Horrific abuse and rape threats are ubiquitous on Indian social media. You only need to scroll through the comments on Twitter posts by prominent female journalists or famous actresses, for instance, to discover how much virulent hatred a confident woman with a voice can elicit. So, while I may mock the fluffy images of 'influencers' in my moments of foolish high-mindedness, I know how desperately we need them. These are women who occupy public space online without apology or permission. The more the merrier.

It's impossible to grow up as a woman in India without knowing what it is like to have to always seek permission to be yourself. Each of us, in our own way, often magnified by caste and class, encounters resistance in finding self-acceptance, achievement and affection. If your experience as a straight woman in this country has been one of bliss, without heartache and self-loathing, I reckon you've inherited an Ambani-esque fortune. Or that you've lived a very protected life. Setting snark aside, let me acknowledge that the fortunate few who've found love and self-contentment without much friction may find limited connection to the stories I've tried to tell. Let me also acknowledge that my stories do not capture the struggles and fandom of women who are not straight, or those who reject gender binaries. The fans I encountered remain trapped by heterosexuality. For now, I hope that you'll digest these everyday stories of women struggling to become themselves. That you'll try to understand why so many women find emotional comfort in an actor as they seek to realize their ambitions for a life of love and dignity. Because in telling me about when, how and why they turn to Shah Rukh, they're telling us about when, how and why the world breaks their heart.

The India I've come to know—through stories, songs and statistics—can only be described as a sisterhood of desperate and disappointed women. And it's not men or mawkish romantic endeavours that stir our cumulative dissatisfaction. The sadness many women experience in their intimate lives speaks to a fundamental failure. The Indian state, our markets and families have waged a sustained campaign of scrutiny and surveillance over the bodies and spirits of women. Even our money and modernity have failed to win us sometimes the most basic human dignities. And through years of experience and cultural reinforcement, what economists would call a series of repeated games, we have learned to expect very little from any of our institutions, of the great edifices of our society. To borrow language from a 1987 Amartya Sen article on gender relations within the household, women have become 'habituated to inequality'. Consequently, we have failed ourselves, teaching ourselves to accept being treated as inferior in public and private life. The preference for and quasi-deification of male babies, for instance, remains rampant amongst men *and* women. We are active participants in discriminating against our own sex—be it how poorly we pay women from lower castes for their labour to how unfairly we survey ourselves and other women; the amount we feed girl infants compared to how we feed the male ego; how we socialize our daughters to prime themselves for the male gaze and become subservient in their own homes.

At this point, I know that many Indian readers will adopt a defensive pose. You'll frown and think that this analysis has not acknowledged the gains from economic growth or the feminist movement in India. You'll insist that reality isn't 'all that bad', that none of your friends displays any symptoms of sexism or self-loathing. You'll insist that 'things are changing', that many women you know are standing up to the patriarchy. You'll mention #MeToo, despite its cripplingly limited effect in India, and Barkha Dutt. Some of you will tell me about the various educated women you meet, the multiple social media debates that suggest how India is changing for its women. You'll demand nuance in how I paint my gloomy picture of the status of women in India today. You'll say #MenToo or, even worse, #NotAllMen.

But I'm too angry and heartbroken to offer any moral ambiguity and equivocation. I find myself in no mood for subtlety or nuance when it comes to describing the women in India. And the data supports my strident lack of balance or sophistication. Let me be clear—*there is no meaningful dimension of well-being on which men and women are equal in India. None.* Within each class and caste bracket, women fall far behind men. All the data on gender in India, despite progress since Independence, confirms that our country is profoundly unequal and that the gap between male and female achievement and access to resources continues to grow.

The Women of India

Deprived groups may be habituated to inequality, may be hopeless about upliftment of objective circumstances of misery, may be resigned to fate, and may well be willing to accept the legitimacy of the established order. The tendency to take pleasure in small mercies would make good sense, given these perceptions and cutting desires to shape (in line with perceived feasibility) can help to save one from serious disappointment and frustration.

—*Amartya Sen, 1987*

In 1974, Vina Mazumdar, the grande dame of Indian women's studies, was part of a 'Committee on the Status of Women in India' that submitted the first official government report on the state of women in the country. It was titled *Towards Equality* and its findings were frightening. Everywhere was evidence of the 'declining status for the large majority of women in the country' including a declining sex ratio, declining employment rate and the rising proportion of women among illiterates.

Inevitably, devastatingly, Mazumdar concluded: 'All our investigations into women's status and the findings of eminent social scientists point to a consistent alliance between patriarchy and hierarchy in maintaining the existing structure of inequalities in our society. The power relations that help to perpetuate monopolistic control of political power, economic power, and knowledge power by a small minority of our population also help to perpetuate certain role models, myths and mystification about women's social, economic and political roles by keeping them out of the arena of legitimate scientific enquiry. This promotion of invisibility of women's actual roles, struggles, views and aspirations have provided a major obstacle to the realization of the vision of equality that took shape during the freedom struggle.' In other words, Indian institutions conspire to silence women, prohibiting us from raising our voices or our expectations. Each aspect of Indian life has become colonized by an old boys' club.

Forty-seven years have passed since this seminal report. Where are we now? The child sex ratio, measuring the number of baby girls born for every thousand baby boys, has dramatically declined from 964 in 1971 to 918 in 2011. Women's literacy levels have increased, but more men are literate and men study many more years than women. The consistent wage gap between men and women, and declining women's employment, show that men are able to earn far more financial independence from their education. Despite how modern the fashion and language of young urban Indians might seem, despite the number of luxury brands present in Indian shopping malls, and activism on social media, women's employment rates have steadily retreated to the same levels as in the 1970s. Nearly all women in India still depend on men or family money for their living.

Despite tomes on the subject of gender gaps, not to mention countless magazine covers in the years since the 1974 report, our institutions continue to silence or dismiss women's experiences of the workplace. Imagine Mazumdar's horror were she to hear that in 2019, the Chief Justice of India could be accused of harassment by a female court officer only for the case to be hastily dismissed as being without 'substance'.

When many young Indian women, mostly part of the social elite, recently raised their voices and told their stories of widespread and unpunished sexual harassment as part of the #MeToo movement, a major Indian female movie star insisted that sexual harassment was not a 'male-female issue'. Her comments were mystifying, not to say annoying. All of these allegations of harassment had been levelled at powerful men. I don't mean to target one actress, but it is a puzzle. Why did an intelligent and articulate popular icon feel the need to silence any acknowledgement of the gendered politics of violence in our country? Why is it so hard for many of us to publicly accept that the market for personal rewards and professional recognition is disproportionately skewed against women who desire success and independence?

During India's COVID-induced lockdown, the fall in women's employment was sharper than men. There were cases of sexual assault within quarantine centres. An eighteen-year-old pupil at a prominent Delhi school was arrested for administering an Instagram account where other young men could exchange and share obscene comments on photographs of their female classmates—teenage girls, lest we forget. The tragic suicide of a gifted male actor degenerated into his girlfriend's character being assassinated for weeks in the Indian media, particularly on the noisy nightly debates on twenty-four-hour news channels. The female actor was eventually imprisoned for two weeks, seemingly to satisfy the bloodlust of a digital lynch mob made up of men *and* women.

No, the situation is simply too dire for nuance. Indian intellectuals often glibly talk of the Bharat–India divide, suggesting that Indians occupy very different countries along the rural–urban spectrum. The data on Indian women's well-being, employment rates and freedom of movement suggests that they live on a different planet, not just country, from their male compatriots. Our political and business leadership remains predominantly male—busy ravaging land, air and water, the very resources that determine how much women toil to care and cook for their homes. The state and the family—the two critical institutions of Indian life—have delegated all the unacknowledged and laborious burden of care to women. Yet, women's work, paid or unpaid, *within* homes, is barely supported or acknowledged by labour laws or infrastructure programmes. Worse, women's interest in pursuing a sense of self outside the home is heavily taxed. Sixty per cent of Indian women are not allowed to travel alone outside their villages or neighborhoods, even to the market or a health clinic. Nearly each one of us has experienced some form of sexual violence. Fifty-three per cent of us are anaemic. Despite increasing educational attainment, women have far less access to jobs, technology, property or communication devices—the oil of twenty-first-century independence.

To make sense of the noisy statistics and to check my own anger and bias, I placed a straightforward question to several feminists, intellectuals, scholars and activists in India: Have things changed in any meaningful way for the female sex? How has the 'status of women' progressed since Mazumdar and her colleagues wrote their report in the 1970s?

My first response came from Jean Dreze, one of India's most recognized economists and activists. Highlighting how tough it is to capture the myriad realities within India in one sweep, he wrote: 'Women's status, as you call it, is not a unidimensional thing and much depends on what you look at—say, women's education levels (which are rising, and certainly contribute to their empowerment) or workforce participation rates (which are declining). In India, social change also tends to be class and caste specific. For instance, if you look at female university students in cities like Delhi, they certainly seem to have more power and freedom than they used to have—like the freedom to marry a person of their choice or to pursue a career of their choice. On the other hand, if you look at a Dalit woman in an agricultural household, the changes would be less striking, though there may be some, associated for instance with lower fertility rates and better access to the mass media. Overall, I would say that there has been some positive change in gender relations in India during the last few decades, but it has been very slow.'

Renana Jhabvala from SEWA reflected on the experiences and lessons of her activism, the work she has done since 1977 for the rights of women workers. 'While women are more educated and healthier than they were in the 1970s,' she said, 'gaps between men and women remain. The key worry for us is that women's access to independence and public life remains curtailed. They barely earn wages for all their labour. Very few have good jobs and even fewer have managed to find success in public life—be it in politics or business. And while I don't think economic liberalization has created this growing male–female divide, liberalization has opened more opportunities for boys. Girls struggle to access these due to strict control from their families. The conversation on freedom for women within families is yet to change radically. Women must speak up. That's key.'

During a panel discussion to launch a book commemorating twenty-five years of India's economic liberalization, Pratap Bhanu Mehta, a leading scholar and public intellectual, declared that the Indian state's handling of women and gender issues had been a 'catastrophic failure'. He joked that the all-male panel debating the pros and cons of economic reform was symptomatic of a larger problem. Every international institution shares his concern. In 2018, Christine Lagarde, head of the International Monetary Fund (IMF) at the time, worried that India had failed to address widening gender gaps. I interviewed Rohini Pande, a development economist studying gender inequality at Yale University. 'The numbers on women's access to jobs seem to be getting worse,' she said. 'What's increasingly worrying is that this issue is barely a political priority. The Indian state can do a lot if it desires. Be it access to phones or jobs, our culture and institutions display tremendous resistance in allowing women more freedom to engage with the world outside their homes.'

Reflecting on the many successes of the women's movement, feminist publisher and writer Urvashi Butalia highlighted the establishment of women jamaats, the role of the movement in addressing caste-based discrimination and the important work of women-led community groups. She went on to say, 'But I think there is a deep lack or a deep dearth of political will, there is no real understanding, among our political class, our bureaucrats, our policymakers, our judges, of how the world can be transformed, and must be transformed, by women's real participation. So, they say the right things (sometimes) and do very little or continue to do the wrong things. If any progress has been made at all, it's been because women have fought for it, they've snatched it and then they've guarded it.'

The interventions of Indian feminists, including the 1974 report, are rooted in the efforts of countless freedom fighters and activists such as Kamaladevi Chattopadhyay. Born in 1903 and a student of sociology, Chattopadhyay has been described by historians as the best-travelled Indian woman of her generation, a representative of a 'coloured cosmopolitanism'. The first Indian woman to compete for political office in 1926, she differed from the Nehruvian conceptual landscape, which understood the engines of the economy to be factories and fields. In her lifetime, as India industrialized, she observed and possibly anticipated the steep decline in women's economic opportunities and the steady devaluation of women's labours. The share of women 'workers' shrunk from thirty-three per cent in 1911 to a meagre twelve per cent in 1971. Several reasons triggered this post-Independence drop in women's paid work: difficulties in capturing and understanding women's labours, population growth, the increased mechanization of the economy, a shift from traditional hand-weaving towards modern mills and factories in which employment was largely offered to men. Chattopadhyay saw the need to acknowledge the home as a site of economic production and augment women's labours through government investments in childcare, crafts and home-based industries. During a sharp exchange with Jawaharlal Nehru on India's Fundamental Rights Resolution, she argued that women workers needed 'attention' instead of 'protection'. She felt that using the word 'protection' made women seem weak. Nehru did not object; his response is one many Indians in 2020 would offer—'There can be no better instance of inferiority complex than Mrs Kamaladevi's objection to the word "protection". I do not understand what is humiliating in "protection".'

Chattopadhyay resisted the notion of protection because she was fighting to overcome the inferior status accorded to women's contributions and experiences of the economy. Following a long struggle for childcare support, a law mandating maternity benefits for women was passed in 1961 providing women in the formal workforce twelve weeks of maternity leave. The legislation was amended in 2017 to expand maternity leave to twenty-six weeks and all enterprises with more than fifty employees were mandated to provide crèche facilities. The amendment also ensured that women's jobs were protected for periods before and after pregnancy. These are vital shifts. However, they still do not recognize childcare as an equal domain to be shared between men and women. There is no corresponding provision requiring the private sector to offer paternity leave. Women in home-based sectors and informal work, the largest chunk of women workers, are also not eligible for the benefits of such laws, which continue to link labour regulations with factories and offices. There are also growing concerns that the 2017 amendment will lead to the private sector hiring even fewer women. And single women who must care for elderly parents with one income (which is invariably less than what a man would earn for doing the same job) are provided no support. So the fight continues.

The Nobel-winning economist Abhijit Banerjee said to me that it was 'hard to overestimate how much damage this history of objectification and oppression has done to the self-esteem of women. Many women have no sense of their own possibility both because they have never had a chance and also because they bear the weight of so much cultural and physical intimidation. Education, media and affirmative action will probably all be key in trying to get them to feel that they can take on the challenges thrown at them by the economy and our very broken society'.

When I asked fan-women about how they saw the 'status of women', none used laws or statistics to explain themselves. They articulated the quality of their lives through the quality of their relationships and the quality of food offered to their children. It seemed as if the latter had improved marginally while the former was in rapid decline. 'There is less love and much more tension everywhere,' Manju had once said to me.

To think that social inequalities aren't driving even privileged women up the wall, to presume discrimination doesn't surface in one's everyday relationship with oneself, to believe that a sense of unworthiness and shame doesn't creep into the way we navigate our romantic lives, to pretend that our interpersonal relationships with partners, fathers, brothers and mothers are immune to structural inequalities and are somehow havens of perfect equality is plain idiocy or, worse, a sinister silence.

According to a study published in the *Lancet* in 2018, suicide rates amongst young Indian women have reached an all-time high. Thirty-seven per cent of all women who died by suicide in the world are Indian; the suicide rate for Indian women is twice the global average. Psychological tests measuring female agency—the degree to which women feel they have control over their lives and can actuate their ambitions—show worrying trends across class and caste groups. According to the WHO, Indians are the most depressed people in the world and women are fifty per cent more likely to suffer episodes of depression than men. Many of us are increasingly unable to cope with the patriarchal structures we have inherited and preserved, whether in the waning forests of Jharkhand or the gated complexes of Gurgaon.

Intimate and Incremental

'Changing how people dress is hugely different from changing how people think.'

—*Shah Rukh Khan, 2009*

About nine years ago, I encountered a young woman called Vibha at the 'Nirbhaya' protests in central Delhi, a mass outpouring of revulsion and anger at the grisly rape and murder of a middle class twenty-three-year-old physiotherapy student by six men on a bus. Vibha was nineteen; she hailed from Rohtak in the prosperous northern state of Haryana, which lies adjacent to Delhi. Two days after our attendance at the protests, the Delhi police would close all metro stations and roads leading to the protest sites and unleash tear gas on those who had still gathered, their candles aloft. Anticipating this sort of trouble, Vibha's mother had accompanied her to the protest as it was 'not safe for a girl to go alone'. These were women from a Jat clan, an agricultural community in northern India that has amassed significant wealth, property and political power through the years. Seven out of the ten Haryana chief ministers have belonged to the community. Jats have historically relied on community-based self-governing councils called khap panchayats. These village councils have gained infamy over the past decade for the strict controls they impose on women's physical movements and their approval of honour killings.

Vibha and her mother had both been shocked and moved to tears by the brutal gangrape and murder of a young woman, who had been given the sobriquet 'Nirbhaya' (the fearless one) by the press, since the law requires that rape victims not be named. The outpouring across the country was a watershed moment in Indian political history as well, with crowds of ordinary voters taking up the cudgels for women's rights, instigating a series of violent protests demanding safety for women in public spaces, and weakening the electoral chances of the ruling Congress-led government. The protest sites were full of angry, anguished upper-class and middle-class women, unable to accept that the female body could become the site for such repeated and grotesque violence.

Claustrophobic among the crush of bodies in the crowd, Vibha's mother complained that she felt dizzy. Mother and daughter had arranged for a taxi to pick them up from a market near the protest site. The taxi driver had to park farther away due to police-imposed road closures. The mobile network was unreliable and Vibha was unable to contact the driver. They were stuck. I was meant to meet a friend for a late drink in Gurgaon and offered to give them a ride home. In keeping with modern Jat wealth, their family home was in a plush gated complex in greater Gurgaon; they had long left behind the source of their wealth—the extensive farmlands in rural Rohtak that were now tended by hired hands. Vibha quickly accepted my offer.

On our way to Gurgaon, a famous old Shah Rukh song was playing on the car stereo. Vibha sang along. I asked her if she was a fan. 'He's too old for me,' Vibha said. 'I like Ryan Gosling.' But, she added, 'I admire Shah Rukh a lot. The way he made it on his own. All the older women in our family get together to watch his films. I have an older cousin who adores him. I think they all want sons like him.'

Through our journey, Vibha talked non-stop. She told me how she was top of her statistics class, how she had many followers on social media, how she had organized for girls from her college to be present at the protest. She struck me as a person composed of appetites and ambitions—desperate to taste the world. Eventually, she made a familiar request, one I had grown accustomed to hearing from north Indian women returning from public spaces—*'Please don't tell our family that you met us at the protest. We had said we were going to the mall.'*

'Papa did not give me permission to attend the protest,' Vibha said. 'But it was important for me to be there. All my friends from college were going, I had urged them to come. As women, we needed to walk together. My mother agreed to join. It's sad we had to lie, but what else could we do?'

I agreed to their request for secrecy. On reaching their house, following a long, frustrating drive, Vibha suggested I have tea with her family. They would offer snacks and tea to my driver as well. The journey to Gurgaon had required all his skill and patience. On Delhi roads, cars seem to exist in order to crush the human spirit through endless traffic snarls. Our drive had been no exception, with the ubiquity of pointless zigzagging by impatient drivers forever on the verge of exploding into a fit of violent road rage. Surinder, my driver, needed a break, and chai sounded terrific. I joined Vibha's father in their sparkling living room, all marble and chandeliers. The walls were lined with photos of family elders—men with sunken hollow eyes and puffed-out chests, women with covered heads and petite frames. Some of the men had served in the Indian army. The Jat community is well-known for military service, agriculture and real-estate acumen. Upon learning of my academic background, Vibha's father was keen to introduce me to his son. I was used to this, as are most Indians who've attended fancy schools—families often want us to help their offspring with application essays. Vibha had a brother, Varun, who was a year younger and had just been admitted to a prestigious college in Delhi University. He had made it through the sports quota as a competitive basketball player who hoped to soon play at the state level.

When we arrived, Varun was taking an evening nap before going out to meet his friends. 'We usually don't disturb Bhaiya,' Vibha said. Still, a domestic worker was sent to summon young Varun. 'Tell the maid to tell Varun, Papa needs to talk to him,' Vibha's father simply released his instructions into the drawing room air without directing his words to any specific person, knowing his demands would be met. Sitting in that room, the unequal family dynamics were evident. It was clear that Varun's movements were barely patrolled, and all the policing in Vibha's home was restricted to her mind and body. Vibha had mentioned her interest in pursuing a business degree during our car journey but her mother had maintained a stoic silence throughout, neither acknowledging nor encouraging her daughter's ambitions. At the time, I thought it was because she was feeling unwell. Now, stuffing my face with biscuits in their living room, I started to think otherwise. No one suggested I dole out career advice to Vibha, even though she was the first woman from her family to attend college.

Twenty minutes had passed when a striking young man entered the room—I could smell expensive cologne and booze on him; perhaps he had begun drinking in the afternoon or perhaps he was still hungover from drinks the previous night. Like most of the young-handsome-rich-drunks in the region, whisky was Varun's poison. His father introduced me and my CV to him and requested that I counsel the young man on his career and education. We women were left with a plate of biscuits and whisky-drenched Varun. Vibha's father had a business meeting at the golf club.

Before I could start asking Varun about his future plans, he turned to Vibha and said, 'Does your new friend have a boyfriend?' Vibha replied 'Bhaiya, don't talk like this now. Please.' Varun turned to me and continued. 'Where are you from?' he asked. 'You don't look like you're from the north.' 'Jharkhand and Bengal,' I responded. My ancestry seemed to get Varun very excited. 'From your surname, your father's Brahmin, no wonder you're good at studies. But you know, our servants and farmers hire brides and maids from both your states, things have become that bad there. So they send their girls to us.' He laughed. The sound of his laughter betrayed his excessive drinking— it was brittle and bold, brassy with the confidence of his family's chandeliers and easy cash. But young and drunk Varun was right.

Back when I met Vibha and Varun, in 2012, Haryana reported birth rates of just 871 women for every thousand men; female foeticide and infanticide, of course, was rife. As a result, rural families had to import paid-for brides from poorer eastern states, such as Jharkhand and Bengal, for help with both farming and fertility. In a survey of 10,000 families in ninety-two villages across Haryana, a local activist group—Drishti Stree Adhyayan Kendra—identified 9,000 such paid-for brides. 'In every village,' wrote the researchers, 'there are over fifty girls that have been bought; some of them as young as thirteen years old, and a very small percentage of the "sold for marriage" women are found to be living a married life. Most are untraceable or exploited as unpaid domestic servants by the agents or men who marry/buy them. There are also instances of girls being resold to other persons after living a married life for a few years.'

'I am sure you have many boyfriends,' Varun interrupted, snapping me out of my sociological reverie. As if everyone hadn't already heard his 'banter', he repeated his remark for his sister's benefit. 'I am sure your friend has had many boyfriends,' he said to her, a grin spreading across his handsome face. Vibha started to say something, but Varun suddenly raised his voice: 'Keep quiet! The grown-ups are talking.' She was stunned into muteness, scared of her younger brother. Varun had shouted at his sister louder than any man I'd heard before. Vibha's father was nowhere to be seen, her mother was a grim-faced spectator. Both women were trembling. Varun's gaze returned to me. 'You know,' he said, his face twisted with contempt, 'here in Haryana, we have a saying about men and women. And about their boyfriends and girlfriends. A key which can open many locks is a great key. But a lock which has been opened by many keys is a bad lock.'

The sexual metaphor was sharp and clear. Varun did not believe in subtlety. 'The only thing that needs a lock and key is your mouth,' I said, almost incoherent with rage. I muttered some meaningless excuse and rushed out of the room. Vibha followed me. She apologized as I was about to enter the large swanky elevator. In tears, she said, 'I was silly to go to that protest, what's the point? These boys at home here will never change. He spoke to you so badly, and I could do nothing. He has no respect for educated women like us. In fact, the more we speak and do. well, the more he hates us. He doesn't even care for my feelings. But he's never like that to guests, he is good at hiding his views. He even gave a speech on how young men must support women's equality on Women's Day at the Jat Bhavan here. Today, he was a bit too open. It must have been the drinking and that we woke him up. I am really sorry.' I was too angry to offer her any coherent words of consolation. Vibha and I exchanged numbers and promised to stay in touch. I never did hear from her. But I wondered about Vibha often. Did her spirit and voice ever change her own home?

Walking back to the car, I knew Vibha would torture herself with the silent burden of remorse about her brother's bad behaviour but that my departure would trigger no guilt or introspection within his smug male heart. He was blessed with beauty and wealth, with all the freedom to deploy his talents, too self-satisfied to waste time on inner reflection. To him, professing support for gender equality in public was simply a way to perform good manners and modernity, to look like he held moral integrity without being moral at all. The world did not incentivize young Varun to investigate his biases. The women in his everyday intimate life would bear the brunt of his authentic feelings. Would Varun ever privately practise the equality he publicly preached at the Jat Bhavan?

A survey amongst students and parents across 314 schools in Haryana was organized in 2014. Led by a team of economists at the Abdul Latif Jameel Poverty Action Lab (J-PAL), the survey was part of an effort to create a baseline to test the impacts of behaviour-change curricula on gender attitudes amongst students by working closely with government-school administrators in the state. The results highlighted the duplicity and self-deception inherent in all our perceptions of the role of women in the world. The good news: nearly ninety per cent of both boys and girls felt that men and women should receive equal treatment and opportunities. The bad news: eighty per cent of boys also felt that men should receive preferred treatment in accessing education opportunities. Fifty-seven per cent of the girls surveyed shared this view. When it came to what those surveyed expected women to do with their energy and time, all politically correct cooing about equal treatment vanished. Eighty per cent of the boys surveyed felt that the woman's 'most important role was of a homemaker' and sixty-seven per cent of the girls concurred.

In 1985, a decade after the release of the disturbing Status of Women Report, Vina Mazumdar wrote again about the 'women's question'. She wondered why the principle of equality enshrined in the Constitution had not been actualized. Why had the 'schools, the legal system and the media failed to develop a culture of equality? Why had trade unions and political parties ignored women's rights and issues?'

Despite moments of mass mobilization and important legal reforms, these questions continue to linger. Our laws and social churnings are yet to manifest wholeheartedly as radical and sustained changes in the way we treat each other in homes, schools or even bus stops. Has the internet dramatically altered us? Do the number of retweets or the attention devoted to popular hashtags provide a reliable signal of ongoing shifts in our daily actions and attitudes? Looking at the repeated episodes of gender-based violence, the drastic drop in female employment and non-stop evidence of discriminatory access to economic opportunity and public space, the answer seems bleak.

Quiz practically anyone in northern India today—including some of the types encountered in this book: the Aristoprat, the school kids of Haryana, the Accountant's parents, young, drunk Varun or even a Bollywood star—about their views and values, and you'll receive sermons on the virtues of treating women as equals. You'll also be told how everyone should treat women fairly within their own homes, in a country where marital rape is not yet a crime. We pay our domestic workers minimum wage, we value women beyond the boys' club formula of beauty, thin-ness and feminine pliancy—thank you very much. It is always someone else who is to blame for social malpractice and gender trouble. It's always 'the government', 'those boys', 'those girls who create trouble', 'dented-painted', 'the neo-liberal conservatives', 'the Lutyens elite', 'those Muslims', 'the Chinky girls who ask for it', 'the poor', 'the uneducated', 'the Gandhis','the Bhakts', it's always the Other. Someone else is always to blame.

Ask us to reflect on our own patterns of intimate behaviour, our friendships, our private family and romantic lives, and we all become squeamish. We point fingers at others, but any glance inward is unwelcome and unnecessary. And yet, all the data on gender-based violence or economic discrimination will show that the home and intimate relationships are where female autonomy is quashed, where the Indian Constitution is crushed, where non-conforming women are taxed, where overt and covert abuse is rampant and self-denial supreme.

Feminist thinker and theorist Nivedita Menon describes the family as the fulcrum of discrimination in India. 'If you bring fundamental rights into a family,' she says, 'and if every individual in the family is treated as free and equal citizens, that family will collapse. Because the family as it exists, is based on clearly established hierarchies of gender and age, with gender trumping age: that is, an adult male is generally more powerful than an older female.' There is a large body of literature on social change. I won't commit here the academic atrocity of furnishing a half-baked literature review. Several comprehensive books do a far better job of taking stock of all the academic literature than I can. Scholars suggest that changing the way we treat each other is not about talk, but fundamentally about moral *action*. In conversations on discrimination in India, politicians and the thinkerati make social change sound like a marketing campaign. Equality becomes a dress that can be advertised, with the hopes that more people will buy it. We do this in our drawing rooms as well, we all become marketing gurus and harp on about how ending discrimination requires a change in 'mindset', a 'trigger' to change our beliefs and views on the world. But, as Varun's women's day speech and the views of young students of Haryana show us, we can all claim to hold liberal beliefs and barely practise them. Thanks to years of media campaigning and the school curriculum, everyone surveyed in the schools of Haryana professed to support gender parity. But translating this professed normative belief—of men and women being allowed equal opportunities—into concrete *action* remains a struggle. Besides, when questioned further, the students surveyed in Haryana retained core patriarchal values. Not unexpectedly, the state reports one of the lowest female employment rates in the country.

Meaningful change in everyday life happens when we start to practise the views we profess. This sounds silly and obvious, but history shows that bridging the gap between saying and doing is tough and protracted. Changing how people expect to be treated and how they treat others isn't like demanding a tax cut or asking people to wear masks or dress in a particular way. Only fools think we can rationalize, cancel, tweet or march our way to a social revolution. Radical change needs oxygen from each one of us. We are required to practise what we retweet, to self-scrutinize, to incrementally partake in impossibly difficult conversations in our own everyday relationships. For change to move beyond people parroting a politically correct aphorism they might have read in a magazine or a bumper sticker towards real shifts in their private behaviour requires repeated and sustained intimate interpersonal dialogue in which discriminatory views are revealed and challenged.

Change involves regular people imposing censure and costs on friends and family members, on making personal acts of discrimination dishonourable and shameful. For the brave, change requires bearing the isolation and costs of resistance. Sometimes, change requires us to be silent, to let someone else have their say. Change will need good faith and generosity. Mindset isn't enough, morality is embodied in how we demonstrate our liberal views in our daily encounters with people, places and our self. Without these intimate revolutions, the best laws and the strongest movements will fail. The realm of everyday intimacy is the true home of social change. It is where all our longing, self-loathing and biases are unveiled. This is the world of deeply private rebellions, within people and within relationships. No platform, no performance. It's where the real battle is. And it's got to be long and ugly.

Private Rebellions

'As long as the self can say "I", it is impossible not to rebel.'

—*W.H. Auden*

Far away from cancel culture and visible sites of resistance, there are private protests in private spaces. Yamini Aiyar, president of one of India's oldest think-tanks, said to me, 'I think we know very little about the changing lives of young women in India because we have stopped studying them for who they are. We know the heroines—the ones who fought against all the odds and became leaders and we know the victims. But the real change is taking place in between—the ordinary women who are dressing differently, who are spending more hours in school than ever before, who are reshaping the rules at home in their marriages, in their relationships with their peers, in their relationships with their in-laws and in their relationships with the working world.'

These ordinary women practising ordinary change are everywhere around us. Encouraged by education and access to information, a new generation of women, with a stronger sense of 'I', hopes for more. They watch films and lust after an actor. They have friends and casual sex. They dare to imagine a self which deviates from their prescribed function as dutiful caregiver. Their professional or personal success has little to do with an online or offline following. With acclaim or public attention. Their hope is not to be noticed at all, or to be noticed in their immediate world on their own terms. Primarily, they just want to be loved, paid well and left alone to do as they please. They seek affordable accommodation and friendly policing systems, not a benevolent patriarch's protection. They seek men and families that can support their desires and ambitions, not treat them solely as providers of family honour, sex, children and care.

My own bias, after reading, research and a couple of decades of regular adult life, is to believe that women's access to an independent income is one of the most powerful tools of resistance against patriarchy. Of course, employment is merely a tool, not a magic bullet. As long as our institutions socialize us to be homemakers and follow caste puritanism, as long as our loved ones tax us for seeking a sense of self beyond beauty and duty, as long as state and society don't show solidarity with the unpaid labours women perform, even the most careerist woman will wish to escape her job, given the opportunity.

A mass female exodus from employment hints at an alarming and apocalyptic future. One where women spend all their time in service of family members and on personal grooming. Research shows that employed women produce more progressive and less narcissistic male children; boys grow up adjusting to the idea that men must help at home, that a loved one may have passions beyond her immediate family, that his female family members do not breathe merely to serve his needs. 'Shah Rukh ki mummy job karti thi (his mother had a job), that's why he is so cool about women,' the Accountant once said. Also, women with jobs are role models for girl children at home, teaching their daughters or sisters to aspire for more than a great body and a great husband. Employed women marry or stay single on their own terms, they might even mingle outside caste boundaries. In societies that prefer men as breadwinners, employment changes women—their self-esteem, their demands from themselves and the world escalate and the dignity they receive and expect also expands. I saw this in the studies I read, I felt it in the fans I met, I know it in myself and my closest female friends. I noticed how small everyday acts of earning your own money and spending it slowly and steadily redefine maryada, the norms for how we treat each other and how we *expect t*o be treated.

Witnessing these deeply private rebellions, I struggle to find solidarity with the vociferous internet sloganeering on 'smashing' the patriarchy. Because the feminism I've seen knows you must chip away at social structures every day. That patriarchy won't collapse with a noisy smash but will gradually unravel. Perhaps it is a sign of how unequal a society we have become that the feminism of my class of Indian elites who live in Twitter Pradesh does not resonate with those who do the hard work of engaging in quiet renegotiations within homes, marriages and friendships. Viscerally, everything I see while grazing social media makes it impossible to reconcile the stylish and loud feminism of the internet with the uncool daal-sabzi version of everyday feminism I have encountered over the past fifteen years of my working life. Feminism that won't catch the eye but that can trigger change.

Unlike Insta-friendly feminism, I have spent much of my adult life enthralled by a feminism that hates public display. A feminism that avoids being photographed because it fears being seen as it does sustained radical things like hold on to a job when your family forbids it, use informal daycare services for your children, abandon arranged marriage in favour of the Delhi Secretariat, watch films without permission or enjoy a 'holiday' from your marriage. This is a feminism that starts with murmurs and ends in roars. It can't do yoga headstands, although it would love to.

13

Madness at Mannat

Main sawalon main hoon, main jawabon main hoon
(I am in your questions; I am in your answers.)

—*Veer-Zaara (2004)*

In January 2019, I take myself to Shah Rukh's palatial home on the poshest corner of the sea-facing Bandra Bandstand in Mumbai. The house is called Mannat, often described as an Urdu word for prayer. Speaking to a few linguists, I learn that the word 'mannat' is derived from Prakrit, a collection of ancient subcontinental tongues used from the fifth century BCE up to the eighth century CE. The root is from the Prakrit 'mann' which implies 'the desiring mind or heart'. There is also the Arabic word 'minnat' (gift, an act of kindness), a cousin of mannat.

Mannat implies acknowledgement, assent, a promise or vow, an expression of desire or intention. The property is an Indian dream: an opulent house of one's own, a landmark to celebrate Mr Khan's conquest of middle-class aspirations, Hindi cinema and real estate. I arrive to offer homage a little after lunchtime. At first glance, everything seems familiar from when I made my original pilgrimage, sixteen years ago.

In 2004, my first visit to Mannat was triggered by failure. I was in Mumbai for a graduate-school interview that ended in a brutal rejection. Ma tried to cheer me up and suggested I divert myself by meeting friends. I had no friends in Mumbai but proceeded to Mannat. It felt like the most natural thing to do. In that period of uncertainty, I did not need human interaction. I required divine intervention. Suddenly, I felt gripped by fandom-fuelled religiosity. If I could not believe in my own abilities, I needed to believe in something. I desperately needed to marvel at society, I needed a spectacle. Darshan would definitely help. Outside Mannat, I found solace in an open-air museum of fellow fans. We were all exhibits, exchanging smiles and glances but no words. There was an air of transcendence and bonhomie, like being at a concert. Young men and women buzzed and bustled about, taking photos and waiting, hoping to catch a glimpse of their hero. It had been an incredible year for Shah Rukh. He had starred in three major box-office hits and his popularity was unparalleled.

In 2019, when I returned, my place in the labour market was far more secure and I'd been able to settle old debts. But Shah Rukh's career was at a crossroads. Approaching his mid fifties, he was deemed too old for the typical romantic film and his recent cinematic experiments weren't paying off. His last film, released a few weeks ago, had flopped hard. The film in question was, ironically, titled *Zero*. Shah Rukh played a narcissistic dwarf who struggles with his fragile façade of self-love while pursuing the affections of an accomplished woman. I watched the film twice and loved most minutes. An empty hall suggested I was in the minority. A series of unsuccessful films had unleashed a stream of 'Shah Rukh's star has faded' prophecies in the muttering media.

While most film critics found little to praise in *Zero*, Baradwaj Rangan, described by the director-producer Karan Johar as the best critic of mainstream Hindi cinema, said *Zero* was the 'bravest romance' he had seen in years. In his review for a prominent Indian daily newspaper, another critic, Raja Sen, hailed the first half of *Zero* as 'flat-out fantastic' and said Khan was 'magic' and 'remains the best lover in the business'. When I asked Sen about the fuss being made over Shah Rukh's fall from box-office grace, he said: 'This so-called dip is because he [Shah Rukh] is committed to radical choices. He has decided to age gracefully on screen. He does films where he lets his female co-stars shine. He seems no longer interested in the logic of commercial cinema and is desperately trying to do different kinds of roles and formats. I'm convinced that ten years from now, even when he is sixty-five, we'll still want to watch him.' Reacting to the news of Shah Rukh's highly anticipated big-budget action release in 2022, Sen, speaking to me in 2021, added: 'After his radical phase was commercially unsuccessful, Khan evidently decided to bring back his aura by starring in the biggest, most obviously mainstream films he could find. His upcoming slate is anything but radical. I'd like to believe the star is playing safe only in order to shine brighter later.'

When we met to discuss her Shah Rukh documentary, Nasreen Munni Kabir reflected on Hindi film's celebrity culture. 'Shah Rukh's stardom,' she said, 'is set in stone. Nothing can change that. These people are legends in their own lifetime, there is no doubt, and there will be no change in that fact. He can do good movies or bad movies, and it won't make a difference. He has reached that pinnacle of stardom. He is like the Beatles—some songs were brilliant, some songs were awful. But the Beatles are the Beatles. And Shah Rukh will always be Shah Rukh.'

Standing outside Mannat in January 2019, I understood what she meant. Despite consecutive commercial failures, the scene outside Mr Khan's home was the same as in 2004. There were nearly fifty people taking photos outside the gate. I counted thirty cars that halted briefly to gawk at the building in the hour that I spent outside Mannat. It was clear that I was visiting a middle-class monument. Shah Rukh's legend appears untouched by his box-office displays. In fact, I sense a deeper reverence. Just like in 2004, young and middle-aged fans mill about. I observed a few young men unsuccessfully try to take selfies with the security guards manning the gate. The house has receded further behind wire-topped walls, far more guarded now than in 2004. Indeed, on that very day, construction workers were adding even more wire to the walls. But no one in the crowd during that hour looked likely to try and breach security, to try and tear down the wall between the icon and the man. We were all too invested in the fantasy. Scanning the crowd, I did not recall as many smartphones or selfies in 2004. But the fifteen intervening years can hardly diminish the sense of nostalgia and euphoria amongst Shah Rukh's fans outside his house. We are all close to our hero, we believe he tells our stories.

In a giddy state of connection and confidence, I approached a mixed group of men and women. They were from Bhopal and were in Mumbai for an entrance exam. 'We saw the Gateway of India,' one of the girls said, 'and then came here.' A young woman with bright pink lipstick added, 'Many of the boys have gone to see Salman's house but we girls wanted to see Shah Rukh.' They're all dressed sharply, wearing the current trends and fixing their hair constantly. None of the ladies have dupattas or cover-ups. One of them is wearing a faux-suede jumpsuit. I don't recall such a keen connection in 2004 to image and style.

On the pavement opposite Mannat, I get talking to a middle-aged woman from Bangladesh. She is accompanied by her father and brother. 'I brought them here,' she smiles and tells me. I ask her if she is a fan, and her response is a toothy grin. 'Yes, of course. There is no one like him.' Her father rolls his sweaty eyebrows in embarrassment.

He says, 'She wanted to take our family to a holiday to Bombay, so she is the boss now. Girls in our homes have become very strong.'

Who's Next?

'The truth is I still fulfil people's desire to see romance on screen. No other guy can romance better than me.'

—*Shah Rukh Khan, 2012*

After my visit, I walk away from Mannat and head towards the rocky beach on Bandstand to sit by the ocean. I see some young men grooving to a new song from an upcoming film called *Gully Boy*. The film features the actor Ranveer Singh as a Muslim rapper from the slums of Mumbai. At the time, Singh was poised to become *the* male icon of popular Hindi film after the roaring business made by his super-macho Christmas 2018 release *Simbba*. He had struck box-office gold with three massive hits in quick succession. *Simbba* was released a week after Shah Rukh's *Zero* and was a resounding pan-national success. Ranveer played the eponymous Simbba, a corrupt, over-muscled policeman who is persuaded to fight the 'good' fight after the brutal rape of a young woman. The film seemed calibrated to have missed the entire #MeToo message in India: the plot essentially comprises gangs of men avenging rape through vigilante violence, while women, whose entire gender these thugs are purportedly 'defending', stand by and watch. The leading lady vanishes after professing love for the hero, only to emerge for song and dance sequences.

I asked the young men listening to the soundtrack of *Gully Boy* if they liked Ranveer Singh and what kinds of films they liked to watch. They were happy to chat. Ranveer, they said, was their favourite. They loved his 'energy' and 'attitude'. I ask them to elaborate on what they meant by his attitude and they sang a song of praise about 'hard work', about the effort he put into his movies and his body. Despite the effort, though, it didn't feel like work. 'He is always having fun,' one of the young men offered. 'It feels fun to watch him.' He went on: 'I like that Thor too. He has a great physique and does action very well.' The men, a group of five in their twenties, included two migrants from Jaipur and Bhubaneswar. They worked together for an online food delivery service. Their bikes were parked at Bandstand and they were enjoying a break before the evening shift. The men were seated near two young women. One of the women worked at a local beauty parlour and the other was a salesgirl in a new organic food store. The girls lived in the same low-income housing complex in Borivali and rode into Bandra together. Intrigued by our conversation, the women joined in. One of the men said that they watched dubbed Hollywood superhero blockbusters like *Thor*, *Iron Man* and *The Avengers* as often as they watched the latest Hindi film at a cheap single-screen hall nearby. Ranveer Singh is no longer competing with the Khans or young Indian actors. Simbba is competing with Thor.

Singh started his film career in 2010 with a slice-of-life movie called *Band Baaja Baaraat*. The film became a critical and commercial success and is now considered one of India's finest contemporary romantic comedies. Ranveer plays a naive, well-meaning man, Bittu, from a farming family in Haryana. Unwilling to work on his family farm, Bittu pleads with an ambitious middle-class young woman, played by Anushka Sharma, to give him a job helping her organize weddings. Together, they achieve tremendous success but fall out after they hook up one night. She is in love with him, and he is unsure of how he feels. Unsure of committing, unsure of what their romance will mean for their business. But all these feelings are unspoken. Instead, they argue. They fight bitterly enough to mutually part ways, only to be reunited when a corporate bigwig insists that only they, as a team rather than individuals, can be trusted to organize his daughter's wedding. During the wedding, Bittu discovers that he is in love with his former business partner. But, it's too late. She has decided to accept an arranged marriage and will be moving to Dubai. In the penultimate scene, the hero apologizes for being scared of love and manages to win back the affections of his beloved. It's a wonderful film, with a fabulous and unapologetically ambitious female lead, full of spunk, song, dance and hilarious Delhi-isms. It is also unusual in its attempt to trace how young north Indians negotiate the meaning of premarital sex when the modern labour market allows young men and women to mingle through work.

But contemporary romance vanished as the main act in Mr Singh's films after the first few years of his career. Three of his biggest hits are historical costume dramas directed by Sanjay Leela Bhansali. While love between a man and a woman plays a role in propelling the storyline forward in each of these films, the organizing principle and pathos is the love of nation or love of community. Romantic achievement is orthogonal to these films. Men and women may love each other, but most of the dialogue is spent on what's 'important'— the valorizing of tradition and honour.

In fact, one of Ranveer Singh's biggest box-office failures was a straight-up romance film where a majority of dialogue was dedicated to establishing male-female friendship and exploring the murky waters of romantic commitment. *Befikre*, a big-budget contemporary romantic comedy set amongst non-resident Indians living in Paris, was directed by Aditya Chopra, who directed Shah Rukh's global-desi romantic epic *DDLJ*. Released in 2016, *Befikre* was promoted as a film full of kisses and 'daring' scenes between Singh and the beauteous Vaani Kapoor. In 1995, *DDLJ* contained no sex. Instead, the hero in *DDLJ* establishes his sanskari values by assuring the heroine that they did not have sex after a drunken night. Fast-forward to the same director's universe two decades later, in which the lead pair hook up within the first few days of meeting, and the hero establishes his decency by apologizing to the heroine for calling her a slut. Still, ultimately, both Shah Rukh and Ranveer must play by the familial rules of marriage—their lover's parents must support the match and approve of them. While *DDLJ* was a genre-bending smash hit, *Befikre* was not.

Back at Bandstand, the men I met raved about Singh's abilities as a rapper in the *Gully Boy* soundtrack. They listened on their phones and were busy repeating the song's hook line—'*apna time aayega*', a generational statement of intent. Our time will come. When I spoke to those boys, the song was three days old and had already been seen by twenty-two million viewers on YouTube. The film would go on to be a major success and Singh would win all the major Indian acting awards.

Since his debut, Singh has starred in twelve feature films in the past decade. In the first ten years of his career, Shah Rukh had appeared in forty-one films. In part, the difference is due to the increased professionalization of the Indian film industry with its now-high production budgets and technical quality. Cinema has moved from loosely defined, largely oral scripts to bound scripts in which stars know precisely what they're doing and when they're doing it. And actors no longer need films to remain relevant, they are ubiquitous in Indian cultural life—on hoardings, news shows and newspapers every day. Their revenue streams are diversified away from film. Most earn money and attention by endorsing brands and appearing at events. In 2018, Adidas organized an India trip for popstar Pharrell Williams to unveil a new collection of sneakers. Ranveer Singh, the Indian brand ambassador for Adidas Originals, played host to Williams. They marketed the shoes while making merry at a Holi party together. Such celebrity relationships with brands are clichéd now. Leveraging mass media and the internet in a country that feasts on celebrities, many Indian film and TV personalities have broadened their reach and their audiences. They are pop culture icons, building empires based on how they dress and how they dance, with little bearing on the films they make or how well they act. Film stars are also heavily managed nowadays, by agents and an impressive public relations machinery. And younger actors are far more accessible through social media than Shah Rukh's generation and those before him ever were.

But there is an arc that links Shah Rukh and Ranveer. Both men have ensured the public knows that they are outsiders. They wear their struggles on their sleeves. In Mr Singh's case, this is a rather remarkable feat of media management, given that he is distantly related to a prominent film family. Like Shah Rukh, Ranveer has spent a fair share of media time through interviews explaining how he had no family connections to help launch him into films. Both have made teary and emotional appearances on TV shows and award ceremonies, both joke about how famous actresses and producers made comments on how they weren't classically handsome and not leading man material, both have ensured we know that they never fit the mould. In their own time, each has deviated from the standard script of the Hindi film hero. Shah Rukh did villainous roles and kickstarted Bollywood's central presence in marketing campaigns for brands. Ranveer has also played villainous roles. Mr Singh's social media antics and outfits are far more provocative than any of his contemporaries. The imagery screams at you, demanding attention. He is fully aware that most ordinary Indians can afford to access his photos or songs far before they can watch his films.

Shah Rukh and Ranveer are both wildly sexy, not in a formulaic pretty-boy way, but with a certain scrappiness. They share a smouldering intensity on-screen. They *want*, so desperately, to entertain and enthral us. To connect with us. When I talked to Nasreen Munni Kabir in her beautiful flat about superstars in India, she said, 'Amitabh was of his time, Shah Rukh is of his time. Salman is of a certain time too. Whoever comes next will represent their time.'

Apna Time Ayega

I would often ask Shah Rukh fangirls what they thought of the younger generation of male actors. The answers were different, depending on who and where they were. No contemporary male actor ever emerged as a common favourite. Urban fangirls liked a newer crop of actors like Rajkummar Rao, Nawazuddin Siddiqui and Ayushmann Khurrana, all doing wonderful, varied multiplex films. The women in Kochi mentioned various Malayalam superstars. Meenal and Sandhya's daughter felt they did not watch enough films to have strong preferences. Most rural women I interviewed preferred the men on TV shows. The growing inequality in India has started to manifest in how Indians now access cinema. Everyone complained about ticket prices. While Lily, living in Simdega, watched movies on TV or a few big-budget films distributed for mass consumption in smaller towns, people like me have access to all kinds of interesting and engaging content tailored to our preferences by Netflix. I've always admired mainstream Hindi cinema for the role it has played in culturally binding and integrating a diverse swathe of Indians. Even today, I can talk to a boatman and a bureaucrat about *Dangal* or *DDLJ*. But as the audience's inclination and ability to pay became more fragmented and diverse, as cinema ticket prices spiralled, Shah Rukh has come to seem like the last film icon many of us shared.

At Bandstand, as the young men continued to wax lyrical about Ranveer Singh, one of our female companions piped up. 'I don't like him that much. Even Tiger [Shroff] just jumps and fights. There is no story or sense.' I asked her about her favourite stars, and she rattled off a list: 'All the heroines are great these days. Priyanka, Kareena, Alia, Kangana, Deepika. I like watching them and how they carry themselves (apne aap ko kaise carry kartein hain). Bilkul professional.'

Actresses in Hindi films have historically received lower pay and fanfare than their male co-stars. But all that's changing because of a crop of new celebrities with longer careers, niche scripts for women, growing market relevance and increasing bargaining power. India's booming fashion economy amplifies the star power and market worth of women in cinema. Their 'looks' are as discussed as their performances. Armed with an international battalion of stylists, trainers, grooming experts and public relations people, India's new female superstars espouse a fuzzy language of female achievement. Some produce their own films, telling innovative stories featuring strong female roles. At the same time, they pay service to the idea that beauty and glamour are the most profitable avenue for women. In an age of impossible female beauty standards and obsessive self-improvement, they urge their fans to refine and better themselves. To help our personal projects of pursuing betterment, they share exercise routines, skincare recipes, diet tips, outtakes from magazine shoots and reading recommendations, aided and abetted by a growing industry of women's fashion and lifestyle magazines.

When I asked Sandhya's daughter and her friends about new movie stars, a few mentioned men, but the fascination was largely female. These first-generation English-speaking teenagers, growing up in the poorest quarters of urban Delhi, did not watch many films, but they watched the women on TV, social media, advertisements and songs. They admired these women, they admired their success. 'They are so focused, we learn from that,' said a fifteen-year-old to me.

Since so many young people used 'focus' when describing these female stars, I asked one teenager to explain what she meant when she used the word. Her answer surprised me. She started talking about Deepika Padukone's public break-up and battles with clinical depression, about how Priyanka Chopra married in her late thirties after finding mega global success, how all these actresses had faced unhappiness because of men and yet continued to *focus* on what was important and thrived in their jobs. 'Boys these days don't care about girls. They are looking for fun everywhere. It happens to actresses also, then I know it's okay for it to happen to me. I look at them and know that I am not alone, that it happens to such beautiful and high-profile women also. I don't know why but it makes us feel better.'

Gold Mendiratta once said to me, 'Everywhere, girls see that female film stars speak openly about having boyfriends and break-ups. A few continue to work after marriage and motherhood. This is very different from when we were younger in the 1990s, when actresses would hide their romances and stop working after marriage. I think this makes it more normal for girls to want and have a boyfriend and good career in real life.' None of the new female superstars is coy about their professional or personal ambitions. They are pragmatic about the challenges of maintaining successful careers and love lives, even for women who look like goddesses. Much like Shah Rukh, the female stars united many women I interviewed in admiration. Shah Rukh played out their mother's fantasies of finding a benevolent husband and breadwinner. India's new-age female superstars played out their own fantasies of female autonomy and achievement.

Fandom, Freedom

'The imagination is the fantastic, the fictional, the unreal, [and] the utopian ... Utopia is the mode in which we radically rethink the nature of family, consumption, government, religion, and so on. From 'nowhere' emerges the most formidable challenge to what-is.'

—*Paul Ricoeur*, 1991

For much of my adult life as a working professional, I thought I was collecting stories about how women see Shah Rukh Khan and his films. In fact, I was collecting narratives of how they saw themselves and those around them. Because none of us know Shah Rukh, and none of us hope to; fantasies are not meant to be tarnished by reality. We made him up and he happily participated in the myth we had created. In imagining Shah Rukh, the women I encountered tried to imagine an alternative to the masculine worlds they occupied. They forged, out of the gossamer fabric of their hopes and dreams, a man who would support freedom and choice for women—whether to work, rest or watch movies. This imaginary world, with its teary-eyed men who wholeheartedly love women with wide open arms, may not be radical, but it is a challenge to the world we currently occupy, in which so many women feel unappreciated, unsafe and unloved.

Through their expressions of fandom, often embarrassing for parents or husbands, some of these women deviated too far from the boundaries of female propriety. Acknowledging fandom meant that a woman was clearly acknowledging that she had a body and that it had desires. That she liked the way a man looked, that she had sexual urges too. I suspect the taboo on female sexuality is the reason why many poor and working-class women framed their fandom for Shah Rukh as being rooted in an appreciation of his hard work and his manners. Some part of their love for the actor was anchored in sex and sexuality—they liked his body, they thought he was handsome, they wouldn't mind waking up next to him. In the absence of a shared indigenous language of bodies and desire, young women would speak the language of Shah Rukh.

What have my travels with Shah Rukh fangirls taught me about our time? That there are no glib answers. No truth that can be uttered in tweets. That modern India is not all that modern for its women. That men too are struggling—to maintain the crumbling façade of masculinity in this new world of insecure jobs and confident women. That economic growth and the dispersion of media technologies have unleashed demands and desires like never before. That jobs take women far away from the safety and oppression of arranged marriages and traditional community life. That factories and families use the tactics of 'benevolent' dictators to control women and their bodies. That moving away from old ways of living and loving

creates paradoxical spaces for joy and bone-crushing loneliness. That
women may leverage their new-found freedom to trap themselves in
toxic romances. That going to the cinema alone in most towns and
villages remains a stigma for women in India. That televisions and
smartphones work in the slums of Delhi but not yet in the villages
of Jharkhand. And the love of a film icon forged during our youth
endures long after our youthful fantasies of love fade. Long after his
own youth fades.

The rise of the religious right highlights how idol worship and
devotion run riot in India. As the ability of organized religion to incite
violence and control the nation's politics grows stronger, its ability
to offer healing and respite to its followers seems depleted. Unlike
their mothers, none of the female fans I followed through the book
looked to the gods for comfort or enchantment. They watched TV or
looked up YouTube videos instead. None imposed traditional Hindu
or Muslim notions of sexual purity on themselves or the women in
their lives. Shah Rukh had triumphed over Jesus. In a country where
everyone voices the grievance of neglect or feels looked down upon,
we need someone to acknowledge us. We need someone to look up
to. That source of awe and acknowledgement for many women in
my generation—certainly not for all, but for many—has been Shah
Rukh Khan.

What have my travels with Shah Rukh fangirls taught me about
our icons? The appetite for the #MeToo movement in India suggests
there is a generation of educated women who are restless for fair
treatment and equal opportunities. They are sick of male deification
and superstardom in Indian culture. They want to be honoured,
admired and respected within their romances and workplaces, not
patronized. They don't need to marry a Shah Rukh, they want to
be Shah Rukh. They want to be as loved as he is. They hope to
dress better, look better and earn better. Pining for a man feels

anachronistic, a romantic relic of the past, where women needed men for survival and status.

More educated than any generation of women before them, with a deeper envy of men's freedoms and a growing appetite for self-reliance, a small swathe of young women finds it worthwhile to struggle and go solo. They are no longer interested in deriving well-being exclusively through marriage and a man's wages, are unwilling to sacrifice an independent life at the altar of love and social norms. While their male friends and lovers idolized politicians and cricketers, the women I observed idolized their own independence.

As for me, I don't find myself relying on Shah Rukh anymore when faced with the daily ignominies of life. I've read enough to know that my pains and desires are not personal faults. Hurt and yearning in our times are artefacts of larger structural forces, and generations of women have faced frustrations and hurdles like mine. Women like me have a diverse pool of cultural resources and friendly solidarities to draw upon. But I still watch each new Shah Rukh interview and each new film, constantly radiating endorsement of a man so far away from me. I can barely wait to see what he does next. We are comrades for life. In private moments, I do return to his oeuvre of talks and songs. To smile when my romantic resilience is tested. To remind myself that men aren't the enemy.

For his fifty-fourth birthday in November 2019, I returned to Mannat. At nearly three in the afternoon, the energy outside Shah Rukh's home was odiously masculine. After fifteen years of research and gossip with female fans, you can imagine my surprise to find a solid wall of men waiting for darshan. '*China se bhi log aate hain*,' said my rickshaw driver about the tourists who also flock to this site of pilgrimage. The area outside Shah Rukh's home was heavily policed. I asked a police officer about the extent of the security and he told me it was needed for 'crowd management'. This was my final visit to Mannat. Shah Rukh's public birthday bash is an annual spectacle in

Mumbai. Fans gather outside his home, hoping to spot the star as he walks out to his terrace to greet the worshipping throng.

Having witnessed the annual birthday tamasha multiple times, a local street vendor told me that he thought women, despite being Shah Rukh's core fanbase, did not feel comfortable standing outside the house and were probably too sensible or too busy to bother. '*Ladies log hi Shah Rukh ko zyada pasand karte hain. Par woh samajhdar hai aur time nahin hain unke paas.*' During the five hours I spent hanging around in the vicinity of Mannat, I counted at least a hundred male and merely ten female pilgrims. The fans were sprawled along the ocean promenade. Most fangirls and fan-women were accompanied by men, but I did spot and speak to three women who had arrived solo. Excited and afraid, each recalled cases of women being molested and injured by a mob of men at the Mannat birthday celebration in 2017. They were acutely aware of the stalker cult surrounding Shah Rukh, that some of the fanboys took their cues from Shah Rukh's portrayals of obsessive lovers who tormented women. The solo female fans knew the risks they faced, weighed the pros and cons, and decided to participate anyway. Their fandom had triumphed over their fear.

Vrinda Kundu, a Bengali twenty-year-old BCom student from Kolkata, had loved Shah Rukh from the age of two. She had joined the mob outside Mannat alone, having done the routine on Shah Rukh's birthday thrice before. Vrinda complained that the police were not allowing fans to approach Shah Rukh's house like they had last year. I asked her why there weren't very many women at the celebration. She laughed and said, 'It's not safe, I guess. Girls don't want to be surrounded and touched in the dhakka-dhakki (push and pull) of so many boys. I am used to the crowds of boys from Kolkata and I have to be brave to see Shah Rukh.' Another solo female attendee, a first-timer, was a twenty-something engineer from Jabalpur in Madhya Pradesh. She worked at a technology firm in Mumbai and lived in Dadar. She clung to her phone for company. 'All you see here are men, men, men. But women love him more. We just can't come out like this,' she told me.

The male fans dominating the landscape were typically in their twenties and hailed from Gujarat, Uttar Pradesh, West Bengal and Maharashtra. Fan clubs from different parts of small-town India were also represented. Shah Rukh has a giant fan following amongst men in Siliguri, which reports the highest share of Shah Rukh searches on Google within India. There was also a vocal group from Aurangabad. I saw Hindu and Muslim fans, all chanting for Shah Rukh. *Bharat ki Shaan, Shah Rukh Khan*. India's Pride, Shah Rukh Khan. Perhaps secularism stands a chance outside Shah Rukh's home on Bandstand. Many of the male fans had saved money for a year to travel and buy custom-made T-shirts for the occasion. One of the young men said that he loved Shah Rukh because he was more brains than brawn. *'Unke paas dimaag hain, body par kam dhyaan dete hain,'* he said, respectfully.

Each time the gates to Mannat opened, these men would surge towards the house, unleashing a tidal wave of masculine energy. As the largely male mob pushed forward, the women ducked for cover. They were either swept aside or swallowed up in the crush. The solo female attendees I interviewed survived the scene, spotted their star and said they would be back next year. They would continue seeking Shah Rukh on his birthday, despite the perils of being pushed around by hundreds of men. 'It would be nice if I find a boyfriend to bring with me next year. But even if I don't, I work in Bombay and my parents don't live here,' said one twenty-six-year-old woman. 'They won't know where I am. It's mad and irrational but I'll still show up alone.'

14

Loveria

Sardi, khaasi na malaria hua. Main gaya yaaron mujhko
love love love loveria hua.
(I don't have a cold, cough or malaria. I have love love loveria.)

—Raju Ban Gaya Gentleman (1992)

Most people see the problem of love primarily as that of being loved, rather
than that of loving, of one's capacity to love. Hence the problem to them is
how to be loved, how to be lovable ... Many of the ways to make oneself
lovable are the same as those used to make oneself successful, to 'win friends
and influence people'. As a matter of fact, what most people in our culture
mean by being lovable is essentially a mixture between being popular and
having sex appeal.

—Erich Fromm, 1956

What is the spiritual function of 'irrational' or 'mad' fandom in our times of short attention spans and cynicism? Why are these sensible women willing to endure tremendous danger and discomfort to wave at an actor from afar? What love does his icon provide?

387

Our tryst with global modernity enables new choices and norms that create their own problems and their own solutions. The opportunity to study, work and find your own partner exposes us to the harsh markets for mates and monies. Philosophers tell us that capitalism has made us all complicit in our own commoditization. Love, as much as labour, has become an object of trade and exchange value—circulating in a marketplace, compelling us to become slaves to the rational logic of incentives, costs and scarcity.

The idea that all social interactions are strategic acts, from which we must extract personal gain, has become common sense. We size people up for what they can offer us. For good or for bad, we condition our affection for another human based on what actions they perform for our welfare. You like my posts, I will be your friend. You withdraw from your career to take care of the children, I will love you forever. You enhance my status in the world outside, I will take care of you. You side with my ex's current girlfriend, I will doubt our friendship. We genuinely believe that feelings such as love or friendship can be summoned and regulated at will, that one can be strategic in how one exercises emotion.

In an important essay, attempting to draw parallels between the writings of Marx and Gandhi, philosopher Akeel Bilgrami highlights how both thinkers were worried by the 'objectification of the relations between human beings themselves whereby they are not mutually seen as subjects to be engaged with but rather—with detachment—as a source of production or a form of value that was at once abstract and material'. In his 1955 classic, *The Sane Society*, psychoanalyst Erich Fromm talked about the 'marketing orientation' of the modern personality, where individuals experience themselves and others purely as commodities—as objects to be consistently marketed or transacted with.

In modern-day heterosexual encounters, humdrum alienation is abundant. The uninspiring language of profit and economics frames our approach towards each other. Within families, women believe they must labour for love. They make deals and bargains with family members to earn access to the world outside. If wealth accords love, a man's income buys him far more love than a woman earning exactly the same paycheck. The per-rupee supply of love varies by gender. Women feel more loved when they toe the patriarchal line, when they prop up powerful men. Feminist scholarship highlights how women kill girl children in the womb, how they endure violence or perform backbreaking hours of housework to secure the love of families. Within families, women are at the greatest risk of losing love if they don't conform to preordained rules and hierarchies. Because love is *capital*, a way to ensure feminine success and survival.

Away from family bonds, in our love affairs, we have all become hyperrational economists. We complain that our partners are not *investing* enough in the enterprise of our pair-bond and any conversation on our love lives degenerates into game theoretic formulations. We leave partners using the framework of *opportunity costs* as we're convinced there are better options out there; we lose weight to become more appealing and *raise our value* in the marketplace. We maintain beauty because attractiveness is an *endowment*, which improves one's chances of finding love.

Love has become a lifestyle product: we love people for the parties they take us to, for what our lovers signal about us. We settle when the biological clock imposes a *constraint*, we play the field and have more sexual pleasure as the *cost* imposed by an unintended pregnancy has been thwarted by contraceptive technology, we measure our success based on the number and types of lovers we've had, we *assess and evaluate* our romantic options as if finding love is like buying a pair of shoes. Unsurprisingly, the world is lonelier than ever, something is profoundly broken in how humans of the opposite sex relate to each other. Love is supposed to defy logic, not be entrapped by it.

Feminists have been troubled by the state of love for generations. They've argued that male power is constructed by the love women give men as mothers and partners. That 'love' confers power, and that the powerful are often loved the most. Indian feminism struggles to explain why so many modern women, those who defy their traditional roles in the economy and fight silent battles at home, have been possessed by the idea of traditional matrimony and romance. They wonder why women hold on to patriarchal men. Some blame the media, Bollywood and actors like Shah Rukh for stirring up fruitless romantic fervour in our women. A few castigate all aspirations for romance as a distraction from the tough job of resistance.

I'm not sure. Yes, most men are walking-talking contraceptives. Modern romance can make one so sad and sceptical that love itself feels like an endeavour fraught with danger and despair. Love inherits all the inequalities of our societies and operates in an unequal and competitive space, where some are more powerful than others. However, the ordinary women I've followed would rather endure the agony of their romantic agency as long as they can enjoy more personal and sexual freedom.

In 2016, Vidya and I had cheered in unison for Shah Rukh's brief guest appearance in *Ae Dil Hai Mushkil*. That cinematic moment, viewed and valued by millions of people, features Shah Rukh playing Tahir Khan, a heartbroken artist who offers a three-minute lecture on the spirit of love. Embodying the notion that love can be a tradeable commodity whose acquisition signifies power, Ranbir Kapoor's character asks Shah Rukh's Tahir, 'Is it easy to love someone when they don't love you in return?' In response, Shah Rukh says 'It's the most beautiful feeling in the world.' Ranbir's character retorts, 'Is it not weakness?' and Tahir says, 'Not at all. One-sided love has a unique power, it is all mine. For me to love someone fully doesn't require the other person's participation. Perhaps there is no greater love. If you must gamble for love, stake whatever you like, why fear? If you win, it's wonderful. If you lose, you haven't really lost.'

The exchange valourizes heartache—there is honour in being heartbroken. Love becomes an attitude of generosity towards oneself and the world, not a self-maximizing transaction between two people. I sense that this scene, and its celebration of romantic abandon, captures the appeal of Shah Rukh's imagery for so many of us. He represents a belief often expressed in many old Hindi film romances that love is a higher spiritual calling. That boy and girl meet and fall so deeply that the boy travels all the way from the UK to Punjab to woo the girl and her conservative family. There is no bargaining or strategizing in how Shah Rukh's characters and his romantic partners decide to love each other. No sexual rival emerges for either party, no caste, no worries about how pragmatic the match is, no bargaining on housework, no fear that career goals won't align. These films are gloriously impractical.

My glimpse into the love lives of Shah Rukh's female fans suggests that more money, co-education, an expanding female interest in exploring professional identities, pornography, greater sexual freedom in conjunction with an unrelenting faith in the male breadwinner and caste endogamy are playing havoc with female self-esteem. Zahira's daughter, Meenal, had kissed and held hands with a Kurmi Bihari Hindu co-worker in 2019. They met through her work as a survey investigator. She was provided accommodation by the survey firm and the boy lived nearby as well. He broke up with Meenal a few months later, citing religious incompatibility. 'Girls get physical only if they like the boy a lot. Boys know that. He knew I was Muslim right from the beginning. But he wanted to have fun, and what was happening between us was nice for him. Boys here will have fun with Muslim girls but marry Hindu ones. They use us. I've realized it's best to be safe, just watch movies and keep a distance from the men around us.'

By December 2019, Meenal had managed to recover from her Bihari break-up. Her female friends from work became primary sources of support and companionship. She contemplated breaking up with Shah Rukh as well. When Meenal expected her hero to be heroic, he turned out to be painfully human. She was hurt by Shah Rukh's silence amidst the Indian government's attempts to implement the Citizenship Amendment Act (CAA) and the National Register of Citizenship (NRC). These government interventions were heavily criticized for discriminating against Muslims and violating the core constitutional values of a secular republic. As students and ordinary Muslim citizens were harassed or killed for protesting the NRC and CAA, India's culturally predominant forces from Bollywood and cricket remained largely silent. Meenal felt her hero was actively letting her down. '*Woh apne kaum ke saath kyun nahi khade ho rahe,*' she said, her first overt reference to religion in all our years talking about Shah Rukh. Why isn't he standing with his own community?

But Meenal could not bring herself to dislike Shah Rukh for too long. It took her two minutes to add, 'Maybe he is helping in a quiet way, in his own way. Maybe, right now, we can't see it. Sometimes it is too tough to say anything out in public. He must be helping. Maybe he can't because he can't take a side, maybe this is a tough time for a Muslim hero to speak.'

In January 2020, Shah Rukh released a new-year greeting on social media. Sidestepping calls to publicly condemn violence and the CAA-NRC, he said he had too many frailties to preach to others. 'I hope Allah is kind to us in spite of ourselves,' he wrote. Meenal was thrilled, '*Achha hai. Kuch to kaha, apne dhang se. Ek din aur bolenge,*' she said. It is good. He said something, in his own way. Someday, he will say more. I was amazed that such a trite apolitical message could make an intelligent woman so utterly ecstatic. At the time, she was busy with a new survey on youth attitudes in public spaces, talking to young men and women at Mumbai's Oval Maidan. I imagined her walking arm-in-arm with Shah Rukh's Twitter feed.

A fangirl's impractical fantasy reveals her reality. Meenal's fantasy of Shah Rukh unequivocally supporting the NRC protests reflects her lived experience of a public culture that does not express unambiguous solidarity with Muslim youth. Her consistent fantasy of Shah Rukh as the apotheosis of a 'good' romantic partner reveals her lived experience of churlish romantic relationships with men who struggle to navigate their new-found sexual possibilities with the slightest consideration.

Once, at a media conclave, I occupied a cheap seat and watched a well-intentioned Delhi heiress ask Shah Rukh why he did not use the power of his iconic status to make movies which 'changed the way people think'. This idea, that mass masala or romance films don't provoke introspection or thought because they do not conform to Western aesthetic codes or aren't gritty depictions of 'issues', is just straight-up condescending and inaccurate. Through watching Shah Rukh and his fan-women, I've seen how his films and celebrity— despite flirtations with toxicity and tradition—bolster many ordinary women's appetite for love and dignity. These women give Shah Rukh's songs and films a good long think. They use his scenes to think about their own lives as well. I have witnessed Shah Rukh stir women's imaginations. His images and idioms nudge young women to expect more from men, more from themselves and the world around them. In response to the heiress, Shah Rukh said that cinema existed for many reasons, one of them being to help audiences and actors escape their realities.

For his fans, Shah Rukh's films and interviews mean whatever they want them to mean: he becomes an archive of all that remains unattainable in banal personal lives; or a call to freedom for working-class fangirls; or a self-help guru for self-helping-women; a soppy balm to soothe the rough-and-tumble of an ordinary female life full of struggle, surveillance and tactical bargaining; an urge to explore bodies and their sexual appetites; or he can serve as the symbol of a metaphysical absence. Each fangirl longs for Shah Rukh in her everyday life—a man manufactured by myth, make-up and movie magic. Sadly, being a fan is dangerous business in many homes in India. Women are chastised for watching him on TV or singing his songs. Their personal phones and televisions are destroyed. And yet, I've witnessed working-class women part with hard-earned wages to watch a Shah Rukh film or to buy new devices to cruise his images in the face of censure from their families and communities for what they considered wasteful spending.

Good women are supposed to surrender their wages to their in-laws or husbands. Good women are supposed to save for their families. Good women are *not* supposed to visit cinema halls alone, and certainly not blow up their savings on fangirling. Many faced violent hostility for merely watching a film without seeking permission from their parents, husbands or in-laws. When I asked these women why they persisted with such costly fandom, their answer was simple: 'We love Shah Rukh, to hell with what our families think.' Their love stories are acts of courage and defiance. They love a man who can never be attained—my modern-age Meeras.

Fifteen years since I unknowingly began the research that culminated in this book, for the women I've followed and chronicled, Shah Rukh remains a spiritual timeout from the alienation, rational trade-offs and determinism of modern life. He continues to provide respite when the world doesn't feel human, when these women feel disposable. When families and workplaces don't treat women as people with desires and rights. When love becomes a chore. A break when practising accountability in intimate interactions feels lonesome. When the moral burden of propelling social change within their immediate relationships becomes too taxing or lonely-making.

At a time when we are so wary of who speaks for whom, so worried about who appropriates whose experience that we risk losing fruitful conversations while stranded on our identitarian islands, I am thankful that Shah Rukh allowed an aspiring academic like me to learn about the lives of women who are so very different from myself. In a country as divided as India, I am grateful that his pervasive iconography allowed us a window into each other's lives, and that he offered us a topic of mutual learning and interest. Obliged that all talk of Shah Rukh liberated me from a researcher's extractive gaze of 'data collection', that his films and songs freed me from having to look at the lives of women through the prism of deprivation and poverty alone. I may have no robust answers or theories, but I've learned to ask better questions. Graphs depicting sales and jobs numbers will never feel the same. I see the economy with greater clarity.

In the dominant language of economics, the women I met mean very little. They are nothing more than faceless members of a tiny numerator which helps calculate India's female employment rate. The tickets they bought to watch Shah Rukh movies are cast as just another financial transaction, helpful for calculating box-office sales. The media they worked so hard to purchase represents another commonplace sales figure for a technology giant or a media empire. Their struggles and labours, embedded in these transactions, are obfuscated and deemed irrelevant. They become simple data points in a graph, valuable for creating an aggregate growth or consumption estimate, one that can be used by corporations, politicians, academics and policy makers to write opinions and fret about the Economy.

Often, when we think of the 'economy,' we think of it as some intimidating notion accessible only to a group of stuffy technocrats and Davos attendees, so precious that it can only be discussed and understood by finance dude-bros, stock-market analysts and know-it-all economists. However, the best economists know that the economy is nothing but our moods and relationships, which define who produces and transacts what. The economy has a rich emotional and ethical life. The economy is made up of the loves and losses of the women I encountered, their fandom and their fantasies—a set of feelings we must be able to conjure up when we look at bland datasheets on jobs, consumption sales or box-office collections. Those statistics represent an ocean of sentiment.

As Mumbai closed down to combat COVID, Meenal's employers announced that they would only be able to support her hostel stay for a month; any additional accommodation fees would be deducted from her salary. Since the trains had stopped running, many of her colleagues decided to organize cars and trucks back home. Meenal was able, though, to move into a work colleague's room in a shared flat in Khar. They spent most of their time on their building's crowded roof. The pandemic had revived her mother's fears, her obsession with finding Meenal a husband. But Meenal was charting a very different path. If she could survive a global catastrophe without a man by her side, it would embolden her to live on her own terms.

Scared by her mother's matchmaking and the virus, she soothed herself with movies and songs on her phone. Unable to spend her savings on the dresses she wanted, Netflix felt like a well-deserved luxury. Meenal planned to watch one Shah Rukh film each week through the lockdown. She giggled at his 'coronavirus song' as well. 'His hair looks great,' she said. Shah Rukh's song was a simple tune, offering jokes and assurance. 'Sab sahi ho jageya,' he sings. Everything will be all right. I suppose movie stars must provide assurances when employers and politicians cannot.

An actor, a man Meenal nor I will ever know, has become the receptacle of so many of our expectations. We expect him to tell us that everything will be okay, we expect him to exhibit moral courage, we expect him to express empathy, we expect him to walk with us. We forget that an actor is a mere mortal. He is crippled by his own celebrity, constrained by the same structures and incentives that guide us. I doubt Shah Rukh can survive our expectations. But real life and its inherent struggle and discrimination create an air of isolation, and a film star makes the loneliness bearable. He offers a glimmer of a possibility, a different way of relating to humans. His iconography offers us metaphors and a new language, a way to express radical expectations of reciprocity and care from families and men.

Honestly, I don't know who the next Shah Rukh will be, or if there will ever be another icon like him. You may not even like Shah Rukh very much. But as our economy and democracy contract, I do know that much struggle lies ahead for women who desire autonomy and achievement. Be it Marx or a movie star, or whoever you admire, our shared future will need icons who unite us in conversation and connection, not those who divide us into spiritual silos. Let us hope that our extraordinary public icons prove worthy of our ordinary private struggles.

Annexures

Panel 1: Distribution of India's Population (All Ages) by Activity Status in Millions: 2018

	Male	Female	Total
1. Population	696.2	661.8	1358
2. Employed	363.0	108.5	471.5
3. Unemployed	24.1	6.8	30.9
4. Students	198.6	162.8	361.4
5. Engaged in domestic duties	5.4	293.6	299.0
6. Labour force (2+3)	387.1	115.3	502.4
7. *Labour force participation (6 as % of 1)*	*55.6*	*17.4*	*37*

Source: Thomas, J.J. (2020). 'Labour Market Changes in India, 2005 to 2018: Missing the demographic window of opportunity?' *Economic and Political Weekly*, Vol. 55, No. 34, pp. 57-63.

Panel 2a: Work Force Participation Rates in India: 1911–1971

	1911	1951	1961	1971
Female	33.7	23.3	28	11.8
Male	61.8	54	57.1	52.5

Source: Guha, et al. (1974) 'Towards Equality: Report. For 1911 and 1951', estimates from Thorner, A. (1962). 'The Secular Trend in the Indian Economy 1881-1951'. *The Economic and Political Weekly*. Vol (4): 28-29-30. 14 July.

Panel 2b: Labour Force Participation Rates (All Ages) in India: 1977–2017

	1977-78	1987-88	1993-94	1999-00	2004-05	2011-12	2017-18
Male-Rural	55.9	54.9	56.1	54	55.5	55.3	54.9
Female-Rural	33.8	33.1	33	30.2	33.3	25.3	18.2
Male-Urban	53.7	53.4	54.3	54.2	57	56.3	57.0
Female-Urban	17.8	16.2	16.5	14.7	17.8	15.5	15.9

Source: NSSO PLFS 2017-18 and EUS for years represented.

Panel 3: Per Cent Share of Workers in Population (All Ages) by Social Group: 1993–2017

	1993-94	1999-2000	2004-05	2011-12	2017-18
Male–SC–Rural	55.4	53.1	54.5	53.9	52.3
Male–SC–Urban	50.5	50.3	53.7	54.5	52.5
Female–SC–Rural	35.5	32.5	33.3	26.2	17.4
Female–SC–Urban	19.9	18.5	20	17.2	17.2
Male–ST–Rural	59.1	55.8	56.2	55.7	53.8
Male–ST–Urban	52	48	52.3	52	49.9
Female–ST–Rural	48.2	43.8	46.4	36.4	27
Female–ST–Urban	23.4	20.4	24.5	19.2	17
Male–OBC–Rural	na	53.2	53.7	53.8	50.5
Male–OBC–Urban	na	53	55.4	54.6	53.2
Female–OBC–Rural	na	30.2	33	23.9	16.8
Female–OBC–Urban	na	16.9	18.5	15.1	14.3
Male–Other–Rural	54.7	52	55.7	55.2	52.2
Male–Other–Urban	52.3	51.8	55	54.9	53.1
Female–Other–Rural	29.7	22.3	26.2	20.1	14.1
Female–Other–Urban	14.5	10.8	13.4	12.9	12.6
Male–Muslim–Rural	49.4	47.8	49.5	49.9	47
Male–Muslim–Urban	50	49.6	52.6	53.2	50.9
Female–Muslim–Rural	16.2	16.2	17.8	15.3	9.9
Female–Muslim–Urban	12.2	9.8	12.1	10.5	7.5

Source: NSSO: PLFS 2017-18 and EUS Reports for each year represented.

Panel 3a: Per Cent Share of Workers in Urban Population (Fifteen Years and Above with Postgraduate Degrees) for Select States 2017–18

	Male	Female
India	77.6	35.7
Delhi	82.5	33.6
Tamil Nadu	82.8	46.3
West Bengal	65.1	39.1
Sikkim	91.4	62.3
Maharashtra	75.3	38.3
Kerala	68.7	57.6
Rajasthan	74.4	26.1

Source: NSO (2019), Annual Periodic Labour Force Survey Report (PLFS) 2017-18*

Panel 3b: Per Cent Share of Population (Fifteen Years and Above) in Select Million-Plus Cities with Regular Salaried/Waged Jobs 2017-18

	Male	Female
Delhi MC	40.1	12.8
Greater Mumbai MC	40.4	15.4
Bengaluru MC	44.5	17.9
Chennai MC	41	15.8
Kolkata MC	42.6	13.7
Coimbatore MC	49	22.9

Source: NSO (2019): PLFS 2017-18**

---

*   For more information, see Table 23 of cited report (pp. A-132). Activity reported based on usual status (principal + subsidiary).

** For more information, see p. A-360 of cited report. Million-plus cities are identified by Census 2011 and fall under municipal corporations within urban regions of states.

Panel 3c: Employment Rates (%) of Urban Indian Women (Twenty–Fifty-five Years) in Top Wealth Quintile by Marital Status in 2019

Unmarried	15.5
Married	6.5
Divorced/Separated	67.8
Widowed	41.9

Source: CMIE 2020

Panel 4: Average Incomes (in Euros) for Selected Countries, 2015

Income Group	US	Western Europe	Brazil	India
All	51940	34341	13702	6669
Top 10 %	244204	127410	75813	36164
Top 1 %	1049180	419052	381473	144891
Top 0.1 %	4840770	1559017	1974917	574652

Source : Assouad, L., Chancel., L and Morgan, M. (2018). 'Extreme Inequality: Evidence from Brazil, India, Middle-East and South Africa'. *World Inequality Database Working Paper 2018/4*. World Inequality Lab. Paris. The estimate is for per-adult income.

Panel 5a: Female Voices in Top 10 Hindi Film Grossers

Film	Year	Number of Female Speaking Characters	Number of Male Speaking Characters	Share of Dialogue for Women (As a % of All Dialogue in the Film)
Hum Aapke Hain Koun	1994	12	12	41
Bahubali 2	2017	5	15	28
Gadar: Ek Prem Katha	1995	8	19	NA
Dilwale Dulhaniya Le Jayenge	1995	10	14	46
Raja Hindustani	1996	6	12	43
Dangal	2016	20	34	31
Border	1997	6	18	28
Kuch Kuch Hota Hai	1998	9	5	60
Bajrangi Bhaijan	2015	8	33	20
Tiger Zinda Hai	2017	9	17	24

Panel 5b: Female Voices in Top 10 Shah Rukh Khan Grossers

Movie	Year	Number of Female Speaking Characters	Number of Male Speaking Characters	Share of dialogue for women (% of all dialogue in the film)
Dilwale Dulhaniya Le Jayenge	1995	10	14	46
Kuch Kuch Hota Hai	1998	9	5	60
Kabhi Khushi Kabhie Gham	2001	17	17	57
Karan Arjun	1995	10	26	27
Dil To Pagal Hai	1997	9	9	49
Mohabbattein	2000	9	18	28
Chennai Express	2013	4	10	38
Devdas	2002	10	14	58
Pardes	1997	13	10	NA
Darr	1993	6	14	33

(Source : Box Office India, https://www.boxofficeindia.com/india-adjusted-nett-gross.php accessed in September 2020. Collections are adjusted for inflation)

Notes on Sources and Reference Materials

PART 1: FANTASIES

Chapter 2: Who Is Shah Rukh?

p.18. Deification of film stars: *Woodcock, George* (1964), 'Indian Film (Review)', *Pacific Affairs*, 37 (3) (Autumn): 330–1, cited in Lawrence, M. ed. (2020). *Indian Film Stars: New Critical Perspectives.* London: Bloomsbury Press.

p. 22. 'big brave message': Rana Ayyub's article is available on the NDTV website at https://www.ndtv.com/opinion/with-3-muslim-characters-a-rebellion-by-shah-rukh-khan-1648365

p. 23. The article authored by Mr Khan on 'Being a Khan' in *Outlook* magazine is available on the NDTV website at https://www.ndtv.com/india-news/read-shah-rukh-khans-article-which-appeared-in-outlook-turning-points-2013-511771

p. 23. The 'Aap Ki Adalat' interview with Rajat Sharma where Mr Khan discusses the Wankhede stadium episode in 2013 is available at https://www.youtube.com/watch?v=DqIO4YCd0_8

p. 24. 'Extreme intolerance' and 'Explain your Indianess': The first Twitter Town Hall with Rajdeep Sardesai in November 2015 is available on

405

the India Today website at https://www.indiatoday.in/watch-right-now/video/exclusive-people-will-throw-stones-if-i-take-a-stand-says-shah-rukh-khan-436287-2015-11-02

p. 24. The interview with Barkha Dutt is available at https://www.youtube.com/watch?app=desktop&v=L9Kb3nzc1Ps.

pp. 24–25. The summary and video footage of the reaction from politicians can be found on the *Indian Express* website (5 November 2015), available at https://indianexpress.com/article/india/india-news-india/no-difference-between-shah-rukh-khan-and-hafiz-saeed-yogi-adityanath/

p. 25. 'nuisance': The *Mid-Day* quote is available in an article on the same subject in *Hindustan Times* (25 November 2015), found at https://www.hindustantimes.com/bollywood/never-said-india-is-intolerant-shah-rukh-khan/story-TcX7o5ZYefPqSf4JSXGkxL.html

p. 27. 'six out of ten audience members were men': Ormax Bollywood Audience Report 2017 and key findings on gender-gaps in footfalls have been published on the Film Companion website (5 April 2017), available at https://www.filmcompanion.in/features/bollywood-features/bollywood-box-office-gender-imbalance-2/

p. 27. Data on share of men and women visiting cinema halls once a month: In urban India, the share of men visiting a cinema hall was thirty-two per cent, compared to only sixteen per cent of women. Unsurprisingly, the gap is larger in rural areas, where only five per cent of women reported going at least once a month to a cinema hall, compared to sixteen per cent of rural men. Table 3.5.1 and Table 3.5.2 (pp. 69–70) of India Report from 2015 National Family Health Survey. IIPS. Mumbai.

Chapter 3: Engineering Shah Rukh

p. 34. 'US$ 2.8 billion film industry': Santoreneos, A. (2019). 'Bollywood, Hollywood or Chinese Cinema: Which film industry makes the most?' Yahoo Finance. 15 May.

p. 35. 'a billion footfalls in 2019': Data on footfalls and share of Hindi language films in overall Indian film revenues for 2019 are from pp. 6,

9 and p. 17 of The Ormax Box Office Report 2019. A copy is available on the Creative First Forum at https://creativefirst.film/wp-content/uploads/2020/05/OrmaxBoxOfficeReport-2019.pdf

p. 35. 'ten per cent growth' and 'Rs 49.5 billion': Data on the growth of the Indian film industry and gross box-office collections for Hindi films are from the FICCI–EY Media Report 2020. A press release is available on the FICCI website at https://ficci.in/pressrelease-page.asp?nid=3667

p. 45. 'Vidya was a demographic anomaly': Share of unmarried and single women from C-2 Table from Census 2011, Registrar General of India.

p. 45. 'a recent survey of urban millennials': YouGov-Mint-CPR Millennial survey. A summary of findings is available on the Centre for Policy Research website at https://www.cprindia.org/projects/yougov-mint-cpr-millennial-survey

p. 46. 'a single daughter remains unusual': Data on share of women who report only one girl child is from the National Family Health Survey 2015. See table below for more details.

Distribution of women with only one living female child by age group and residence in India, NFHS 2015–16				
	Total	<30 years	30-39 years	40+ years
% of women with only one female living child: Total	7.84	9.52	6.74	5.24
% of women with only one female living child: Urban	9.27	9.77	9.59	7.77
% of women with only one female living child: Rural	7.08	9.39	5.13	3.8

Source: Calculations shared by Rajib Acharya and Sapna Desai at Population Council using NFHS 2015 data

p. 47. Data on jobs, salaries and social security from the 'Annual Report of the Periodic Labour Force Survey (PLFS) 2017–18' published by the Ministry of Statistics and Programme Implementation, Government of India, in May 2019. (i) The share of women with regular salaried/waged jobs (activity code 31) aged 30–34 years from

Table 15, p. A-61. (ii) The share of 15–59-year-old men and women in urban Delhi who are reported as workers (with any job) from Table 17, p. A-68 (iii) The range of monthly earnings for urban female regular salaried/wage earning workers in Delhi from Table 42, page A-262 till A-265. These have been rounded off for presentation in the text. (iv) Share of women workers with written contracts from Statement 19, p. 70 of the main report. (v) Analysis on share of workers earning more than Rs 50,000 from Ishan Anand and Anjana Thampy, using PLFS data. A summary is available through an op-ed on the Mint website (6 August 2019) at https://www.livemint.com/politics/policy/most-regular-jobs-in-india-don-t-pay-well-plfs-1565075309032.html

p. 49. 'summon the sublime': Sidhar Wright, N. (2015). *Bollywood and Postmodernism: Popular Indian Cinema in the 21st Century*. Edinburgh: Edinburgh University Press.

p. 60. 'India has lowest rates of social mobility': India ranked 76 out of 82 countries ranked by the World Economic Forum Global Social Mobility Index Report for 2020. Available on the World Economic website here: http://www3.weforum.org/docs/Global_Social_Mobility_Report.pdf

p. 64. 'under five per cent file income tax': *Financial Express* news reports (21 September 2020) here https://www.financialexpress.com/economy/only-1-of-india-pays-income-tax-govt-shows-proof-tax-evasion-still-a-major-roadblock/2088141/

p. 64. 'eight per cent of Indians have college degrees': C-8 Series Census of India (2011), Registrar General of India.

p. 64. Kapur, Devesh (2010). 'The Middle Class in India: A Social Formation or Political Actor?' in Julian Go ed. *Political Power and Social Theory*. Vol. 21. Bingley, UK: Emerald Group Publishing Limited. pp.143–69.

p. 65. Maryam Aslany (2019). 'The Indian middle class, its size, and urban-rural variations', *Contemporary South Asia*, 27:2, 196-213, DOI: 10.1080/09584935.2019.1581727 and summary available on Mint (24 April 2019) at https://www.livemint.com/news/india/the-anatomy-of-india-s-middle-class-1556088919798.html

p. 65. 'Delhiite spends Rs 3,298 per month': Average monthly per capital expenditure for Delhi from Statement 4U Page 54 of NSS Household Consumption Expenditure Survey Report (2014) released in Feb 2014. NSS Report 555.

p. 65. '"middle-income" populations': Pew Research Center (2015). *A Global Middle Class Is More Promise than Reality.* Washington, D.C.

p. 66. Anand, I. and Thampi, A. (2016). 'Recent Trends in Wealth Inequality in India'. *Economic & Political Weekly*, 51(50): 59-67.

p. 67. 'women hold twenty per cent of wealth in India': p. 26 of Credit Suisse Research Institute (2018). 'Global Wealth Report 2018'. Switzerland.

p. 68. Chancel, Lucas and Piketty, Thomas, 'Indian Income Inequality, 1922-2015: From British Raj to Billionaire Raj?' (November 2019). *Review of Income and Wealth*, Vol. 65, pp. S33-S62, 2019. https://ssrn.com/abstract=3619370http://dx.doi.org/10.1111/roiw.12439

Chapter 4: An Actor and an Aristoprat

p. 79. *Statistical Straitjackets*: Please see the annexures for detailed tables on data cited in this section on jobs. All estimates in the book use usual status (principal+subsidiary). For details, read methodology section of the PLFS or EUS reports cited in annexures. A valuable explanation of the data is provided by Himanshu (2011) and G. Raveendran (2008). References are provided below.

p. 80. 'sixty-six per cent of Indian women's labour goes unpaid': World Economic Forum (2017). *The Global Gender Gap Report.* Switzerland (p. 177, India Profile)

p. 80. '3.26 billion hours of unpaid work': Oxfam International (2020). *Time to Care: Unpaid and Underpaid Care Work and the Global Inequality Crisis.* Oxford University Press.

p. 80. 'six out ten women in unpaid housework': See Table 15 from Annual Period Labour Force Survey (henceforth PLFS) 2017–18, p. A-60. 'Unpaid housework' includes 'attended to domestic duties only' (code 92) and 'attended to domestic duties and was also engaged in free collection of goods (vegetables, roots, firewood, etc.), sewing, tailoring, weaving, etc. for household use' (code 93). Using the same dataset, a 2021 working paper by Ruchika Chaudhury from IWWAGE shows that 68 per cent of urban Indian women (between the ages of fifteen to fifty-nine years) were engaged exclusively in domestic duties in 2017 and 2018.

p. 80. Himanshu (2011). 'Employment Trends in India: A Re-examination', *Economic and Political Weekly*, Vol. XLVI, No. 37. 10 September.

p. 80. 'historic low': Statement 8 on p. 53 of PLFS Report 2017–18. Estimates for those above fifteen years of age.

p. 80. 'women reported the highest ever unemployment rate': Statement 33 on p. 85 of PLFS Report 2017–18.

p. 80. 'job-loss growth': Kannan, K.P. and Raveendran, G. (2019). 'From Jobless Growth to Job-Loss Growth: Gainers and Losers during 2012-2018.' *Economic & Political Weekly*, 54 (44): 38-44.

p. 80. small mercy of no further decline: Ministry of Statistics and Programme Implementation, Government of India, *Annual Report of the Periodic Labour Force Survey (PLFS) 2018-19*, June 2020. The data showed a marginal increase in rural workforce participation for women from 17.5 per cent in 2017 to 19 per cent in 2018. Urban female employment had remained steady between 14.2 per cent in 2017 to 14.5 per cent in 2018. Patterns of gender gaps in employment remained similar to 2017. The latest data from the PLFS for 2019-2020, released in July 2021, shows an increase in women's work force participation (those fifteen years and above) to 28.7 per cent. However, male workforce participation is at 73 per cent. Even in urban Delhi, share of women (fifteen to fifty-nine years) working or looking for work is 17 per cent. The same estimate for men is 79.9 per cent.

p. 80. Urban impact of pandemic on women: 'Quarterly Bulletin of Periodic Labour Force Survey: April to June 2020', available at http://mospi.nic.in/sites/default/files/publication_reports/PLFS_Quarterly_Bulletin_April_June_2020.pdf. See Statement 2 on p. 3

of the report. The estimates are not directly comparable to the 2017 employment statistics as those rely on 'usual status' with a reference period of one year as opposed to the bulletin which reports only on 'current weekly status' with reference period of one week. However, the pattern is a useful indication of trends following the pandemic.

p. 81. 'report published by economists at Azim Premji University': See Figure 3.5 on p. 64 of Azim Premji University (2021). 'State of Working India 2021: One Year of Covid-19', Centre for Sustainable Employment, Azim Premji University; Deshpande, A (2020a), 'The Covid-19 pandemic and lockdown: First order effects on gender gaps in employment and domestic work in India', GLO Discussion Paper No. 607; Deshpande, A (2020b), 'The Covid-19 pandemic and gendered division of paid and unpaid work: Evidence from India', IZA Discussion Paper No. 13815.

p. 83. '14.9 million urban workers': Kannan, K.P. and Raveendran, G. (2019). 'From Jobless Growth to Job-Loss Growth: Gainers and Losers during 2012-2018.' *Economic & Political Weekly*, 54 (44): 38-44.

p. 83. For a detailed review of India's employment estimations, please see Krishnamurty, J. and Raveendran, G. (2008). 'Measures of Labour Force Participation and Utilization'. Working Paper Series. National Commission for Enterprises in the Unorganized Sector, Government of India. New Delhi.

p. 83. 'seventy-seven per cent of India's labour force is male': See Panel 1 in Appendix and Thomas, J.J. (2020). 'Labour Market Changes in India, 2005 to 2018: Missing the demographic window of opportunity?' *Economic and Political Weekly*, Vol. 55, No. 34, pp. 57-63.

p. 83. 'women accounted for 10.7 per cent of the workforce in 2019': Vyas, M. (2020). 'Female workforce shrinks due to economic shocks'. CMIE Economic Outlook. 14 December. Available at https://www.cmie.com/kommon/bin/sr.php?kall=warticle&dt=2020-12-14%20 12:48:29&msec=703

p. 84. 'seventy-one per cent of women between 30-34 years in domestic duties': Table 15 on p. A-58 from Annual PLFS 2017-18. For 1993 estimates, see Table 30 (B) on p. A-116 from NSS Report 409 on Employment and Unemployment 1993-94, NSSO. March 1997.

p. 84. 'less than a quarter of India's wealthiest women work': Statement 12 on p. 60 of PLFS 2017-18.

p. 84. workforce participation rates for fifteen–fifty-nine-year-olds: See Table 17 on p. A-68 in PLFS Report 2017–18.

p. 86. 'about 0.5 per cent of urban working women': The government published a National Classification of Occupations 2004, available at https://labour.gov.in/sites/default/files/CodeStructure.pdf. To calculate the share of urban working women in the 'media', I combined the following occupation codes for the estimate: (i) Code 521 'Fashion and Models' (employs 0.07 per cent of all urban working women) (ii) Code 347 'Artistic, Entertainment and Sports Associate Professionals' (employs 0.23 per cent of all urban working women) and 245 'Writers and Creative or Performing Artists' (employs 0.24 per cent of all urban working women) from Table 25 (p. A-147) in the PLFS 2017-18 Report. The following occupations fall under the umbrella of Code 245: Authors, Journalists and Other Writers (2451); Sculptors, Painters and Related Artists (2452); Composers, Musicians and Singers (2453); Choreographers and Dancers (2454); Film, Stage and Related Actors and Directors (2455). The following are included under the group of Code 347: Decorators and Commercial Designers (3471); Radio, Television and Other Announcers (3472); Street, Nightclub and Related Musicians, Singers and Dancers (3473); Clowns, Magicians, Acrobats and Related Associate Professionals (3474); Athletes, Sports Persons and Related Associate Professionals (3475). There are no sub-groups under Code 521.

p. 87. 'survey by CSDS': CSDS- KAS Report (2017). 'Attitudes, Anxieties and Aspirations of India's Youth: Changing Patterns.' New Delhi.

p. 87. 'Research Institute for Compassionate Economics': Coffey, D., Hathi, P., Khurana, N. and Thorat, A. (2018). 'Extreme Prejudice: Evidence from a New Survey'. *Economic and Political Weekly*, 53 (1): 46-54.

p. 87. Pew Research Center (2021). *Religion in India: Tolerance and Segregation*. Washington, D.C.

p. 87. 'Sanskritization': Srinivas, M.N. (1956). 'A Note on Sanskritization and Westernization, Far Eastern Quarterly', 15, 4:481-496. Reprinted in M.N. Srinivas. (2002). *Collected Essays*. New Delhi: Oxford University Press.

p. 89. 'India in bottom five': World Economic Forum (2020). 'The Global Gender Gap Report'. Switzerland, p. 12.

p. 90. 'Accustomed to reading statistics…': Bhattachrya, Pramit. 'India's Richest 20% Account for 45% of Income'. Mint, 2 December 2016. https://www.livemint.com/Politics/AvHvyHVJIhR0Q629wkPS5M/Indias-richest-20-account-for-45-of-income.html

Chapter 5: An Elite Composite

p. 114. 'Abandoning all expectations…': 'Shah Rukh Khan is ruining women's lives. This one did something about it', *Hindustan Times*, 19 April 2018. https://www.hindustantimes.com/bollywood/shah-rukh-khan-is-ruining-women-s-lives-this-one-did-something-about-it/story-XaN1PDEFyvyTgjEkb5fk6H.html

p. 116. 'motherhood penalty': Das, Maitreyi Bordia; Zumbyte, Ieva. (2017). 'The Motherhood Penalty and Female Employment in Urban India'. Policy Research Working Paper; No. 8004. Washington, DC: World Bank.

p. 117. 'discouraged workers': Das, M.B. (2006). 'Do Traditional Axes of Exclusion Affect Labor Market Outcomes in India?' Social Development Paper 97, Washington, D.C.: World Bank.

p. 117. 'urban women spend five hours on chores': International Labour Organization (2018). *Care Work and Care Jobs: For the Future of Decent Work*. Geneva. Data on India being in the bottom five countries measured by time spent by men in domestic duties and care-giving roles from p. 45 of the same ILO report.

p. 139. 'separate sphere': Lundberg, S., & Pollak, R. A. (1997). Separate Spheres Bargaining and the Marriage Market. In L. Haddad, J.

Hoddinott, & H. Alderman (Eds.), Intrahousehold Resource 35 Allocation in Developing Countries: Models, Methods and Policy (pp. 75-84). Baltimore and London: The Johns Hopkins University Press.

Chapter 6: Adventures in Accounting

p. 146. Share of women in accounts globally: Catalyst, *Quick Take: Women in Accounting using Bureau of Labour Statistics and EuroStat data* (June 29, 2020).

p. 146. Share of women in accounting in India: Hairharan S (2014). 'At 50,000, 22% of CAs in India are Women'. *Times of India*, 29 November, accessed here: https://timesofindia.indiatimes.com/india/at-50000-22-of-cas-in-india-are-women/articleshow/45313255.cms

p. 146. Number of women CAs: Institute of Chartered Accountants in India. *Women at ICAI Platform portal dashboard* accessed in 2020.

p. 171. 'women need permission': India Spend (2017). '65% Indian Women Literate, 5% Have Sole Control Over Choosing Their Husband'. 17 February

p 173. 'hidden tax': Mullainathan, S. (2018) 'The Hidden Taxes on Women'. *The New York Times*. 2 March.

Chapter 7: A Girl Called Gold

p. 182. 'twelve per cent of commercial pilots are women in India': Manju, V. (2018). 'Women Pilots' Percentage in India is Twice That of the Global Average'. *The Times of India*. 8 November.

p. 183. Johari, A (2016). 'The Glamorous Lives of '80s Airhostesses in India'. *Quartz India*. 4 February.

p. 183. treatment of in-flight crew: Katakam, A. (2003). 'A Case of Discrimination'. *Frontline*. 24 October.

p. 183. 'woman becomes the first flight in-charge at Air India': Kalpana Sharma. (2011). 'The Other Half – Another Battle Won'. *The Hindu*, 27 November. Available at https://www.thehindu.com/opinion/columns/Kalpana_Sharma/the-other-half-another-battle-won/article2659397.ece

p. 184. Masoodi, A. (2016). 'Living the High Life'. Mint. 1 July.

p. 184. growth of airlines: National Transport Development Policy Committee (2012). 'Report of Working Group on Civil Aviation Sector'. Ministry of Civil Aviation, Government of India. June; Phadnis, A. (2016). 'India Flies High in Domestic Air Traffic Growth. *Business Standard*. 7 July.

p. 184. Times News Network (2009). 'Air India Sacks Ten Airhostesses For Being Overweight'. *The Times of India*. 6 January.

p. 184. Miller, M. (2015). 'Air India Grounds 130 Flight Attendants "for Being Overweight".' *Independent*. 16 September.

p. 184. A.W. (2018). 'SpiceJet's Cabin-crew Recruitment Is Accused of Being Sexist'. *The Economist*. Business Traveler Gulliver. 30 August.

p. 184. Indo-Asian News Service (2018). 'Maneka Gandhi Asks Air India To Sensitise Male Staff on Female Colleagues'. NDTV.com. 24 August.

p. 196. 'Claiming Comfort in Public Space': Save the Children (2018). 'WINGS 2018: World of India's Girls – A Study on the Perception of Girls' Safety in Public Spaces'. New Delhi. 15 May.

p. 199. 'An entire issue of *India Today* in 2011 on abs and Westernized body': Rathnam, S., Rege, P. and Bamzai, K. (2011). 'Rise of the Navel'. *India Today*. 13 June; Datta, D. (2007). 'Craze for Abs'. *India Today*. 15 October.

p. 205. Illouz, Eva (2012). *Why Love Hurts: A Sociological Explanation*. Polity Press, Cambridge.

p. 215. '"love" was a far more frequent reason for the murder of women than terrorism': Thakur, A. and Dhawan, H. (2019). 'Love Third Biggest Murder Motive in India'. *The Times of India*. 18 November.

p. 215. National Crime Records Bureau (2018). *Crime in India 2018. Volume I*: pp xii. Ministry of Home Affairs. New Delhi

Chapter 8: Lost in Liberalization

p. 231. 'broad theories for women dropping out of Indian workforce': Chaudhary, R. and Verick, S. (2014). 'Female Labor Force Participation in India and Beyond'. International Labour

Organization, ILO DWT for South Asia and Country Office for India. New Delhi: ILO, 2014; ILO Asia-Pacific working paper series, ISSN 2227-4391; 2227-4405 (web pdf)

Chaudhary, R. (2021). 'Working or Not: What Determines Women's Labour Force Participation in India?' IWWAGE Working Paper Series. April.

p. 231. 'education effect': Das, M.B. and Desai, S. (2003). 'Why Are Educated Women Less Likely to Be Employed in India? Testing Competing Hypothesis'. Social Protection Discussion Paper No. 0313. The World Bank.

p. 231. 'underestimation effect': Sudarshan, R.M. and Bhattacharya, S. (2009). 'Through the Magnifying Glass: Women's Work and Labor Force Participation in Urban Delhi'. *Economic and Political Weekly*, Vol. 44, No. 48, pp. 59-66; Mondal, Bidisha, Ghosh, Jayati, Chakraborty, Shiney and Mitra, Sona. (2018). 'Women Workers in India – Labour Force Trends, Occupational Diversification, and Wage Gaps'. Centre for Sustainable Employment Working Paper 3. Bengaluru: Azim Premji University.

p. 231. 'structural transformation': Chatterjee, U., Murgai, R. and Rama, M. (2015). 'Job Opportunities along the Rural-Urban Gradation And Female Labor Force Participation in India'. *Economic & Political Weekly*, Vol. 50, 26-27: pp. 5-10

p. 232. 'care and cultural barriers': 'What Kinds of Jobs Do Indian Women Perform?': To simplify, there are two ways the NSS data helps us understand the occupational profile of workers. First, we can use data on the industries/broad sectors which engage workers. As per the 2017 PLFS (Table 26 on p. A-150), in urban India, 25 per cent of women are employed by manufacturing, 10 per cent are in the retail trade sector (includes jobs in shops or as salespeople), 15 per cent are engaged by the education sector. Nearly 6 per cent are employed within the health and social-work sectors. However, this data does not elaborate on the types of tasks/occupations being performed. For instance, not all women employed by the education industry are teachers. Therefore, the NSS creates a second method of classifying workers based on their occupations. The details I present on professions draws on this data (p. A-147 Table 25 in PLFS 2017). Note that to estimate 'professionals', I combine division 1-4 (this includes legislators, managers, professionals, clerks and technicians). For nurses, I include associate staff and midwifery support. (Code 223 and 323). Despande, A. and Kabeer, N. (2019). '(In)Visibility, Care and Cultural Barriers: The Size and Shape of Women's Work in India.' Discussion Paper Series in Economics Number 4/19. Department of Economics. Asoka University. Sonepat.

p. 232. 'education effect': Bhalla, S.S., and Kaur, R. 2011. 'Labour Force Participation of Women in India: Some Facts, Some Queries.' Working Paper 40, Asia Research Centre, London: London School of Economics and Political Science.

p. 232. '19 per cent of jobs for women': p. 23 in Kapsos, Steven, Silberman, Andrea and Bourmpola, Evangelia. (2014). 'Why Is Female Labour Force Participation Declining So Sharply in India?'. ILO Research Paper No. 10. ILO. pp 14 Available at: http:// www.ilo.org/wcmsp5/ groups/public/---dgreports/--- inst/documents/publication/ wcms_250977.pdf

p. 232. rural women's value as producers of their children's nutrition and human capital: Afridi, F., Dinkelman, T. and Mahajan, K. (2016). 'Why Are Fewer Married Women Joining the Work Force in India? A Decomposition Analysis over Two Decades'. IZA (Institute for the Study of Labor), Discussion Paper No. 9722.

Chapter 9: Surveyors

p. 241-42. SEWA membership and history: SEWA Bharat Annual Report, 2019

p. 242. Aggarwal, A (2007). 'Impact of Special Economic Zones on Employment, Poverty and Human Development.' Working Paper No. 194. New Delhi: Indian Council for Research on International Economic Relations.

p. 242. Women working in SEZs: Tejani, S. (2011). 'The Gender Dimension of Special Economic Zones' in Farole, T. and Akinci, G.

(ed.) *Special Economic Zones: Progress, Emerging Challenges and Future Directions*. World Bank. Washington, D.C., p. 257.

p. 242. women's SEZ employment in 2008: Singh, D. (2011). 'Role of SEZs in Employment Generation, Export Promotion and Attracting Investment' in *An Analysis of Special Economic Zones in India: A Case Study of Haryana*. Doctoral thesis. Patiala: Department of Economics, Panjabi University, p. 115.

p. 242. 'government data': Department of Commerce (2020). *Fact Sheet on Special Economic Zones*, available on http://sezindia.nic.in/. Ministry of Commerce and Industry, Government of India.

p. 242. 'working women with written contracts and eligible for social security in 2018': Statement 16 from Annual Periodic Labour Force Survey, 2018-19, NSO, Government of India.

p. 244. Data on home-based workers from WIEGO paper: Raveendran, G. (2020). 'Home-Based Workers in India: A Statistical Profile'. WIEGO Statistical Brief No. 23. June 2020.

p. 246. Agarbatti exports: Bajaj, Manjul. (1999). 'Invisible Workers, Visible Contribution. A Study of Home-Based Workers in Five Sectors across South Asia'. Background paper presented at Regional Policy Seminar on Women Workers in the Informal Sector in South Asia: Creating an Enabling Policy Environment. Kathmandu, Nepal, 18-20 October; ET Online (2018). 'Agarbatti Industry's Exports Nears Rs.1000 Crores in FY18'. *Economic Times*. 6 June.

p. 245-46. Segregation and urbanization in Ahmedabad: Mahadevia, D., Desai, R., Vyas, S. (2014). 'City profile: Ahmedabad'. Centre for Urban Equity Working Paper 26. Ahmedabad: CEPT University.

p. 245-46. Bapunagar and riots: Chandhoke, N. (2009). 'Civil Society in Conflict Cities: The Case of Ahmedabad'. London School of Economics and Political Science (W.P 64, series 2, November). www.crisisstates.com

p. 252. Intra-household bargaining: Agarwal, B. (1997). '"Bargaining" and Gender Relations. Within and Beyond the Household. Feminist Economics'. 3 (1), 1-51

p. 252. Folbre, N. (1997). 'Gender Coalitions: Extra Family Influences on Intrafamily Inequality' in: Alderman, H., Haddad, L. and Hoddinot, J. (eds). *Intrahousehold Allocation in Developing Countries*. Baltimore, MD: Johns Hopkins University Press, pp. 263-74.

p. 252. perceived contribution: Sen, A. (1990). 'Gender and Cooperative Conflicts' in Tinker, I. (ed.) *Persistent Inequalities. Women and World Development*. New York and Oxford: Oxford University Press, pp. 123-49; Kabeer, N. (1999) 'Resources, Agency, Achievements: Reflections on the Measurement of Women's Empowerment'. Development and Change, Vol. 30: 435-464

Chapter 10: The Boredom of Manju

p. 274. Rural Roads Project or Pradhan Mantri Gram Sadak Yojana: Asher, Sam, and Paul Novosad. 2020. 'Rural Roads and Local Economic Development.' *American Economic Review*, 110 (3): 797-823.

p. 275. share of rural men engaged in agriculture: Nikore, M. (2019). 'Where are India's Working Women? The Fall and Fall of India's Female Labour Participation.' *The Times of India*. 14 October.

p. 283. Jain, Devaki (1985). 'The Household Trap: Report on a Field Survey of Female Activity Patterns' in Devaki Jain and Nirmala Banerjee (eds). *Tyranny of the Household*. New Delhi: Vikas Publishing House, pp. 215-248.

p. 283. Jain, Devaki and Chand, Malini. (1982). 'Report on a Time Allocation Study, its Methodological Implications.' Paper presented at the Technical Seminar on Women's Work and Employment. New Delhi: ISST.

p. 284. Time Use Surveys: Deshpande, A. (2021). 'What Did You Do in the Last 24 Hours?' *The India Forum*. 1 January.

p. 284. Jain, Devaki. (1996). 'Valuing Work: Time as Measure', *Economic and Political Weekly*, Vol. 31, No. 43. 26 October, pp. WS46-WS57

p. 284. National Statistical Office (2020): 'Time Use in India-2019'. Available at http://mospi.nic.in/sites/default/files/publication_reports/Report_TUS_2019_0.pdf

p. 288. Foreign tourism from India to Switzerland: Mathew, Liz. (2018). 'Switzerland to honour Sridevi with statue'. *The Indian Express*. 8 September.

Chapter 11: A Tale of Two TVs

p. 316. 'The Era of Consumer A.R.T: India's Media and Entertainment Sector'. Mumbai: FICCI-EY. March 2020.

p. 316. 'Playing by New Rules: India's Media and Entertainment Sector Reboots in 2020'. Mumbai: FICCI-EY. March 2021.

p. 316. TVs in 2017: 'Reimagining India's Media and Entertainment Sector'. Mumbai: FICCI-EY. March 2018.

p. 316. Access to streaming content, hours of use: *Film Companion*. 'Ormax OTT Audience 2019 Report' summarized on the Film Companion website at https://www.filmcompanion.in/features/ bollywood-features/7-revelations-about-indias-ott-space-from-ormax-medias-ott-audience-report-2019/

p. 317. 'the vast digital gulf between men and women': Mehrotra, K. (2018). 'Internet in India: Gaping Gender Gap'. *The Indian Express*. 8 August.

p. 317. Households with TV: 'India Report from 2015 National Family Health Survey'. Mumbai; IIPS, p. 34, Table 2.8.

p. 317. 'Seven out of ten women report watching TV': 'India Report from 2015 National Family Health Survey'. Mumbai: IIPS, p. 55, Figure 3.3

p. 318. Oxford Poverty and Human Development Initiative (OPHI) (2018). 'UN's multi-dimensional poverty indicators: Global MPI 2018'. University of Oxford.

p. 319. women, farming and land in Santhal Parganas: Rao, N. (2017). 'Good Women Do Not Inherit Land' in *Politics of Land and Gender in India* (1st ed.). New Delhi: Routledge.

p. 330. Conditions of work for domestic workers: Neetha, N. (2013). 'Paid Domestic Work: Making Sense of the Jigsaw Puzzle'. *Economic and Political Weekly*, Review of Women Studies, Vol – XLVIII, No. 43, 26 October; Neetha, N. (2013). 'Minimum Wages for Domestic Work:

Mirroring Devalued Housework'. *Economic and Political Weekly*, Review of Women Studies, Vol – XLVIII No. 43, 26 October.

Chapter 12: An Equilibrium of Silly Expectations

p. 350. *Towards Equality* report: Guha, P., Kara, M., Shyam, S., Dogra, N., Mahajan, V., Dube, L., Hasan, S., Haksar, U., Sarkar, L. and Mazumdar, V. (1974). 'Towards Equality: Report of the Committee on the Status of Women in India'. Ministry of Education and Social Welfare, Government of India.

p. 350. Mazumdar, V. (1985). 'Emergence of the Women's Question in India and the Role of Women's Studies'. New Delhi: Centre for Women's Development Studies.

p. 353. communication devices: Barboni, Giorgia, Field, Erica, Pande, Rohini, Rigol, Natalia, Schaner, Simone and Troyer Moore, Charity. 'A Tough Call: Understanding Barriers to and Impacts of Women's Mobile Phone Adoption in India.' October 2018.

p. 355. 'coloured cosmopolitanism': Slate, N. (2009). '"I am a colored woman": Kamaladevi Chattopadhyaya in the United States, 1939–1941'. Contemporary South Asia. Volume 17 (1) Annual Conference Edition of the British Association for South Asian Studies.

p. 355 steep decline since 1911 of women workers: See Panel 2a in Appendix

pp. 355-356. Nehru: Sarkar, L. (1988). 'Nehru and Gender Justice'. Paper Presented at National Seminar on Nehru and the Constitution: Ministry of Law and Justice and Indian Law Institute, 30-31 December, cited in Mazumdar, V. (1998). *An Unfulfilled or a Blurred Version? Jawaharlal Nehru and Indian Women*. New Delhi: Centre for Women's Development Studies.

p. 357. mental health and suicide: Dandona, R., Kumar, G.A., Dhaliwal, R.S., et al. (2018). 'Gender Differentials and State Variations in Suicide Deaths in India: the Global Burden of Disease Study 1990–2016'. *Lancet Public Health*; 3: e478–89; National Mental Health Survey of India, 2015-2016. 'Prevalence, Patterns and Outcomes'. Supported by Ministry of Health and Family Welfare,

Government of India, and implemented by the National Institute of Mental Health and Neurosciences (NIMHANS), Bengaluru; Roy, S., Morton, M., and Bhattacharya, S. (2018). 'Hidden Human Capital: Self-efficacy, Aspirations and Achievements of Adolescent and Young Women in India'. World Development, *111*, pp. 161-180.; World Health Organization (2018). 'Depression in India: Let's Talk'. New Delhi.

p. 362. JPAL Study: Dhar, Diva, Tarun Jain, and Seema Jayachandran. (2018). 'Reshaping Adolescents' Gender Attitudes: Evidence from a School-Based Experiment in India.' NBER Working Paper No. 25331. December.

p. 365. Menon, N. (2012). *Seeing Like a Feminist.* New Delhi: Zubaan Books.

p. 368. 'employed women produce more progressive children': McGinn, Kathleen L., Mayra Ruiz Castro, and Elizabeth Long Lingo. (2019). 'Learning From Mum: Cross-National Evidence Linking Maternal Employment and Adult Children's Outcomes.' Work, Employment and Society 33, No. 3. June, pp. 374–400

Chapter 13: Madness At Mannat

p. 377. Shah Rukh had appeared in forty-one films: Wikipedia, https://en.wikipedia.org/wiki/Shah_Rukh_Khan_filmography#Feature_films

Chapter 14: Loveria

p. 388. parallels between the writings of Marx and Gandhi: Bilgrami, A. (2014). *Secularism, Identity and Enchantment.* New Delhi: Permanent Black, p. 151.

Quotes and Epigraphs

p. vi. 'And I am quite free': Murty Classical Library of India (2015). Mutta. *Therigatha: Poems of the First Buddhist Women.* Tr. Charles Hallisey. Harvard University Press.

p. vi. 'The economic gender gap': World Economic Forum (2020). 'The Global Gender Gap Report'.

p. vi. 'Their fantasies are': Verghis, S. (2013) 'The Sahib of Cinema: Bollywood star Shah Rukh Khan'. *The Australian*. 10 August.

p. xi. '*Koi na koi chahiye*': Lyrics by Sameer

p. xi. 'We really don't need more people around us': Shah Rukh Khan (2020). @iamsrk on Instagram. 'Lockdown Lessons'. 16 May 2020.

p. 3. '*Uljhan bhi hoon teri*': Lyrics by Irshad Kamil

p. 13. Nandy, A. (1981). 'The Popular Hindi Film: Ideology and First Principles'. *India International Centre Quarterly, 8*(1), pp. 89-96.

p. 13. Shah Rukh Khan (2017). 'The Quest for Love and Compassion'. TED2017 Vancouver. 27 April.

p. 33. Pathak, A. (2016). 'The SRK Interview - Part 1: "As Long As India Makes Films, People Will Watch Shah Rukh Khan".' *Huffington Post India*. 1 July at https://www.huffpost.com/archive/in/entry/the-shah-rukh-khan-interv_n_10765942

p. 38. Warhol, A. (1977). *The Philosophy of Andy Warhol (From A to B and Back Again)*. New York: Harvest.

p. 48. Shah Rukh Khan (2015). 'Life Lessons: Lecture at Edinburgh University'. The text is also available on the Indian Express website at https://indianexpress.com/article/entertainment/bollywood/shah-rukh-khans-speech-university-of-edinburgh-bollywood/

p. 59. SRK interview with Rajeev Masand on CNN-IBN from 2011 available at https://www.youtube.com/watch?v=ducxQhLVwIY

p. 75. Crane, S. (1899). 'A Man Said to Universe. *War Is Kind and Other Lines.*' Project Gutenberg. https://www.gutenberg.org/files/9870/9870-h/9870-h.htm

p. 112. Krishnamurti, J. (1977). Public Lecture in Ojai. 3 April. Available at https://www.youtube.com/watch?v=J5VppejtjCI

p. 177. '*Udi udi jaaye*': Lyrics by Javed Akhtar

p. 229. 'In my late 20s...': Shah Rukh Khan (2017). 'The Quest for Love and Compassion'. TED2017 Vancouver. 27 April.

p. 229. 'We keep talking about modern India...' The first Twitter Town Hall with Mr Sardesai in November 2015 is available on the *India*

Today website at https://www.indiatoday.in/watch-right-now/video/exclusive-people-will-throw-stones-if-i-take-a-stand-says-shah-rukh-khan-436287-2015-11-02

p. 241. Dickinson, E (1863). 'The Loneliness One Dare Not Sound' in *The Complete Poems of Emily Dickinson* (ed. Thomas H Johnson). Boston: Little, Brown and Company.

p. 265. '*Chand ne kuch kaha*': Lyrics by Anand Bakshi

p. 345. Chaitanya, T. (2017). 'SRK: Why Only a Feminist? I'd Like to Be a Woman'. *Femina*. 9 January. Available at https://www.femina.in/celebs/indian/srk-tries-to-reduce-gender-disparity-34582-1.html

p. 350. Sen, A. (1987). 'Gender and Cooperative Conflicts'. UNU WIDER Working Paper 18. Helsinki.

p. 358. India Today Conclave. Q&A Session with Shah Rukh Khan. 2009. New Delhi. Available at https://www.youtube.com/watch?v=i6mcguPa4p8&t=51s

p. 367. Auden, W.H. (1944). *For the Time Being: A Christmas Oratio*. Princeton: Princeton University Press, 2013 edition.

p. 370. '*Main sawaalon main hoon*': Lyrics by Javed Akhtar

p. 374. Gangwani, R. (2012). 'I Cried for Hours-SRK'. *Filmfare*. 11 December.

p. 381. Ricouer, P. (1991). *From Text to Action: Essays in Hermeneutics II* (tr. Katherine Blamey and John B. Thompson). Illinois: Northwestern University Press, p. 184.

p. 387. '*Sardi, khaasi na malaria hua*': Lyrics by Mahendra Dehlvi

p. 387. 'how to be lovable': Fromm, E. (1956). *The Art of Loving*. Thorsons, 2010 edition.

Index

Padukone, Deepika, 71, 199, 212, 379–380
Pande, Rohini, 354
pandemic, 12, 31, 66–67, 72, 80–81, 86, 215, 281, 342, 396, *see also* COVID-19 crisis
Pardes (1997), 125, 134, 259, 291
parents, 46–51, 53–54, 56–57, 60–64, 95–97, 122–124, 153–154, 157–160, 165, 170–172, 175–176, 190–197, 211–213, 255, 305–307
Paris, 209, 217, 376, 402
partners, 77, 93, 115, 121, 204–205, 221, 236, 244, 276, 328, 357, 388–390; finding, 45
part-time workers, 83
patriarchy, 8, 77–78, 87–88, 100, 141, 234, 241, 313, 349–350, 368–369
pedestrian human activity, 106
Pepsi, 275, 277, 287, 291
Phillips, Adam, 109
Phir Bhi Dil Hai Hindustani (2000), 20
physical perfections, 178, 215
Piketty, Thomas, 68
placement agents, 326
Planning Commission, 55, 82, 164–166
Popova, Maria, 140
Population, distribution by activity status 398t; with regular salaried/waged Jobs 401t

porn, 39, 201–202, 226, 391
portrayal, 27, 179, 222, 311
poverty, 98, 142, 395
Prabhas, 25, 329
Pradhan Mantri Gram Sadak Yojana (PMGSY), 274
pragmatism, 4, 47, 234
Pratham, 278
Presidential Bodyguards (PBG), 77
prestige, 69, 102, 134, 174
privileged, 7, 36, 63–64, 69–70, 72–73, 77, 90, 92, 322, 331
professional life, 11, 148, 233
property, 54, 56, 67, 69, 89, 250, 252, 319, 353, 358, 370; rights over, 67, 100; rights of Hindu women, 67
proposals, 146, 168–169, 193, 264. *See also* marriage; matrimony
psychological break, 168
public: bravado, 218; charisma, 18
Pulse Polio programme, 276–277
purchasing power, 65, 101
Pushpavalli, 61

Rab Ne Bana Di Jodi (2008), 264, 333
Raees (2017), 177, 213
Raju Ban Gaya Gentleman (1992), 19, 123, 387
Rampur, 273–274, 276, 279–280, 283, 285–286, 288–289, 295–296, 298–301, 303–304, 306,

About the Author

Shrayana Bhattacharya trained in development economics at Delhi University and Harvard University. Since 2014, in her role as an economist at a multilateral development bank, she has focused on issues related to social policy and jobs. Prior to this, she worked on research projects with the Centre for Policy Research, SEWA Union and Institute of Social Studies Trust. Her writing has appeared in the *Indian Express*, *Economic & Political Weekly*, *Indian Quarterly* and *The Caravan*. She lives in New Delhi.